Adventure Journalism
in the Gilded Age

# Adventure Journalism in the Gilded Age

*Essays on Reporting from the Arctic to the Orient*

Edited by KATRINA J. QUINN,
MARY M. CRONIN *and* LEE JOLLIFFE

*Foreword by* MICHAEL S. SWEENEY

McFarland & Company, Inc., Publishers
*Jefferson, North Carolina*

*This book has undergone peer review.*

LIBRARY OF CONGRESS CATALOGUING-IN-PUBLICATION DATA

Names: Quinn, Katrina J, editor. | Cronin, Mary M.
(Mary Margaret) editor. | Jolliffe, Lee, editor.
Title: Adventure journalism in the Gilded Age :
essays on reporting from the Arctic to the Orient /
edited by Katrina J. Quinn, Mary M. Cronin and Lee Jolliffe.
Description: Jefferson, North Carolina : McFarland & Company, Inc.,
Publishers, 2021 | Includes bibliographical references and index.
Identifiers: LCCN 2021022086 | ISBN 9781476680552 (paperback : acid free paper) ∞
ISBN  9781476642093 (ebook)
Subjects: LCSH: Journalism—United States—History—19th century. | Press—United
States—History—19th century. | Reporters and reporting—United States—
History—19th century. | Voyages and travels. | BISAC: LANGUAGE
ARTS & DISCIPLINES / Journalism
Classification: LCC PN4864 A37 2021 | DDC 071.309/034—dc23
LC record available at https://lccn.loc.gov/2021022086

BRITISH LIBRARY CATALOGUING DATA ARE AVAILABLE

ISBN (print) 978–1–4766–8055–2
ISBN (ebook) 978–1–4766–4209–3

On the cover: *insets* Eliza Scidmore and companions at the summit of Mt. Fuji
(*Jinrickisha Days*, p. 185; photograph by Herbert George Ponting, c. 1905;
Library of Congress, Item cph.3b16850); Frederick Wadsworth Loring
(1848–71), a promising young newspaper editor and author from Boston
(photograh by Timothy H. O'Sullivan, National Archives, VCN: 106-WA-145);
*background* Yosemite's Glacier Point Rock, photograph by Isaiah West Taber,
1880–1900 (Rijksmuseum, Objectnummer: RP-F-2012-96-228).

Printed in the United States of America

*McFarland & Company, Inc., Publishers
Box 611, Jefferson, North Carolina 28640
www.mcfarlandpub.com*

# Table of Contents

v

# Foreword

## Michael S. Sweeney

Much of our collective memory of the developmental years of the United States is built upon our ancestral wanderlust and what nineteenth-century pulp novelist Horatio Alger called "luck and pluck."

To begin with, the Europeans who first came unto the shores of North America, meeting the natives who had been there for thousands of years, knew they faced long odds and numerous hazards. They came anyway, figuring the dangers were the price one paid for a chance at a better life.

Those who stayed behind in Ireland, England, France, Scandinavia, and so on, also may have felt the siren call of adventure luring them westward, but for whatever reason chose safety first. Thus, one might argue that the first Euro-Americans had self-selected for traits of novelty and risk. Think in terms of evolution: Those who braved slow, risky wooden ships to come to America carried something like the gene for travel, gambling, and adventure, and they bred it into the following generations.

Those who colonized the Eastern Seaboard did not remain content to stay behind the barrier of the Appalachian Mountains. They pushed westward, eager to see what lay behind the next hill, and the hill after that. Fulfilling manifest destiny, the new Americans populated the nation from ocean to ocean, displacing the natives along the way.

Luck and pluck. Who survived and who died. And among those who survived, who found ways to prosper. These are details of chance that built the United States, particularly during the age of exploration and expansion.

It is easy to forget today, when one can hop a plane in New York and land in Chicago in less than two hours, just how arduous and long a journey could be in the time of riverboats and railroads. And that was just for travel between cities. Huge sections of North America, and the world, remained *terra incognita,* beyond the reach of any form of mechanized transportation, well into the twentieth century.

Yet as the blank areas of the maps slowly became etched with exotic names—Yellowknife, Death Valley, Cheyenne—cities and heartlands prospered and became home to millions who worked in factories and farms. Not all could risk the cost of wandering.

For them, adventure journalism provided vicarious thrills. For the cost of a penny or two, a meatpacker in Chicago or a garment worker in New York could grasp hours of entertainment by reading about exotic people and places that had the benefit of being real, not fictional. They could dream of a world beyond the lives to which they had become rooted, perhaps scratching the itch of that wanderlust gene that had long slept dormant.

I read the accounts of adventure journalism in this book, and I find myself thinking, "Wow. Does that sound like fun." (I include the tragic explorations here, as nobody set out to find the North Pole thinking, "Well, I'll surely die along the way.") Reporters got *paid* to go on exotic adventures and tell their stories to audiences eager to read them. And not only were these stories the kind that built individual reputations, both for newspapers and for their reporters and editors, but they also served to construct a shared identity of what it meant to be Americans: bold, Christian, rational conquerors of the wild.

These adventure journalists played many roles. They were interpreters and guides. They were investigators and sociologists. But primarily, I think, they were actors in stage plays of their own authorship. They had to find a story, of course, but they also had to assign it meaning, acting like the omniscient narrator of *Our Town* or the observant Ishmael of *Moby Dick*. Being an actor meant being active—taking a key role in the unfolding drama. The traveling reporters knew that they served as proxy for the ordinary reader, which meant taking time to explain how they got the story and, against all odds, got it back to the printing presses of civilization, again and again. This put the readers in their shoes, making the story resonate even more strongly.

And finally, let us not forget the role of bard. Adventure journalists, as this book makes clear, wrote for you and me. Not a scientific society nor an academic press. They took pains to, as Frank Leslie said, "Never shoot over the heads of the people." Their care in reaching out to their audiences paid dividends for the publishers who sent them into the wilderness, and for readers who found their understanding of the world beyond the next hill expanded far enough to form a new construct of what it meant to be "American."

# Preface

KATRINA J. QUINN

The Gilded Age saw the emergence of issues which still characterize our national discourse: multiculturalism and national identity, the tenuous balance of technology and the environment, scientific innovation and discovery. These issues, and more, were discussed and dissected by the nation's great mass medium, the nineteenth-century press. And as the nation expanded its role on the world stage, as the reach of its economic, military, and technological interests grew, newspapers took on new roles that would replace Civil War battlefields with ideological clashes and experiential panoramas of unbounded proportion.

The rhetorical role of the press in the formation of a global nation of the twentieth century cannot be underestimated. What was the nation to be? And what was the stage on which it would act? Enabled by the massive machinery of the late–nineteenth-century press, and often propelled by the deep-pocketed and ambitious titans at its helm, adventure journalists of the Gilded Age set out to take a look. This book is the study of these remarkable men and women and an exploration of the adventure journalism genre. It seeks to position Gilded Age journalists squarely within their historical and cultural milieu, in a time of expanding scientific, economic, political, and perceptual boundaries. Thus themes connected to manifest destiny, American exceptionalism, and the technology of travel figure prominently in the text—demonstrating, once again, the continuing relevance of journalism history, which informs contemporary discourses of American national identity and the nation's place in the world by preserving these moments of purposeful engagement.

To the nineteenth-century reader—perhaps a laborer, factory worker, teacher, or farmer, in his or her intimate environment, facing intense and immediate struggles—the vast world must have seemed impossibly remote. And yet there it was in the newspaper: the journalist, buoyed by ships and stages, tumbling into mines and scrambling up mountains, traversing arctic snowdrifts and sultry jungles, in the far corners of the globe. Thanks to the adventurers, just a few weeks, or a month, or two, away, the world was right there at your fingertips. Measurable, palpable, these stories brought the world to the doorsteps of the individual, and conversely took the reader on a global adventure, shaping nineteenth-century Americans' perceptions of the world and of themselves.

This book is the result of collaborations fostered at the Symposium on the 19th-Century Press, the Civil War, and Free Expression, where the work of these authors was first presented. Directed for more than 25 years by Dr. David B. Sachsman, the George R. West, Jr., Chair of Excellence in Communication and Public Affairs at the University of

Tennessee at Chattanooga, the symposium serves as an incubator for timely and relevant historical research. We are also indebted to the authors of these essays, who have taken a fresh look at this valuable historical record to re-introduce Americans to their forebears, some of the most daring real-life adventurers to grace the pages of the Gilded Age press.

# Introduction

Katrina J. Quinn, Lee Jolliffe
*and* Mary M. Cronin

Welcome to a time when being a reporter might mean bushwhacking into Africa in search of the origin of the Nile or sledding across Siberia in the dead of winter, hoping to rescue a Polar expedition lost at sea. And welcome to a time when your editor might suddenly decide you had best go off around the world at a day's notice or ride in a lurching stagecoach for 2,000 miles through uncharted territory, all for the good of circulation back home.

Many American newspaper publishers of the North had grown spoiled—rich and spoiled—during the Civil War. Ever-faster printing presses had allowed them to feed a public insatiable for war news. The reasons people read shifted during wartime; no longer did people read to feel informed. Getting the newspaper became a matter of urgency, as families combed every inch of newsprint looking for the name of a loved one at war, for mention of particular local regiments, and for a sense of the overall progress of the conflict. So spoiled were publishers by the huge wartime circulations that something had to be found to keep readership at peak levels once the guns were silenced, to keep those new presses running at full capacity and pay for the capital investments made in that machinery. Fortunately, another investment, this time national, in railroads and telegraph lines, might prove to be of help.

As the late nineteenth century saw dramatic expansion of technology and communication, the rise of a financially prosperous middle class, and greater personal mobility, American journalists of the Gilded Age set off on adventures by land, sea, and rail to uncover, witness, and explore increasingly accessible corners of the globe. Their reporting corresponded to other adventures: nation-building and empire-building; technological and scientific discoveries; and a transformation in the role of the press in bringing stories to a progressively diverse reading public. Their work was undertaken during an era in which the U.S. government, while still rebuilding a once-divided nation, was reasserting itself on the world's stage.

This book seeks to define and explore the genre of post-war adventure reporting and highlight the men and women who pursued it. Adventure journalism engaged the journalist in a journey or experience that was outside the normal for both the reporter and his or her readers. We propose that the term "adventure journalism" denotes both a method (an adventure) and content (discussion of that adventure), and suggest that the reader must be able to perceive the method/content as an "adventure" to qualify as adventure journalism. Objective reporting on the South Seas or from the Alaskan wilderness,

5

for example, would not be adventure reporting without the dramatic struggle of the journalist to acquire the story.

Adventure journalism therefore implies a small or large degree of danger, risk, or struggle, generally in a remote location. Indeed, the genre proposes a significant intersection with sensationalism, since adventures by definition display sensational content. No mundane or familiar experience would qualify as an "adventure"; thus the wilder the adventure, the more risky it was, the more colorful or exotic the people and places … the more attractive the subject as the focus of nineteenth-century adventure reporters.

Lee Jolliffe identifies these individuals as "people who seek out or are sent out to find adventure, place themselves on-stage as players in events, and report back to the periodical press about the events they witness and generally participate in."[1] Characteristics of adventure journalists included bravery, industry, and self-sacrifice, but an essential characteristic of the reporter was his or her role as an outsider in the reported environment. This allowed the journalist to see, interpret, and translate for the readers.

Implicit to this model is a consciousness of boundary-crossing: from the normal and familiar to the new and unfamiliar. Boundaries in this sense include geographic boundaries, but also cultural or environmental boundaries, and urban or economic boundaries. Because of the importance of the reporter as the boundary-crosser in the reported story and on behalf of the readers, he or she becomes part of the story, inserting himself or herself into the location/landscape/experience. Sometimes, the reporter's position as an outsider could lead to enhanced risk or, alternately, comic situations. The reporter furthermore serves as a surrogate for the readers in the adventure. He or she is witness, and may attempt to convey the experience through descriptions of people and places, unfamiliar procedures or rituals, etc., often resulting in a narrative or literary component to the reportage.

It must be noted that nineteenth-century adventure journalism was before all faithful to the reporting impulse and reporting methods of the era. Thus it was episodic, responsible to the public trust, and committed to truth-telling. In other words, while there is great commonality between adventure journalism and, for example, nonfiction travel narratives or other works, the reporting purpose is an *a priori* condition of the genre, which deliberately sought the acquisition of news.

## Tradition of Adventure Writing

The journey or adventure story is among humanity's greatest archetypal tales, manifest throughout history in fictional and nonfictional works, taking on a variety of narrative forms. Epochal works such as Homer's *Odyssey* established the journey motif as well as the traveler-hero figure, embodied with the bravery, intelligence, and resourcefulness needed to wrestle with the natural world and its inhabitants. Ancient works of nonfiction adventure provide scientific accounts of travel or geography,[2] with nonfiction adventure texts appearing more frequently in the late Middle Ages and early Renaissance. Surviving works often relate official diplomatic or commercial expeditions, as in the Asian adventures of Marco Polo in the thirteenth century or the Holy Land pilgrimage of Conrad Grünenberg in the fifteenth century, and were produced in small quantities.[3] As time went by the circle of travel broadened. In the sixteenth century, the English writer Richard Hakluyt published eyewitness accounts of explorers to North America, a

Like other journalists of his day, Frederick Wadsworth Loring (1848–71), a promising young newspaper editor and author from Boston, accepted an opportunity for adventure with "the greatest eagerness and enthusiasm." He was well-suited for adventure. From Death Valley, he wrote his *Appletons' Journal* editors that despite being "bootless, coatless, every thing but lifeless" after a "fortnight of horrors," he found himself nevertheless "well and cheerful" ("Table-Talk," *Appletons' Journal*, Dec. 9, 1871). Just days after this photograph was taken, Loring and his companions were ambushed and murdered by Apaches near Prescott, Arizona (photograph by Timothy H. O'Sullivan, National Archives, VCN: 106-WA-145).

work which may have accelerated support for colonization of the continent.[4] Fifty years later, Sir Thomas Herbert wrote an account of his years in Africa and Asia, having served as a member of Charles I's embassy in Persia, with multiple editions of his book published.[5] Indeed this was a global phenomenon, as travelers from Asian and Arabic countries recorded their adventures as well.[6] Travelers inscribed works in the form of letters, poetry, or journals, and were often motivated by a moral or educational impulse, a role the press would take on in the nineteenth century.

With increasing mobility particularly among the upper classes, the figure of the literary adventurer took hold during the seventeenth and eighteenth centuries, establishing the travel narrative as a fixture in popular literature. Prominent British authors such as Daniel Defoe,[7] Samuel Johnson,[8] and James Boswell[9] published popular nonfiction travel books. Well-to-do women adventurers of the period, such as the inveterate English horseback traveler Celia Fiennes, also wrote detailed memoirs of their trips, but their work was generally not published until later, a gendered difference in distribution and readership which persisted until the nineteenth century.[10] Exceptions include the prolific Lady Mary Wortley Montagu,[11] who published colorful accounts of her life in Turkey, where her husband was British ambassador, and Mary Wollstonecraft,[12] who in 1795 traveled to Scandinavia in pursuit of a pirated ship. Her popular account of this trip, *Letters Written During a Short Residence in Sweden, Norway, and Denmark*, was published the following year and translated into four languages.[13]

Among the prominent upper-class literary adventurers of the eighteenth century was Lady Mary Wortley Montagu (1689–1762). She intentionally engaged notions of travel writing—as well as the unique perspectives of a woman traveler—in her work. Addressing her reader, she noted, "You will perhaps be surpriz'd at an Account so different from what you have been entertaind with by the common Voyage-writers who are very fond of speaking of what they don't know" (from XXXII, Adrianople, April 1, 1718) (engraving by S. Hollyer after J.B. Wandesforde. New York: Derby & Jackson, Bildarchiv Austria, Inventarnummer: PORT_00103897_01).

The nineteenth century saw the burgeoning of adventure writing as opportunities for travel and publishing expanded. Although global exploration and the age of European colonization began centuries earlier, exploration of the world's remote places continued into the nineteenth century. However, the funding, personnel, and means of promotion changed substantially. While cartographers had sketched most of the coastlines of the world's continents as well as the Pacific islands by the dawn of the nineteenth century, two of the world's biggest colonial powers—Great Britain and France—had ceased government funding for exploration. Private groups, including the Royal Geographical Society (based in London), came to the fore, raising funds for civilian explorers to continue the discovery and mapping of the globe, especially the interiors of Africa, Asia, South America, and the polar regions.[14]

These privately funded expeditions brought fame to many explorers, including Sir Richard Francis Burton,[15] Dr. David Livingstone, and Sir John Franklin, whose three-year search during 1845–1848 for the famed Northwest Passage and subsequent disappearance in 1847 led to more than fifty search and rescue missions.[16] Much of the men's acclaim (and, in some cases, notoriety) came from mediated sources. Groups like the Royal Geographical Society promoted the expeditions via public talks and provided information that the media reprinted. The explorers often publicized themselves—and profited handsomely—from their written accounts and public lectures.[17] Mediated sources also allowed these Anglo and European explorers to craft images of themselves as dashing, heroic men of action during an era where the idea of "manhood" was being rethought publicly. The concept of a strenuous life that focused on out-of-doors activities was not only celebrated and promoted during the latter decades of the nineteenth century but also linked to racial dominance. Anglo-Saxon writers put forth a vision that white males were superior physically, emotionally, spiritually, morally, and culturally to other races.[18]

Readers could also follow the real-life adventures of well-known novelists such as Charles Dickens,[19] Mary Shelley,[20] and Robert Louis Stevenson,[21] who brought narrative adventure into the mainstream with their popular works. Even those not principally known as writers, such as French diplomat Alexis de Tocqueville, earned their place in history with works that described travels through distant lands as well as the cultural and political institutions that shaped them.[22] Widely read works of missionaries and scientists included Lutheran missionary Karl von Gutzlaff's 1834 book, *Journal of Three Voyages Along the Coast of China in 1831, 1832, and 1833*, and the 1868 work of English writer and artist Frederick Whymper, *Travel and Adventure in the Territory of Alaska*, which sold thousands of copies.[23] Prominent women adventurers of the period included Isabella Frances Romer, who published a book of European travels in 1843 and, in 1846, an account of a trip to Egypt, Africa, and the Middle East,[24] as well as well-known adventurer Isabella Bird, who published many articles and a dozen books about her travels to Australia, the Sandwich Islands, the American West, India, Asia, Africa, and the Pacific.[25]

In America, those of the adventuring mindset found plenty of opportunities right at their doorsteps, producing well-circulated books with increasing frequency during the nineteenth century. Popular works of exploration and adventure of this period were published by writer and politician Henry Marie Brackenridge, who traveled in Louisiana, South America, and the western United States.[26] Geographer and geologist Henry Rowe Schoolcraft was another well-known explorer who made excursions into territories west of the Mississippi River, publishing several of his journals, especially *Journal of a Tour into the Interior of Missouri and Arkansaw* in 1821.[27] One of the first American literary figures who recorded trips west of the Mississippi was Washington Irving, who published *A Tour on the Prairies* in 1835.[28] Among the best-selling adventure books of the Old West was historian Francis Parkman's *The Oregon Trail: Sketches of Prairie and Rocky-Mountain Life*, which established him as a leader in the development of narrative history.[29] These popular books fueled the nineteenth-century reading public's interest in remote places and the adventures of the authors to reach them.

In light of the great public interest in adventure writing, it was to be expected that the works of these men and women would be carried in the periodical press, taking the form of travel correspondence. One of those published adventurers was wealthy artist George Catlin, known for his portraits of Native Americans in the 1830s. Catlin's correspondence from five trips to the West was published in the *Spectator*, the *Daily Commercial Advertiser*, and other publications.[30] In 1871, the *Atlantic Monthly* published a series of articles under the title "Mountaineering in the Sierra Nevada," by a wealthy young traveler, Clarence King. The articles proved so successful that they were collected in a book the following year, subsequently published in many editions both in the United States and England.[31]

By the mid-nineteenth century, adventure correspondence such as this was a regular feature of the American press, feeding the reading public's hunger for information about new parts of the continent and the world. This interest was fueled by political expansion—with nine states admitted to the union between 1830 and 1860, and twelve more between 1860 and 1900—as well as by a perceptual expansion, as Americans by the thousands moved into and settled the West. As the Gilded Age dawned, writers and intellectuals put forth a new view of the American West, seeing it as a vast and vital spiritual resource, a space free from the corruption brought on by civilization.[32]

## Journalists Take the Stage

Nineteenth-century journalists stepped into the role of the adventuring hero en masse. However, something was different about the work of journalist-adventurers. Journalists did not write for their king or the gov-

A groundbreaking woman journalist, editor, and feminist writer, Margaret Fuller (1810–50) was already well-known by 1844, when she was hired by Horace Greeley as the first-ever book reviewer in journalism history at the *New-York Tribune*. Fuller was the *Tribune*'s first female foreign correspondent, traveling to Europe in 1846. Returning to the U.S. in 1850, she drowned in a shipwreck off the shore of Fire Island, New York (daguerrotype by John Plumbe, 1846, National Portrait Gallery, Smithsonian Institution, Object number: NPG.2007.386).

ernment, for a close circle of friends, for their church or a scientific community; instead, they wrote intentionally and enthusiastically for the readers, an expanding population as circulation numbers swelled. They wrote with a commitment to content that was newsworthy and reader-driven, connected, perhaps, to current events, but also an event of itself. Their audience was a mass audience—strangers, but familiar by nationality or perhaps by region; people, including the working class, the vast majority of whom would never themselves have a chance to travel but who would gladly partake in an adventure of the imagination. Journalists themselves, of course, were not privileged in the sense that the English aristocracy or American upper-classes would be, and they brought the eyes and ears of the masses to bear on great adventures around the globe.

This democratization of the adventure text meant journalists were not writing journals or government surveys, or poetry, or fiction. In contrast to artists, explorers, government emissaries, or the idle rich, journalists were in the writing business. They brought skills of observation, an investigative mind, a commitment to truth-telling, description and details, and a sense of news—what in this day's adventure was important, unique, etc.

They had the motivation for adventure reporting, as the number of newspapers, particularly dailies, exploded through the nineteenth century, and content was needed.[33] Journalists also had the credentials that granted them access to remote villages or unusual people, to serve as an eye-witness for their readers, inhabitants of a nineteenth-century world that was quickly transforming.

Adventure journalism thus came of age with the profession itself. Although correspondence from others had been included in newspapers for many years,[34] James Gordon Bennett institutionalized this practice when he hit upon the idea of internalizing the correspondent—placing paid staff in Europe and several American cities as early as 1838. It was thus a short leap for journalists to purposefully take to the road to find their own stories, a practice that was honed in the fires of Civil War and that blossomed in new directions in the post-war period. Motivated by a desire for adventure but also facilitated by changes in technology and a sense of public duty, journalists were on a mission to acquire the "best news and the most."[35] And thus the northeastern newspapers sent their reporters on the road, across the border, and around the globe. It was a financial gamble that paid off, as circulations grew. Adventure reporting proved so popular that many authors collected their correspondence to be published again as books, often in multiple editions.[36] Albert Richardson's *Beyond the Mississippi* was one of the

In the business of writing, adventuring journalists did so under tents, from bouncing stages, in the rain, and—in this 1872 image of William McKay of the *San Francisco Bulletin*—on the battlefield alongside two Warm Spring Indian scouts (National Archives, VCN: 111-SC-82307).

most popular, according to *Publisher's Weekly*, with more than a quarter million copies printed.[37]

## *Thematic Elements*

The work of American adventure journalists in the Gilded Age is characterized by situational paradigms related to their unique cultural, nationalistic, scientific, technological, and philosophical locus in history. In the business of articulating the world as they saw it, that agency carried assumptions related to national identity, manifest destiny, Anglo-American cultural and racial superiority, technological change, growing concerns about nature and the environment, and so on. These are the themes that emerge from the work of our adventure journalists of the Gilded Age, whether their travels took them to Mexico, South America, Africa, Asia, the Arctic, or the American West.

Among the prominent ideological constructs reflected in the work of these Gilded Age authors is the idea of manifest destiny. From its earliest days, the nation had expanded westward, an economic and nationalistic crusade accelerated with discoveries of mineral wealth in Colorado, California, and elsewhere. Manifest destiny demanded an acquisition and a purification of territory and national concept, leaving as its casualties many Native Americans and their traditional cultures. The construct established an essential coherence among post-war Americans, North and South, East and West, working toward an idealized American national identity, finding a place for those American populations who may not share a regional heritage but who would share a common inheritance.

Because the American community was comprised of disparate elements, it was the work of cultural architects to define what America would be. Just as Lincoln, Whitman, and others laid the rhetorical foundation of the American nation-state during the Civil War,[38] the process continued afterward as the nation began its collective march toward a bright and blessed destiny.[39] From de Tocqueville through twentieth-century political scientist Benedict Anderson,[40] of course, the role of newspapers in defining that community has long been acknowledged. After the Civil War, the nation saw a mobilization of journalists who took inventory of what was won, measured its value, and projected its future. The adventure journalists of this book, and others, were among these legions, and their footsteps across the continent and across the globe called them to come to terms with the physical and ideological boundaries of the nation. It's also relevant to note that nations are defined as well in juxtaposition to those identified as *other* both within and without—in the case of our adventure journalists, Native Americans, but also immigrants and unfamiliar global populations.

While adventuring journalists were acutely aware of encounters with human and socio-cultural others, they were thrust upon environmental others as well, a theme which conflated smoothly with a growing awareness and understanding of the natural world. Much like personal letters, diaries, and journals, adventure reporting provided ample descriptions of the methods, technologies, routes, and, often, the inconveniences of travel; in other words, the traveler was intimately in contact with environment and his or her passage through it. Thus environment was a significant player not only in the adventuring act but in the perceptual machinery of the adventurer. Stalking through brush, sweltering in the heat, heaving on the waves, an adventure journalist's account of the environment was personal, intimate, at times dominating and at times dominated. The environment was an obstacle to be overcome but also worthy of reporting, the source of rich descriptive narrative, and a personal connection to the reader, who could envision himself or herself in this context.

Although many readers would never travel themselves, the technologies of travel matured through the nineteenth century, with journalists taking advantage of improved roads, bridges, canals, and vehicles as time went on. Where travelers had once knocked at the door of a remote farmhouse or cabin for accommodations, later travelers could look forward to a serendipitous tavern or lodging house as transportation routes were formalized. As railroads sprung up in the 1840s and 1850s, access to distant regions was improved, though reporters' passage to remote quarters was still facilitated by stagecoach and horse through most of the century. Ocean travel, conducted by cargo ship prior to the 1840s, was revolutionized with the advent of dedicated passenger ships and regularized service, with a growing list of amenities by the 1860s. These ships carried reporters to Europe, the Caribbean, Asia, and the South Seas.

With the technology to penetrate the farthest corners and cultures of the globe, journalists were well-equipped to execute the global mission of their profession. The role of the press had evolved during the mid–nineteenth century, according to Hazel Dicken-Garcia, from one which benefited the individual to one which could "aid ... the

Despite the significant evolution of transportation technologies in the nineteenth century, many journalists venturing into remote landscapes still faced daunting challenges. Even well-engineered roads of the 1870s, including this one across the Beaver Head River between Ogden and Helena, Montana, seem a bit precarious by today's standards (photograph by William Henry Jackson, 1871, National Archives, VCN: 79-JAG-9).

world,"[41] keeping pace with and indeed driving broad American reform movements. Dicken-Garcia finds this mission to have emerged in the 1840s and 1850s, an era when broad reform movements were taking flight: social reform, especially in urban areas; a temperance movement launched early in the century and gaining steam throughout; educational reform; reform of mental institutions and prisons; women's suffrage; and of course, abolition.

By the Gilded Age, the newspaper was more than a recorder of quotidian goings-on, according to a columnist in the *North American Review*, but instead it recorded "the daily history of the world and record of the doing of mankind, political, commercial, social, artistic...."[42] The newspaper served as a "vast popular educator," bringing news from the most remote corners of the globe.[43] Incentivized by such a noble duty, serving a growing readership, and buoyed by a growing infrastructure that could finance and staff ambitious reporting ventures, newspapers such as the *New York Herald,* the *New-York Tribune,* and *Frank Leslie's Illustrated Newspaper* set about pursuing stories on the national and global stage that could fulfill the newspaper's mission to educate the public, shape public opinion, and drive public policy.

Buttressing innovation in the transportation industry, scientific discoveries fueled the popular imagination as well as the adventuring impulse of daring reporters. A deeper understanding of the natural world, including theories of evolution and genetics, infused a new meaning to reporters' observation of remote ecosystems and plant life. New insights into anthropology and ethnography would have prompted and shaped encounters of reporters with exotic peoples and cultures. And innovations in visual technologies—from the first photograph and the first daguerreotype, produced in 1826 and 1835 respectively, to the first demonstration of high-speed photography in 1851, the development of halftone reproduction in the 1880s, and moving pictures in 1888—meant photography and reproduction were on a dazzling trajectory, launching an era of visual reportage. As a profession, photojournalism came of age in the Civil War, and spread its wings in the Gilded Age, with some photographs of the period presented in newspapers as woodcuts until technology allowed for halftone reproduction beginning in 1880.[44] Press photographers could finally capture images of the lakes and mountains of the continent, and eventually of sites around the world.

The dangers and trappings of exotic environments provided a contrast to a sense of American pride rooted in the environment. Where ancient civilizations had histories, artifacts, and monuments to mark great accomplishments and outline a national being, in America these ideas had to be cultivated from raw materials of land, people, and innovation. Journalists contributed to this rhetorical tapestry by articulating a sense of national pride connected to landscape, a construct Merle Curti labeled *monumentalism*.[45] The environmental movement, furthermore, was taking shape after the publication of *Man and Nature* by George Perkins Marsh in 1864, and the designation of Yellowstone, in 1872, as the first national park. Adventure journalists were in a unique position to become witnesses to national wealth tied to land in the form of extent, grandeur, and mineral resources.[46]

The monumentalism exuded in these works was closely tied to the theme of American exceptionalism, which affirms the superiority of American ideals, systems, ontologies, and virtue. This theme was present as well in the works of global adventurers, who found themselves in socio-cultural settings that contrasted starkly with the advantages and comforts and Christian ideals of American society. The others of the world were refracted through the lens of American exceptionalism as journalists took their skills

3993   Glacier Point Rock, 3201 feet. -Yosemite Valley.   *Taber* Photo., San Francisco.

Unlike the Gilded Age tourists who would daringly pose on Yosemite's Glacier Point Rock, most Americans relied on the accounts of writers and artists to convey the majesty of the nation's greatest natural monuments—sights which "inspire the mind with sensations of sublimity…," not to mention national pride. *St. Cloud* [MN] *Journal*, Aug. 6, 1868) (photograph by Isaiah West Taber, 1880–1900, Rijksmuseum, Objectnummer: RP-F-2012-96-228).

of observation but also their judgmental sense of propriety, of civilization, of taste, and of culture. Images of natives scantily clad, or of rakish behavior, tales of meager accommodations or habiliment, unrefined social behaviors, heathenistic rites, and so on, were fascinating to the journalists and the readers alike as they stood in contrast to American ideals.[47] The journalist served as a conduit of information to the reader, and in this role, was a stable, familiar viewer entering the exotic milieu. Thus adventuring journalists articulated not only an ideology that defined America, but an epistemology that positioned the rest of the world as relative to an American standard.

## Our Itinerary

This collection takes a critical look at the work of American adventure journalists as they traveled across America and around the world, arguing that the genre emerged partly in an effort to bolster circulation but also in connection to broader social, political, cultural, and scientific movements. The book does not seek to be exhaustive, but instead provides essays that investigate the work of individual journalists. Each study seeks to address the adventure category broadly, using individuals as examples or case studies of broader findings. Theoretical and interdisciplinary approaches can also be found, as the works of adventure journalists were indeed themselves multidisciplinary. The book excludes the associated but distinct categories of war reporting, adventure journals, and historical fiction.

The first part of the book, "Adventures at Home," presents studies of adventures by rail, trail, and sea, brought to the reading public in the form of narrative journalism accompanied by engravings and later, as printing processes improved, photography. These journalists reported from the far corners of North America with adventures to Alaska and even the Arctic. Katrina J. Quinn shows us the American West via newly cut trails and trundling stagecoaches and then via early railroad travel, as reporters heeded publisher Horace Greeley's admonition to "Go west, young man." During their rough-and-tumble travels, journalists—even Greeley himself—would suffer the mishaps of the trail—stagecoach rollovers, luggage dropped into rivers, buffalo hunts, and very occasional battles with Native Americans. Luckily for reporters, railroads would soon offer somewhat more comfortable travel, at least to places along their ever-expanding routes. Mary M. Cronin takes us from New York City to San Francisco by rail with magazine publisher Frank Leslie and his entourage of reporters and illustrators, who filled up his complimentary Pullman Palace car. Leslie's magazine accounts of the trip show his business acumen, as he identifies opportunities for expansion, but also make clear his lens of Anglo-American superiority and manifest destiny. The mountains and prairies streamed by the rail coach windows as Leslie and his colleagues feasted inside on champagne, oysters, and other succulent fare.

While most adventure journalists pursued their stories above-ground, Katrina J. Quinn takes a deep dive with reporters into the mines of America, among the era's most dangerous terrains. At a gold mine near Bodie, California, reporter J. Ross Browne said he thought of sunshine and of widows and orphans as he descended a rickety ladder several stories downward—having refused the alternate method of descent, which was being lowered in a big wooden bucket secured by rope to a blind horse. Copper, coal, iron, and of course, silver and gold mines drew some reporters as inexorably as Alaska or Africa drew others. Mining held all the era's notions of masculinity and strength: qualities such as individualism, a strong work ethic, coarseness, strength, resourcefulness, mastery of material things, exuberance, and confidence, according to Frederick Jackson Turner.[48]

Another journalistic impulse in exploration of the growing United States was focus on its waters, specifically its rivers. One of the most famous reporters of this era, James Creelman, chose to travel the Mississippi River from a launch point on the Ohio River downriver to New Orleans and the Gulf of Mexico. What made Creelman's choice of adventures so exciting to readers was his companion, Irish explorer and stunt celebrity Paul Boyton. For their trip, Boyton used his own invention, a unique rubber rescue suit, rather than a boat. Essay author Crompton Burton takes us along, as Creelman travels more than 1,500 miles by steamer, train, and rowboat, chasing the bobbing Boyton and fending off floating steamboat debris, ice floes, and even hungry alligators, to report the feat for the *New York Herald*.

The acquisition of Alaska in 1867 by U.S. Secretary of State William Seward had not resulted in much Congressional interest in sending out the ubiquitous geological survey teams that had been key to mapping and claiming the western mainland. Seward's Folly had not seen many visitors until the gold rushes of the 1890s took hold of the public imagination—and the plans of W.J. Arkell, the editor of *Frank Leslie's Illustrated Newspaper*. Arkell envisioned a *Leslie's* expedition, exploring and sending back frequent dispatches and drawings of the Alaskan interior. What actually happened was that the explorer journalists were "green, urban tenderfoots who took unnecessary risks." They refused to wait out snowstorms and insisted on traveling through the winter months. For quite some time, readers back home believed the team had been lost in Alaska's unforgiving winter. Mary M. Cronin joins Gilded Age readers in following the *Leslie's* Alaska adventure and sharing literal cliff-hangers from these reporters.

Like the *Leslie's* Alaska adventurers, Chicago newspaper columnist Teresa Howard Dean had no business setting out for the frontier. But her prominence and readership helped her convince her editors to support a trip to South Dakota to visit the Sioux Indians immediately after the Battle of Wounded Knee. *Chicago Herald* Editor Jimmy Scott gave her a small revolver, a Pullman ticket, and press credentials. Paulette D. Kilmer here describes Dean's travels as she reported the tragic Sioux visit and, later, the World's Columbian Exposition of 1893 and San Francisco's California Midwinter Exposition of 1894, treating each as if it were a world-circling trip, with exhibits and peoples gathered from around the globe.

The second section of this book, "Globetrotters," presents studies of adventures to the far corners of the globe by reporters sent abroad by publishers hungry for the most terrifying adventures in the most exotic locales. Though Thomas Knox was first made famous as the war reporter who was court-martialed by General William T. Sherman—Sherman hated newspaper reporters and saw them as spies—Knox was later to be known as an intrepid explorer, travel writer, and celebrity, whose travels to Asia and Siberia made him the stuff of legend. William E. Huntzicker follows Knox's sea voyage across the Pacific to the Orient, where Knox took an almost anthropological view of the "natives" he found there. Jennifer E. Moore will also take readers on a Pacific voyage, with a bored young reporter, then-unknown Mark Twain, as he explores Hawaii (then called the Sandwich Islands). In Hawaii, Twain's interviews with tattered survivors of the wrecked and burnt clipper ship *Hornet* made him a household name.

The phrase "Dr. Livingstone, I presume" would forever embarrass reporter Henry Morton Stanley, whose treks in Africa were far more serious than the suddenly popular phrase would have suggested. James E. Mueller reports on Stanley's trips to Africa and their enthusiastic reception back home, travel tales made all the more fascinating to readers by their extreme attention to detail, what Stanley himself called "minutia." Sponsored by the *New York Herald*, Stanley's first trip to Africa included a search for the missing doctor, missionary, and explorer, David Livingstone. Stanley's crew battled disease, hostile tribes and dangerous animals on a year-long, 700-mile journey from the eastern coast to reach a village called Ujiji near Lake Tanganyika, to find the doctor. Also featured in this essay is Stanley's second trip to Africa, to chart its waterways. With 300 men—reduced to 175 by "dysentery, famine, heart disease, desertion and war"—Stanley soldiered on and we, like his nineteenth-century readers, travel with him.

*National Geographic* reporter and photographer Eliza Ruhamah Scidmore also traveled widely and to exotic locales, publishing accounts of her trips regularly and widely. James E. Mueller takes us along on Scidmore's most famous Gilded Age adventures to Alaska in 1883–84; to Japan on multiple occasions beginning in the 1880s; and, in the 1890s, to Java, an island of present-day Indonesia. From Alaska, Scidmore provided her readers exhilarating tales of life aboard a ship navigating through dangerous glacial waters—tales so popular that she is widely credited with helping to launch Alaska's cruise ship industry. Scidmore's favorite port of call was Japan, the scene of one of her most vivid and dangerous adventures, the treacherous ascent of Mount Fuji. In Java, she braved her guide's constant harping on "Snakes! Snakes!" to traverse the jungles and climb Mount Papandayan.

Full of daring and drama, Gilded Age attempts to reach the North Pole were a source of good newspaper copy and avid readership. Crompton Burton explores reportage from an ill-fated North Pole expedition, a publicity stunt of James Gordon Bennett Jr. A boisterous publisher who inherited his wealth and his newspaper, Bennett had discovered that funding expeditions—the more perilous the better—was a fine hobby and an effective circulation-builder. Bennett had already sent two excursions to the North looking for a Northwest Passage, and now, paying no heed to such crucial elements as the seasons, Bennett hired a crew and bought a run-down ship, the *Jeannette*, and off the explorers went in the autumn of 1879, to immediately become ice-locked and eventually suffer starvation, hardship, and death. The stories Bennett had sought from the North Pole were not to be, but the search for the lost crew of the *Jeannette* lasted for months, as the U.S. government and various publications sent expeditions in hopes of finding survivors. The search became a saga that included a mad dash across Siberia in winter, with reports arriving from far-flung Asian telegraph stations as reporters looked for any news of the *Jeannette*.

Not to be overlooked, and concluding the Globetrotters section of the book, is perhaps the most memorable of the Gilded Age adventure journalists, Nellie Bly, pen name of Elizabeth Jane Cochrane. Bly is well-known today for her 'round the world trip, attempting to beat the Jules Verne fictional "record"—and succeeding. Early in her career, though, Nellie Bly took a train to Mexico, where she reported on the people and cultures of our neighbor to the South, which she found to be quite exotic. Her trip was full of adventure and immersion, for example, dressing in a borrowed riding costume to visit the stunning Chapultepec Castle, guarded by soldiers. She described a Mexican bull-fight in all its gory pageantry, and took a flat-bottomed boat to see the Floating Gardens of Xochimilco. This lesser-known adventure reporting, explored here by Jack Breslin and Katrina J. Quinn, introduced contemporary readers to topics such as Mexican history, food, customs, and myths. Little did she know that her next trip would take her so much farther.

## Legacy of Gilded Age Adventure Journalists

The legacy of the adventure reporting craze of the Gilded Age was a new vision of what journalism could be to a nation. Regions that had seemed remote and inaccessible were now more familiar, thanks to these reporters. They not only told the story of the homeland as had their predecessors, but also connected readers to a widening world of possibilities, helping to smooth a way for the nation's tentative steps onto the world stage.

As the twentieth century dawned, it was not yet 50 years since Horace Greeley sat under his India-rubber blanket on the Colorado frontier, not yet 100 years since Lewis and Clark first crossed the continent. It was to be another century of adventure, danger, and conflict, during which the spirit of discovery pushed Americans still onward and outward, with reporters the scribes of this ongoing adventure. Twentieth-century newspapers would formalize the adventure journalism blueprint with legions of foreign correspondents who would envelop the far corners of the globe, a role coming into maturity by World War I along with new publishing technologies, photo reproduction, and moving pictures.

This collection invites twenty-first century readers to join some of the most daring and innovative Gilded Age adventurers on their journeys. The reportage provides a window to a past that is at once historic and yet familiar, with troubadour-journalists telling the story of the great American nation, no matter where the next bold adventure would lead.

## Notes

1. Lee Jolliffe, "Adventurer Journalists in the Gilded Age," *Journalism History* 42, no. 1 (2016): 3.
2. Pausanias (c. 110–180) *Description of Greece*; Gerald of Wales (1146–1223) *Itinerarium Cambriae* (Journey Through Wales, 1191); *The Travels of Sir John Mandeville* (c. 1356), an imaginary account of travels in Asia based on a variety of true sources about the eastern countries; Christopher Columbus (c. 1450–1506), journal of the first voyage (1492–1493).
3. *The Travels of Marco Polo* (1254–1324) was written by Rustichello da Pisa in 1300; Rustichello da Pisa, *The Travels of Marco Polo*, trans. by William Marsden (New York: AMS Press, 1968). Grünenberg (d. 1494) wrote his travelogue in 1486.
4. Richard Hakluyt, ed., *Divers Voyages Touching the Discoverie of America and the Ilands Adjacent unto the Same, Made First of All by Our Englishmen and Afterwards by the Frenchmen and Britons: With Two Mappes Annexed Hereunto* (London: Richards, 1582); Quarto.; John Winter Jones, ed., *Divers Voyages Touching the Discovery of America and the Islands Adjacent* [Hakluyt Society; 1st Ser., no. 7] (London: Hakluyt Society).
5. Sir Thomas Herbert, *A Relation of Some Yeares Travaile, Begunne Anno 1626.* (London: Stansby and Bloom, 1634). See staffblogs.le.ac.uk/specialcollections/2015/01/07/17th-century-adventures-in-travel-writing/. Newer Edition: *Some years travels into divers parts of Africa and Asia the Great describing more particularly the empires of Persia and Industan: interwoven with such Remarkable Occurrences as Hapned in these Parts During these later times* (London: A. Crook, 1665).
6. See, for example, *Inscribed Landscapes: Travel Writing from Imperial China*, trans. Richard E. Strassberg (Oakland: University of California Press, 1994) and Nabil Matar, *In the Lands of the Christians: Arabic Travel Writing in the 17th Century* (New York: Routledge, 2003).
7. "A tour thro' the whole island of Great Britain," first published in three volumes between 1724 and 1727. Daniel Defoe, *A Tour thro' the Whole Island of Great Britain*, 4 vols. (London: Brown, Osborne, Hitch, and Hawes: 1762).
8. Samuel Johnson, *A Journey to the Western Islands of Scotland* (Dublin, Ireland: Thomas Walker, 1775).
9. James Boswell, *The Journal of a Tour to the Hebrides* (London: Henry Baldwin, 1785).

10.  Fiennes compiled her memoir in 1702, according to Kat Eschner of the Smithsonian, but it was not publicly available until a century later. See Kat Eschner, "See 17th-Century England Through the Eyes of One of the First Modern Travel Writers: Celia Fiennes traveled and wrote about her adventures—including a bit of life advice." www.smithsonianmag.com/smart-news/see-1600s-england-through-eyes-one-first-travel-writers-180963536/. That publication was rediscovered by a descendant and republished in the late nineteenth century, at the height of the adventuring craze. See Richard Cavendish, "Birth of Celia Fiennes," *History Today* 62, no. 6 (June 2012): unpaginated. www.historytoday.com/richard-cavendish/birth-celia-fiennes

11.  *Lady Mary Wortley Montagu: Selected Letters*, edited by Isobel Grundy (New York: Penguin, 1997). These letters were plainly intended for public distribution, according to Grundy, as they were extensively revised.

12.  Wollstonecraft (1759–1797) was a well-known English writer, author of *A Vindication of the Rights of Woman* (1792), and mother of writer Mary Shelley. Mary Wollstonecraft, *A Vindication of the Rights of Woman* (London: J. Johnson, 1792).

13.  See *The Complete Works of Mary Wollstonecraft*, edited by Janet Todd and Marilyn Butler (London: William Pickering, 1989) and Anka Ryall and Catherine Sandbach-Dahlström, *Mary Wollstonecraft's Journey to Scandinavia: Essays* (Stockholm: Almqvist & Wiksell International, 2003).

14.  Duggard, *Into Africa*, 88.

15.  Burton (1821–1890) was at once an English explorer, geographer, translator, writer, soldier, orientalist, cartographer, ethnologist, spy, linguist, poet, fencer, and diplomat. Key works include Sir Richard F. Burton, *First Footsteps in East Africa; or, An exploration of Harar* (London: Longman, Brown, Green, and Longmans, 1856) and Sir Richard F. Burton, *Personal Narrative of a Pilgrimage to El-Medinah and Meccah.* 3 vols. (London: Longman, Brown, Green, and Longmans, 1855–56).

16.  Many works have been written about nineteenth-century British explorers. Among the more current works are Owen Beattie and John Geiger, *Frozen in Time: The Fate of the Franklin Expedition* (Vancouver, BC: Greystone Books, 2014). On rescue efforts launched to locate Franklin and his men, see pages 50–72, 88–90. On African explorers, see William Harrison, *Burton and Speke* (New York: St. Martin's Press, 1982); Martin Dugard, *Into Africa: The Epic Adventures of Stanley and Livingstone* (New York: Broadway Books, 2003).

17.  Tim Jeal, *Stanley: The Impossible Life of Africa's Greatest Explorer* (New Haven: Yale University Press, 2008), 469.

18.  Gail Bederman, *Manliness and Civilization: A Cultural History of Gender and Race in the United States, 1880–1917* (Chicago: University of Chicago Press, 1995), 4–13; Saxton, *The Rise and Fall of the White Republic*, 343.

19.  *American Notes for General Circulation* (London: Chapman and Hall, 1842) and *Pictures from Italy* (London: Bradbury & Evans, 1846).

20.  Mary Shelley, *Rambles in Germany and Italy, in 1840, 1842, and 1843* (Breinigsville, PA: Nabu Pubic Domain Reprints, 2011).

21.  *Travels with a Donkey in the Cévennes* (Boston: Roberts Bros., 1879).

22.  Although sent to America by a request of the French government to study the prison system, de Tocqueville spent nine months traveling through the United States and Canada to collect material for *Democracy in America* (1835).

23.  Dugard, *Into Africa*, 33; Edward Rice, *Captain Sir Richard Francis Burton: A Biography* (Cambridge: De Capo Press, 2001), 2–3, 419–422.

24.  Isabella Frances Romer, *A Pilgrimage to the Temples and Tombs of Egypt, Nubia and Palestine in 1845–6* (London: R. Bentley, 1847).

25.  The prolific Bird produced many works during her lifetime, including *The Englishwoman in America* (1856), *Six Months in the Sandwich Islands, amongst the Palm Groves, Coral Reefs and Volcanoes* (1874), *A Lady's Life in the Rocky Mountains* (1879), and *Unbeaten Tracks in Japan: Travels of a Lady in the Interior of Japan* (1879), among others.

26.  Henry Marie Brackenridge, *Views of Louisiana, Together with a Journal of a Voyage up the Missouri River, in 1811* (Pittsburgh: Cramer, Spear and Richbaum, 1814). Brackenridge followed in the frontier footsteps of his father, Hugh Henry Brackenridge (1748–1816), who settled in Pittsburgh in 1781, when it was a village of 400 residents, and founded the University of Pittsburgh and the *Pittsburgh Gazette*, now the *Pittsburgh Post-Gazette*.

27.  The full name of Schoolcraft's published journal is *Journal of a Tour into the Interior of Missouri and Arkansaw, from Potosi, or Mine a Burton, in Missouri Territory, in a South-West Direction, toward the Rocky Mountains; Performed in the Years 1818 and 1819* (London: Sir Richard Phillips and Co., 1821). During the time Schoolcraft (1793–1864) was tramping through the Ozarks, potential settler John Stillman Wright published cautionary letters from his 1818–1819 trip to what was then considered the "West"—Ohio, Indiana, Illinois and parts of Kentucky. The resulting book, *Letters from the West; or a Caution to Emigrants* (Salem, NY: Dodd & Stevenson, 1819), documents his disillusionment after finding so much of the territory already in the hands of disreputable speculators.

28.  Irving spent a month on the prairies of Oklahoma.

29. Francis Parkman, *The Oregon Trail* (1846), edited by Bernard Rosenthal (New York: Oxford University Press, 1999), ix. Parkman was so widely respected that Theodore Roosevelt's four-volume history of the frontier, *The Winning of the West* (New York: G. P. Putnam's, 1889–1896), was dedicated to him.

30. George Catlin (1796–1872), *Letters and Notes on the Manners, Customs and Conditions of the North American Indians, 1844*, ed. Peter Matthiessen (New York: Penguin, 1989). Many of Catlin's paintings are exhibited at the Smithsonian Museum of the American Indian in Washington, DC.

31. Clarence King, *Mountaineering in the Sierra Nevada*, 1872, edited and with a Preface by Francis P. Farquhar, 1935 (Lincoln: University of Nebraska Press, 1997). King set out for California in 1863, after graduation from Yale, taking the train to its end in St. Joseph, Missouri, and continuing to Virginia City, Nevada, by horseback.

32. David Hamilton Murdoch, *The American West: The Invention of A Myth* (Las Vegas: University of Nevada Press, 2001), 25.

33. According to Frank Luther Mott, there were about 200 newspapers in the United States in 1800, with 3000 by 1860. Rowell suggests there were as many as 20,000 newspapers and periodicals, all told, by 1900. See Frank Luther Mott, *American Journalism: A History of Newspapers in the United States Through 250 Years, 1690-1940* (New York: Macmillan, 1941), 216; *American Newspaper Directory* (New York: George P. Rowell, publisher, March 1900), vol. 32, issue 1; *National Newspaper Directory and Gazetteer* (Boston and New York: Pettingill & Co., 1899); H. L. Mencken, *Newspaper Days, 1899-1906* (Baltimore: The Johns Hopkins University Press, 1996); and William E. Huntzicker, *The Popular Press, 1833-1865* (Westport, CT: Greenwood Press, 1999).

34. In the 1820s, journalist Anne Royall spent four years traveling in the young state of Alabama, publishing a collection of letters from the trip in 1830. Anne Royall (1769–1854), *Letters from Alabama on Various Subjects* (Washington: 1830). See Elizabeth J. Clapp, *A Notorious Woman: Anne Royall in Jacksonian America* (Charlottesville: University of Virginia Press, 2016). Alabama was granted statehood December 14, 1819.

35. Mark Wahlgren Summers, *The Press Gang: Newspapers and Politics, 1865-1878* (Chapel Hill: University of North Carolina Press, 1994), 16.

36. An interesting inversion of the older tradition of publishing serialized books in the periodical press.

37. *Publisher's Weekly*, Iss. 655, Aug. 16, 1884, 216.

38. See Melinda Lawson, *Patriot Fires: Forging a New American Nationalism in the Civil War North* (Lawrence: University Press of Kansas, 2002).

39. See Geoff Eley and Ronald Grigor Suny, eds., *Becoming National: A Reader* (New York: Oxford University Press, 1996). See especially Eley and Suny, "From the Moment of Social History to the Work of Cultural Representation," 3–38; and Prasenjit Duara, "Historicizing National Identity, or Who Imagines What and When," 151–178.

40. Benedict Anderson, *Imagined Communities: Reflections on the Origin and Spread of Nationalism* (New York: Verso, 1983). For more on the role of cultural elites in articulating national identity, see Ernest Gellner, *Nations and Nationalism* (Ithaca: Cornell University Press, 1983).

41. Hazel Dicken-Garcia, *Journalistic Standards in Nineteenth-Century America* (Madison: University of Wisconsin Press, 1989), 155.

42. Dion Boucicault, "At the Goethe Society," *North American Review* 148 (March 1889); 336–337. Qtd in Dicken-Garcia, 159.

43. O. B. Frothingham, "Voices of Power," *Atlantic Monthly* 53 (February 1884), 176–182. Qtd in Dicken-Garcia, 159.

44. The first halftone photograph, of "Shantytown, New York," was printed in New York's *Daily Graphic* on March 4, 1880. See Joshua Brown, *Beyond the Lines: Pictorial Reporting, Everyday Life, and the Crisis of Gilded Age America* (Berkeley: University of California Press, 2002), 267–68.

45. Merle Curti, *The Roots of American Loyalty*, 1946 (New York: Russell & Russell, 1967).

46. For more on landscape and national identity, see Katrina J. Quinn, "The Rocky Mountains, Yosemite, and Other Natural Wonders: Western Landscape in Travel Correspondence of the Post-Civil War Press" in *After the War: The Press in a Changing America, 1865-1900*. Sachsman, David B., ed. (New York: Transaction, 2017), 127–140.

47. The sense of moral superiority made reporting of potentially distasteful or lewd information possible because it was presented in the guise of reporting as a dissociated or objectified occurrence. These subversive themes were common but often disguised in nineteenth-century periodical literature, dime novels, and even mainstream literature.

48. John Mack Faragher, ed., *Rereading Frederick Jackson Turner: "The Significance of the Frontier in American History" and Other Essays* (New Haven: Yale University Press, 1994), 53–55.

# PART I

# Adventures at Home

# Adventure Reporting from America's Western Rails and Trails, 1860–1880

Katrina J. Quinn

Four years before he advised Civil War veterans to "Go west, young man," 48-year-old *New-York Tribune* editor Horace Greeley set out for the Pacific, in 1859. Traveling by rail to the Missouri River at St. Joseph, he continued by stagecoach, foot, and mule for another 2,000 miles to introduce his readers to the wonders of the continent.

Greeley's trip set the stage for other journalists. So many, in fact, that in an *Atlantic Monthly* review of Samuel Bowles's 1865 *Across the Continent,* well-known writer and abolitionist Thomas Wentworth Higginson declared, "Since Mr. Greeley set the example, it has been the manifest destiny of every enterprising journalist to take an occasional trip across the continent, and personally inspect his subscribers."[1] As a group, these westering journalists were highly energetic, but not all young, not all wealthy, and not all male. What they shared was the reporter's hunger for adventure in the endless quest for a good story.

This essay explores the works of Greeley and other "enterprising journalists" who took the rails and trails to the American West during the 1860s and 1870s, including Albert Deane Richardson of the *New-York Tribune*; Fitz Hugh Ludlow writing for the *New York Evening Post*; Joseph Pratt Allyn writing for the *Hartford Evening Press*; Bowles of the *Springfield Republican*; Grace Greenwood of the *New-York Times*; and Amos Jay Cummings of the *New York Sun*. Over this period, we see the adventures of these reporters move from stagecoach and trails to an accelerated but fettered path of the railroad, resulting in texts that display divergent narrative pace, content, and thematic prominence. This shift corresponds to a cultural transition from travel to tourism during the century, an evolution explored by scholars like Daniel J. Boorstin, who claim that the shift brought an associated swing in subjectivity from active traveler to passive tourist.[2]

This essay also investigates the motivation and technologies of travel and reporting, the content and structure of the reportage, and the prominent role of the journalist as eyewitness and author. These adventurers took their readers to America's verdant plains and towering mountains, and introduced them to their western countrymen. They provided insight to the natural and future economic resources of the continent and highlighted the risks and dangers of western rails and trails that made reporting from the nineteenth-century West an adventure, indeed.

Each of these authors produced articles that can be called epistolary and literary. Epistolary, because they are addressed to a familiar reader, one who shares language and a semiotic framework through which to process information; one who, while absent from the author, is rhetorically active in the text as an explicit addressee, for whose edification and entertainment the article is written. All of the authors studied here make explicit reference to their readers and to their reading experience, perhaps to their memories of a certain person or place, and to their indulgence for an extended digression or description. Many letters also carry a date and place of composition, and perhaps a salutation of the reader or a closing *adieu*, adopting additional common practices of private letter writers.

The articles are also highly literary, strong examples of nineteenth-century literary journalism, a category in which the author takes a personal role in the story while maintaining a deliberate reportorial stance. Adopting narrative and rhetorical techniques generally associated with fiction, literary journalism is characterized by this subjective author as well as an oscillating narrative voice that embraces both objective reportorial and subjective content.[3] Extended descriptions, dialogue, analepsis, and other narrative structures are present in these works. The articles also exhibit a common narrative framework that encompasses a ritualistic departure; the hardships and inconveniences of travel; episodic accounts of places; and an evocative return journey with time for reflection. In this way, they closely resemble the popular nonfiction travel books of the day.

As a literary form, Carol Marie Greene argues, the newspaper travel letter combined nineteenth-century journalism, customs of nineteenth-century travel, travel writing, and ideologies of travel that are intellectual, experiential, and spiritual as well as physical.[4] Yet the genre exhibits significant breadth in style and content, with articles during this period delivering diverse thematic content tied to national identity. Sara Mills points to gendered variation in the authorial voice, with women more likely to be constrained in their expression than male writers.[5] Other distinctions include the factual vs. the sentimental author, with our adventuring journalists falling primarily into the former group. For Mills, the traveller's gaze is the subjective look of imperialism. Mills's approach has implications for adventuring journalists, engaged in writing national narratives in the age of manifest destiny.[6] Barbara Korte agrees, arguing that "nineteenth-century travel writing was characterized by its self-consciousness and by its promotion of values (expedition, heroism, and so on) central to empire."[7]

Germane to this discussion is the definitive work of political scientist and historian Benedict Anderson, who argues that because a nation encompasses so many individuals who may never come into contact, nationalism is largely imagined, and develops through shared narratives and cultural practices, with newspapers playing a central role.[8] Eric Hobsbawm supports Anderson's paradigm of the *imagined community* but adds that the recognition of the community engenders a desire among citizens to seek out evidence of its existence: "Merely by dint of becoming a 'people,' the citizens of a country … found themselves seeking for, and consequently finding, things in common, places, practices, personages, memories, signs and symbols."[9] Armed with this evidence, individuals could affirm and recreate in reality a community that was once merely imagined.

Our adventuring reporters were among those gathering that evidence. Because of the broad audience for adventure journalists, their work had direct implications for nation-building and contributed to the myth of the West.[10] As witnesses to the expansion of civilization and the conquering of the wilderness at the very moment of naissance, and bringing the journalist's eye and commitment to truth-telling, adventuring reporters produced articles that formed the core of this myth. Within their stories, published in newspapers and inside leather bindings, lay the hallmarks of myth: the journey and the hero; obstacles and rituals; and iconic signs and landscapes. The reporters themselves became the heroes, undertaking a journey that marked the landscape with the individual footstep and that took possession of it through rhetorical means. Our heroes crafted adventures to seek the mythic signs of *westernness*: rivers, mountains, and monumental landscapes; spare cabins with frugal settlers; hirsute frontiersmen; herds of buffalo; violence and solitude; Indians, Mormons and miners.[11] But they also revealed complexities in the western idiom as they debated the nature of Native Americans as Indian attackers and "noble savages"; considered the interplay of economic resources, technological innovation and wilderness; and constantly looked ahead, both spatially and temporally—conveying a sense of perpetual beginnings.

The power of this myth was its resonance with archetypal tales and its concomitant participatory character. The journey was ritualistic in the sense that it was a shared experience for many travelers, engaged by many more through the reading act. Biblical overtones are conveyed as the travelers confront moral challenges, and, through imagery, relayed the blossoming of gilded cities, the toils and sacrifice of the players on the frontier stage, and the blessings of providence. As fully ordained scribes, our journalistic heroes fit into the paradigm of *Americanness* themselves, the subjective centerpiece of the narrative, in constant motion, and always positioned as subjective outsiders. David Seed explains the implications of the subjective traveler, who "situates him/herself in a relation to those observed," a position which is "charged with ideological implication" for the individual's text and for the cogenerated myth.[12]

What these journalists brought to the myth-building process was a timely audience of thousands, readers who were also countrymen and women who could follow the journey and acknowledge their role as characters in an unfolding national narrative. Our authors sent their correspondence back to eastern newspapers with the closest courier, and their columns were reprinted, in whole or in part, in newspapers across the country. The stories proved so popular that many of these journalists collected their letters and reprinted them in book form, "rescued," in the words of Samuel Bowles, "from the destined oblivion of daily journalism to figure in covers."[13] These books were the subject of favorable book reviews and reading clubs, with many selling multiple thousands of copies in multiple editions. Their reach was far and sustained, driving national conversations not only about the adventure, but also about American identity and citizenship.

Horace Greeley set the stage for the westward journalistic adventure.[14] Curious and ambitious, and a proponent of western expansion, Greeley had long intended to make a trip to the West, he recalled in his autobiography, and hoped that upon announcing his plans, a companion would step forward to accompany him.[15] But when none did, he set off, alone, on May 9, 1859, California-bound. Greeley was an early supporter of the Transcontinental Railroad, and his biographers share the perspective that advocacy of this project, along with economic development of the West, was among his principal motivations.[16] Greeley took the railroad from New York to St. Joseph, crossing the Missouri to Atchison by steamer, deploring the fetid atmosphere of closed sleeping cars. He soon found himself sleeping in tents or under the stars, however, taking refuge beneath trees or within make-shift shelters, drinking from fresh springs or, more often, muddy, briny, or brackish streams.[17]

## *Striking a Trail*

Like the other authors in this sampling, Greeley's journey was replete with adventure. Greeley was among the first American travelers to strike upon some mountain trails, with some opened as recently as weeks before his arrival. As a result, his ride was truly treacherous—he sustained a significant injury to his leg when his stagecoach overturned—and accommodations were scarce. Approaching Leavenworth, Kansas, for example, Greeley and fellow passengers were disembarked so that the stagecoach could be lowered down a precipitous bank. Meanwhile, he tells us, "the passengers severally let themselves down a perpendicular bank by clinging to a tree, and crossed a deep and whirling place above the ford, on the vilest log I ever attempted to walk…." Hazardous river crossings were commonplace, and later in the journey, Greeley even lost his trunk in Sweetwater Creek after the lead mules became disoriented and agitated, much to Greeley's chagrin.[18]

Readers couldn't get enough of first-person journalistic adventures on America's rails and trails, a modality launched by *New-York Tribune* editor Horace Greeley, pictured in his top hat and trademark duster coat (photograph by Mathew Brady, Library of Congress, Item cph.3c10105).

Charting the progress of civilization across the continent was a common thematic interest of these westward-bound adventure journalists. Greeley often measured this development in terms of populations and structures, enumerating businesses and homes to quantify progress. He found that "Junction City, Kansas has a store, two hotels, and some thirty or forty dwellings, one of which is distinguished for its age, having been erected so long ago as 1858."[19] Although Denver had burst forth a full year before, Greeley found upon his arrival that its architecture was comprised merely of log cabins; its hotel, The Denver House, boasted "walls of logs, a floor of earth, with windows and roof of rather flimsy cotton-sheeting; while every guest is allowed as good a bed as his blankets will make. The charges are no higher than at the Astor and other first-class hotels, except for liquor—twenty-five cents a drink for dubious whisky, colored and nicknamed to suit the taste of customers."[20] In light of these doubtful accommodations, he and his accidental travelling companion, Albert D. Richardson, "jumped a cabin."[21] Luxurious it was not, at 12 by 12 feet, but it did boast a fireplace, a chair and table made of unstripped wooden logs, and a mattress—far better, in Greeley's estimation, than the ramshackle hotel.

Greeley stated explicitly what other writers may have only inferred, that as he withdrew farther and farther west, away from "civilization," he himself was transformed "toward the primitive simplicity of human existence," which he presented in a timeline noting the sequential disappearance of chocolates, morning newspapers, baths, wash-bowls, barbers, chairs, beds, and finally benches, until he found himself sleeping in the wagon under an India-rubber blanket.[22] He described a "tavern" which "consisted of a crotched stake which, with the squatter's fence aforesaid, supported a ridge-pole, across which some old sail-cloth was drawn, hanging down on either side." The resulting structure, "some six by eight feet, and perhaps from three to five and a half feet high," was generously equipped with two whisky barrels, several glasses, and a menu consisting of "three or four cans of pickled oysters and two or three boxes of sardines, but nothing of the bread kind whatever."[23] The tents, the hardships, the Spartan accommodations—these function as mythic signs of westerness in the works of Greeley and his ilk, who painted for their readers a rhetorical picture of the adventuring life in the West.

Albert Richardson famously met Greeley on this trip when by chance the *Tribune*

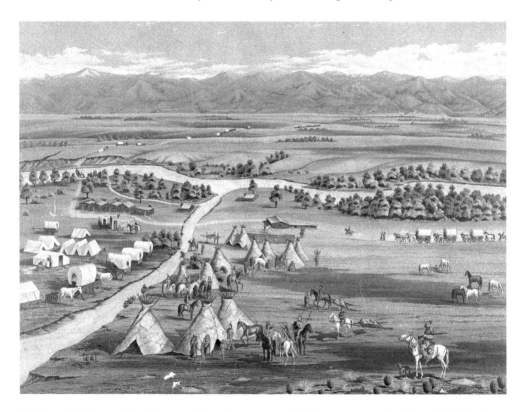

**Still part of Kansas Territory and less than a year old, Denver was a hard-scrabble "forlorn and desolate-looking metropolis" when Horace Greeley and Albert Richardson arrived on June 6, 1859 ("Denver in 1859." Collier & Cleveland Lithograph Co., Library of Congress, Item cph.3b49610).**

editor boarded Richardson's stagecoach on the newly minted Leavenworth and Pikes Peak Express en route to Denver.[24] By 1859, Richardson was a veteran adventurer, having moved to Kansas Territory in 1857 to report on the border violence for the *Boston Journal* in the wake of the improvident Kansas-Nebraska Act of 1854. Perhaps even more than the other adventurers, Richardson just could not sit still and was among the most dedicated of the adventuring journalists of the Civil War era, undertaking a pair of trips-on-assignment into the Confederacy, first in 1861 and again in 1863, when he was captured by the Confederates and held in prison for more than eighteen months until a daring wintertime escape. Richardson was soon on the road again, heading to the Pacific with three other newspapermen—Bowles; U.S. House of Representatives Speaker Schuyler Colfax, formerly editor of the *South Bend* (Indiana) *Tribune;* and Illinois Lieutenant Gov. William Bross of the *Chicago Tribune*—in 1865. While his companions returned East, Richardson continued his adventures in Utah, Montana, Idaho, and Oregon, then back to New York by way of Panama, in January 1866. Later that year, Richardson took off again to revisit Kansas and Nebraska, this time by train.[25]

The voice and structure of Richardson's reporting, like the adventure reporting of other adventuring journalists, embodies a sense of unfolding action as it was largely written *en route,* preserving at an inscriptional level the germinating adventure. Greeley, for example, emphatically wrote his letters from the road, noting at one point that he was writing "on a box in the mail company's station tent," after his stagecoach overturned.[26] This *en route* modality mimics the narrative sequencing of a travel journal or diary, but was intensified by the requisite timeliness of journalistic publication. Most columns were given a dateline of the author's location and date, a designation often retained in later book form. The content appears in a loosely chronological order but is not comprehensive, instead focusing on what the author found to be significant, dramatic, or comical, and digressing on a regular basis into mini narratives, background, conversations, landscapes, or the quotidian details of daily subsistence, as might a familiar letter to family and friends. The result was a supple narrative structure that could be digested by newspaper readers as standalone adventures or as "chapters" in the complete account of a journey, as in Richardson's *Beyond the Mississippi,* published in 1867 and again in 1869, as well as in the collected works of Greeley, Ludlow, Bowles, and others.

Richardson's text is a strong example of how the author positions himself as the protagonist of his or her adventuring journeys, taking possession of the archetypal character of the explorer, setting out to conquer the wilderness. Since the time of Odysseus, the explorer motif has been used to prove one's manliness, to demonstrate a domination of the natural world, and to enact survival of the fittest. Thus Richardson and his kindred journalists deliberately sought opportunities for solitary travel, for experiences that would be seen as novel, challenging, or dangerous. During Richardson's maiden voyage beyond the Mississippi in 1857, for example, he traveled by horse, boat, or stage, often unaccompanied, without a discernible roadmap for himself or for the reader. In one instance, he approached three cabins before securing accommodations for the evening, the first "occupied by a brawny Indian" who motioned him along; the second with three beds already full of travelers; and finally, the third, the home of the "Widow C---," where Richardson finally "slept refreshingly in one bed, while a hen with a brood of chickens occupied another."[27] Without a stable itinerary, the adventure takes on the character of spontaneity, with Richardson making do with whatever shelter and accommodations presented themselves.

Yosemite was a regular stop for adventure journalists, but it wasn't all business. "Our companions from San Francisco proved rich in song and sentiment; good-nature flowed and over-flowed," Bowles of the *Springfield Republican* mused. "We … grew steadily barbaric and dirty; laughed at dignity; and voted form and ceremony a nuisance" (*Across the Continent*, 232–33). Pictured in July 1865 are Bowles, standing, top left; in the second row, Colfax, seated third from left; Bross, seated third from right; acclaimed landscape architect Frederick Law Olmsted, center; and Richardson, reclining jauntily in the front (photograph by Carleton Watkins; used with permission of CarletonWatkins.org).

## *Iconography and the Western Experience*

Not all of the journalists traveled alone, including Fitz Hugh Ludlow, art critic for the *New York Evening Post*, who accompanied famed artist Albert Bierstadt to the West in 1863.[28] Ludlow and Bierstadt traveled from Atchison, Kansas, through the buffalo country of the Plains; into gold mines, to the top of Pike's Peak and into the Garden of the Gods; through the Rocky Mountains to Salt Lake City; into the Yosemite Valley for an indulgent, seven-weeks' stay; and finally by horse into Oregon and to the Columbia River Valley. While the trip afforded Bierstadt a healthy portfolio of popular artistic work, Ludlow's writings were as eagerly consumed by eastern reading publics, reprinted in newspapers and monthlies across the country, including the *San Francisco Golden Era, The Circular,* and the *Atlantic Monthly*, and later collected in a popular book, *The Heart of the Continent*, in 1870.[29]

The trip continued the construction of the western myth. Like Greeley and the other adventure journalists, Ludlow manifested a significant appreciation of landscape in his writings, one of the dominant ideological constructs associated with the West. At the side of Bierstadt, it must have been easy to spot the picturesque, majestic, or sublime in the landscape, but to convey it through words was another task entirely. "As well interpret God in thirty-nine articles as portray it to you by word of mouth or pen," Bowles wrote of the Yosemite in 1865.[30] Thus Ludlow and other adventuring journalists regularly found themselves engaged in the poetic, using literary devices to capture the inexpressible. And "so it was here," as Ludlow caught his "first view of Mormondom" and the Wasatch Mountain Range in Utah. "The view was not explicable by the ordinary ideals of terrestrial scenery; it was a fairy phantasm, a floating cloud, a beatific dream of paradisiacal ranges, let down out of heaven, not builded out of earth." Ludlow, like his adventuring peers, was well aware of the shortcomings of language to capture these scenes. "These gross comparisons come as near the impression as words of mine can," he wrote, "but my reader must take a step in idealism for himself, and imagine all these gems glorified by distance into the spirits of themselves."[31]

Ludlow was also taken by the notion of the western *experience*, suggesting a growing stabilization of that concept in the sense of ideology as well as itinerary by the Civil War era. He captured scenes of camping under the stars, "smoking my pipe, with a sense of perfect rest"[32]; plunging up and down sharp ravines in a bouncing stage;[33] and taking a dip in the briny Great Salt Lake, because avoiding it, he knew, would be the source of great shame in the future.[34] Ludlow even participated in a buffalo hunt—he with his rifle and Bierstadt with his "color-box"[35]—while visiting the Comstock Ranch in Nebraska.[36] A staged affair, the hunt was a conspicuous and graphic element of the western myth, intended in part to position the creatures for Bierstadt's scrutiny, but also in part to immerse the visitors in the fantasy. Ludlow described the experience in romantic, grandiose terms: "I never knew the ecstasy of the mad gallop until now. … Now we were plunging with headlong bounds down bluffs of caving sand, fifty feet high, and steep as a fortress glacis, while the buffalo, crazy with terror, were scrambling half-way up to the top of the opposite side." If his horse were to stumble, Ludlow predicted, "I should be trampled and gored to death. I should be wiped out like a grease-spot, and [his horse] Nig with me, for the terror of the herd was too extreme…."[37] The action, the emotion, the danger, all were part of the adventure of the West.

Another iconic western adventure was coming face-to-face with Native Americans, whose spirit echoed through the writings of nineteenth–century westering journalists more than their human forms may have appeared on the trail. Both professional and amateur writers wrestled with the threat of attack, but actual encounters were usually peaceful. This was not completely true for Joseph Pratt Allyn, however, a correspondent for the *Hartford Evening Press* from 1863 to 1866, during his tour of Arizona and other portions of the Southwest.[38] Allyn, a judge appointed by Abraham Lincoln to serve in Arizona Territory, was conscripted by his friend, the *Press*'s editor, Charles Dudley Warner, to write letters for the *Press*. Allyn was sent to the Southwest, in part because of chronic ill health, but Nicolson notes that did not deter him from pursuing rigorous adventures, sometimes riding horseback instead of in a wagon to facilitate spontaneous diversions to places off the beaten path.[39] Thus Allyn's letters are packed with adventures among deserts, ancient ruins, mines, caves, rivers, and canyons, bringing him into close contact with Mexicans and Native Americans.[40]

In January 1864, Allyn rode horseback with a small party of men from the First California infantry en route to Fort Whipple, built just a month before by members of that company.[41] After crossing a wide valley, the group came upon a note, stuck to a tree—"deposited," Allyn observed, in "this strange post office"—announcing Apache hostilities ahead. Advancing with great watchfulness, the group proceeded safely to their camp-site.[42] The situation was not so peaceful the following month, when Allyn joined notorious rancher King S. Woolsey on a pioneering expedition into the Verde Valley.[43] As gunfire was heard, one of the men shouted, "'For God's sake get under cover, you'll get hit.'" A skirmish with a small band of Native Americans was taking place. In his account of the encounter, Allyn remembered the scene as one of bravery and sacrifice on the part of one man, "just falling back from the bank of the stream facing us, and discharging his arrows…. The Indian was on this side of the river and his squaw with an infant was on the other side. The Indian made a brave, noble fight to give her time to get away. By this time, others came up and the scene beggars description…. Everybody saw Indians, shots were flying thick and fast."[44] Later, Allyn learned the woman and child were killed with the same bullet when a soldier "mistook her for a man."[45]

For most of the western traveling adventure journalists, however, encounters with Native Americans were generally uneventful, despite reports of violence and a sense of constant threat. Such was the case for *Springfield Republican* publisher Samuel Bowles, who set out for the Pacific, first, in 1865, by stagecoach and horse, and later, in 1868 and 1869, by stage and rail.[46] Just before his departure from Lawrence, Kansas, in 1865, Bowles and his party received word of multiple attacks along the stage line, one upon a group of former soldiers and the other upon a civilian stagecoach, and later saw evidence of previous attacks in the form of burned buildings and multiple reports of atrocities from near and far.[47] During his 1868 trip to Colorado, his party was again unmolested, despite escalating tensions that resulted in a night spent in expectation of imminent attack outside of Denver. In Bowles's mind, however, it was an episode of poetic fortune as it made "the circle of our Colorado and border travel experience … complete."[48]

While his reporting interests spanned topics such as federal Indian policy, economics, and regional development, Bowles' adventure was an immersion in the heroic, the mythic, the monumental, and the sacred that was America. In the mountains, the adventurer not only appraised their image, as one might in the presence of a Bierstadt painting, but also purposefully engaged their spirit by enacting a mountain experience:

> …now, two weeks from home, I am sporting familiarly under their shadows, following tediously up their sides, galloping in the saddle around their summits, drinking from their streams, playing snow-ball in June with their imperishable snow banks, descending into their very bowels, and finding companionship and society as various and as cultured and as organized as in New England; cities of thousands of inhabitants, not only at their base, but away up in their narrow valleys, eight and nine thousand feet above the sea level![49]

For Bowles, as for other adventuring journalists in the age of expansionism, the mark of human progress on the wilderness was not only a sign of "improvement" but also a testament to the resourcefulness of the citizenry. Thus, as Greeley drew comparisons between the dirt-floored Denver House hotel and New York's Astor Hotel, and as Richardson enumerated the dwellings of a remote outpost, so did Bowles marvel at signs of development in the West. From Colorado, he reported mining towns perched in the mountains, some boasting populations of six or seven thousand, squeezed into narrow ravines, "on streets the narrowest and most tortuous that I ever saw in America; some houses held up in dizzy hights on stilts, others burrowed into the stones of the hill…," exactly where one might expect a town never to stand. But Bowles found these towns to be "thriving, orderly, peaceable, busy, supporting two of them each its daily paper, with churches and schools, and all the best materials of government and society that the East can boast of," a testament to the determination of the population and the inexpressible wealth of the mountains.[50]

## *Trails to Rails*

After the completion of the Transcontinental Railroad, the adventure changed, as hero-journalists rode upon fixed iron tracks instead of meandering horses and bouncing stages. With conveyance accelerated and considerably more comfortable, the spirit of adventure was retained as journalists found improved access to remote outposts. Among the post–Spike travelers was Grace Greenwood, a reporter for the *New-York Times,* who had previously rambled about Europe on assignment for the newspaper.[51] Now, in 1872, her adventure to the American West produced stories that largely harmonized with the epic excursions of her journalistic predecessors, which readers perceived as highly personal and clever.[52] A reviewer in the *Overland Monthly and Out West Magazine* noted the unique perspective that a female author brought to the trip: "Feminine eyes see very much that masculine eyes scorn to take note of, and these thousand-and-one little items tell the true story."[53] Another review, in the *Christian Union,* affirmed the power of the hero-journalist to engage readers in the mythic journey. The reviewer was transported, he explains, away from his own passage on a train, to another, "the ideal journey, in a book, but a journey most vividly realized at every instant, abounding in excitement, made inspiring by the colossal outspread panorama of nature, brimming, with fun, across the plains and mountains which lie towards the sunset."[54]

Like other adventuring reporters to the West, Greenwood endeavored to engage the mythic, and did not let gendered limitations get in the way of a good story, particularly when that story investigated one of the West's most iconic nineteenth-century industries, mining. Northwest of Denver, for example, Greenwood entered Colorado's great Caribou Mine, a staple of the western reporter's adventure. "[E]scorted by a gallant young miner," she agreed to enter via a vertical shaft, "which I bravely descended in a bucket, and with my own hand chipped off a bit of silver ore, which I expect my posterity will piously preserve."[55] Journalists to the West were regular visitors to mines, which became a composite sign of mineral wealth, technological innovation, and mastery of the natural environment in the name of the national treasury. But mines also embraced the complex idiom of the stalwart frontiersman facing danger and a hostile environment. In California, Greenwood and a party of friends visited the New Almaden quicksilver mines in the Santa Cruz mountains. Adhering to the narrative format of adventure journalists generally, Greenwood's account of the experience began with a departure, snapshots of her promenade through labyrinthine tunnels, and finally an assessment of its meaning:

> We rode in ore-cars, on blocks of wood, which made the most reliable sort of seats. We were drawn by a stout and serious-minded mule, and each fellow of us carried a lighted candle stuck in a split stick. Thus we plunged into the darkness and the silence of inner earth, and woke the sullen echoes with laughter and merry shouts, and called out with our flickering torches momentary gleams from crystals imprisoned in the dull rocks for ages, dreaming of the light.

The experience is articulated as though Greenwood were half-way around the world in an exotic land—which, to her eastern readers, indeed she was. "[I]t had a strange wild look, and we all had a sense of something adventurous and mysterious, and delightfully awful and Arabian-Nightish, about the expedition," she wrote. "We forgot that we lived in a prosaic Christian land, and in virtuous Tammany times, and should hardly have been surprised to come upon the cave of the 'Forty Thieves,' with all their treasure in it ; or, when we turned back to the day, to have found the door of the tunnel closed against us."

Greenwood acknowledged the epic proportions of her journey on the rails and trails of America, as she drew parallels between her mine expedition and her previous grand adventures. "I have had many a grand drive in my day," she remembered. "I have driven in the Corso in carnival time ; my elegant hired hack figured in a procession miles long, going to a Queen's prorogation of Parliament; I have driven to weddings and races and reviews and fashionable funerals; but," compared to her trip into the New Almaden mine, "never have I enjoyed a drive as I enjoyed this. It was rough, but royal,—full of exhilaration and jollity."[56]

Like Greenwood, Amos Jay Cummings, of the *New York Sun*, took a sprawling tour of the American West by railroad in 1873.[57] By then, the impromptu adventure of traveling west had been largely mitigated by railcars, dining cars, and commercial maturation of western outposts. As a result, the journalist's attention pivoted

Grace Greenwood rode into the quicksilver mine at New Almaden, California, in an ore car—perhaps this one—during her visit in 1873 ("In the Tunnel, New Almaden," by Carleton E. Watkins, 1875, the Miriam and Ira D. Wallach Division of Art, Prints and Photographs, New York Public Library, ID G89F341_006F).

toward the significant or colorful people and events along the way instead of the perils of the journey itself. He had more time to consider fellow passengers, views from the windows, and overheard conversations. The journey also took on more of a contrived character, with planned excursions rather than impulsive or unanticipated adventures.

Cummings' columns are full of anecdotes, from the train to the gold mines, but it's more a *search for adventure* (as in a planned expedition to the Great Salt Lake), or a *reported adventure* (as in a supper-time confrontation between a trapper and a conductor in Ellis, Kansas, when the conductor "endeavored to persuade the trapper into an endorsement of his peculiar views by drawing a revolver upon him," followed by a round of shooting, scrambling among the passengers, and a disordered reboarding of the train),[58] or a *missed adventure*—marked, for example, by white gravestones, denoting "spots where [Indians] had massacred parties of whites,"[59] than an embodied adventure as readers saw in the reports of Greeley or Richardson.

Like other adventuring journalists, Cummings made pointed observations about his western countrymen, and occasionally took an opportunity to engage them in conversation, letting them speak directly to readers in the East. Embellished with descriptions of clothing, language, and behaviors, these individuals take on metonymic western signs that distinguish them from their eastern counterparts. Early in his travels, for example, Cummings notes a group of "citizens" at the train depot in Denver, sporting "flannel shirts and buckskin trousers, measuring a footprint in the mud."[60] The fervor with which these individuals engage in their seemingly trite investigation set them up as hapless and perhaps a bit dotty. But the tables are turned when Cummings has the opportunity to interview a Canadian settler in Manitou, Colorado, an individual whom Cummings portrays as a "sound-headed, practical man." The interview was purposeful, with Cummings tapping into his reportorial instincts in the interest of collecting information for farmers "in the States," or back east, and presenting the interview as direct conversation between "City Farmer" (Cummings) and "Mr. Ouelette."[61]

Cummings' narrative includes a wide cast of western characters who mark the landscape with their human struggles, triumphs, and quirks. For example, these characters include the dignified Colorado hotelier "Judge Castello," described as "portly as the Hon. Judge Anthony Hartman of your city, but his nose is much larger and his face is more flushed, though he drinks less beer"[62]; the storytelling attorney Wilbur F. Stone of Colorado Springs, who "sat with his heels upon a square table" as he spun his tales;[63] the "courteous and agreeable sheep herder" J.J. Armijo, who gave Cummings a detailed overview of the sheep-herding business;[64] and restaurateur Charles Yeomans of Salt Lake City, "built like a fifty-year-old Adonis" and yet a "confirmed bachelor."[65] Both Brigham Young and his estranged wife, Ann Eliza Young, are interviewed at great length and, like many of the less notable subjects, quoted directly.[66] This effort to seek out and give voice to westerners capitalized on the literary dimensions of the epistolary form to bring the adventure to life and compose a national tapestry of citizenship through the writer's western adventures.

## Authors of the Myth

In 1869, as he wrapped up a new edition of his popular *Beyond the Mississippi*, Albert Richardson noted, "Authors and census-takers must be swift of foot to keep pace with progress beyond the Mississippi."[67] Much had changed in the year since his last trip, and Richardson had much to add. But his comment captured the impulse of the adventuring journalist on the rails and trails of America, more than Higginson's snide comment about "inspecting [one's] subscribers." For why, after countless personal adventures were recounted, after hundreds of columns were printed and reprinted, after dozens of leather-bound books were dedicated to these tales of the West—after all this, why was the reading public still eager for more?

Our adventuring journalists surely could answer that question, for their reporting shows that the adventure was never the same. Each time a journalist took to the rails and trails, a new America was discovered. Imperfect, inconsistent, unsure, the myth was constantly evolving, and the participatory dimension of the myth added to its appeal. Unlike journalists who traveled the seven seas or who swept past the most remote outposts aboard the Orient Express, westering journalists were writing for a reading public who could, should the spirit of adventure move them, leap aboard a train or stagecoach and recreate the correspondent's step. In fact, the power of the myth was that it was moved from the realm of archetype into the realm of possibility with the technological innovations of the period.

The westward-bound journalist-heroes of the Gilded Age were in search of the mythic but also authors of the myth. They scrambled into stagecoaches, mounted horses, camped under the stars. They spent weeks or months on the road as journalistic witnesses, recording evidence of the developing nation and its endless natural wonders. As adventurers, they inserted themselves into a journey that was already iconic in its rhetorical construction. As authors, they composed a narrative of a national identity which embraced all Americans, including their readers, in its consummation. As journalists, they uncovered evidence of nationhood by purposefully pursuing epochal signs of westernness in landscape, citizenry, and civilization. Their reportage preserves the spirit of the adventure and secures their seminal role as troubadours of the American West.

NOTES

1. T. W. Higginson, "Reviews and Literary Notices" [Review of *Across the Continent*, by Samuel Bowles], *Atlantic Monthly* 17 (1866): 524–25.

2. Daniel J. Boorstin, *The Image: A Guide to Pseudo-events in America* (New York : Harper & Row, 1961). For more on tourism of the nineteenth century, see John Sears, *Sacred Places: American Tourist Attractions in the Nineteenth Century* (New York: Oxford University Press, 1999) and Marguerite S. Shaffer, *America First: Tourism and National Identity, 1880–1940* (Washington, DC: Smithsonian Institution Press, 2001). For more on the semiotics of the tourist, see Jonathan Culler, "The Semiotics of Tourism," in *Framing the Sign: Criticism and its Institutions* (Oxford: Blackwell, 1988).

3. For more on literary journalism and epistolarity, see Katrina J. Quinn, "Exploring an Early Version of Literary Journalism: Nineteenth-century Epistolary Journalism," *Literary Journalism Studies* 3, no. 1 (2011): 33–52 and "Reconsidering the Public Letter in Epistolary Theory: The Case of Samuel Bowles (1865)," *The CEA Critic* 77, no.1 (2015): 97–119.

4. Carol Marie Greene, *Letters Home: Newspaper Travel Writing of Kate Field, Mary Elizabeth McGarth Blake, and Grace Greenwood*. PhD diss., Indiana U of Pennsylvania, 2001.

5. Sara Mills, *Discourses of Difference: An Analysis of Women's Travel Writing and Colonialism* (New York: Routledge, 1993). For another rich look at women's unpublished travel narratives of the early Republic, see Susan Clair Imbarrato's *Traveling Women: Narrative Visions of Early America* (Columbus: Ohio University Press, 2006).

6. For more on travel literature from a colonialist perspective, see David Spurr, *The Rhetoric of Empire: Colonial Discourse in Journalism, Travel Writing, and Imperial Administration* (Durham, NC: Duke University

Press, 1993); Harry Liebersohn, "Recent Works on Travel Writing," *The Journal of Modern History* 68, no. 3 (1996): 617–628; and Sharon Bohn Gmelch, ed., *Tourists and Tourism: A Reader* (Long Grove, IL: Waveland Press, 2010).

7. Quoted in David Seed, "Nineteenth-Century Travel Writing: An Introduction," *The Yearbook of English Studies* 34 (2004): 1–5. See Barbara Korte, *English Travel Writing: From Pilgrimages to Postcolonial Explorations*, trans. Catherine Matthias (New York: Palgrave Macmillan, 2000).

8. Benedict Anderson, *Imagined Communities: Reflections on the Origin and Spread of Nationalism* (Rev. ed. London: Verso, 1991), 6.

9. E. J. Hobsbawm, *Nations and Nationalism Since 1780* (New York: Cambridge University Press, 1990), 90.

10. For more on the myth of the West, see Henry Nash Smith, *Virgin Land: The American West as Symbol and Myth* (Cambridge, MA: Harvard University Press, 2001), Richard Slotkin, *Fatal Environment: The Myth of the Frontier in the Age of Industrialization, 1800–1890* (New York: Harper Perennial, 1994), and Arthur K. Moore, *The Frontier Mind* (New York: McGraw-Hill, 1963). For a deeper analysis of the contributions of Samuel Bowles and his western adventures in the development of a post-war national myth, see Katrina J. Quinn, "'Across the Continent … and Still the Republic!' Inscribing Nationhood in Samuel Bowles's Newspaper Letters of 1865," *American Journalism* 31, no. 4 (2014): 468–489.

11. For more on the rhetorical construction of the tourist, see Jonathan Culler, "The Semiotics of Tourism," *Framing the Sign: Criticism and its Institutions* (Oxford: Blackwell, 1988).

12. Seed, "Nineteenth-Century Travel Writing," 1.

13. Bowles, *Across the Continent: A Summer's Journey to the Rocky Mountains, the Mormons, and the Pacific States, with Speaker Colfax* (Springfield, MA: Bowles & Co., 1865). Bowles's companions on this trip were journalists as well, namely Schuyler Colfax, speaker of the U.S. House of Representatives and former editor of the *South Bend Tribune*; William Bross, president of the *Chicago Tribune* and lieutenant governor of Illinois; and Albert Richardson, reporter for the *New-York Tribune*. While all travelers published correspondence from the trip in eastern newspapers, Bowles, Bross, and Richardson also published their correspondence in book form after their return to the East.

14. Greeley (1811–1872) was arguably the most influential of the great nineteenth-century editors, serving at the helm of the *New-York Tribune* from 1841 until his death. Greeley's letters from the 1859 trip to the Pacific, particularly his famous interview with Brigham Young, were reprinted in newspapers across the country. In 1860, he collected the letters in a book, *An Overland Journey, from New York to San Francisco, in the Summer of 1859* (New York: C. M. Saxton, Barkerm, & Co.; San Francisco: H. H. Bancroft, 1860), adding a final chapter, which advocates for a Transcontinental Railroad, after his return to New York.

15. One individual did step forward, Greeley recalled, "but his wife's veto overruled his not very stubborn resolve." Horace Greeley, *Recollections of a Busy Life* (New York: J. B. Ford & Company, 1868), 360.

16. See L.D. Ingersoll, *The Life of Horace Greeley* (Chicago: Union Publishing Co., 1873), 335; Henry Luther Stoddard, *Horace Greeley, Printer, Editor, Crusader* (New York: G. P. Putnam, 1946), 187; and William Alexander Linn, *Horace Greeley: Founder and Editor of the New York Tribune* (New York: D. Appleton and Co., 1912). For a more recent source, see Robert C. Williams, *Horace Greeley: Champion of American Freedom* (New York: New York University Press, 2006).

17. See Greeley, *An Overland Journey*, pages 4–5, 152, 157, and others, including much of dispatch 24, "From Salt Lake to Carson Valley," 219–232. Greeley mentions how he became sick after drinking from a brook outside of Laramie (157), but later drew the line at the Humboldt River water, "about the most detestable I ever tasted. I mainly chose to suffer thirst rather than drink it" (230).

18. Greeley, *An Overland Journey*, 157. Greeley's trunk was eventually recovered and returned to him. See Greeley, *An Overland Journey*, 281–82.

19. Greeley, *An Overland Journey*, 60–61.

20. Greeley, *An Overland Journey*, 136.

21. Greeley, *An Overland Journey*, 137. "Jumping a cabin" denotes taking possession of a seemingly uninhabited structure, a practice which was common due to the transient nature of many settlers in the West. Richardson also recounted this episode in his memoir, *Beyond the Mississippi*, 184–185.

22. Greeley, *An Overland Journey*, 85.

23. Greeley, *An Overland Journey*, 61.

24. Born in Franklin, Massachusetts, Richardson (1833–1869) worked for a number of papers before being recruited by Greeley in 1859 to write for the *Tribune*. Ten years later, Richardson was shot in the lobby of the newspaper by the estranged husband of Abby Sage McFarland, with whom he had become romantically involved. He died days later after a deathbed marriage ceremony performed by well-known abolitionist clergyman Henry Ward Beecher.

25. Richardson collected the correspondence from these trips, publishing *Beyond the Mississippi: From the Great River to the Great Ocean. Life and Adventure on the Prairies, Mountains, and Pacific Coast*, in 1867. A second, expanded edition was printed in 1869.

26. Greeley, *An Overland Journey*, 158.

27. Richardson, *Beyond the Mississippi*, 111–113.

28. Ludlow (1836–70) was an author and journalist, for a time art critic at the *New York Evening Post*, and

best known for his book *The Hasheesh Eater* (1857) and for his work and personal struggle with opioid addiction (Fitz Hugh Ludlow, *The Hasheesh Eater: Being Passages from the Life of a Pythagorean* (New York: Harper Bros., 1857). Bierstadt (1830–1902) was one of the best-known landscape artists, a member of the Hudson River School movement, and traveled several times to the American West.

29.  Fitz Hugh Ludlow, *The Heart of the Continent: A Record of Travel Across the Plains and in Oregon, with an Examination of the Mormon Principle* (New York: Hurd and Houghton, 1870).

30.  Bowles, *Across the Continent*, 223.

31.  Ludlow, *Heart of the Continent*, 214.

32.  Ludlow, *Heart of the Continent*, 89.

33.  See Ludlow, *Heart of the Continent*, 200–201.

34.  See Ludlow, *Heart of the Continent*, 313, 399–404.

35.  Ludlow, *Heart of the Continent*, 34.

36.  A homestead inhabited by a "true frontiersman" and his children—"one of the best, truest, kindest families of pioneer people we met in our whole journey, and having no equals for typical character or native goodness in our experience." Ludlow invoked the writing act when he took part of a "rainy Nebraska day" to make textual "portraits" of the Comstock family "for my readers." (*Heart of the Continent*, 24).

37.  Ludlow, *Heart of the Continent*, 72–73.

38.  See John Nicolson, ed., *The Arizona of Joseph Pratt Allyn: Letters from a Pioneer Judge: Observations and Travels, 1863–1866* (Tucson: University of Arizona Press, 1974), 5. Connecticut-born Allyn (1833–69) was appointed to the Supreme Court of Arizona Territory by Abraham Lincoln.

39.  Nicolson, *The Arizona of Joseph Pratt Allyn*, 41.

40.  Unlike the other journalists in this sample, Allyn's twenty-four letters were sent over the course of three years, 1863–66, and were written under the name "Putnam," a pseudonym he had used in correspondence from Washington while serving as a Congressional clerk.

41.  Named after Amiel Weeks Whipple, a Civil War Union General, Fort Whipple was a U.S. Army post built near what would later be Prescott, Arizona.

42.  Nicolson, *The Arizona of Joseph Pratt Allyn*, 63.

43.  The rancher Woolsey was appointed an officer in the Arizona militia and gained fame for his brutal attacks on Apache tribes. He later was central in the founding of the Democratic Party in Arizona.

44.  Nicolson, *The Arizona of Joseph Pratt Allyn*, 88–89.

45.  Nicolson, *The Arizona of Joseph Pratt Allyn*, 89–90.

46.  Bowles (1826–1878) was a frequent traveler, visiting Europe on four occasions. His correspondence was printed in the *Springfield (MA) Republican* but also in newspapers across the country, including the *Atlantic Monthly*. He collected the letters from his 1865 trip in *Across the Continent: A Summer's Journey to the Rocky Mountains, the Mormons, and the Pacific States, with Speaker Colfax* (Springfield: Bowles & Co., 1865). Correspondence from his trip to Colorado was published in *The Parks and Mountains of Colorado: A Summer Vacation in the Switzerland of America, 1868* (Springfield: Bowles & Co., 1869). In light of the completion of the Transcontinental Railroad, selections from these works were reprinted in 1869 as *Our New West: Records of Travel Between the Mississippi River and the Pacific Ocean* (Hartford, CT: Hartford Publishing Co., 1869). The same year he also published a collection of his *Atlantic Monthly* columns as *The Pacific Railroad—Open, How to Go, What to See: Guide for Travel to and Through Western America* (Boston: Fields, Osgood, & Co., 1869).

47.  Bowles, *Across the Continent*, 6–7, 10–11.

48.  Bowles, *Parks and Mountains*, 142–44. A series of Arapahoe raids led Acting Colorado Gov. Frank Hall to send a series of telegrams to warn the Colfax party of imminent danger, and recommending that they remain in the mountains temporarily. Pickering provides context for this scene in his 1992 edition (*Parks and Mountains* [Norman: University of Oklahoma Press, 1992], notes p. 226–28). Compare this experience to that of Horace Greeley, who, nine years earlier, was eager for an Indian encounter: "I have been passing, meeting, observing and trying to converse with Indians almost ever since I crossed the Missouri..." (Greeley, *An Overland Journey*, 117).

49.  Bowles, *Parks and Mountains*, 31.

50.  Bowles, *Across the Continent*, 34.

51.  See also "From Eight Days in the Yosemite," published July 27, 1872, in the *New-York Times*. Also available in *Snowy Range Reflections: Journal of Sierra Nevada History and Biography* 4, no. 2 (2012). Greenwood (1823–1904) was the first woman writer and reporter on the payroll of the *New-York Times*. She was a frequent adventure journalist, traveling to Europe for the *Times* in 1852. See Grace Greenwood, *Haps and Mishaps of a Tour in Europe* (Boston: Ticknor, Reed, and Fields, 1854), a work that remained in publication for the next four decades.

52.  Greenwood's letters were later published as a book, *New Life in New Lands: Notes of Travel* (New York: J. B. Ford, 1873).

53.  "Current Literature," *Overland Monthly and Out West Magazine* 11, no. 1 (1873): 103.

54.  "Books and authors," *Christian Union*, April 9, 1873, 7, 287.

55.  Greenwood, *New Life in New Lands*, 82–83.

56.  Greenwood, *New Life in New Lands*, 293–95.

57.  Cummings (1838–1902) served in the Army during the Civil War, then worked at various New York

newspapers, before serving as a U.S. Congressman. His westward trip, beginning in late May 1873, was not his only adventure. According to Milanich, Cummings' other trips took him to exotic destinations such as Nicaragua in 1857, Florida several times including 1873, England and Paris between 1879 and 1882, and New Orleans in 1885. See Amos J. Cummings, *A Remarkable Curiosity: Dispatches from a New York City Journalist's 1873 Railroad Trip across the American West*, ed. Jerald T. Milanich (Boulder: University Press of Colorado, 2008), and Amos J. Cummings, *Frolicking Bears, Wet Vultures, and Other Oddities: A New York City Journalist in Nineteenth-Century Florida*, ed. Jerald T. Milanich (Gainesville: University Press of Florida, 2005).

58. "Over the Kansas Plains. The Level Paradise South of the Missouri River," *The Sun*, June 6, 1873, 3.

59. Cummings learned that attacking Indians "rarely appear upon the line of the road" and "seem to have given up the thing for good…" (*Ibid.*).

60. "Over the Kansas Plains. The Level Paradise South of the Missouri River," *The Sun*, June 6, 1873, 3.

61. "A Canadian in Colorado. A Farmer's Experience at the Base of the Rocky Mountains," *The Sun*, July 7, 1873, 3.

62. "The Petrified Stumps. Stone Trees in the Heart of the Rocky Mountains," *The Sun*, July 5, 1873, 3.

63. "The Fate of a Gold Seeker. Surprising Adventures of an Oberlin Graduate," *The Sun*, July 28, 1873, 3.

64. "SHEEP. The Growing of Wool and Mutton in New Mexico," *Chicago Daily Tribune*, July 8, 1873, 5.

65. "The Funeral Postponed. Tears From the Eyes of the Hardest Mormon," *The Rutland Daily Globe*, Oct. 6, 1873, 1.

66. These interviews appeared in several letters from Cummings and were widely reprinted. See Cummings, *A Remarkable Curiosity*, 237–248, 251–260, 263–271, and 289–295.

67. Richardson, *Beyond the Mississippi*, 572.

# From Gotham to the Golden Gate

*Promoting American Expansion, Exceptionalism,*
*and Nationhood by Railroad*

MARY M. CRONIN

Publisher Frank Leslie was determined to get out of New York City during the hot summer months of 1877—and to make it pay. Like many of his fellow publishers, Leslie had grown rich and become dependent upon the massive circulation that his illustrated weekly had achieved during the U.S. Civil War.[1] With the conflict over and readers no longer feeling as urgent a need to stay informed, Leslie had to find stories that appealed to readers. He decided that an adventure, replete with the sensationalism and exotica that his readers desired—albeit a carefully planned and comfortable one—might boost his flagging finances.

The publisher settled on a transcontinental railroad trip. The journey seemed just the ticket. The Central Pacific Railroad provided Leslie, his wife Miriam, and a coterie of reporters and illustrators with free travel in a first-class Pullman Palace car, as well as complimentary hotel accommodation at stops along the route. In exchange, the railroad would receive lavish publicity from the multi-part series to be published in *Frank Leslie's Illustrated Newspaper* (hereafter, *Leslie's*).[2] Appearing from July 1877 to May 1878, the celebratory "Across the Continent" series served up a healthy dose of national pride and touted American technological and cultural superiority during an anxious era that was fraught with political, social, cultural, and economic upheaval.[3]

Leslie knew his readers were eager for news and illustrations about distant and exotic locales that would provide exciting, entertaining copy, but also deliver a sense of worldliness.[4] His working-class and middle-class readers had long enjoyed the publisher's vision of the illustrated news format: rapid reporting complemented by smartly executed illustrations. And unlike some of the more high-class publications of the day, which often talked down to the masses, Leslie's motto was "never shoot over the heads of the people."[5] His middle-of-the-road approach presented news that often was sensational, exotic, or both. The result was an entertaining publication that "presented a vivid and lively picture of the American scene."[6]

The new railroad series, too, would offer *Leslie's* readers a mix of romantic, mythic, and realistic portrayals that, collectively, depicted American ingenuity and technology and lauded citizens' hard work and individualism. Publisher Leslie had long recognized the unique and mythic allure of the American West.[7] He had sent reporters and sketch artists to western locales with regularity before and after the war years. The discovery of gold in Colorado made it a source of fascination for readers who learned about the territory in such stories as "Sketches at Pike's Peake," in the August 20, 1859, edition and "Life and Scenes in Denver, Colorado," for the October 25, 1873, issue. As historian William E. Huntzicker has noted, "Leslie took hundreds of thousands of Americans to places they had never been before."[8]

Over the course of ten months, the new series allowed readers to enjoy, in vicarious fashion, a detailed view of their expansive, swiftly changing nation—from the Hudson River Valley, through the Midwest, the Great Plains, the far West, and on to the rollicking city of San Francisco—while also experiencing a train journey that many could not afford.[9] The installments served to illustrate the possibilities of western tourism a few years before the massive middle-class tourism boom of the 1880s. The American West was of particular interest to travelers; the region's vastness, its unusual flora, fauna, and geological features, and its sheer distance from the more populated East Coast fascinated Americans and foreigners alike.

Then, too, western geography was uniquely intertwined in the national mindset with the concept of American exceptionalism. As historian Michael J. Hostetler has stated, "For most of the nineteenth century, Americans conceived of their special role and destiny in the world to be intimately connected to westward geographical movement."[10] And although Leslie's journalistic sojourn lacked a degree of arduousness and was far from impromptu, the "Across the Continent" series remains an exemplar of the adventure journalism form for its serialized nature, for the often-sensational copy that introduced readers to the colorful characters and scenery of the American West, and particularly for the center-stage role of the Leslies and their artists as they set out to travel, witness, interpret, and report upon their experiences for their readers.[11]

## Across the Continent at "Twenty Miles an Hour"

Prior to the formal start of the series, *Leslie's* editors provided an early visual puff for the journey, an illustration in the April 28, 1877, issue, which showed a crowd of well-dressed well-wishers waving goodbye as Leslie was about to enter his train car at New York City's train station. The elaborate Wagner Sleeping Car, in which his party would spend many hours, had been renamed "The Frank Leslie." A promotional editorial from July 23, 1877, announced the series' start and promised readers both entertainment and knowledge: "Our readers may congratulate themselves upon the opportunity thus to be placed before them of obtaining newer and more accurate knowledge of the natural features of the Great West and the Pacific Slope than have ever before been available."[12] The piece ignored the reality that many journalists and authors had already taken the same journey and had published articles or books detailing their experiences.[13] Yet, as historian Deirdre Murphy states, the *Leslie's* series' length, the massive number of accompanying illustrations, the sheer amount of territory the Leslies travelled, and the large readership that resulted made the series a notable one.[14]

Like other nineteenth-century works of adventure and travel, the series provided readers with a blend of "journalism, autobiography, fiction, history, anthropology, and political analysis; a smorgasbord of interpretation and experience."[15] Readers expected that travel literature would prove educational, abounding in factual detail and penned in a manner that demonstrated that writers were sharing their discoveries with readers.[16]

ACROSS THE CONTINENT ON THE PACIFIC RAILROAD.—DINING SALOON OF THE HOTEL EXPRESS TRAIN.—See Page 301.

While their fellow travelers spent uncomfortable nights sleeping upright in regular Pullman train seats, shared washing and grooming facilities, and frequently had only twenty to thirty minutes to down meals and drinks at train stations, Frank and Miriam Leslie and their staff slept and lived in walnut-paneled comfort, complete with a personal chef, servants, and the finest linens, crystal, and china (*Frank Leslie's Illustrated Newspaper*, Jan. 15, 1870, Library of Congress, Item 99614012).

The *Leslie's* series followed these conventions. The series also occurred as the literary realism movement was emerging and the romanticism of an earlier generation was being pushed aside.[17] Long drawn to *Leslie's* for its perceived realism, readers turned to the weekly news publication for exciting stories that came with the publisher's promise that his illustrated newspaper would depict people, places, and events as they were—though publisher Leslie never explained that artistic license was taken at times.[18]

Like other works of adventure journalism, "Across the Continent" articles focused on boundary-crossing. The series' three writers—Leslie; his wife; Miriam, and noted children's book author Bracebridge Hemyng—used East Coast culture and society as the yardstick from which they judged the lives and livelihoods of other Americans. The railroad journey and the subsequent reporting provided the requisite sense of distance common to travel and adventure writing. As they traveled west, the journalists' reports and illustrations presented readers with familiar and unfamiliar scenery, animals, individuals, and lifestyles, giving readers a sense of the nation's vast and varied physical and human landscape. Serving as interpreters and guides for their readers, the *Leslie's* staff escorted readers across geographic and cultural boundaries, serving as central figures not only in the narrative but also in many of the series' illustrations, placing them most assuredly at the center of the adventure.

The series opened with a convention commonly used by travel writers and explorers, the ritualistic departure, which evoked the subjects' excitement at leaving and provided enough emotional sentiment to hook readers.[19] As literary scholar Jeffrey Alan Melton has stated, the best travel and adventure writers of the nineteenth century used the departure convention to welcome readers and invite their participation on the journey. Given the crowded field that was nineteenth-century travel literature, the establishment of a close relationship was necessary.[20] But though they were genteel explorers in the truest sense of the term, the reporters and illustrators took their task to investigate and report upon "every place of interest on the route" seriously, although, at times, superficially, since they frequently had a mere thirty minutes to a few hours to investigate communities before their train departed.[21]

For all its promotional fanfare, the series acknowledged the class-based discrepancies that existed for travelers. Quite unlike the experiences of early settlers, the publisher, his wife, and their staff traveled in comfort, dining on champagne, oysters, and other succulent fare, while taking in the nation's sights and sounds.[22] While Frank and Miriam Leslie and their staff slept and lived in walnut-paneled comfort, complete with a personal chef, servants, and the finest linens, crystal, and china, however, their fellow travelers spent uncomfortable nights sleeping upright in regular Pullman train seats, were forced to share washing and grooming facilities, and frequently had only twenty to thirty minutes to down meals and drinks at train stations—the only source of food for the common railroad passenger. A February 9, 1878, article expressed regret that the Leslies' fellow passengers traveled like sardines in a box. "It is a pathetic thing to see …," the article noted.[23]

The series continued *Leslie's* practice of visually depicting newsworthy people and places, while providing readers with images and text that often—but not always—fit their expectations of the nation's western region. Hearty settlers, hard-working miners, colorful yet defeated Indians, curious Mormons, exotic Chinese, unusual animals, and almost unearthly, majestic scenery were depicted throughout the ten-month-long series.[24] Taken collectively, the series contributed to post-war nation-building by demonstrating to readers that Americans had brought civilization to land that once was wilderness and exploited nature's bounty—conclusive proof of America's exceptionalism to *Leslie's* readers. The series' authors and illustrators adhered to commonly-held beliefs in manifest destiny and Anglo-American superiority in representing that identity.[25] Occasionally, however, the series' three writers challenged popular viewpoints, or admitted that their own perceptions had been colored by widely-held stereotypes.

Replete with detailed descriptions and statistics, the series delivered the factual knowledge that readers of the time desired.[26] From many stops along the route, the series provided details about the populations of burgeoning towns, lists of major businesses, and descriptions of buildings and the materials with which they were constructed as a means of quantifying national progress.[27] The July 21, 1877, installment, for example, explained how Chicago's modern water filtration system kept minnows and fish spawn out of the city's water supply. The *Leslie's* team took readers along for an informational walking tour to explore a dam, the water authority's massive steam pumps, and its tunnel system. The same installment also took readers through Chicago's stock yards and charted their growth via detailed statistics, including the fact that five million feet of lumber had been used to repair the stockyards and to build more chutes. True to the series' congratulatory nature, the article touted the city's "wonderful development, in the short space of forty years." Its citizens were represented as innovative, and, in high praise, the article's author called Chicago "eastern" in development.[28]

Later installments also reflected the educational nature of adventure journalism and travel writing. Two full months' worth of installments were devoted to Virginia City, Nevada, where much of the nation's silver was mined and smelted. An editorial published on February 23, 1878, plugged the March and April installments, telling readers that they would learn about "the source of our silver" and promising "a splendid four-page panoramic view of Virginia City, Nevada." The detailed narrative of silver's journey from mine to coin, including details of the chemical process, would bore many modern readers, but such lengthy explanations were commonplace in nineteenth-century travel literature.[29]

Although the articles introduced readers to the diverse flora, fauna, geographic features, and people of the nation, the Transcontinental Railroad was itself a prominent fixture in most of the articles as proof of the country's technological superiority[30] In a clear nod to the railroad executives who funded part of the journey, most installments featured illustrations that depicted the Leslies' train at stations from the party's send-off in New York to the train's final terminus in Oakland, California, located next to a dock where ferries for the trip across the bay to San Francisco were lined up.[31] Other images depicted elaborate trestle bridges, including a spider-like iron one that soared 130 feet over Dale Creek in Wyoming, as visual proof of American ingenuity.[32] Not surprisingly, two articles puffed the nation's two main railroad titans, Cornelius Vanderbilt and George Pullman. New York City's railroad station was portrayed in an early article as "an appropriate monument to the enterprise of America's great railroad king," Vanderbilt, because "it bespoke the extent and importance of that mighty artery of trade and commerce over which we were about to be conveyed."[33] A later installment from Chicago lavished praise on Pullman, who met the journalists and explained the latest technological marvels of his train cars.[34]

Indeed, the completion of the transcontinental line in 1869—the first in the world—reinforced Americans' beliefs in their own exceptionalism.[35] The monumental task was upheld also by writers and politicians as a demonstration of Anglo-American superiority, with vast stretches of wilderness settled and native peoples pacified, even though two often-derided immigrant groups—the Irish and the Chinese—built much of the railroad line.[36] The railroad's completion, therefore, was rich with symbolism. The line was portrayed by many nineteenth-century writers, including the Leslies and British journalist and explorer Henry M. Stanley, as more than a technological triumph; it was a "true harbinger of civilization" and proof of America's shining future as an industrialized nation.[37] As historian Stephen E. Ambrose has stated, not even the mighty steamboats, which also helped shorten distance and accelerate transportation, were given such an accolade.[38]

Two installments involving train stations provided readers with visual and textual proof that the railroad had helped tame and transform America's wilderness. The November 3, 1877, installment included an image of a large cage with two mountain lions located outside of the Green River, Wyoming, train station. Travelers, who were given twenty minutes to purchase refreshments and view the station's exhibit of western gems, minerals, and petrified wood, seemed to spend much of their time entranced by the cats. Men and women stared at the mountain lions from a distance, while small children drew closer and uttered "shrieks of ecstasy" as the cats snarled at their visitors. The author of the installment was impressed by the creatures, stating, "They are splendid creatures, tawny yellow, like the lion, but maneless, and as large as the common panther which they very closely resemble."[39] A similar scene appeared in the May 11, 1878, issue. The journalists beheld a caged grizzly bear at the Lathrop, California, train station. The article noted the bear was "a magnificent creature, full grown and … in perfect condition" despite its captivity, with a silky, tawny-gray coat.[40]

## Landscape, Westward Expansion, and American Exceptionalism

Although European visitors to the United States were far more tempered in their enthusiasm for and far less convinced of the nation's greatness, American writers often used their country's varied landscape and its vast resources as proof of the nation's exceptionalism, and the "Across the Continent" series was no exception. The series' authors evoked a significant appreciation of landscape from the very first article. The Hudson River Valley's beauty had long been appreciated by travelers, and the series gave the region

TWENTY MINUTES FOR REFRESHMENT—PASSENGERS VISITING THE CALIFORNIA LIONS AT GREEN RIVER STATION.

ACROSS THE CONTINENT.—THE FRANK LESLIE EXCURSION TO THE PACIFIC—INCIDENTS OF TRAVEL FROM FORT STEELE TO GREEN RIVER. FROM SKETCHES BY OUR SPECIAL ARTISTS.—SEE PAGE 138.

**Like their readers, the Leslies viewed the caged mountain lions from a safe distance. Descriptions of unfamiliar flora and fauna of the West were a regular part of Gilded Age frontier reporting (*Frank Leslie's Illustrated Newspaper*, Nov. 3, 1877, Library of Congress, Item 90712207).**

its due.[41] But the vast, thundering presence of Niagara Falls left the Leslies and their staff, like writers before them, grasping for the right words to describe the scene.[42] The first installment described the Niagara River and the subsequent falls in biological terms: "… we approached the great cataract, whose unceasing work it is to throb like a mighty artery as it pours the floods of the Erie into the bosom of the Ontario." Lacking the right, poetic description, the unknown author merely said, "…Niagara at all seasons is indescribably magnificent." The Leslies had taken a special excursion to the Falls, and the July 7, 1877, installment described their activities in detail, including a snowball fight after they found snow still on the ground in April. They also boarded an incline railroad, which resembled open sleigh carriages, down to a base near the river for a better view of the falls.[43]

The Leslies and their staff rejoiced as the scenery from their train window turned into the "true West" of their imaginations, and they shared that joy with readers in the September 1, 1877, installment, proclaiming that the West began at the Platte River Valley in Nebraska. "With Omaha we leave behind us the last suggestion of life in the States, and drink in the first breath of grandeur and savage freedom of the Plains," the installment's author told readers before describing the area's "desolate ranches … the silvery Platte" and its "steep, dark bluffs."[44] The scenery in Wyoming proved more unusual and inspired one of the series' authors to wax romantic at its unique rock formations:

> The buttes around Green River are wonderful in size, shape, color, and variety; there are towers, castles, and cathedrals, bulbous knobs and excrescenses, colossal mushrooms, "giant's clubs" and "giant's teapots," forts, temples, tombs, and shapes of things unknown, possibly, in the heavens above and certainly in the earth beneath; all carved out of rich red and brown and cream-colored limestone, strata upon strata of varying color. The river sweeps in great curves, washing a white, sandy beach with its clear, emerald-green waters—the brightest, richest green that ever flashed in sunlight, caught from the color of the shale over which it runs. Every foot of ground for miles above is rich with fossil flowers, ferns, fishes, and even insects, buried in every layer of shale, waiting for the treasure-seeker's hammer.[45]

Like travelers before and after them, the Leslie party delighted in the nation's landscape, which rarely disappointed. The series' authors blended realism and romanticism in their descriptions as they marveled at the changing scenery and sought the proper superlatives to describe it. The series, at times, provided readers with a sprinkling of dreamy romanticism that celebrated nature when the scenery or the subject warranted the authors to wax poetic. While journeying across Wyoming, for example, the October 13, 1877, installment described "a new world of red granite buttes … short, steep canyons … [and] stunted pine-trees clinging here and there along the tawny ridges of the divide…."[46] But Americans did more than appreciate their country's scenic beauty; they used their landscape to define their nation as a unique in the world, and thus took pride at its unique natural features.[47]

Through landscape, the twin themes of American exceptionalism and manifest destiny played out in the *Leslie's* series, which also lauded the hard-working individuals who tamed the wilderness and made use of its timber, minerals, and crops. The task was a necessity in a nation that was rapidly industrializing and whose citizens needed the raw materials for their budding consumer culture.[48] The *Leslie's* staff, therefore, hailed the ingenuity and energy of countless, often-unnamed Americans, and upheld the growth of cities, towns, and mining communities as proof of the nation's exceptionalism. Using eastern cities as a benchmark, the journalists provided detailed statistics and gave out praise for the growth of midwestern and western cities. After admiring the intricate locks on the Erie Canal at Lockport, New York, as a remarkable feat of engineering,[49] the Leslies and their sketch artists marveled, in turn, at the thriving cities of Rochester, New York; Toledo, Ohio; Chicago, Illinois; Omaha, Nebraska; and a host of other cities and towns, viewing all as hives of activity and technological ingenuity. Readers learned, for example, that Toledo's enormous grain elevator had a 1.5 million-bushel capacity, and that the city had sixteen mills in operation, many of which were devoted to producing flour—clearly examples of "Yankee thrift and enterprise."[50]

Chicago and Omaha were particularly lauded for their progress and their citizens' industry. For example, a July 21, 1877, installment noted that in forty years Chicago had grown from "a small aggregation of balloon-shaped log-cabins" to a true city of 450,000 inhabitants. And, those citizens had built the current city with its "wide, lighted avenues" despite having encountered "extraordinary obstacles" in their quest to build a city out of marshy land.[51] A similar August 18, 1877, article praised Omaha's 20,000 people, portraying them as an "enterprising population" who had built many fine public buildings with imposing exteriors. A few dilapidated buildings caught the party's eye and ire, particularly a handful of third- and fourth-rate hotels, which drew criticism.[52]

Even as the Leslies and their staff discovered the West of their imaginations in Wyoming, complete with cowboys, stagecoaches, and a mixed population that included Chinese and other immigrants, the party continued to judge recently constructed communities by northeastern standards. An October 13, 1877, installment gave Cheyenne, Wyoming, mixed reviews. While the *Leslie's* staff admitted their pleasure at seeing the march of civilization, only two or three of the city's blocks "look solidly respectable" with their neat brick buildings, a large hotel, and stores with attractive window displays. The rest of the city failed to measure up. It "soon drops such mimicry of the 'effete East' and replaces into a bold disregard of architectural forms and proprieties," the article's author noted with displeasure.[53] In another example, the Nevada desert, though stark, was turned into a descriptive treat by one of the series' authors who, accustomed to the bustle of New York City, acknowledged the land was lonely and empty, but expressed an appreciation of the "glaring white flats and tufted grey sage," and the brown sand hills. Readers were told that miles and miles of such scenery had put many of the train's occupants to sleep, but the author was drawn to the land and romantically contemplated the desert's quiet solitude, stating its "bareness is the very grandeur and tragedy of desolation."[54]

In an age before inexpensive, portable cameras allowed visitors to depict their travels for themselves, *Leslie's* sketch artists were central to the series' success.[55] One particularly eye-catching illustration, titled "The Palisades of the Humboldt River," depicted Nevada's Twelve-Mile Canyon's steep walls, enormous rock formations, and, at its bottom, a river flowing through it. The image visually demonstrated that the wilderness had been conquered since the Transcontinental Railroad curved through the narrow gorge and into the wilderness beyond. The accompanying article acknowledged the role of the railroads in taming the West, stating the canyon had been "untraveled even by a horseman before the rails of the Central Pacific Road."[56]

## Portraying the West's Inhabitants: Settlers, Indians, and Chinese

The *Leslie's* series encouraged readers to follow Horace Greeley's maxim and "Go West," pointing to the Great Plains and the far West as safety valves that could solve the problem of overpopulation in eastern cities. After observing a throng of settlers in Omaha and Council Bluffs, the author of the August 18, 1877, installment encouraged readers, especially unemployed ones, to head West and work hard. "Your prairie-farm will be a saving's bank," the article noted, adding the land was "splendid" and the railroad "extends ample facilities to the farmer." Large tracts of land were still available for individuals who were willing to work hard, the article proclaimed, before telling readers that successful settlers had gotten rid of their temporary sod houses and built tidy wood homes for themselves.[57] The journey also allowed *Leslie's* journalists to praise the industry and resilience of the nation's post-war population. Readers saw farmers, miners, loggers, ranchers, and a host of urban workers exploiting the landscape for the good of the nation. Substantial brick hotels and blocks of large, well-filled stores appeared in such cities as Council Bluffs, Iowa, and Freemont, Nebraska—lands where Indians once roamed.

Illustrations provided visual proof of this success. A sketch from Freemont depicted huge piles of lumber near the town's train station and white men laboring in a community that already had a large, wooden grain elevator and a big windmill.[58] Illustrations also contributed to the mythic status of the individual settler. The "Across the Continent" series was published during an era of changing pictorial representation, during which a broadening readership, including an increasing number of immigrants entering the middle class, wanted more realistic portrayals and objected to traditional, pre-war depictions that relied heavily on stereotyped physiognomic codes.[59] Thus, from the varied occupants of the regular train cars to the teeming masses of immigrants at the Nebraska train station, and even in street scenes in each city and community the journalists' visited, most individuals were depicted with uniquely different faces, different poses, and of different dress that identified their class status. Even the numerous Virginia City, Nevada, silver miners depicted in the March 9, 1878, were clearly displayed as unique individuals, although artist Thur de Thulstrup represented the bare-chested men's musculature in classical proportions. Their half-nakedness was shockingly erotic by nineteenth-century standards.[60]

The February 2, 1878, article was devoted entirely to another group encountered by the Leslies on their adventure: railroad tramps. The article told readers that no sketch on railroad travel would be complete without a sketch devoted to tramps, their lives, and their attempts to ride the Union Pacific and Central Pacific Railroad cars for free. And, while the author noted he was amused at every station watching the tramps' "tricks" to try and get a ride, *Leslie's* sketch artists revealed the dangers that the tramps caused. One illustration showed several tramps attempting to throw a conductor from the train's roof after he had climbed up to remove them. Another image revealed that railroad personnel could be equally violent where tramps were concerned, with a conductor on a rear platform attempting to shove tramps off the train at a stop as they tried to board for free.[61] A large image in the same issue demonstrated the illustrated press' uneven attempt at post-war visual realism. The scene, which depicted railroad tramps sitting around a fire, made clear to readers that the tramps included native-born Americans, as well as immigrants from several nations. Men dressed in Russian, German, American, and Irish attire were striking different poses and all, except the Irish, were shown with distinctive facial features. The Irish continued to be depicted as simian, complete with stereotypical pipes and bowler hats.[62]

*Leslie's* artists did not shy away from the tawdry and sensational aspects of Western life. A risqué stage show at a music hall in Cheyenne, Wyoming, depicted a cross-section

The *Leslie's* reporters found promising signs of civilization in the West of the late 1870s, including developing commerce, transportation systems, and culture—despite the dancing girls and the "unconventional" audience at this Cheyenne theater (Frank Leslie's Illustrated Newspaper Oct. 13, 1877, Library of Congress, Item cph.3a-05839).

of white settlers. Men and women dressed in proper Victorian attire chatted at tables, some ignoring and some eyeing a dancing girl whose skirts were immodestly high. Gamblers, miners, and other rough types also were present, imbibing their favorite alcoholic beverage, or playing cards. The illustration accompanied a detailed article which compared the facility to its eastern counterparts: "The house, for all its cheap finery of decoration, its barbaric red and yellow splashes of paint, and its bizarre Venuses and Psyches posing on the walls, is marvelously clean; the audience wholly masculine, is unconventional (let us put it courteously), but not riotous."[63]

Cheyenne offered *Leslie's* reporters and illustrators, and, subsequently, readers, a western experience that was both real and mythic. While the sturdy, stone façade of the three-story Inter-Ocean Hotel and the globe-like street lamps demonstrated that both Anglo-civilization and a degree of respectability had arrived in the far West, an image showing a wide dirt street with its stagecoach, nearby timbered buildings, and the city's denizens, which included men clad in western dress shouldering rifles and a forlorn, blanket-clad Indian sauntering alone, suggested that although civilization had encroached on a formerly untamed land, its triumph was not yet complete.[64] The accompanying article noted that the reporters and artists were so enjoying the western culture that they had hoped to find, that they were "...loath to leave these stirring, crowded streets!" The article's author, possibly Hemyng, appealed to the readers' imaginations with a colorful description of Cheyenne's streets that would have been at home in a dime novel:

Look at that rich dash of color in the dusty street—a Mexican rider on a fierce, little mustang, his great, white sombrero rolled up at the side, his long, wild hair blown back, his scarlet cravat flying and the wind whirling out his great, blue cloak, show the purple jacket underneath, the silver-buckled belt, the stamped leather stirrups, the flashing silver spurs, and the gleam of a pistol at his side—there! He has gone, with a clatter of hoofs and a cloud of dust; and no one turns to look after him except us "down-Easters."[65]

Like previous adventure journalists on the rails and trails of the West, the Leslies anticipated encounters with Native Americans as part of their Western adventure. For the *Leslie's* staff and their readers, Indians personified the West like no other people. In both articles and illustrations, the depictions of Native Americans relied on earlier physiognomic codes and constructions as well as original and, at times, perhaps, more accurate depictions. Many of the illustrations depicted the individuality of native people with unique dress, poses, and facial features. But writing during an era in which the federal government was ignoring treaties and openly battling Native Americans on the western plains, however, the series' authors regularly used common, pejorative terms such as *barbarous* and *savage* when referring to Native Americans. The series noted that once "the iron tracks of the railway" brought civilization to an entire country, the action relegated native inhabitants to the past. Many illustrations demonstrated this by showing native people off to the side of the pictures, staring as the train passed them by. The Indians' subjugation, much like the brutal suppression of striking laborers, fit a common political narrative in the post-war environment, when many citizens saw violent repression as necessary means to stop those who stood in the way of the nation's industrial purpose.[66]

Despite the racial references that were so common at the time, the journalists and their fellow train passengers were thrilled, rather than fearful, when encountering Native Americans. A first glimpse of an Indian village, seen from the train window, led a reporter to label the Indians as "picturesque" and state that the Native Americans and their shaggy ponies were "not an unpleasant sight."[67] But when stereotyped expectations of Native peoples were not met, the series' authors voiced their disappointment. For example, the author of the January 19, 1878, article evinced surprise that some Indians worked for the railroad. The reporter seemed disappointed that the men did not fit the popular culture image that had been thrust upon them. The men were working, not begging, the article stated, adding that the Indians who were loading up a freight-car had no war paint on their faces and that their bodies were not wrapped in blankets. Mixing grudging acceptance and the common racism of the time, the article stated:

> True, they work in a rather languid manner, but still it is work, and so far a refreshing spectacle; and we are told that a small number of them are regularly employed, there upon the railroad, co-laborers with the Chinese, and receiving the same rate of wage—one dollar per day—with this difference, however, that the Celestial 'finds' himself his pork and rice, the staff of his life, and the Indian is generously allowed to draw his ration from the Government.[68]

When the train stopped in Humboldt, Nevada, for passengers to have their lunch, many of the train's female passengers immediately crowded around a group of "civilized" Indians on the platform. The article expressed both the excitement of seeing living relics of the nation's past as well as disdain at their presence: "For the first time, we feel a thrill as the sight of a genuine savage, for this party is gorgeous in buckskin and beadwork, the men having eschewed the regulation black hat, tied on with a dirty string, and one of them has actually a bow and quiver of arrows slung at his back." The natives were members of the Shoshone Tribe. One woman, described as the only "comely" female, spoke

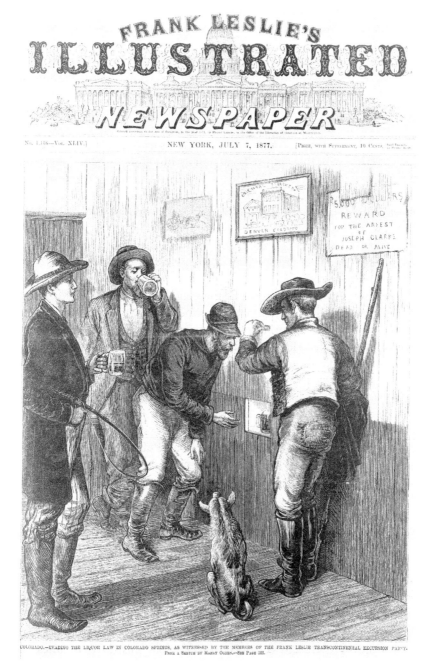

COLORADO.—EVADING THE LIQUOR LAW IN COLORADO SPRINGS, AS WITNESSED BY THE MEMBERS OF THE FRANK LESLIE TRANSCONTINENTAL EXCURSION PARTY.
FROM A SKETCH BY HARRY OGDEN.—SEE PAGE 303.

In the American imagination—and in *Leslie's* "Across the Continent"
series—western life was characterized by contrasts: the advance of civilization and the wild life of the frontier. The tension between law-and-order and
a taste for whiskey is brought to life in this sketch by Harry Ogden, published July 7, 1877, showing four men "evading the liquor law in Colorado
Springs, as witnessed by the members of the Frank Leslie transcontinental
excursion party" (Frank Leslie's Illustrated Newspaper, July 7, 1877, Library
of Congress, Item cph.3c19251).

English and was peppered with questions by the Anglo passengers.[69] The stop gave the train riders what they wanted: a western experience that met their expectations and fit their stereotypes.

Another minority group—the Chinese—also was portrayed with curiosity and ambivalence, reflecting the common prejudices of the day in both illustration and text.[70] The February 9, 1878, installment delivered the exotica that *Leslie's* readers expected in describing Chinese working on the railroad line outside of Reno, Nevada, but it also made clear that the Asian immigrants were far inferior to white workers. The workers were described as "bare-legged, ragged, dressed in a sort of hybrid mixture of Chinese and Caucasian styles, with their pig-tails twisted up out of the way, and their great straw platter hats tied under their chins." While the *Leslie's* staff saw the Chinese as a cultural curiosity, the journalists also displayed their derision toward the "Celestials," admitting "an ever-fresh delight" in laughing at and mocking the workers' "pigeon English," but, at the same time, worrying that the Chinese were not as docile as they looked. After poking fun at the workers, the reporter stated, "…they scorn a response, but sit cackling among themselves in their own queer chopped-up language, replete, probably, with opprobrious epithets for the 'white devils.'"[71]

When the *Leslie's* staff encountered Chinese again, in Colfax, California, several of the male staffers showed their deep disregard for the Chinese by walking into their homes and businesses uninvited. The immigrants did not stop them, preferring to ignore the rude reporters. The staff described how a Chinese butcher chopped up meat, while next door several Chinese sat around a table eating rice and meat and drinking tea from "the most seductive dark-blue cups." Readers learned the railroad workers' homes were little more than "dreary" shanties and huts, which compared unfavorably to the homes occupied by white residents that the journalists witnessed during a stop in Sacramento.[72]

But *Leslie's*, like its rival, *Harper's Weekly*, had long reinforced popular viewpoints on race via illustrations and the accompanying text.[73] Publisher Leslie held to an editorial policy that all people—native born and immigrants—were worthy unless they proved themselves otherwise. When the latter occurred, *Leslie's* illustrators and reporters often engaged in stereotypical portrayals. For example, Irish immigrants often were portrayed with simian features and seen as lazy, cunning, or hard-drinking.[74] Reader participation was crucial in the development and acceptance of such visual and textual stereotypes. As historian Joshua Brown has noted, the illustrated press' contribution to stereotyped portrayals relied upon regular and prolonged viewership of such images.[75] *Leslie's* often used what's been termed "binary opposites" in its verbal and visual portrayals of whites and racial minorities, a practice the magazine continued in the "Across the Continent" series. By their very use, binary opposites purposely reaffirmed the dominance of white individuals, while subordinating all other western residents as "others."[76] Part of the reason, certainly, was that the reporters and sketch artists often had only thirty minutes to an hour to wander through frontier communities while the train was being serviced at the station, but dominant racial ideologies also were at work.

When "The Frank Leslie" arrived at the end of the track in Oakland, California, its notable passengers transferred to a ferry for the final leg of the journey, by water, to San Francisco. Upon their arrival, presented in the May 18, 1878, magazine, the author joyously proclaimed, "we welcome civilization yet again," but the reporter seemed overwhelmed by that civilization after journeying through the wide-open valleys and deserts of the West. The bustling streets thrummed with vendors, newsboys, and carriage drivers, while the steep hills upon which the city was built displayed an odd sense of urban planning—homes and retail establishments "curiously" interspersed around warehouses. Yet, the Leslies and their staff proclaimed that the buzzing West Coast city offered them "All the life and stir of New York streets … and more besides."[77]

## Delivering American Identity

The 1877 "Across the Continent" series served as one of the last hurrahs for the illustrated press. The invention of the half-tone process, which allowed publications to inexpensively reproduce photographs, soon spelled the demise of wood engravings as a source of pictorial reproduction.[78] The genteel adventure also ultimately bankrupted the publisher. Although the journalists received complimentary railroad travel, Leslie's tab for the lavish meals and other expenses incurred during the journey exceeded $15,000. The Financial Panic of 1877 further put the publisher's finances in the red and forced him to accept a trustee to oversee his publishing empire's fortunes.[79]

But the three-month journey had allowed publisher Leslie and his readers to celebrate Anglo-American expansion and ingenuity. During a time of tremendous political corruption, uncertain race relations, and economic strife, when Americans undoubtedly needed a celebratory series that did not focus on the nation's post-war ills, the "Across the Continent" series delivered a mix of myth and realism that depicted an America that many readers wanted and expected to see. Readers viewed a nation that was actively on the move in the decade after the Civil War and a country that was emerging as a technological powerhouse, as hard-working native-born citizens and immigrants used the country's vast resources in their quest to achieve manifest destiny. The *Leslie's* adventure provided a glimpse of a nation on the cusp of a consumer culture whose western cities and communities were quickly acquiring the comforts of their eastern counterparts. Yet, readers also saw a frontier that was in part still raw, a land that still served as an escape from urban woes, with a landscape that would awe generations of adventurers to come.

## NOTES

1. Lee Jolliffe, "Adventure Journalists in the Gilded Age," *Journalism History* 42, no. 1 (2016): 2.

2. Richard Reinhardt, *Out West on the Overland Train: Across-the-Continent Excursion with Leslie's Magazine in 1877 and the Overland Trip in 1967* (Secaucus, N.J.: Castle Books, 1967), 5. The Leslies and reporter Bracebridge Hemyng gushed throughout the series at the lavishness and modernity of their train car and the first-class hotels in Chicago, San Francisco, and other communities in which they spent time.

3. Although the last article under the title of "Across the Continent" appeared on May 25, 1878, *Leslie's* ran a short story on June 15, 1878, under the headline "Overland to the Pacific" that told of the party's arrival at the Palace Hotel in San Francisco. A large illustration in the June 28, 1878, issue puffed the Palace Hotel by showing the hotel's "Grand Court" entrance where carriages arrived. A later, July 20, 1878, issue depicted a view of Sansome Street in San Francisco with a subsequent article that told of the city's trade and financial operations. The article clearly was penned by one of the three "Across the Continent" authors, but the article was not labeled as such. For more on social and cultural conditions at the time, see Paul Boyer, *Urban Masses and Moral Order in America, 1820–1920* (Cambridge: Harvard University Press, 1978), 70, 123; Ari Hoogenboom, *Rutherford B. Hayes: Warrior and President* (Lawrence: University Press of Kansas, 1995), 286–293; William Gillette, *Retreat from Reconstruction, 1869–1879* (Baton Rouge: Louisiana State University Press, 1979), 323–331; Douglas R. Egerton, *The Wars of Reconstruction: The Brief, Violent History of America's Most Progressive Era* (New York: Bloomsbury Press, 2014), 308–318; Phillip S. Foner, *The Great Labor Uprising of 1877* (New York: Pathfinder Press, 1977), 8–9; Stuart Creighton Miller, *The Unwelcome Immigrant: The American Image of the Chinese, 1785–1882* (Berkeley: University of California Press, 1969), 169–175, 194–199; Erika Lee, *At*

*America's Gates: Chinese Immigration during the Exclusion Era, 1882–1943* (Chapel Hill: University of North Carolina Press, 2003), 26.

4. Jeffrey Alan Melton, *Mark Twain, Travel Books, and Tourism: The Tide of a Great Popular Movement* (Tuscaloosa: University of Alabama Press, 2002), 19; Cindy S. Aron, *Working at Play: A History of Vacations in the United States* (New York: Oxford University Press, 1999), 151.

5. Joseph Becker, "An Artist's Interesting Recollections of Leslie's Weekly," *Leslie's Weekly* December 14, 1905.

6. Frank Luther Mott, *A History of American Magazines*, II, 1850–1865 (Cambridge, Mass.: Harvard University Press, 1938), 465.

7. Many eastern publishers, including the *New York Tribune*'s Horace Greeley, headed west as much out of personal curiosity as for circulation reasons. For more, see Katrina J. Quinn, "'I turn my face westward tomorrow': Adventure Reporting from America's Western Rails and Trails, 1860–1880," paper presented to the 2016 Annual Symposium on the 19th Century Press, the Civil War, and Free Expression, Chattanooga, TN, 1.

8. William E. Huntzicker, "Picturing the News: Frank Leslie and the Origins of American Pictorial Journalism," in David B. Sachsman, S. Kittrell Rushing, and Debra Reddin van Tuyll, *The Civil War and the Press* (New Brunswick, NJ: Transaction Publishers, 2000). 322.

9. The $300 ticket did not include a sleeper berth. For the same price, Americans could travel to Europe and journey in greater comfort. Marguerite S. Shaffer, *See America First: Tourism and National Identity, 1880–1940* (Washington, D.C.: Smithsonian Books, 2001), 17; Aron, *Working at Play*, 140. See the installment published on August 25, 1877, for a look at first-class travel, and the February 9, 1878, article for a lengthy glimpse at how lower- and middle-class citizens traveled. The latter article struck a sympathetic tone toward regular travelers.

10. Michael J. Hostetler, "Henry Cabot Lodge and the Rhetorical Trajectory." in *The Rhetoric of American Exceptionalism. Cruical Essays, eds.* Jason A. Edwards and David Weiss (Jefferson, N.C.:McFarland, 2011), 119–120.

11. Katrina J. Quinn, "'I turn my face westward tomorrow,'" 9.

12. *Frank Leslie's Illustrated Newspaper*, June 23, 1877.

13. Katrina J. Quinn, "'Across the Continent … and Still the Republic!' Inscribing Nationhood in Samuel Bowles's Newspaper Letters of 1865," *American Journalism* 31, no. 4 (2014): 468–489; Jerald T. Milanich, ed. *A Remarkable Curiosity: Dispatches from a New York City Journalist's 1873 Railroad Trip across the American West* (Boulder: University Press of Colorado, 2008); Benjamin Franklin Taylor, *Between the Gates: A Train Journey from Chicago to San Francisco* (Chicago: S.C. Griggs and Co., 1878); Grace Greenwood, *New Life in New Lands: Notes of Travel* (New York: Ford, 1873); Albert D. Richardson, *Beyond the Mississippi: From the Great River to the Great Ocean. Life and Adventure on the Prairies, Mountains, and Pacific Coast* (Hartford: American Publishing Co., 1869); Samuel Bowles, *Across the Continent: A Summer's Journey to the Rocky Mountains, the Mormons, and the Pacific States, with Speaker Colfax* (Springfield, MA: Bowles, 1865). Robert Taft provided a detailed discussion of illustrated periodicals' discussions of transcontinental travel in his 1953 book. See Robert Taft, *Artists and Illustrators of the Old West, 1850–1900* (New York, 1953).

14. Deirdre Murphy, "Like Standing on the Edge of the World and Looking Away Into Heaven," *Common-Place* 7, no. 3 (2007), available online at: common-place.org/book/like-standing-on-the-edge-of-the-world-and-looking-away-into-heaven/ (accessed June 9, 2017).

15. The quote is from Melton, *Mark Twain, Travel Books, and Tourism*, 22–23; Sears, *Sacred Places*, xii.

16. Melton, *Mark Twain, Travel Books, and Tourism*, 22–23, 25, 30; Mulvey, *Anglo-American Landscapes*, 199.

17. Although the realism movement became a force in literature in the early 1880s, realism had earlier practitioners, including those writing for the periodic press. Brenda Murphy, *American Realism and American Drama, 1880–1940* (New York: Cambridge University Press, 2008), 1; Amy Kaplan, *The Social Construction of American Realism* (Chicago: University of Chicago Press, 1992), 8.

18. Huntzicker, "Picturing the News," 313, 320–321; Brown, *Beyond the Lines*, 70–71; Kevin G. Barnhurst and John Nerone, "Civil Picturing vs. Realistic Photojournalism: The Regime of Illustrated News, 1865–1901," *Design Issues* 16, no. 1 (2000): 61–64.

19. Melton, *Mark Twain, Travel Books, and Tourism* 24–25.

20. *Ibid.*, 24.

21. The quote is from *Frank Leslie's Illustrated Newspaper*, June 30, 1877. For more on the concept of genteel explorers, see Hanna, Jr., "The Genteel Explorers," 73.

22. The Leslie's lavish Pullman Palace Car, its staff, wine cellar, cooking facilities and other modern conveniences were detailed in the August 25, 1877, installment of the series. An earlier, July 21, 1877, installment detailed the lavish meals served to the publisher and his staff. For more on the luxuriousness of train travel, see Archibald Hanna, Jr., "The Genteel Explorers; or, When the Covered Wagon Became a Pullman Palace Car," *Yale University Library Gazette* 54, no. 2 (1979): 72.

23. *Frank Leslie's Illustrated Newspaper*, February 9, 1878. On first and standard-class train travel distinctions, see Ambrose, *Nothing Like it in the World*, 24.

24. Miriam Leslie put out a well-received book of their journey in 1877 titled *California: a pleasure trip from Gotham to the Golden Gate, April, May, June 1877.*

25. Hostetler, "Henry Cabot Lodge and the Rhetorical Trajectory," 119–120; Richard Hofstadter, *Social Darwinism in American Thought* (Boston: Beacon Press, 1983), 172–173. For the development of beliefs in the superiority of Anglo-Saxons in America, see Reginald Horsman, *Race and Manifest Destiny: The Origins of American Racial Anglo-Saxonism* (Cambridge: Harvard University Press, 1981).

26. Mulvey, *Anglo-American Landscapes*, 244.

27. Hanna Jr, "The Genteel Explorers," 77.

28. *Frank Leslie's Illustrated Newspaper*, July 21, 1877.

29. *Frank Leslie's Illustrated Newspaper*, February 23, 1878 and March 2, 1878.

30. Shaffer, *See America First*, 20.

31. *Frank Leslie's Illustrated Newspaper*, May 18, 1878.

32. *Frank Leslie's Illustrated Newspaper*, October 20, 1877.

33. *Frank Leslie's Illustrated Newspaper*, July 7, 1877.

34. *Frank Leslie's Illustrated Newspaper*, August 25, 1877. Pullman is depicted in this issue on page 417. The same issue also featured elaborate illustrations of the Leslies' first-class travel, including the wine closet and sommelier, the Leslies' personal chef, and the other servants and their tasks.

35. Mulvey, *Anglo-American Landscapes*, 240.

36. Stephen E. Ambrose, *Nothing Like it in the World: The Men Who Built the Transcontinental Railroad, 1863–1869* (New York: Touchstone Books, 2000), 17–18; Shaffer, *See America First*, 20.

37. Henry M. Stanley, *My Early Travels and Adventures in America and Asia*, Vol. I (London: Sampson Low, Marston, 1895), 88.

38. Ambrose, *Nothing Like it in the World*, 25–27.

39. *Frank Leslie's Illustrated Newspaper*, November 3, 1877.

40. *Ibid.* Also see *Frank Leslie's Illustrated Newspaper*, May 11, 1878.

41. For more on what Niagara Falls and the Hudson River Valley meant to antebellum tourists, see Sears, *Sacred Places*, 49–50.

42. Mulvey, *Anglo-American Landscapes*, 206.

43. *Frank Leslie's Illustrated Newspaper*, July 7, 1877.

44. *Frank Leslie's Illustrated Newspaper*, September 1, 1877.

45. *Frank Leslie's Illustrated Newspaper*, January 19, 1878.

46. *Frank Leslie's Illustrated Newspaper*, October 13, 1877.

47. Sears, *Sacred Places*, 5.

48. Shaffer, *See America First*, 16. Shaffer notes that changes wrought by industrialization, especially changes in production and distribution practices, transformed both "patterns and interactions of daily life," as well as the public's views of time, space, and distance. Both antebellum era and post-war illustrators and painters intertwined the scenery and nationalism in illustrations. See Angela Miller, *The Empire of the Eye: Landscape Representation and American Cultural Politics, 1825–1875* (Ithaca, NY: Cornell University Press, 1993), 10–11.

49. *Frank Leslie's Illustrated Newspaper*, July 7, 1877.

50. *Frank Leslie's Illustrated Newspaper*, July 14, 1877.

51. *Frank Leslie's Illustrated Newspaper*, July 21, 1877.

52. *Ibid.* Also see *Frank Leslie's Illustrated Newspaper*, August 18, 1877.

53. *Frank Leslie's Illustrated Newspaper*, October 13, 1877. The Leslies were more approving of longer-established Midwestern cities, including Council Bluffs, Iowa. An August 18, 1877, issue praised the city's development, touting its "substantial brick hotels" and its "blocks of large and well-filled stores."

54. *Ibid.*

55. Hanna, Jr., "The Genteel Explorers," 77.

56. *Frank Leslie's Illustrated Newspaper*, January 5, 1878.

57. *Frank Leslie's Illustrated Newspaper*, August 18, 1877.

58. See *Frank Leslie's Illustrated Newspaper* for August 18, 1877, and September 1, 1877.

59. Brown, *Beyond the Lines*, 170–171.

60. *Frank Leslie's Illustrated Newspaper*, March 9, 1878.

61. *Frank Leslie's Illustrated Newspaper*, February 2, 1878.

62. *Ibid.*

63. *Frank Leslie's Illustrated Newspaper*, October 13, 1877.

64. *Ibid.* Similarly, the January 19, 1878, installment also showed the rough-and-ready exotica of the West that easterners craved. Images from the installment showed the daily stagecoach to Winnemucca, Nevada, from Boise City, Idaho, with its passengers, mailbags, and guards. The accompanying article stated the departure of the stagecoach has become "one of those vignette pictures of frontier life to which we have grown accustomed." The journey covered 275 miles.

65. *Frank Leslie's Illustrated Newspaper*, October 13, 1877.

66. Shaffer, *See America First*, 16.

67. *Frank Leslie's Illustrated Newspaper*, September 15, 1877.

68. *Frank Leslie's Illustrated Newspaper*, January 19, 1878.

69. *Frank Leslie's Illustrated Newspaper*, January 19, 1878.

70. Mary M. Cronin and William E. Huntzicker, "Popular Chinese Images and 'The Coming Man' of 1870: Racial Representations of Chinese," *Journalism History* 38, no. 2 (2012): 87.

71. *Frank Leslie's Illustrated Newspaper*, February 9, 1878.

72. *Frank Leslie's Illustrated Newspaper*, May 4, 1878.

73. Brown, *Beyond the Lines*, 79, 91, 113, 122.

74. David R. Spencer, "No Laughing Matter: 19th Century Editorial Cartoons and the Business of Race," *International Journal of Comic Art* 11 (2009): 206; Brown, *Beyond the Lines*, 100–102, 106–107.

75. Brown, *Beyond the Lines*, 71.

76. Stuart Hall, "The Spectacle of the 'Other,'" in *Representation: Cultural Representations and Signifying Practices*, ed. Stuart Hall (London: Sage, 1997), 234–235; Alan Trachtenberg, *Shades of Hiawatha: Staging Indians, Making Americans, 1880–1930* (New York: Hill and Wang, 2004), 23.

77. *Frank Leslie's Illustrated Newspaper*, May 18, 1878.

78. Brown, *Beyond the Lines*, 173.

79. Reinhardt, *Out West on the Overland Train*, 18.

# "Into the Dark Abyss"

## Gilded Age Adventure Reporting from the Mines of America

### Katrina J. Quinn

With a hurried glance at the sunny landscape and "a thought of home and the unhappy condition of widows and orphans, as a general thing," *Harper's New Monthly Magazine* correspondent J. Ross Browne entered the vertical shaft of a gold mine near Bodie, California, in 1864, desperately clinging to a series of dilapidated ladders. He had turned down an alternate method of descent—a bucket lowered by a blind horse—after observing "with horror ... the rickety wooden bucket and the flimsy little rope that was to hold us suspended between the surface of the earth and eternity...."[1] But Browne quickly regretted his ladder-choice as he descended several hundred feet into the earth, fearing that at any moment a rung would give way, or that he would lose his footing, or his grip, or perhaps his consciousness, and plunge through the darkness to the bottom of the shaft.

Later, Browne would find it "a little remarkable that I am now alive to tell the story of my adventures. I penetrated more shafts in the earth, was dragged through more dangerous pits and holes in wooden buckets, was forced to creep over more slippery ledges, rich in mineral deposits, and to climb up a greater number of rickety ladders than I would like to undertake again for less than a thousand shares in the 'Empire Gold and Silver Mining Company.'"[2]

While adventure reporting of the late nineteenth-century took other newspaper correspondents to the farthest corners of the globe, some chose to stay closer to home, traveling down into the mines of America. Copper mines, coal mines, iron mines, and especially silver and gold mines presented rich opportunities for daring reporters of the Gilded Age, descending by ladder, bucket, coal car, and hydraulic lift, without much in the way of equipment—outside of an often-uncertain candle. Like Browne, these correspondents were in search of a great adventure, but also sought to tell stories of the nation's industry and ingenuity.

This essay examines mine adventure reporting from 1860 to 1875—an age of manifest destiny, technological innovation, and nation-building.[3] It finds that this reportage presents a consistent methodological impulse, with correspondents deliberate in their plans to report on mining, equipped with a specific set of interests and questions to be answered. The reportage also reflects consistencies in narrative framework, beginning with an explanation of the reporter's motivation and his or her descent into the mine;

continuing with the subterranean experience and an assessment of technology and production; and concluding with a perfunctory exit.

Just as the structure of their stories is highly consistent, journalists and correspondents who wrote about mine adventures commonly adopted a reporting style that was highly literary and personal, and often sought to convey a multisensory experience to their readers. Thus the reportage provides rich descriptions not only of the underground environment but also the personal experience of heading down into an alien sub-terrain. The "otherness" of the reporters in many ways echoes the position of their contemporaries writing from more traditional adventure destinations across the globe, and establishes a common subjectivity with readers.

Finally, readers of mine adventure journalism would have encountered important thematic elements related to national identity during an age of manifest destiny. Qualities that marked American national identity—qualities such as individualism, a strong work ethic, coarseness, strength, resourcefulness, mastery of material things, exuberance, and confidence, according to Frederick Jackson Turner[4]—all were reported to be in abundance in the mines of America.[5]

## Mine Adventure Reporting in Context

From the earliest colonial settlements, Americans have engaged in mining for materials such as silver, lead, copper, iron, and more, with settlers near Jamestown, Virginia, shipping iron ore to England as early as 1608, according to industrial historian Albert S. Bolles.[6] While mining was nothing new in the nineteenth-century, the industry blossomed in the antebellum period as the United States saw unprecedented physical, economic, and political growth. The industry further expanded as new resources were discovered in newly settled western regions and as technology led to more accessible—and certainly more profitable—efforts.

Although the history of America is studded with rich strikes of gold, silver, and other minerals, mining became a dynamic part of the American idiom in the mid–nineteenth-century with such extraordinary events as the California Gold Rush of 1848–55,[7] the discovery of silver at the Comstock Lode in 1859,[8] and the Pike's Peak Gold Rush of the same year.[9] Although working conditions remained crude and dangerous, the mines fueled westward expansion and the development of the railroad, while mining camps were among the first outposts of civilization. Technological advances led to new opportunities, with the iconic miner of the forty-niner era, panning alone in a California river, replaced by commercial shaft mining and large-scale industrial operations over the course of just a few years.

As the industry grew, so did the impact of the mining idiom on the American psyche as it resonated with emerging concepts of nation, wealth, and technological innovation following the Civil War. In April 1865, in fact, as Speaker of the House of Representatives Schuyler Colfax was about to leave on a transcontinental journey, mining was among the chief concerns of President Abraham Lincoln, who asserted that the nation would soon be "the treasury of the world." Lincoln believed the nation's mineral wealth to be virtually inexhaustible. "Tell the miners from me," Lincoln instructed Colfax, "that I shall promote their interests to the utmost of my ability; because their prosperity is the prosperity of the Nation."[10]

Gilded Age reporting from the mines of America echoed these themes and

In the scramble for wealth, mining boomtowns like Deadwood, South Dakota, with their wooden buildings, provisioners, and saloons, sprung up throughout the West. In the case of Deadwood, pictured here during the Black Hills Gold Rush in 1876, the settlement was made illegally, on land granted to the Lakota by the Treaty of Fort Laramie (photograph by S.J. Morrow, National Archives, VCN 165-FF-2F-15).

introduced readers to the environmental and technological riches of the nation. Because the mining concept was connected to fortune and danger, to windfalls and disasters, and because it featured authors engaging in action-packed and sometimes dangerous adventures, mine reportage capitalized on mid–nineteenth century interests in the exotic and subversive. It was a natural fit in an age of sensationalism, as ambitious editors looked for scintillating content to drive post-war circulation.

Among the notable figures undertaking a mining adventure were some of the most prominent newspaper editors, reporters, and correspondents of the era. Editors included such well-known figures as Schuyler Colfax, speaker of the U.S. House of Representatives and former editor of the *South Bend (IN) Tribune,* who traveled to the Pacific in the summer of 1865, and his companion Samuel Bowles, of the *Springfield (MA) Republican.* Frequent traveler Amos Jay Cummings, editor of the *New York Sun,* visited a number of mines during his sweeping trip of the West in 1873. Also reporting from the mines were well-known Civil War and Gilded Age reporters, including Grace Greenwood of the *New-York Times*, Albert D. Richardson of the *New-York Tribune*, and Dan De Quille, writing in the *San Francisco Golden Era* and later an editor of the *Territorial Enterprise* in Virginia City, Nevada. *Harper's New Monthly Magazine* was among the leaders in publishing mine adventures, with numerous stories appearing throughout the 1860s and 1870s. Among the well-known correspondents writing about mine adventures for *Harper's* were J. Ross Browne, whose multi-installment series, called "A Peep at Washoe," was published in 1860, and William V. Wells, who had been among the eager forty-niners, and was sent by the publication to write about the evolution of the industry eleven years later. Auber Forestier, writing for the *Saturday Evening Post*, and Joseph Pratt Allyn, writing under the pseudonym "Putnam" for the *Hartford Evening Press,* were among others retained as correspondents for publications across the country. These individuals were accompanied by scores of lesser-known or small-town reporters and even anonymous correspondents who climbed, squeezed, crouched, and crawled in the darkness, hundreds of feet beneath the surface of the earth.

Acutely aware of the substantial economic potential of the mining industry for the future of the country, these writers were dedicated to the collection of verifiable news. They reported extensively on the financial prospects of the mines, the role of the business owners, the quality of the ores, systems for processing and transporting the metals, accessibility to markets, the trading prices of company shares, and the geologic or economic history of the region. Auber Forestier, for example, writing for the *Saturday Evening Post,* reported on the geological structure of the quartz vein in Grass Valley, California, the number of men at work in the mine, and the physical construction of the shaft and tunnels.[11] Throughout his lengthy *Across the Continent* newspaper series of 1865, Samuel Bowles dedicated multiple columns to the western mining industry's economics and innovations, hoping to motivate investment by and emigration of his eastern readers.[12]

But news was only part of the mining story. While newsgathering may have prompted the reporters' attention, the true allure of mine reporting lay in the adventure itself. Venturing into a dark shaft without a certifiable bottom, creeping through the darkness to find a glimmering cavern of ores, lighting upon a subterranean civilization of laborers after miles of serpentine passageways, crouching in the darkness beside a rocky chasm, climbing for what seemed like hours toward a pinprick of light—these were the emergent stories from the mines of America, not merely about the economic or technological riches of the nation, but about the encounter of the human psyche with the subterrestrial unknown.

## Into the "Cavern of Darkness"[13]

While the mine adventure was universally transformative for untested visitors, the transformation occasionally began prior to entering the mine. One colorful example came from the pen of the dignified George McKendree Steele, corresponding for *The Ladies' Repository* in 1871, who described the amusing process of donning "miner's garb" for a trip into the Calumet Copper Mine in Upper Michigan:

> I … took off my own clothes and got into a good thick pair of drawers, over which I drew on stout duck trowsers. I also put on a good warm undershirt and over it a coarse loose jacket. Then a pair of heavy and capacious boots at one end of my person, and at the other a thick, clumsy hat, which had evidently seen service both as a covering and a helmet, and was thoroughly incrusted with a coating of clay and grease, completed my array. A tallow candle, with a ball of plastic and adhesive clay rolled around the lower end, so that in ascending and descending the ladder it might be readily fastened to the hat, was placed in my hand, and I was in the full uniform of, and no doubt was as prepossessing as, the average miner.[14]

More often, reporters had surprisingly little or no preparation before descending into a menacingly dark shaft or muddy pit. Take, for example, Joseph Pratt Allyn, who recalled that he had barely time to remove his overcoat and the loose items from his pockets before scurrying after his companions into a dark shaft at the Mowry Mine, a silver mine in Santa Clara County, Arizona.[15]

Like participant reportages generally, mine adventures exhibit a chronological structure, typically beginning with a ritualistic descent or entrance into the mine by rope and bucket, coal car, ladders, or other arrangements. Grace Greenwood recounted one of the more genteel entrées, taken at the New Almaden quicksilver mines in the Santa Cruz mountains in 1873.[16] Greenwood and her party rode "in grand style" in ore cars, seated upon blocks of wood, and drawn by "a stout and serious-minded mule…. Thus we plunged into the darkness and the silence of inner earth…."[17] No doubt Greenwood appreciated this route after being lowered in a bucket at Colorado's Caribou Mine the previous fall.[18]

Not all mine adventurers were so lucky, however, with most entering by more treacherous and disconcerting means. In a very Freudian passage, a reporter for the *Weston (WV) Democrat* recalled, "We descend the shaft with a disagreeable feeling of going, we know not whither, save somewhere into the depths of a black pit which yawns beneath us."[19] A writer for *Appletons' Journal of Literature, Science and Art* described his descent in a bucket, relating both the process and his personal experience, noting both an "unpleasant sensation of vacancy" and a sense of "closeness" in the narrow space, amplified by the darkness. The use of present tense verbs and the pronoun "you" serve to generalize the action and incorporate the reader: "Now and then it occurs to you that a stone might fall from the wall, and break your head; that the rope, stretched by the weight it supports, the oscillations of which are perceptible, may also break, or the bottom of the tub may fall out." The writer described the panic of some newcomers to the mine, who "cower down in the bottom of the bucket, where they remain motionless through fear, and it is sometimes necessary to turn the bucket over to get these stupefied people out…."[20]

With adventure reporting lying outside the realm of the familiar for both the adventurer and the reader, the text frequently took on literary conventions to capture the phenomenal experience. For example, a correspondent for the *Circular* described his experience in the Barytes Mine in Cheshire, Connecticut, in 1861, with rich multi-sensory imagery: "The guide goes through the small hole in the floor, and we follow, all alive with caution, but not with fear. The wet and slimy ladder, the dripping and gurgling of water, the red glare of the candles, the shouts of the delayed miners coming up, the thunder of slamming trap-doors over head, the grinding of the ascending and descending buckets,

**Journalists such as Albert Richardson may have felt displaced in strange underground environments, but not thesee Pennsylvania coal miners and their mule, working "three miles underground" (Photograph by Strohmeyer & Wyman, Aug. 19, 1895, Library of Congress, Item cph 3a14861).**

the smell of the mine, and the asthmatic breathing of the pumps all go to flood one with a torrent of novel sensations."[21] Readers could easily perceive a sense of disorientation in Joseph Allyn of the *Hartford Evening Press* as he entered the Apache Chief Mine in Arizona. His language paints a surreal environment and bespeaks a mounting sense of panic:

> Slowly you are lowered down, until the light of day disappears and somehow an impression steals on you that perhaps you won't get back, your candle burns dimly or most likely won't burn at all, for the air is very impure; you reach the bottom where two or three naked figures are drilling by the pale flicker of two or three candles kept burning by a stream of air forced down the pipe that runs alongside of the track. In the dim light it seems as though you were shut up here without an exit and the figures of the miners flitting about are weird and unnatural. Their cautious salutations destroy that illusion, you strain your eyes, try to see something, all the rocks look alike to you, and grasping a piece freshly knocked off, you scramble back to the car and strike the pipe as a signal to be hoisted out—at least that's about what I did.[22]

Descriptions of the descent, therefore, not only accounted for the individual's passage but also conveyed the complex cognitive realignment to the subterranean environment. For Samuel Bowles, visiting the Gould & Curry Mine in Virginia City, Nevada, "[i]t seemed a very long journey, and the nerves had to brace themselves. The most stolid person, stranger to such experience, will hardly fail to find his heart beating a little quicker, as he goes into these far-away, narrow recesses in the bowels of the earth."[23]

The extreme discomfort of the reporter in the mine environment could also provide fertile ground for self-deprecating humor that could elicit a rhetorical connection to the distant reader. One correspondent used present-tense verbs and an engaging narrative style to bring the adventure, and the adventurer's perspective, to life. The passage also mirrors the pace of the author's experience itself by stopping and starting, a clever rhetorical trick that keeps the readers in suspense:

> You look between your feet and think that the guide's candle is getting away from you. Down you go a little more swiftly. It is only going down a ladder after all. Down, down, down, when shall we get somewhere? 'Hold!' Here is a lot of miners on a platform waiting to go up. Guide carefully hands you over a frightful hole bridged by a plank or two. Down again; just room enough to get along—planking close to one elbow and the great pump-shaft close to the other. 'Hold!' some one shouts—you are on his fingers. 'Hold!' you shout, for some one is on your fingers. The ladder is as dirty as ever; the water drips and plushes; how jealously you protect your candle, which here seems much like reason's dim candle in a benighted world.[24]

Contrast the stopping and starting of the descent by ladder in this passage with Dan De Quille's wild plunge into the "bowels" of the Ophir Mine on another mine excursion, vis-à-vis a miniature, steam-powered rail car on a 45-degree declined track. De Quille, one of the great western newspapermen and humorists of the nineteenth century, wrote at length about his mine adventures. In this passage, Perry C., De Quille's companion, "stowed himself in the bottom of the car ... and I piled in on top of him, with one knee stuck into his ribs, an arm clutching the top of the car and the other round his neck, with my chin *hooked* over his head ... we were as snugly packed as a pair of sardines." After orders to "let'r rip," the car was propelled at a terrifying rate down the rail: "We went thundering along, and I managed to twist my head half-round and see out of the corners of my eyes as we rushed through the dazzling flash of an occasional lamp fixed on the roof that the passage down which we were coursing, was ceiled with plank kept in place with beams and braces, and that it would not be necessary to raise my head to any great altitude to get my scalp taken." The scene unfolds as the car lands at the base of the track:

> Bump! and the car has stopped. Hearing a considerable amount of loud laughter, I raise my head and open my eyes ... and some half-dozen bearded miners are standing about us with candles flashing and flaring in their hands, all laughing fit to split their sides. What at, I didn't know ... but it is barely possible that they may have discovered something ludicrous in the manner in which we were stowed away in our box, and in our lying as still as a pair of pet kittens for some time after the car was down—waiting to be sure the thing had lit![25]

Once underground, reporters were challenged to navigate through the labyrinthine and often claustrophobic environment. Allyn described the contortionist pathways as sometimes "high enough to walk erect in, then you had to stoop, sometimes to crawl, after which you would emerge into a chamber...."[26] A similar scene was drawn for readers of the *Circular*: "Here the lead is a huge vault, there the walls come together as if ready to crush us. 'Look out for your heads'; each man successively echoes 'heads' to the one behind him; and we all stoop to go under the timbers that support the mass of material excavated above."[27]

The reporter often made an explicit connection between the physical environment and his or her mental state. "Once at the bottom, there is a damp oppressive feeling in the air," wrote a reporter in the *Weston (WV) Democrat* of March 31, 1862. "[T]he rock over-head drips dirty water down upon us, and occasionally an icy stream crawls down our back, sending a disagreeable shudder from head to foot. Of course we get bewildered; the light from the little lamp in our oil skin hat is very dim and smoky, and casts a sort of uncertain radiance for about three feet in advance, throwing great black shadows which leave us in a kind of unpleasant doubt whether or not we shall suddenly step into some abyss and disappear forever into the bowels of the earth."[28]

When journalists attempted to convey the convoluted magnitude of the mines, their writing adopted analogous structures. Bowles described entering the Gould & Curry Mine with a sentence that reflects its byzantine structure: "At last we reached the scenes of the ore and the work after it; and among these we clambered and wandered about, down shafts to this or that level, and then out on side tunnels through the vein in both directions; up again by narrow, pokerish ladders to a higher set of chambers, in and out, up and down, till we were lost in amazing confusion."[29] Like the *Appletons'* writer before him, the *Weston Democrat* correspondent recounted his odyssey with present tense verbs, building narrative momentum that could immerse the reader in the author's experience: "We trudge through countless leads, now scrambling over timbers, then compressing ourselves into incredibly small compass in order to crawl through the narrowest of openings. There is a conglomeration of coal dust and mud under foot that sticks to our shoes like glue. We trip over the rails, and bruise every square inch of our bodies against the sharp angles of the rough walls, while our hands and faces, within a very few minutes, partake of the somber hue of our surroundings."[30]

Adding to a sense of the exotic were sensory components such as sound and light. An otherworldliness was the effect of lighting, with journalists noting the play of flickering lantern lights creating ghostly shadows as the miners worked and moved. Also contributing to a sense of the exotic was the use of animals in the mines, where one reporter noted "Liliputian [sic] mules, which are kept in the mine, and appear as lively and healthy as if they lived above ground."[31] Horses and mules were used to draw ore in and out of tunnels, for raising and lowering personnel, and for transporting equipment. After a blast in a West Virginia coal mine, for example, mules were brought in to haul the debris. "We hear the noise of their hoofs approaching, mingled with the sounds of blows and an alarming chorus of expletives on the part of the drivers," the correspondent remembered. "[A]fter arguing sometime with their attendants, mule fashion, by drumming on the wagons with their heels, refusing to stir, or manifesting an unconquerable disposition to lie down, they are at length persuaded, through the agency of a club or by being banged about the head with a lump of coal, that resistance is useless, when they reluctantly start off on a slow jog trot."[32]

Reporters were amazed by the widespread use of new technologies in creating and operating the mines, a nod to the role of human ingenuity in mastering the landscape in service to the nation. Albert Richardson praised innovations in excavation technology at the silver mines of Virginia City, Nevada, where sledgehammers had been replaced by a new machine that "seizes … and chews" the ore "with its iron teeth to the proper fine-ness, like bits of cheese."[33] In terms of headframe works that cleverly improved the safety of miners entering a shaft, both Richardson and Samuel Bowles admired a "safety cage," from which metal arms would project when in free-fall. When a suspension line was cut as a demonstration, "The heavy car fell two or three feet, and then suddenly stopped. Two strong arms of steel darting out horizontally struck into the wall on either side, and held the burden firmly over the dark abyss! It was precisely like a falling man throwing out his hands to grasp the nearest object—a marvelous counterfeit of human instinct."[34]

Flooding was another threat in mines in the East as well as the West, but inventors developed a variety of ways to address it. On a tour of Colorado's Bobtail Mine, Amos Cummings learned that while water poured in at a staggering rate of 250 gallons a minute, the foreman had invented a pump that could siphon off twice as much, a triumph of ingenuity. "There is nothing to prevent the miners from following the crevice down to China if their pumps are big enough," Cummings proclaimed.[35] Also addressing the water issue was the proposed six-mile-long Sutro Tunnel, to provide drainage from and access to the Comstock mines of Virginia City, Nevada. Grace Greenwood and her party proceeded about a half mile into this tunnel, to where the construction crews were blasting their way through granite. Greenwood "liked the boldness and the daring of it. ... It was some thing stupendous, yet practicable and feasible...."[36]

Other engineering successes touted in the newspapers included complex hydraulic ventilation systems; pan amalgamation, known as the Washoe process, and other processing techniques; square set timbering, which Richardson guessed accounted for more lumber within the Gould & Curry Mine than in the entire city of Virginia above it; arrastre apparatus for crushing ore; and a mortise-and-frame machine for joists—inventions, Richardson asserted, that were the "productions of practical working miners" and evidence of common American ingenuity.[37]

Like their readers, mine reporters were amazed by the amount of wealth generated in the mining industry, especially in the silver and gold mines of the West—"a shrine," Dan De Quille wrote of the Ruby Vein, "for a miner to worship at! Here he might drill in a hole, and crawling into it, literally roll in wealth."[38] But while the miners were surely too busy and exhausted for such a frivolous diversion, men and women of the press were highly conscious of the rich environment. De Quille painted a dazzling and somewhat embellished picture for his readers: "Think of passing up a flight of silver stairs to a silver walled palace!"[39] In reality, even the most lucrative of the silver mines was not lined in glistening silver; it took a bit of imagination to recognize what was to be the wealth of the nation, waiting to be extracted from the earth. "In the dull, unattractive form of ore, the silver is there, and the metallurgist with his furnace is the magician who is able to bring forth the glittering metal ... in the solid bars he is able to produce, we have weighty and tangible evidence of the almost incalculable riches hidden beneath the dingy, sootlike covering of these ores.... The very floor on which we walk, notwithstanding its dinginess, is one of silver," he wrote, "the very dirt and dust that receives the imprint of our footsteps surpasses in richness the famed Pactolian sands."[40]

Mine reporting explicitly connected the wealth of the mines to the wealth and destiny of the nation. After outlining the unlimited potential of California mining for his *Harper's* readers, William V. Wells made the connection plain, instructing his readers to "think not of the youngest sister of the Republic as a creature of premature and unhealthy growth but as a child blooming in her freshest charms, and smiling in the confidence of a glorious future."[41] Bowles admired the miners and asserted that they "worked with the energy and enterprise of the American people, stimulated by the great profits sure to be

While visitors relied on dim candles to illuminate the dark hollows of a typical nineteenth-century mine, in the hands of the renowned photographer Timothy O'Sullivan, it is easy to picture Virginia City's Gould & Curry Mine as De Quille's "silver walled palace" (De Quille, *The Washoe Giant*, 130–31). O'Sullivan used a flash of burning magnesium to illuminate the mine. (1867, National Archives, VCN: 77-KS-1-15).

realized from wise and persevering use of the opportunities."[42] Indeed, to the editors, reporters, and correspondents who saw them, the mines of America were most certainly poised to become the treasury of the world.

## Foreigners in a Foreign Land

Like Gilded Age adventurers in far-away outposts of civilization around the globe, mine reporters found themselves in a foreign land among foreign people and drew anthropological portraits of the natives. Like actual human residents of foreign cultures and nations, miners were depicted as having their own observable behaviors and customs, presented in clear contrast to the invading and civilized visitors. In anticipation of an encounter with the miners, multiple reporters whimsically referred to them as gnomes—humanoid spirit-creatures inhabiting the underworld, and a popular literary figure of the era.[43]

The irony of this representation is that it was soundly discounted by the reporting. The correspondent for the *Weston Democrat* was surprised by the appearance of the coal miners: "Soon we encounter a party of miners, rough, hardy-looking men, far healthier than we should believe would be the case with beings whose labor is carried on away from the light of day."[44] Miners were generally depicted as good-natured, as when De Quille and his companion landed at the base of their coaster track. Richardson found the miners in a Granby, Missouri, lead mine to be industrious and agile. "Some were quarrying out the metal; others blasting it from 'pockets' in the rock," he wrote. "In one place they were lying flat upon their backs, digging it with picks from the roof of a passage a foot high; in another they were perched up in a gallery, breaking off the blocks and rolling them down."[45] Reporters from Hillsboro, Ohio, were told by a mine supervisor that "the health of miners in this country is better on an average than that of any other class or workmen, which he attributed to the uniform temperature and pure air in which they labor."[46] While it is to be expected that a mine supervisor might misrepresent the working conditions in his mine, the reporting on the subject generally agreed that miners were hearty, happy, and productive.

In further contrast to the narrator journalist, who was positioned as the foreigner in this environment, the miners appeared to be quite at home, even in the midst of heat and danger. The *Democrat* correspondent noted that when explosives were ready to be detonated and the visitors had scrambled to take cover, the miners "lounge lazily out of the way, forming a little group by themselves, and puff quietly at their pipes." The blast was then triggered: "A flash—then a deep muffled explosion, which echoes through the long caverns, and is followed by the rumbling and crash of the falling *debris*—clouds of dense sulphurous smoke fill the chamber, rising up to the roof and curling away toward the shaft." As the visitors huddled out of sight, the miners calmly waited for the smoke to disburse and then casually resumed their work. The author was amazed by the easygoing attitude of the miners as they handled explosives "in close proximity to the unguarded flames of the lamps," even while "coolly smoking or chatting."[47]

Despite popular culture depictions of mining camps as lawless or wild, mine reporting unambiguously depicted the miners-at-work as a categorical symbol of industrial success and the triumph of civilization. Superintendents and other supervisors were consistently described as men of good character who offered hospitality to their visitors. De Quille described his guide to the Gould & Curry mine as "gentlemanly and attentive"[48] and had higher praise for Mr. Deidesheimer, a foreman in the Ophir Mine of Virginia City, Nevada, "a most gentlemanly man and accomplished mining engineer, who politely volunteered to show us through the works."[49] After a tour of several hours in the Ophir, De Quille was even more taken with his tour guide: "If you should be so lucky as to secure Mr. Deidesheimer for your guide, you will find him indefatigable in pointing out and explaining whatever is worthy of notice, and withal good-humored, pleasant, and gentlemanly, with no end of patience in answering questions."[50]

After a day in the mines, Greenwood noted her surprise at finding a number of

In the works of adventure journalists, western miners—hailing paradoxically not only from eastern states but also from around the world—were depicted as symbolic of American national identity: brave, industrious, confident. Framed by halos of the mining shafts, these Comstock miners certainly appear heroic in this photograph by Timothy O'Sullivan, whose body of work, with its unprecedented "visual and emotional complexity," according to the Smithsonian American Art Museum, "far surpassed the demands of practical documentation" (National Archives, VCN: 77-KS-1-13).

educated men among the laborers. "In some localities," she reported, "three out of five of the practical miners are college-bred men. Two ex-professors of Yale are said to be mining at Caribou."[51] After touring the Caribou mine in Colorado, Greenwood was invited to dine with the miners at a boarding house. Her description of the meal and the company reveal profound connection of the miners with civilization and nation:

> That evening we sat down to supper with a goodly company of "honest miners,"—men in rough clothes and heavy boots, with hard hands and with faces well bronzed, but strong, earnest, intelligent. It was to me a communion with the bravest humanity of the age,—the vanguard of civilization and honorable enterprise. I believe that Caribou is remarkable, even in this wonderful country and time, for the orderly, moral, and intelligent character of its people. Born after the evil reign of excitement and reckless speculation was past, mining life here is sober and laborious and law-abiding; we, at least, saw no gambling, no drunkenness, no rudeness, no idleness. A New England village, resting under the beneficent shadows of the school-house, an Orthodox church, and the county jail could not present a more quiet and decorous aspect.[52]

At another dinner with miners from the Terrible Lode in Colorado, Greenwood acknowledged, "It was, I confess, something of a surprise to me to find all these 'Terrible' fellows so intelligent, so well dressed, so agreeable. Transformed from gnomes into very agreeable fellow-creatures, they passed with ease and dignity from the 'shaft ' to the stairway, and from the 'drift' to the drawing-room."[53]

With the exception of superintendents and guides, rarely did the reportage address the miners as individuals; instead, they were textualized as a composite symbol of human industry, at once conjoined with the earth and yet masters of it. In reality, many were misfits, adventurers, restless Easterners, and immigrants from Europe and Mexico, but through a strange alchemy of eye-witness reporting in which the reporters acknowledged their own displacement, miners became the prosaic heroes of the mine adventure story. In *Harper's*, J. Ross Browne argued, "The life of the miner is one of labor, peril, and exposure; but it possesses the fascinating element of liberty, and the promise of unlimited reward. In the midst of privations amounting, at times, to the verge of starvation, what glowing visions fill the mind of the toiling adventurer! Richer in anticipation than the richest of his fellow-beings, he builds golden palaces, and scatters them over the world with a princely hand."[54] Subject to the great democratization of the mines through shared physical labor, exposure to danger, common appearance and a shared micro-culture, as well as a shared role in the nation's destiny, they, too, were refined into the American of Frederick Jackson Turner, part of the industrial machinery of the Gilded Age.

## A Window into the Gilded Age

Having survived several hours of rigorous perambulations through the chambers and levels of the Gould & Curry Mine, and after mastering a "sensation of faintness" while climbing a final vertical ladder of 120 feet, Albert Deane Richardson popped out of the shaft and into the air and light again.[55] Like other mine adventurers, he felt a sense of relief in addition to physical exhaustion. However, the return of an adventuring reporter from an unknown environment to a known environment also demanded a moment of rhetorical reconciliation, a re-engagement of normalcy as pen was set to paper to share the experience with the readers of America.

Mine reporting was at its core the writing of an American parable, full of romance and inspiration. Driven by a reportorial imperative and a responsibility to enlighten or entertain the reading public, correspondents on mine adventures connected with readers by reflecting cultural values, conveying nationalistic themes, and sharing their personal adventures. Copper mines, coal mines, and especially silver and gold mines—these were the stuff of legend and newsprint in the Gilded Age. Reporting from the mines of America presented an intense microcosm of—a literal submersion into—pressing themes of innovation, technology, national wealth, manifest-destiny, and the strength and resourcefulness of the American people. Adventure journalism provided the window into the underground monuments that would make the Gilded Age truly gilded.

NOTES

1. J. Ross Browne, *Adventures in the Apache Country: A Tour Through Arizona and Sonora, With Notes on the Silver Regions of Nevada, Illustrated by the Author* (New York: Harper & Brothers, 1869), 15.

2. Browne, *Adventures*, 13. The son of an Irish newspaper editor, Browne (1817 or 1821–1875) was a regular correspondent for *Harper's Magazine* while also holding government positions and publishing books of his adventures at home and overseas.

3. Primary sources were acquired through a search of the *American Periodicals* database from ProQuest, the *Chronicling America* archive, housed at the Library of Congress, the *California Digital Newspaper Collection, Cooperative Libraries Automated Network Digital Collections* provided by the Nevada State Library, and the *Making of America* archive at Cornell University Library. Additional material was collected from the published works of journalists who collected their newspaper stories in popular travel books. The search was delineated by the years 1860–1875 and by search terms such as "into the mine" and "below the earth." Sources were considered if they presented a first-person account of a trip into a mine appearing in a periodical or published by a journalist during this period. Private correspondence, second-person accounts, and objective reporting on the mining industry or technology were not included.

4. John Mack Faragher, ed., *Rereading Frederick Jackson Turner: "The Significance of the Frontier in American History" and Other Essays* (New Haven: Yale University Press, 1994), 53–55.

5. Few studies have touched on mine reportage in more than a peripheral way. One exception is Floyd's *Claims and Speculations: Mining and Writing in the Gilded Age,* a broad study of mining writing and representation that addresses journalism as part of a spectrum that includes literature, folklore, and popular culture. See Janet Floyd, *Claims and Speculations: Mining and Writing in the Gilded Age* (Albuquerque: University of New Mexico Press, 2012). The topic of mine reporting is occasionally raised in studies of Western journalism and in biographies of prominent Western journalists. See Richard A. Dwyer and Richard E. Lingenfelter, *Lying on the Eastern Slope: James Townsend's Comic Journalism on the Mining Frontier* (Miami: Florida International University Press, 1984); Dwyer and Lingenfelter, eds., *Dan De Quille: The Washoe Giant* (Reno: University of Nevada Press, 1990); Lawrence I. Berkove, ed., *The Sagebrush Anthology: Literature from the Silver Age of the Old West* (Columbia: University of Missouri Press, 2006); and Janet Floyd, "The Feeling of 'Silverland': Sagebrush Journalism in Virginia City's 'Flush Times.' *Media History* 19, no. 3: 257–269.

6. For comprehensive information on the history of mining and other industries, see Albert S. Bolles, "Mines and Mining, and Oil," in *Industrial History of the United States, from the Earliest Settlements to the Present Time: Being a Complete Survey of American Industries [...]" (*Norwich, CN: Henry Bill Publishing, 1889), Book IV, 667–780.

7. Approximately 300,000 ambitious miners, known as "forty-niners," hailing from the eastern U.S. and abroad, settled in California between 1848 and 1855.

8. A "silver rush" to the Mount Davidson region of Nevada, beginning in 1859, launched one of the most lucrative mining operations of all time. Chuck Lyons of *Wild West Magazine* writes, "By mid-1875 the partners' holdings were estimated at about $1 billion—*in 1875 dollars...*," with one of them still ranked among the wealthiest Americans of all time. See Lyons, "The Bank Crowd and Silver Kings Made a Fortune From the Comstock," April 2015 (tinyurl.com/hmpafxe).

9. The Pike's Peak or Colorado Gold Rush of 1858–61 brought 100,000 gold seekers known as "fifty-niners" to the region. See S. M. Voynick, *Colorado Gold* (Missoula: Mountain Press Publishing Company, 1992), 61–62.

10. *Washington Daily Morning Chronicle*, Aug. 7 1865, in a column reprinting Colfax's speech in Virginia City, Nevada, on June 26. President Lincoln met with Schuyler Colfax to discuss the trip mere hours before he went to Ford's Theater on April 14, 1865. "Don't forget, Colfax," the president said, "tell those miners that that is my speech to them [that western resources should be quickly developed], which I send you. Let me hear from you on the road, and I will telegraph you at San Francisco. Pleasant journey and good bye." Qtd in Willard H. Smith, *Schuyler Colfax: The Changing Fortunes of a Political Idol* (Indianapolis: Indiana Historical Bureau, 1952), 207.

11. Auber Forestier, "More About California: An Expedition Underground," *Saturday Evening Post*, June 11, 1870, 3; republished in *American Periodicals* database. Forestier was a pseudonym for Aubertine Woodward Moore (1841–1929), a writer, musician, and prolific translator of French, German, and Scandinavian novels and music. In 1870, she wrote a series of travel letters during a trip to California for the *Saturday Evening Post*. From 1900 to 1911, she served as music critic for the *Wisconsin State Journal*.

12. Samuel Bowles, *Across the Continent: A Summer's Journey to the Rocky Mountains, the Mormons, and the Pacific States, with Speaker Colfax* (Springfield, MA: Bowles, 1865). Bowles (1826–1878) was editor of the *Springfield (MA) Republican* and widely held as one of the most influential editors of his day.

13. From Dan De Quille, "The Wealth of Washoe," *The Golden Era*, March 31, 1861. De Quille was the pen name of William Wright (1829–1898), who achieved national acclaim in 1876 for his book, *History of the Big Bonanza: An Authentic Account of the Discovery, History, and Working of the World Renowned Comstock Silver Lode of Virginia City, Nevada* (Hartford, CT: Amerian Publishing/A. L. Bancroft, 1870). De Quille wrote for San Francisco's *The Golden Era* and, for more than 30 years, Virginia City's *Territorial Enterprise*. For more on DeQuille, see Richard A. Dwyer and Richard E. Lingenfelter, eds. *Dan De Quille, The Washoe Giant: A Biography and Anthology* (Reno: University of Nevada Press, 1990).

14. G.M. Steele, "DOWN IN A COPPER MINE," *The Ladies' Repository; a Monthly Periodical, Devoted to Literature, Art and Religion,* August 1871, 85–89. George McKendree Steele (1823–1901), D.D., LL.D. was president of Lawrence University in Appleton, Wisconsin, from 1865–1879.

15. Connecticut-born Allyn (1833–69) was appointed to the Supreme Court of Arizona Territory by Abraham Lincoln. See *The Arizona of Joseph Pratt Allyn: Letters from a Pioneer Judge: Observations and Travels, 1863–1866*, ed. John Nicolson (Tucson: University of Arizona Press, 1974).

16. Quicksilver is another term for mercury. The mining of quicksilver in California predated the discovery of gold, with the mercury mine at New Almaden the first commercial and ultimately most profitable mine of any type in the state. See Andrew Scott Johnston, *Mercury and the Making of California: Mining, Landscape, and Race, 1840–1890* (Boulder: University Press of Colorado, 2013).

17. Grace Greenwood, *New Life in New Lands: Notes of Travel* (New York: J. B. Ford and Company, 1873), 293. Greenwood (1823–1904) was the first woman writer and reporter on the payroll of the *New-York Times*. She was a frequent adventure journalist, traveling to Europe for the *Times* in 1852. See *Haps and Mishaps of a Tour in Europe* (1854), a work that remained in publication for the next four decades.

18. Greenwood, *New Life*, 82–83.

19. "Blasting in a Coal Mine," *Weston (WV) Democrat*, March 31, 1873, 1.

20. No author, "Underground Life; or, Coal-Mines and Miners," *Appletons' Journal of Literature, Science and Art,* April 10, 1869, 3–4.

21. A. B., "A Careful Man Visits a Mine," Circular, February 7, 1861, 3; Barites comprise a group of minerals used in mining and the production of paints and other chemical-based products.

22. "Letter XII," *Harford Evening Press*, Oct. 14, 1864.

23. Bowles, *Across the Continent*, 317–18.

24. A. B., "A Careful Man Visits a Mine."

25. Dan De Quille, "The Wealth of Washoe," *The Golden Era*, March 31, 1861.

26. "Letter 18," *Arizona of Joseph Pratt Allyn*, 192.

27. A. B., "A Careful Man Visits a Mine."

28. "Blasting in a Coal Mine," *Weston (WV) Democrat*, March 31, 1873, 1.

29. Bowles, *Across the Continent*, 318.

30. "Blasting in a Coal Mine," *Weston (WV) Democrat*, March 31, 1873, 1.

31. "Jackson and Jackson County," *The Highland Weekly News* (Hillsborough, Ohio), May 18, 1871. 2. The story provides an account of a tour of the Star Furnace in the town of Jackson in south-central Ohio by a group of four reporters including Mackley, of the *Standard*; Piatt, of the *Cincinnati Commercial*; Eyler of the *West Union Defender*; and Raper, of the *Vinton Record*.

32. "Blasting in a Coal Mine," *Weston (WV) Democrat*, March 31, 1873.

33. Albert D. Richardson, *Beyond the Mississippi: From the Great River to the Great Ocean.... New Edition* (Hartford: American Publishing Company, 1869), 375.

34. Richardson, *Beyond the Mississippi*, 375, and Bowles, *Across the Continent*, 317.

35. Amos J. Cummings, "In the Golden Gulches," in Cummings' *A Remarkable Curiosity: Dispatches from a New York City Journalist's 1873 Railroad Trip across the American West*, ed. Jerald T. Milanich (Boulder: University Press of Colorado, 2008), 175. Cummings (1838–1902) held editorial positions at the *New-York Tribune* prior to moving to the *Sun*, for which he reported from the American West and Europe. He served multiple terms in the U.S. House of Representatives. See also Amos J. Cummings, *Frolicking Bears, Wet Vultures, and Other Oddities: A New York City Journalist in Nineteenth-Century Florida*, ed. Jerald T. Milanich (Gainesville: University Press of Florida, 2005).

36. Greenwood, *New Life*, 180–81.

37. Richardson, *Beyond the Mississippi*, 376.

38. De Quille, *The Washoe Giant*, 128, referring to the Gould & Curry.

39. De Quille, *The Washoe Giant,*132.

40. De Quille, *The Washoe Giant*, 130–31. De Quille is referring to the Pactolus River in the ancient state of Lydia, now in Turkey. The river was famous for its golden sands and appears in the myth of King Midas, who washed himself in the river to free himself of his curse.

41. Wm V. Wells, "How We Get Gold in California," *Harper's New Monthly Magazine*, Vol XX Iss 119 (April 1860), 616. Wells' reporting emphasized the evolution of mining infrastructure and technology, Wells having been among the individuals who headed to California during the 1849 Gold Rush.

42. Bowles, *Across the Continent*, 41. For more on Bowles's contribution to a sense of national identity in the immediate postwar period, see Katrina J. Quinn, "'Across the Continent...and still the Republic!': Inscribing Nationhood in Samuel Bowles' Newspaper Letters of 1865," *American Journalism* 31:4 (2014), 468–489.

43. Nathaniel Hawthorne and William Cullen Bryant were among those featuring gnomes in their works of fiction and poetry.

44. "Blasting in a Coal Mine," *Weston (WV) Democrat*, March 31, 1873.

45. Richardson, *Beyond the Mississippi*, 212.

46. "Jackson and Jackson County," *The Highland Weekly News*, May 18, 1871.

47. "Blasting in a Coal Mine," *Weston (WV) Democrat*, 1.

48. De Quille, *The Washoe Giant*, 126.

49. De Quille, *The Washoe Giant*, 129.

50. De Quille, *The Washoe Giant*, 134–35.

51. Greenwood, *New Life*, 92–93.

52. Greenwood, *New Life*, 81.

53. Greenwood, *New Life*, 106.

54.  J. Ross Browne, "A Peep at Washoe," *Harper's New Monthly Magazine*, CXXVII, Vol. XXII, December 1860, 10. Browne (1821–75) was a regular contributor to *Harper's*, writing about Western mining regions in the "A Peep at Washoe" series, *Harper's New Monthly Magazine*, CXXVII, Vol. XXII, December 1860, 1–17; January 1861, February 1861; "A Visit to Santa Cruz," *San Francisco Daily Evening Bulletin* (Vol. XVII, no. 51, December 7, 1863); "Down in the Cinnabar Mines ," *Harper's New Monthly Magazine*, Vol. XXXI, October 1865); and more.

55.  Richardson, *Beyond the Mississippi*, 376.

# Float Along the Frontier

*Down the Missouri with Captain Paul Boyton,*
*James Creelman, and the* New York Herald

CROMPTON BURTON

In the autumn of 1881, *New York Herald* publisher James Gordon Bennett Jr. and his newspaper's editors faced something of a dilemma. In an embarrassment of riches, their pages were filled to capacity with no fewer than three scintillating and problematically simultaneous sensations, each capable of commanding its own decks of screaming and exaggerated headlines. Ongoing coverage of the murder of President James Garfield was obviously worthy of as much space as the staff could spare, but two other curiosities, both of the newspaper's own manufacture, were hard to deny a prominent position as well. The disappearance of the Bennett-sponsored U.S. Arctic Expedition and a perilous journey through the heart of Indian country also packed plenty of appeal for *Herald* readers. Deciding which of the three trending topics to feature and which to merely maintain posed quite a challenge especially when editorial considerations demanded choices between an insane assassin, starvation and death on the Polar ice pack, and staring down the Sioux chief who massacred General George Armstrong Custer's Seventh Cavalry.

It was the misfortune of Captain Paul Boyton and *Herald* reporter James Creelman that their 64-day, 1,500-mile float down the Yellowstone and Missouri rivers occurred at precisely the same time. As a consequence, the paper's editors were compelled to relegate it to second-class status at its precise moment of triumph, which perhaps explains why the story enjoys very little notoriety in today's popular literature. As a result, their epic journey has yet to be fully appreciated for its own dramatic qualities and the popular appeal it held for Bennett's readership over an extended period of time.

This is more than a little surprising given that Boyton, a well-known showman and adventurer, was equal parts Dr. David Livingstone, P.T. Barnum, and Harry Houdini; he had been a daring and romantic figure even before attracting and holding the imagination of *Herald* readers following along with his aquatic activities. Born in Ireland's County Kildare in 1848, Boyton spent the better part of his childhood in Pittsburgh, where the confluence of the Allegheny, Monongahela, and Ohio rivers provided him the perfect playground in which to indulge his obsession with swimming. Serving as a yeoman in the Union Navy during the Civil War, he went on to become a salvage diver, lifeguard, and merchant seaman, experiences that uniquely qualified Boyton to meet the considerable challenges he faced on his most fabulous float ever.

73

*Herald* readers were already very familiar with the Big Muddy, as the Missouri was popularly known. The newspaper's headlines in March and April 1881 described a river gone wild as a result of heavy winter snows and rapid melting that created devastating ice jams. Articles featured narratives of desperate dashes of frightened townspeople to higher ground in such settlements as Yankton and Vermillion in the Dakota Territory, and it was into this raging torrent and the imaginations of the journal's readers that Boyton proposed to launch himself, in a buoyant rubber suit, for a river voyage from Glendive to St. Louis.

To be clear, the actual timing of the float fell well after the waters had receded, but the power of the Missouri was firmly established in the minds of *Herald* readers even if the more pressing challenge to Boyton would be the changes in the channel resulting from the river jumping its banks for miles in every direction. Navigating these new and uncharted twists and turns proved to be a recurring theme in the dispatches to come, and the innovative rubber suit Boyton first discovered during a chance meeting with inventor C.S. Merriman years before became almost as much the story as the perilous exploits of America's "Fearless Frogman."[1]

## Early Exploits of the Fearless Frogman

Adapting the vulcanization process of Charles Goodyear for his own designs, Merriman originally developed a rubber suit intended to serve as a lifesaving device for steamship passengers. Much as Boyton appreciated its potential applications in the rescue of drifting survivors, he was quick to seize upon its entertainment and exhibition value as well. Weighing approximately thirty-five pounds with five air chambers providing buoyancy, the Merriman Suit enabled its occupant not merely to float with the current or the tide, but also to make steady forward progress with the use of a double-bladed paddle and even a small sail.

Anxious to put the newly created "safety dress" to the test, Boyton set out to cross the English Channel wearing it in the spring of 1875. After his first attempt failed, he successfully navigated the choppy waters between Cape Grisnez and Folkestone in twenty-three hours, arriving to the cheers of a considerable crowd early in the morning of May 29. As much as the "American Sea Walker" had proven the Merriman Suit worthy of wide acclaim and subsequently earned lucrative engagements for future demonstrations, he also found himself the object of great interest by Bennett and the *Herald*. Coverage of the Channel crossing served as the newspaper's introduction of the plucky adventurer to its readers, and there were more than a few exciting episodes still to come.[2]

In fact, when Boyton later returned to the United States and scheduled an aquatic exhibition at the Cunard dock in Jersey City on January 20, 1876, it was not at all surprising the *Herald* showed more than a passing interest, even if it did hand the assignment to one of its newest and least-experienced reporters, James Creelman. Little did Bennett's editors know that in connecting the entrepreneur and the enterprising correspondent, they were launching a relationship that would bring them no small amount of sensational copy in the future.

Born in Montreal on November 12, 1859, James Creelman displayed an active interest in journalism from a very young age. Before reaching his twelfth birthday, he ran away to New York where he eventually earned appointment to Bennett's *New York*

*Herald* while still a teenager. The *Herald* proved the perfect learning environment. Creelman eagerly accepted any and all assignments, developing a flair for reporting and writing that later earned him celebrity status among nineteenth-century journalists.

While Bennett prohibited bylines, the page-eight story in the journal's edition of January 21, 1876, bears a familiar stamp and may quite possibly be one of Creelman's first published articles. In it, he highlighted Boyton's entertaining exhibition at the Cunard dock, which included calmly perusing the latest edition of the *Herald* while floating offshore—much to the delight of a waterfront crowd numbering in the thousands.

As a result of the brief encounter, Boyton and Creelman formed a lasting friendship that kept the Captain in the headlines and the correspondent among the ranks of the period's most prolific adventure journalists. From time to time, they reunited for a new chapter in the ongoing coverage of the "suit of rubber clothing." In January 1879, for instance, Creelman joined his friend on a New York Harbor float and "dropped himself deliberately into icy waters off the Battery, and went cruising around in a sort of jumble of darkness, loneliness, shark stories and ice cakes."[3] The *Herald*'s lock on the "graphic story" became a reliable resource by which to generate boosts and bumps in circulation. And when the "Water Fiend"

PAUL BOYNTON
*Champion Deep Sea Swimmer*

Stuntman Paul Boyton (not *Boynton*) made his reputation crossing the English Channel. But the 21-mile crossing—choppy though it may be—would not prepare Boyton for his 64-day, 1,500-mile float down the Yellowstone and Missouri rivers. What was he thinking? (cigarette card for W.S. Kimball & Co., 1887, Library of Congress, Item 2018646103).

announced his upcoming navigation of the Allegheny, Ohio, and Mississippi rivers in the spring of 1879, James Creelman was the obvious choice to cover the ambitious journey to New Orleans.[4]

In the end, only Creelman was able to stick with Boyton and his story over the journey's entire 80 days, 1,500 miles, and seven-state itinerary, telegraphing sensational copy home to the *Herald* at stops from the Ohio Valley to the Gulf of Mexico. Content to chase Boyton by train, rowboat, and steamer rather than float alongside in his own rubber suit, the young reporter filed vivid descriptions of dodging floating ice, surviving thundering falls, and eluding vicious alligators. Creelman's final dispatch described Boyton's tumultuous hero's welcome in New Orleans on April 27, 1879. Celebrated in the columns of the newspaper the next day, the arrival of the adventurer and the "Herald Correspondent" in the Crescent City was applauded as "the finish of one of the most remarkable of all human feats of endurance."[5]

## The Most Daring Float Trip Yet

More daring exploits were yet to come. Two years later, Boyton announced his greatest challenge to date: a float down the Yellowstone and the Missouri all the way from Glendive, Montana, to St. Louis. It was on this grueling 64-day, 1,500-mile excursion that the reputation of the "Frog Man's" erstwhile companion James Creelman was cemented as not merely a prolific, but a prominent adventure journalist of the first stripe, delivering a serialized saga from the frontier of the American West.

There is some disagreement about just how Creelman met up with Boyton at Bismarck, Dakota Territory, in September 1881. According to Dave Walter's *Montana Campfire Tales*, it was an almost serendipitous or chance encounter, while Boyton himself recalled that Creelman was actually assigned to "accompany him the rest of the way and write up the Indian country" for the *New York Herald*. The latter explanation seems the most plausible, especially upon examination of correspondence between the two preserved within the James Creelman Papers at Ohio State University in Columbus. In a letter from Boyton to Creelman from Red Wing, Minnesota, dated August 28, 1881, the Captain sought to firm up plans for the journey and determine if Creelman was available to cover the stunt for the *Herald*. "I have not written to Bennett yet, but will do so," promised Boyton. "If you would write to Bennett too it would make it more binding—I could start on the Yellowstone and make a few hundred miles of still-mysterious river before entering the Missouri."[6]

Boyton left nothing to chance in persuading his friend to accompany him. "The trip will be one of the grandest I ever attempted," he gushed. "We could go from St. Paul by rail to a point on the Yellowstone and then commence a voyage that would exceed all I have done before." Showman he might have been, but Boyton was also an entrepreneur counting his pennies. He admonished, "If you come, the *Herald* must pay all your expenses, but out-side of RR fare, it will be very little."[7] Finally, Boyton appealed to Creelman's single-minded focus on bringing the story back to his newspaper without the added distractions that had marked their progress on the Allegheny, Ohio, and Mississippi, when the reporter acted as Boyton's pitchman during frequent stops for fundraising and satisfying the curiosity of crowds along the riverbank. This time there would be "no lectures, 'no moral show,' no excursions." The Captain closed, declaring, "I do hope you can come."[8]

Creelman was familiar with the territory Boyton proposed to traverse, having been assigned by the *Herald* on two separate occasions to investigate the massacre of General George Armstrong Custer and his Seventh Cavalry at the Little Big Horn in 1876.[9] Indeed, as recently as August 10, 1881, Creelman had reported upon encounters with the subdued war chiefs of Sitting Bull and the Sioux nation from Fort Yates.[10] While it is clear James Creelman was ideally positioned to deliver exclusive coverage of his good friend Boyton by virtue of their relationship, it was no accident either that he was equally well-placed geographically because of his assignment to sustain the memory of Custer and the storied

Seventh. There can be little doubt that the journalist was more than a little intentional in being present in Bismarck awaiting the arrival of "the Incredible Floating Man."[11]

On September 28, "Beaver Boyton" stepped ashore in Bismarck, having already traveled more than 400 miles on the Yellowstone and Missouri Rivers. Fatigued from battling stormy weather and enduring thirty-six-hour stretches out on the water, he laid over just long enough to renege on his promise to limit extracurricular activities. The very next evening he lectured to an overflow crowd in the town's opera house, an event described in detail by the *Bismarck Tribune* on September 30.[12]

The very same day, the two travelers left Bismarck by river, bound for St. Louis, Boyton in his rubber suit and Creelman trailing not far behind in a canvas canoe named "Baby Mine."[13] The trip would be characterized by all of the requisite elements of adventure journalism and Bennett's classic serialized adventures: the race against time, the

Chasing Boyton along the Missouri was just one of many journalistic adventures for James Creelman, who would make his career writing from such far-flung destinations as Korea, China, Haiti, Cuba, Paris, Rome, and Manila. See Creelman's 1901 memoir, *On the Great Highway: The Wanderings and Adventures of a Special Correspondent* (Library of Congress, Item 2016856307).

conspiracy of the elements, simmering unrest among the native population, savage cultures with strange and mysterious traditions, evil and misery aplenty, and hundreds of miles to navigate before journey's end in St. Louis. The ambitious itinerary required a grueling pace to complete the journey before winter descended upon the Great Plains. The initial stages of their float also demanded they count upon the hospitality of the U.S. Army at several of its frontier outposts to sustain them in their quest. Boyton already knew something of such arrangements, having stopped at Fort Buford where the Yellowstone meets the Missouri, and again at Fort Berthold just above where the Knife River joins the Big Muddy, feeding its southern course into the heart of the Dakota Territory. With future layovers possible at Fort Yates, Fort Hale, and Fort Randall before running for home past Pierre, Yankton, Sioux City, Omaha, St. Joseph, and Kansas City, the floating travelers depended upon the military to provide more than mere rest, recovery, and provisions. Of even greater value to Creelman and the *Herald*, each of the forts offered the true lifeblood of the adventure reporting: a telegraph office.

As the duo floated out of sight from Bismarck, there were no galleries of spectators as there had been in the previous trip, along the Ohio and Mississippi, and Boyton was reminded of the intense feelings of isolation and loneliness he experienced in the first days of his previous paddle, traveling 600 miles alone. Those feelings, shared with his correspondent companion, provided a significant element of Creelman's first dispatch to the *Herald* from Fort Yates, dated October 1, 1881. Arriving at the fort two days out of Bismarck, Creelman summarized "Paul Boyton's Experience Along the Yellowstone River" for *Herald* readers, bringing them up to speed and moving the narrative of the rapidly unfolding adventure into the present. Almost wistfully, Boyton recalled, "No one can appreciate how utterly lonely a man can become when floating through these immense solitudes." But if Boyton had been longing for companionship on the upper reaches of the Missouri, such was not the case at Fort Yates and the Indian Agency, where he and Creelman encountered Sioux chiefs Rain-in-the-Face, Gall, Low Dog, Long Soldier, and Flying By, among others.[14]

Such ready subjects did more than merely keep Boyton company; they provided Creelman an opportunity to continue his education on the "Indian question" and allowed him to provide sketches of life on the Great Plains for his editors back in New York. Of particular interest was revisiting the transfer of Sitting Bull to Fort Randall and, at the urging of his hosts, an appeal for more troops to deter the Sioux from attempting another uprising. "When I saw the whole forces on dress parade this morning and then turned my eyes to the tents of the 3,000 Indians who are encamped three miles away in full sight, the utter helplessness of the command was impressed upon me strongly," he wrote. "I have been requested by the army officers here and elsewhere to call public attention to this matter."[15]

The appeal for reinforcements along with the travel narrative from Fort Yates ran in the *New York Herald* October 22, 1881, its twenty-two-day telegraph voyage suggesting just some of the challenges associated with sending adventure reports home to the East Coast newspapers. Coupled with Creelman's report on the urgent need to outdistance winter's icy blast, the notion that another Little Big Horn remained a possibility rendered his Fort Yates dispatch the perfect vehicle to sustain the full attention of the readership to upcoming serial installments from the frontier.

When *Herald* editors next received word from Boyton and Creelman, the telegram came from Pierre, present day capital of South Dakota, on October 11. Arriving at the settlement in the "midst of a hurricane" twenty-five days into the journey, the paper's correspondent detailed the physical rather than psychological demands of the trip. He noted that "up to the present time, the Captain has lost forty pounds in weight, but nothing in spirits." Also contained within the article was the sort of travelogue detail for which Bennett's reporters and their narratives had become famous. Capturing a rare moment on the way down the river, Creelman wrote, "The water was as smooth as glass." He continued, "And when we floated in among a number of white swans with oars flashing in the moonlight, and the whole flock flew upward, with shrill cries, startling the cranes that stalked in the shadows and sending clouds of cackling geese and ducks whirling up from every gloomy nook and ravine, the picture was perfect."[16]

As descriptive as Creelman was in painting a picture of migratory birds on the wing, he was equally detailed in chronicling efforts to introduce the white man's civilization to the Sioux. Noting a stop at Fort Bennett and an overland trip to the Cheyenne Agency, he described the tribe's practice of burying its dead in the branches of trees, pronouncing the tradition "disgusting" and no longer tolerated once the Agency was established. Similarly, he highlighted the opinion of the local agent who lamented the ongoing failure of efforts to provide schooling for Indian boys, remarking, "They are very apt pupils and can

Creelman's reporting from the Boyton float captured more than his water-logged companion. Near Fort Randall, Dakota Territory, he shared a long pipe with Sitting Bull in his tent—possibly this one, where the great chief is pictured with his "favorite wife," according to the original stereograph card. "There was an inexpressible dignity in the strong face of the old chieftain, as he stood there on the prairie," Creelman later wrote (Creelman, *On the Great Highway*, 294) (Bailey, Dix & Mead, c. 1882, Library of Congress, Item cph.3a30334).

comprehend ideas with wonderful accuracy, but their prejudice against white people is so great and unconquerable that education would be thrown away did we not know that it is gradually raising the standard of Indian intelligence."[17]

The societies of the Sioux and Cheyenne were not the only cultural studies offered up in the dispatch from Pierre. Stealing a page from his days as a crusading journalist in New York exposing graft and corruption, Creelman devoted significant attention to an overnight stay with a rancher while in transit. During the layover, Creelman and the Captain came into direct contact with "A New Phase of Slavery" when he discovered "How White Men Buy and Work Their Indian Wives." Finding sensation in describing the disreputable domestic life of their host, Creelman delivered a scathing indictment of the practice of white settlers purchasing Indian women at the agencies, keeping them in servitude, forcing upon them hours and hours of labor each day, and beating them when their behavior displeased their owner. "This system of female slavery is much more extensive than the public generally suppose," Creelman claimed. "Scores of white men are accumulating wealth from the physical labor of these poor women and their children." He closed dramatically, "This is a phase of the Indian question which is kept in the background, but it is a fruitful source of evil and misery which needs immediate attention."[18]

A pattern subsequently emerged in Creelman's correspondence from the Great Plains. His next few dispatches would begin with descriptions of the float while the second section of each telegram was dedicated to cultural sketches of the circumstances in which the Native Americans found themselves five years after Custer's defeat. Reflection on the "Indian question" constituted a part of multiple letters, highlighting the irony that while the float was designed to be a spectacle—to grab the attention of *Herald* readers—it also opened western territories to Creelman's and in turn his readers' attention. For example, arriving at Fort Hale numb with cold and fatigue, the *Herald* correspondent dedicated precious space in his October 15 installment to the massive beaver populations whose activities contributed to the growing difficulty in navigating the river. "It is a mistake to suppose that the beaver is almost extinct in America," Creelman wrote. "The banks of the Missouri are completely hived with beaver holes, and on the tributary brooks they are numbered by hundreds of thousands."[19]

But then, after delivering due diligence on the progress of the adventure, Creelman related details of his visit to the nearby Crow Creek Agency, where he discovered the domestication of the Yanktonai tribe. His highly detailed copy noted that "within two years there have been 200 houses *built by the Indians*" and "Nearly all the chiefs have taken land claims, and some of them are now actually engaged in farming." Creelman observed, "It was a strange comment on the barbarism of the Indians to see a tattered tepee pitched within ten feet of a warm log house, the occupant of the latter sitting on his own doorstep and watching the misery of his less progressive brother." Such vignettes hinted at not only the ongoing advance of the United States' notion of civilization across the frontier, but also its potential benefits and uneven outcomes in replacing the old ways with the new.[20]

To this point in the *Herald*'s coverage of "Boyton's Progress," Creelman's reporting was almost equal parts adventure and assimilation of the Native American people into white society, but this was about to change. On a balmy autumn afternoon a few days out from Crow Creek, Creelman followed Boyton into Fort Randall, and it was there that they encountered the great Sioux chief, Sitting Bull. As was standard, the opening paragraphs of Creelman's October 19 telegram back to New York featured a full share of details from out on the water, everything from makeshift repairs on the now worn and frayed rubber suit to unusual flocks of sea gulls circling overhead. In fact, Boyton was moved to exclaim, "It is a good sign, for we must have travelled south faster than the cold weather. If this keeps on we shall get to St. Louis before winter commences in earnest."[21]

A "dual sunset" phenomenon, the result of raging prairie fires, also enjoyed special notice in the article which ran in the *Herald* on October 29, as did a harrowing account of Boyton becoming trapped in one of the Missouri River's many mires. "Toward midnight we became entangled in a maze of sand bars, and at one place the Captain was caught in the quicksand," Creelman wrote. "He tried to extract his feet from the stinking mass, but a strong power seemed to be sucking him downward." Only some quick thinking by Boyton averted disaster when he "inflated his dress to its fullest capacity and the increased buoyancy enabled him to struggle free." But the balance of the Fort Randall dispatch was not about riverine trials and travels so much as it was given over at great length to an interview with the architect of one of the greatest military disasters in American history.[22]

In techniques later to become something of a trademark, Creelman provided context aplenty in describing not only the circumstances in which he found Sitting Bull, but the appearance and mannerisms of his subject as well. "Whatever may be said of Sitting Bull," Creelman observed, "he certainly has the appearance of a man born to lead men." Anxious to further frame the Uncapapa chief for his readers in the East, the correspondent cast a sympathetic eye with yet another choice detail. "He has none of the impudent swagger of Gall, or the treacherous expression which distinguishes Low Dog and Rain-in-the-Face." Remarking further on Sitting Bull's modesty and dignity, Creelman created a striking portrait for his readers well before he posed his first question.[23]

Another of Creelman's special signatures was to insert himself into his stories, and it was at this point in his dispatch that he deftly included an item designed to confirm his eyewitness participation and his proximity to famous personages. When introduced at last, Sitting Bull was informed he was in the presence of a *Herald* reporter and, upon learning he could speak to the American people if he so desired, pumped Creelman's hand repeatedly. Promotion of both newspaper and correspondent was complete.

Eventually positioned across from the hostiles' leader in his teepee, Creelman noted Sitting Bull's physical appearance in great detail and later allocated significant space in his letter describing the chief's height, weight, and dress. What then unfolded in the columns of the newspaper ten days later was a striking sketch of a proud tribal leader "telling the simple story of a retreating race" in a provocative interview format that enabled Sitting Bull to hold forth on subjects ranging from his escape to Canada, the recent assassination of Garfield, and his desire for his people to attain U.S. citizenship.[24]

"I have lived a good while and seen a great deal and I have always had a reason for everything I have done," said the chief. "Every act of my life has had an object in view, and no man can say I have neglected to think." There was no question that Sitting Bull was particularly thoughtful in considering the potential benefits from this interview with Creelman. Sitting Bull declared the allegiance of his people to the "Great Father" and stated for the record, "In my act of surrendering I consider that I have wiped the blood from my hands and washed myself entirely of the past."[25]

Creelman's selection of quotes bolstered the article's theme of indomitable American will by highlighting the complete submission of the savage Sioux chief. "Give me a reservation and I promise that all of my people shall dress in white men's clothes and give up their savage life entirely," he proclaimed. "I have little influence now, because I am helpless, but I promise a complete reform in the Sioux people if the government will aid me."[26]

## "Preparations ... to Receive Him"

With Sitting Bull's disclaimer received back in New York and winter fast approaching, it was with a sense of great urgency that Boyton and Creelman eventually took their leave at Fort Randall to make for St. Louis. Paddling hard in favorable weather conditions, they reached Sioux City a week later, welcomed back to civilization by a crowd of more than 5,000 curious onlookers. It was in Sioux City that the content and format of Creelman's published dispatches became less the presentation of a Great Plains travelogue and socio-economic commentary and more a series of abbreviated updates featuring frenzied glimpses of celebrations in support of the Big Muddy's conquering heroes.

Indeed, for the next half dozen stops along the Missouri River, *Herald* articles chronicling the progress of the Captain and the correspondent ran under greatly reduced headlines and with only modest mention of the float. Readers learned in Creelman's October 26 telegram from Sioux City little more than the size of the crowd, enthusiasm of local dignitaries at the town's landing, and safe passage through "the great whirlpool near Vermillion, Dakota Territory, in which it was predicted that both would be lost." Even so, the newspaper's reporter and adventure advance man did set the stage for Boyton's arrival in still-distant St. Louis, hinting that "The towns along the river are greatly excited at his approach and preparations are being made everywhere to receive him."[27]

Battling stormy waters and treacherous snags, the Captain and the correspondent next landed at Omaha where their arrival was welcomed by a crowd that Creelman estimated at more than 20,000 people. "By Telegraph to the Herald," he sent along news to New York on October 30 announcing the huge turnout and describing the resulting crush along the riverfront that caused one man to faint. Beyond that, however, there was scant detail in the next day's edition.[28]

As it turned out, Bennett's *Herald* was forced to share its exclusive with another newspaper of the very same name, Omaha's *Daily Herald*. Eager to present its own "Fascinating Narrative of his Adventures with Indians, Sportsmen and Snags," and unafraid to differ from Creelman on the count of well-wishers present at the wharf-side welcome—"not far from a thousand people"—the local journal assigned one of its reporters to visit the Captain at the Canfield Hotel to secure fresh narrative rather than settle for clips from out-of-town news exchanges. In an interview for its November 1 issue, Boyton described afresh everything from his rubber suit and departure from Glendive to his encounters with mud banks, blowing sand, and freezing cold. And there was an angle Creelman had yet to visit. The Captain, it seemed, was anxious to divulge his plans to author some work of his own. "I am writing a book and shall publish it myself in three different languages—French, German and English—describing 20,000 miles and ten years in a rubber suit," he offered, even as he prepared to deliver another fundraising lecture that same evening.[29]

Omaha was a two-paper town in the autumn of 1881, and its version of the *Herald* was, in turn, faced with competing coverage of the celebrated visit by its local rival, the *Daily Bee*. In that paper's November 3 edition, the send-off for the "intrepid swimmer" from the day before was prominently featured along with mention of the potential for a new stop on Boyton's schedule. "He received a telegram from Brownsville yesterday offering him fifty dollars and the receipts to lecture there and this he accepted," claimed the *Bee*. "At St. Joe he will only stop to get his mail."[30] Indeed, after arriving in St. Joseph, Missouri, four days out of Omaha after dark on November 6, Creelman accounted for their delay in a dispatch published in the *New York Herald* the next day, allowing that while their original intention had been to paddle non-stop to St. Joe, windy conditions had necessitated a layover in Brownsville. Whether such was truly the case or the inducement offered for the lecture was the more powerful incentive to linger up the river, there was no doubt Bennett's correspondent and his editors were busily building to what they hoped would be an appropriately grand finale for the float.

Boyton's and Creelman's journey now more closely resembled a victory tour than a voyage of discovery. How else might one explain the sensational flourishes contained within the closing graph of the paper's November 7 article? Buried on page seven it might have been, but the description of the local constabulary being overwhelmed by the spontaneous enthusiasm of the "cheering mob" in St. Joe and "the navigator" being hoisted up upon the shoulders of the crowd was matched by the urgency in Creelman's claim that the journey would be completed on the 17th, "even if, as the captain says, he has to skate a part of the distance on the ice."[31]

Anticipation was indeed building along the river route down the Missouri, but it was not just curious crowds or enterprising local reporters awaiting Boyton's arrival in Kansas City. Already moored at the town levee was the *St. Jacob's Oil*, a steamer hired by Vogeler & Company to not only promote its product, a liniment as pungent as it was popular, but to support its number-one spokesman, the Captain. In a number of items running in papers as far afield as the *Inter-Ocean* of Chicago and *San Francisco Chronicle*, his testimonials were more about advertising than adventure as he extolled the virtues of the unguent as critical to his standing up to the trials of his float. "From constant exposure I am somewhat subject to rheumatic pains, and nothing would ever benefit me until I got hold of this Old German Remedy," he enthused in a November 13 article in the *Chronicle*. "I would sooner do without food for days than be without this remedy for one hour."[32]

An entrepreneur able to turn his notoriety to good advantage in the lecture hall as well as in endorsement, Boyton was an effective pitch man to be certain, but despite the efforts of Creelman and the *Herald*, he was not universally beloved, as readers of the *Kansas City Star* soon discovered. When the *Star*'s reporter climbed aboard the *St. Jacob's Oil* and interviewed its bored and cranky crew, killing time as they waited to steam upriver to escort Boyton into town, he was somewhat surprised to learn that they had little patience for all the hoop-la and adulation shown their fellow employee. "It'd suit me just as well if he never got here," said one sailor. "May the devil get him on the way." Pressed further as to why he was so negative about the hero of the hour, the crewman exclaimed, "He expects us to do everything for him and we have enough to do without that." Caustically, the Missouri mariner remarked, "He don't do this thing for fun. Of course, he's paid by Vogeler & Co. to advertise their medicine."[33]

Eventually, the capitalistic Captain arrived in Kansas City and Creelman's dispatch reflected no traces of impatience or disappointment in his reception. "Captain Boyton arrived here to-day and met with a reception on the river banks from thousands of people," the *Herald* correspondent wired the home office on November 9. "He left St. Joseph yesterday morning and did not make a halt until this morning. During the night he suffered intensely from the cold."[34] Similar cables were forthcoming from Missouri mile markers like Boonville, Hermann, and St. Charles as Creelman and Boyton raced for St. Louis through rising waters and falling temperatures. Each letter "By Telegraph to the *Herald*" emphasized the frigid conditions of the advancing season and counted down the number of miles remaining until reaching the Mississippi and finishing "the greatest aquatic voyage that has ever been attempted."[35]

One of these dispatches, a November 17 wire from Hermann, Missouri, was among the shortest in the serialized account of the navigation of the Missouri. At less than a dozen lines, its brevity and less-strident tone seem significantly out of character, especially with the triumphant arrival in St. Louis less than a week away. As will be seen later in the pages of the newspaper, appearances can be deceiving, and Creelman never did lose his ability to manufacture excitement and sensation even if his editors apparently suffered from fatigue with the float rivaling that of its participants.

There are differing versions of the journey's conclusion downriver. According to the hometown *Globe Democrat*, when Boyton and Creelman finally set foot on solid ground in St. Louis at 4 p.m. on the afternoon of November 20, the frigid temperatures decidedly chilled local interest. "There was no stir of any kind and the termination of the voyage was rather an inglorious end for 'the climax of a lifetime,' which is how the Captain billed the trip," read the paper's summary.[36]

Inexplicably, the *St. Louis Republican*, on the other hand, presented an entirely different picture of the arrival of the two rivermen, agreeing only with the time at which they came ashore. "The bridge was thronged with people as he passed under and thousands were watching him from the levee front," read the item, which was eventually picked up in a limited number of other newspapers such as the *San Francisco Bulletin*. "He was received at a landing near the foot of Market Street by a number of his St. Louis friends and escorted to one of the hotels, where he changed his clothes, took supper, and afterward received his callers."[37]

Whatever the case, the *New York Herald's* modest eleven-line announcement of their arrival lacked even a single decked headline. "Boyton's Feat" generated faint notice on page seven despite the dispatch claiming "great excitement" and the river bank "thronged all day long with people anxious to see the famous navigator end his voyage." Whatever the reality of the reception, it was not of sufficient sensation to displace breaking news from the nation's capital, where the prosecution was closing its case against Garfield assassin Charles Guiteau. Neither did it manage to interrupt the latest from the Navy's Arctic relief expedition that reported no sign of the steamer USS *Jeannette*. Rendering space even more at a premium were a variety of other stories that included fatal boat accidents, ferryboat fires, lynchings, rescues at sea, upheaval at Tammany Hall, and a bride left deserted during her wedding night.[38]

Throwing chronology and continuity to the wind and, in this case, the waves as well, the editors finally found available column inches for Creelman and "Boyton's Long Swim" the last week in November. The float down the majestic waterways simply packed too much punch to be overlooked entirely. "Down the Missouri" went the newspaper's readers one final time "Paddling in an Icy Current" on a "Perilous Journey." And those were just the headlines.[39] Dusting off dispatches from almost a full month before, the *Herald* revisited the dash of Boyton and Creelman as they had sought to cover the last few hundred miles of the journey and outdistance winter's icy blast. From Yankton to Omaha to St. Joseph and finally on into St. Louis, the stories of "Boyton's Long Swim," "Boyton's Paddle," and "Captain Boyton's Latest Feat of River Navigation" made their way back onto the top of the page and returned in sharp detail to the overactive imaginations of *Herald* readers, thus representing a fitting albeit tardy testimonial to the intrepid adventurers.[40]

Playing a central role in such a reprise of the voyage's highlights, *Herald* editors reached deep to find five decked headlines worthy of their edition of November 28, the last in which dense columns of details from the Great Plains were featured. "Enthusiastic Greetings and Cheery Salutes on the Weary Downward Way" and "Skirting the Vine-clad Hillsides of the American Rhine" topped a November 17, 1881, telegram sent from Hermann, Missouri, where German settlers had been building vineyards and wineries since the 1850s. It seems Creelman had not grown clipped and cranky in the waning weeks of the trip once its end was in reach. Rather, he had forwarded multiple columns from Hermann several days before, detailing everything from the "Baby Mine" freezing in place on the river to navigating by starlight and passing by hundreds of bobbing lanterns held by those not wanting to miss sight of "a black, shark-like body, which rose upon a wave, gleamed in the light for a moment, waved its hand and passed on at the rate of nearly seven miles an hour."[41]

## End of the Adventure

Not by any failure of the correspondent did *Herald* coverage seemingly wear thin along the homestretch. As the use of Hermann cables appears to demonstrate, the journal's experienced editorial staff apparently cherry-picked selected pieces of telegrams to run in the moment and some to save for later. Their motivations for abandoning immediacy for expediency with such decisions are interesting to contemplate. Perhaps by presenting more abbreviated updates in the adventures' final days they sought to artificially quicken the pace of the voyage to re-energize waning interest after almost two months of continuous coverage. This seems unlikely, however, given the resolve with which Bennett and his newspaper stuck with adventures from Africa and the Arctic over months and even years versus the float's more modest eight weeks. They might have seen value in not competing with themselves and diminishing the impact of the trip's final installments by jamming valuable narrative into the shrinking spaces between insane assassins and mysterious disappearances on the Polar ice pack.

Whatever the case, true to a pledge made during the journey, Boyton figuratively, if not literally, broke his paddle in two, never to float so far down another river for the rest of his life. A proposed navigation of the Amazon prominently mentioned in the immediate aftermath of completing the voyage never came to pass. Instead, he swapped his rubber suit for P.T. Barnum's center ring and a sea lion show that became the main attraction at an amusement park built on the site later developed into Coney Island. But if the Missouri float trip was the Captain's finale, it was Creelman's debut as one of the age's most talented and tenacious interviewers, a reporter who could be counted upon to corner even the most elusive of subjects and bring the story home.

James Creelman went on to become not only a master interviewer, but an iconic war correspondent credited with a number of the most sensational stories published in American newspapers of the late nineteenth century. Present at Port Arthur in 1894 and again at El Caney during the Spanish-American War, his accounts of atrocities and battlefield heroics remain among the most oft-quoted examples of Yellow Journalism in the study of the nation's press during the period. Eventually, his bulging portfolio featured more than enough material to write an entire book—which is exactly what he did, publishing his long-anticipated memoirs to modest critical acclaim in 1901.

Featured prominently within the pages of *On the Great Highway: The Wanderings and Adventures of a Special Correspondent* were sketches of famous people and momentous events, including an entire chapter devoted to the encounter with Sitting Bull. There was only passing reference to the circumstances that delivered the correspondent to his highly acclaimed interview with the Sioux chief. Briefly recalling the series of dispatches that captured the attention of *Herald* readers for several weeks in the fall of 1881,

Creelman allowed, "I had paddled down the muddy waters of the Missouri with Paul Boyton, the adventurous traveller [*sic*], who spent his time floating along the rivers of the world in an inflated rubber suit." It was faint praise indeed for a friend who played such an important role in advancing the correspondent's career and placing him in a position to file highly prized copy in frontier-sized installments. Boyton was also responsible for facilitating the conversation with Sitting Bull at a time when competition for interviews with famous personages was becoming keen and the quotes were considered something of a coup.[42]

For all that, the Captain had no need to play a second to Creelman's lead. In fact, his own personal reminiscences were commercialized a full eight years before those of the correspondent. Released in 1893, *The Story of Paul Boyton—Voyages on All the Great Rivers of the World* referenced an impressive resume of its own with recollections of famous floats down the Rhine and the Po and across the Straits of Gibraltar in addition to the navigation of the Yellowstone and Missouri.

While it is true that taken in tandem, the two obscure memoirs of bygone heroes may fail to resonate with modern audiences, the flowery prose of Creelman and Boyton should not be dismissed out of hand. Embedded within the volumes' overly descriptive passages reside notable tales of bold adventure, daredevil risk-taking, and wide-eyed wonder that sold editions of the *New York Herald* by the tens of thousands. Dated though they may be, the retrospectives speak from another time in the American experience well worth remembering: when the advance of civilized influence even within the young nation's own borders remained a popular theme, and the taming of indigenous peoples and the wilderness they so grudgingly surrendered spoke to important feelings of national pride and identity. It was an age in which readers were anxious to find refuge from so much pushing and progress.

In the instance of Paul Boyton and James Creelman, they sought to indulge their pursuit of escapism with a man dressed in a rubber suit and a "stripling of a writer for a New York newspaper" trailing behind in a canvas canoe. With such adventurers and journalists feeding their flights of fancy, newspaper readers of the Gilded Age were more than willing to follow along in the wake of such a serialized saga and vicariously travel around each and every bend in the Missouri, thrilling to each and every twist in an unabashedly sensational story.[43]

### NOTES

1. Peter Lyon, "The Fearless Frogman," *American Heritage Magazine*, Volume II, Issue 3, April, 1960.
2. *New York Herald*, May 25, 1875; *New York Herald*, May 30, 1875.
3. "A Journalist Afloat," *New York Herald*, January 26, 1879.
4. *Memphis Commercial Appeal*, April 12, 1879.
5. *New York Herald*, April 28, 1879.
6. Boyton to James Creelman, Red Wing, Minnesota, August 28, 1881, The James Creelman Papers, Ohio State University Libraries, Rare Books, and Manuscripts.
7. *Ibid.*
8. *Ibid.*
9. *New York Herald*, July 7, 1876. The Battle of Little Big Horn was a story Bennett felt he still owned and not without good reason. A little more than five years before, the *Herald* paid more than $3,000 for a 50,000-word dispatch telegraphed over a twenty-four-hour span, enabling the newspaper to break one of the greatest scoops in the annals of American journalism. On July 7, 1876, just three days after the young nation celebrated its centennial in Philadelphia, *Herald* headlines screamed, "Custer's Terrible Defeat" and "The Cause his Fearless Daring."

10. *New York Herald*, August 10, 1881.

11. David Walter, *More Campfire Tales: Fifteen Historical Narratives* (Helena, MT: Farcountry Press, 2002), 31.

12. *Ibid.*, 30.

13. Paul Boyton, *The Story of Paul Boyton—Voyages on all the Great Rivers of the World, Paddling Twenty-Five Thousand Miles in a Rubber Dress* (Milwaukee: Riverside Printing Co., 1892), 325.

14. *New York Herald*, October 22, 1881.

15. *Ibid.*

16. *New York Herald*, October 23, 1881

17. *Ibid.*

18. *Ibid.*

19. *New York Herald*, October 28, 1881.

20. *Ibid.*

21. *New York Herald*, October 29, 1881.

22. *Ibid.*

23. *Ibid.*

24. James Creelman, *On the Great Highway: The Wanderings and Adventures of a Special Correspondent* (Boston: Lothrop, Shepard Co., 1901), 295.

25. *Ibid.*, 299

26. *New York Herald*, October 29, 1881.

27. *New York Herald*, October 27, 1881.

28. *New York Herald*, October 31, 1881.

29. *Omaha Daily Herald*, November 1, 1881.

30. *Omaha Daily Bee*, November 3, 1881

31. *New York Herald*, November 7, 1881.

32. *San Francisco Chronicle*, November 3, 1881

33. *Kansas City Star*, November 5, 1881.

34. *New York Herald*, November 10, 1881.

35. *New York Herald*, November 17, 1881.

36. *St. Louis Globe Democrat*, November 21, 1881.

37. *St. Louis Republican*, November 21, 1881.

38. *New York Herald*, November 21, 1881.

39. *New York Herald*, November 24, 1881; *New York Herald*, November 28, 1881.

40. *Ibid.*; *New York Herald*, November 25, 1881; *New York Herald*, November 28, 1881.

41. *New York Herald*, November 28, 1881.

42. Creelman, *On the Great Highway*, 297.

43. *Ibid.*, 295.

# "An Almost Undiscovered Country"

## Frank Leslie's *1890 Alaska Expedition and the Tradition of Gilded Age Adventure Journalism*[1]

### MARY M. CRONIN

In the early months of 1890, W.J. Arkell, the editor of *Frank Leslie's Illustrated Newspaper* (hereafter, *Leslie's*), decided to do what the U.S. government had rarely done and sent a team of three men to explore the interior of Alaska, a place he termed "an almost undiscovered country."[2]

Fierce competition for readers among America's metropolitan press during the Gilded Age led a number of publishers to fund expeditions to the earth's remaining unexplored and underexplored places in exchange for exclusive reports laden with exotica that would awe and inform readers.[3] *New York Herald* publisher James Gordon Bennett Jr. had established the standard for doing so by dispatching journalist Henry Morton Stanley in the early 1870s to locate and resupply the famed British explorer Dr. David Livingstone, who had been reported missing in Africa. When Stanley succeeded, many American newspapers tipped their editorial pens in homage to Bennett. The *Buffalo Express* called the expedition "the most extraordinary newspaper enterprise ever dreamed of."[4] Stanley's first-person accounts of his exploits across the mysterious and dangerous continent, which were serialized throughout the spring of 1872, led the *Herald*'s circulation to soar as readers thrilled to the journalist-explorer's often-harrowing adventures through column after column of the newspaper.[5]

Arkell wanted—and needed—to achieve similar publicity and circulation success for *Leslie's*.[6] A number of new, inexpensive magazines designed for mass readership had emerged in the 1880s, providing competition at a time when *Leslie's* circulation had dipped to 67,000, down from 100,000 in 1860.[7] The illustrated newspaper was still solvent, though, its finances buoyed by advertising revenues, so its editor spared few expenses for the expedition he hoped would both mimic and rival Stanley's triumph. Arkell thus hired Edward Glave, a young Englishman who had worked with Stanley in Africa for several years before embarking upon a successful lecture tour during which he detailed his exploits along the Congo River. Glave, a former accountant who tired of London, had distinguished himself as a fine hunter and explorer while in Africa. He also had substantial artistic talent and would serve as one of the Alaska expedition's sketch artists. With Glave hired, Arkell puffed the expedition's potential in an April 5, 1890, editorial, stating,

The icebergs of Glacier Bay were a far cry from the Congo River basin, where Edward Glave had served H.M. Stanley in Africa, yet the young explorer accepted an invitation from *Leslie's* editor W. J. Arkell to take his chances on a new adventure. Glave admired Alaska's wild landscape, thick forests, and rugged mountains, with "fantastic, jagged peaks all snow-clad at the summit" (Library of Congress, Item ppmsc.01994).

"It is not unlikely that the result will be second only to that of Stanley's explorations in Africa."[8]

E. H. Wells, a reporter who had mapped the Fortymile River, which ran along the Alaska-Canadian border, and rafted the Yukon River in 1889 on assignment for the E.W. Scripps newspapers, was put in charge of the expedition. The expedition's third member, an astronomer-turned-journalist, Alfred B. Schanz, was recruited because he had a background in the sciences and history.[9] The men were joined in San Francisco by Jack Dalton, a mountaineer who had been to Alaska, and Frank B. Price, a sailor with Arctic experience. Outfitted with the best photographic equipment available, plus materials to make artistic sketches, the journalists were instructed to write "graphic narratives" of their adventures and produce illustrations "of the strange sights they met" for the readers back home.[10]

The often-richly illustrated articles were serialized during 1890 and 1891.[11] The series achieved the publicity that Arkell craved—but in an unexpected way. While American newspapers and magazines hailed the expedition at its outset,[12] the difficulties inherent in communicating with *Leslie's* New York City office from the interior of Alaska led to unfounded stories in the nation's press that two members of the expedition—Wells and Price—had perished. In reality, the men had taken Schanz, who became ill in late June 1890, to a trading post that had a doctor, then continued their explorations along the Fortymile River, meeting with gold miners before journeying overland to explore the

Tanana River.[13] In September, they arrived at St. Michael, a Russian settlement on the west coast of Alaska, but had no means to communicate their whereabouts to New York and remained unaware that readers and journalists across the nation feared the worst, declaring them lost and probably dead.[14] Their "disappearance" made headlines, as did their "reappearance" the following spring when the men made their way to Kodiak for a return trip to Port Townsend, Washington, via one of the first steamships to reach Alaska in the spring.[15]

In an age when middle-class travelers were seeking new destinations to visit and post–Civil War American society sought to resume its nationalistic goals of "conquest, colonization, and territorial expansion," an Alaska expedition was not only a safe gamble, but a welcome one.[16] As historian Melody Webb notes, Alaska "was not only as exciting as Africa, but was much closer and American."[17] Gilded Age editors advanced this very sentiment. For example, the *Wilkesbarre (PA) Record* editor welcomed the *Leslie's* expedition, stating, "Our own continent offers opportunities for exploration quite as surprising as anything to be hoped for in Africa." Similarly, the *Utica (NY) Herald's* editor said he was looking forward to the expedition's "experiences and discoveries," adding "…it cannot fail to be a most interesting narrative to both the scientific world and the general public."[18]

The *Leslie's* Alaska series provides an excellent case study of Gilded Age adventure journalism. The reporters constructed uneven narratives that blended first-person adventure journalism, naturalist and ethnographic observations, historical information, and political commentary, while also elaborating on Alaska's resources.[19] The reporters also embraced commonly held stereotypes of the American West and its inhabitants, while promoting territorial expansion in the cause of manifest destiny. This essay argues that Alaska's "newness" to the American nation and its vast spaces and resources led journalists to construct narratives that included views more commonly expressed in the first half of the century: that Alaska, as a frontier location, was a wild and savage place that could and should be tamed by individuals of Anglo and European stock for the betterment of the American nation.[20]

## Adventure Journalism in the Popular Press

Americans' fascination with travel literature, especially about locations within the country, is almost as old as the nation itself.[21] As the edge of the American frontier continually moved westward, books and articles about travelers' and pioneers' experiences were rushed into print.[22] Some of these were produced by pioneers and journalists, but travel literature by notable writers sold briskly, particularly works by Charles Dickens, Margaret Fuller, Mark Twain, Horace Greeley, and *Springfield (MA) Republican* publisher Samuel Bowles, all of whom discussed western sites and vistas, native peoples, the newly arrived settlers, and frontier customs, as well as the authors' personal experiences.[23] Importantly, such writing usually provided readers more than merely descriptive discourse. The books and articles often articulated the authors' views on the larger issues of the day, including the meaning of nationhood, nation-building, manifest destiny, and class and race relations.[24] Such writing, therefore, led to an imagined West that influenced the reading public.[25]

Frequently, those writers (and many citizens) located their identity in their relationship to the land.[26] The vastness of the American West evoked America's power and promise. The frontier also was where many Americans located the nation's core values and ideals. The land held a bounty of richness for those individuals who were independent enough, rugged enough, and of sound enough character to work and better themselves. The frontier, therefore, held promises both real and mythical, and the press played an important role in creating this mythic West. As David H. Murdoch has said, "The conquest of distant lands and their savage inhabitants became standard fare for adventure stories and, when projected eventually by the Yellow Press, stimulated what one contemporary called 'spectatorial lust.'"[27]

The public also needed such mediated travelogues. Although the Civil War and the Reconstruction Era were over, late nineteenth-century America remained racially divided and suffered from a host of economic, industrial, social, cultural, and political changes and upheavals. The West—both as a geographic location and as a mediated construction—remained a safety valve of sorts, a region, Murdoch notes, "...where the borderline between fact and fantasy was as unclear as the frontier between savagery and civilization.... Then, [too] nostalgia for the lost wilderness and the end of the frontier became bound up with nostalgia for a simpler America."[28]

Following the U.S. Civil War, a resumption of exploration and western settlement demonstrated America's power and resurgence to the world, while the funding of expeditions by the nation's publishers demonstrated the parallel power, influence, and resources of the press during the Gilded Age. Popular magazines and newspapers, aimed at average readers, provided a home for much travel and adventure stories during this period. *Harper's Monthly*, *Scribner's*, and two Leslie publications, *Frank Leslie's Illustrated Newspaper* and *Frank Leslie's Popular Monthly*, were among the popular magazines that devoted an increasing amount of copy to travel and adventure stories.[29] As historians David W. Bulla and David B. Sachsman have noted, America's Gilded Age publications often grew profitable from a rising tide of new, urban immigrant readers if their staffs provided entertaining copy.[30] Adventure journalism stories fit this bill.

The purchase of Alaska from Russia in 1867 for $7,200,000 (which worked out to two cents an acre) by U.S. Secretary of State William Seward allowed further expansion and exploration, although Seward's actions initially were ridiculed by many members of the public, the press, and some politicians who derisively called the decision "Seward's Folly" and "Seward's Icebox."[31] Some publications did herald the purchase, seeing it as another step toward manifest destiny.[32]

Alaska's vast size meant there was plenty of territory for journalists to explore. Seward's purchase of Alaska expanded America by 663,300 square miles, adding thirty-nine mountain ranges and more than 12,000 rivers.[33] Editor Arkell knew that the reading public, awash with dime novel tales set in the western frontier, as well as more genteel literature and adventure and travel stories from the periodic press, would thrill to a series of illustrated narratives that revealed the largely uncharted Alaskan interior: a territory rich with unusual animals, colorful natives, and dramatic, but often-treacherous, landscape. Such content had long been *Leslie's* stock-in-trade, and the editorial tradition continued after the founder-publisher Frank Leslie died in 1880.[34]

Although Arkell promised readers exciting stories and touted the exploratory nature of the expedition, the *Leslie's* journalists were not the first to investigate or to report on Alaska's interior. Scientific, military, and privately funded exploration of the territory began in the 1600s when the first Russians sailed to the region. Several nineteenth-century explorers produced popular guidebooks and accounts that sold well, bringing publicity to Alaska and its resources.[35] A few publications, including the *Century Magazine* and the *New York Times*, also sent reporter-explorers to the territory prior to the *Leslie's* expedition.[36] The *Leslie's* series, with its distinctive woodcut illustrations and substantial copy, however, was among the most detailed of the popular press accounts.

## *The* Leslie's *Alaska Trip: Tenderhorns in the Wilderness*

The *Leslie's* series drew upon such national yearning, while allowing its reporter-explorers to imbue their narratives with the traditional values of heroic endeavor—self-reliance, courage, chivalry, and honor.[37] The images that accompanied the articles also helped visually establish the journalists' ruggedness and manliness. For example, the June 27, 1891, issue of *Leslie's* depicted Wells and his team navigating the Taku River rapids. The September 5, 1891, issue of *Leslie's* portrayed Wells as a man of action, outfitted in western attire in an Alaskan forest, bent slightly forward with a rifle in search of game. The September 26, 1891, issue depicted the men and their Indian guides vigorously paddling through a river with a swift-flowing current.

All told, these journalists covered a vast amount of territory, especially after splitting into two parties. They visited the Chilkat Valley and the Katmai region, then paddled or portaged a number of rivers, including the Yukon River, the Fortymile River, the Tanana River, the Taku River, the Alsek River, the Kuskokwim River, and the Nushagak, Mulchatna, Tatshenshini, Kakhtul, and Holitna Rivers. The men also continued their journeys during the dangerous winter months, traveling via sleds with dog teams to further explore the southwestern portion of Alaska.[38]

The two teams reunited at Kodiak in the spring of 1891 for the journey back to Seattle. The journalists had covered several thousand miles via boats, rafts, dog sleds, and snowshoe. They visited and wrote about members of several tribes, including the Tlingit, Athabascan, Yup'ik, and Chilkat tribes; drew maps; recorded observations of the territory's flora, fauna, people, and geography; and attempted to ascertain the depths of several lakes. Schanz, who was accompanied for a while by trader John W. Clark, helped conduct a census of the inhabitants of mining towns and native villages along the Nuskagak River, an unexpected duty, but one that allowed him to spend time with local whites and natives.[39]

Since the journalists were living and working during an era where Americans valued and celebrated the socially constructed mythology of the frontiersman, editor Arkell was more than willing to make use of such stereotypes. Despite the men's relatively limited Arctic credentials, Arkell referred to his reporters as explorers. The series, Arkell said in a June 20, 1891, editorial, "will be a most thrilling record of an extraordinary series of adventures, describing the perils of travel on land and water; over the ice and snow by raft, dog-sleds, and on foot. Some of the explorers' escapades were marvelous; in fact, the whole diary of the trip is marvelously interesting."[40]

Although the *Leslie's* journalists often faced arduous conditions as they traveled on land and via rivers, their serialized accounts demonstrate that the reporters, far from being true explorers, were green, urban tenderfoots who took unnecessary risks. The men chose to explore all winter, rather than wait out the snow storms and frigid temperatures at trading posts, then resume their exploration during the spring when travel conditions improved. Schanz grew angry in mid–October 1890 when he could not secure "willing and competent guides" among the native men for winter travel and was forced to spend some time at Fort Alexander, a trading post in the Nushagak River region.[41]

Later, when Schanz succeeded in persuading several guides to accompany him, the decision almost cost the journalist and his men their lives. Deep snow, blizzards, and an inadequate supply of food took their toll as the men journeyed across the Tanana Basin, with Schanz determined to explore the territory, regardless of the dangers involved. "No living being could exist an hour exposed to the full force of such a storm, and later on the trip we had to 'run for it' repeatedly," he admitted in discussing one particular blizzard.[42] Every member of the team suffered from frostbite, several sled dogs were lost to storms and wolves, and the men almost starved to death. Schanz acknowledged in an October 10, 1891, article that he misjudged the team's food supplies, not realizing that both people and dogs needed a high calorie diet in the extreme cold. Only the charity of native peoples from several remote villages, who took the explorers in and shared their precious winter food stocks, led to the party's survival during their ill-fated February and March 1891 explorations.[43]

The difficult winter journey led Schanz to combine two dueling mediated images of Alaska, portraying it as a region of great natural beauty, but one that remained dangerous, savage, and untamed. A chastened Schanz noted in the November 7, 1891, issue of *Leslie's* that the men's bleeding feet, bloated faces, aching arms, and emaciated condition left them numb to the natural splendor of Petroff Falls on the Noghelin River. "It was one of nature's gems of beauty, but in our condition not even the charms of such a scene would awaken adequate appreciation."[44]

Schanz put his inexperience to good use, however, passing off new experiences as exotica to readers. For example, the journalist awoke with a start one March morning to the sound of what he thought was artillery, only to discover that thick river ice had warmed to the breaking point. Although the journalist was unaware of the noise that occurred during the spring ice thaw in Alaska, he turned the event into the type of colorful tale that his editor back in New York City desired.[45] Wells also acknowledged in a florid style the hardships that befell his team during winter travel, using hyperbole to paint a picture of Alaska as a wild and untamed place. "Strange events were in store for us—events that would force us to travel several thousand miles further than had been planned. The phantom of starvation was to beckon at us in a mountain trap, in a game-forsaken region. Adventures were to befall us in swift succession," he noted in the first installment of his narrative.[46]

Like Schanz, Wells also turned dangers caused by his inexperience with wilderness travel into the exciting copy that was expected by *Leslie's* readers. After building a raft in June 1890, Wells, Schanz, Frank Price, and a guide known as Indiank packed it to overflowing with "blankets, guns, field-glasses, coats, cameras, pantaloons," food stuffs, a smaller canvas boat, and other provisions, then attempted to navigate the fast-flowing Taku River (the journalists referred to it as the Tahk) despite underwater boulders, protruding riverbanks, and partially submerged logs. Wells told readers their "theory of navigation" was a simple one—avoid the boulders, riverbanks, and logs. The journey, Wells admitted, was not uneventful, but despite the journalists' mistakes, Wells portrayed himself and his colleagues as virile men of action using a florid, purple-prose style in a June 27, 1891, installment:

> Meanwhile I had jumped into the canvas boat and cast it loose from the raft, rowing some distance ahead and keeping a sharp lookout for obstructions. The current was running eight knots, and a collision meant destruction to the boat. But despite my watchfulness, I got into

On occasion misjudging the weather, the distance, or their supplies, the inexperienced *Leslie's* staff depended on their native guides to navigate through hundreds of miles of unfamiliar and unforgiving Alaskan wilderness. These Tagish or Tlingit guides are resting their oxen on the Dyea Trail, 1897 (Library of Congress, Item cph.3a31293).

> a scrape. Rounding suddenly a short bend I saw that I was in the jaws of a small but vigorous cascade that, splitting around a huge rock, ran roaring and throbbing into a boiling pot-hole beneath. There was no chance to retreat.[47]

Wells' narrative continued in breathless style, taking readers on the ride with him in his flimsy boat as "a tall, angry breaker was in waiting," smashing into his craft with a terrific blow and throwing him head over heels. Eventually, the men brought their two boats to shore to make camp for the evening in a valley whose "panoramic beauty" left Wells in awe.[48]

In a later article, published on September 19, 1891, Wells used the same breathless literary style to describe the "exciting experience" of turning the sled dogs loose to run down a steep, icy hill, while the explorers used the weight of the packed sleds to pull them down the hillside. One of the native guides, named Sas-sut-ka, was thrown off his sled and dragged downhill as he clung to the sled's rail. "It was a ride long to be remembered and not frequently repeated," the journalist said in hindsight.[49]

## Touting Tourism

Although the accounts of their winter journeys might have given readers pause about visiting Alaska, the journalists made clear at the start that Alaska had great potential for tourism—during the territory's summer months. Wells noted in a June 27, 1891, article that the Taku River was navigable for steamboats for at least four times the navigable distance of the Tagish River.[50] He also, in a June 20, 1891, account, denounced as "absurd" the popular stories that portrayed the "icy fastness" and "frozen terrors" of Alaska. He explained in measured tones that such stereotypes were based on accounts by tourists who traveled via steamboat near Mount St. Elias and Sitka, where "an imposing wall of glaciers and snowy mountains" could be seen.[51] A "different kind of country" could be found in the interior, Wells noted, describing in romantic terms the "gigantic mountains, great rivers, and picturesque scenery." He then switched to a pragmatic observation, stating that in his opinion, a railroad to bring tourists and goods was not only practicable, but could be constructed at "moderate expense." Both the territory's landscape and its levels of winter snowfall were similar to those found in western Canada, a region that already had railroads, he said.[52]

Articles by Glave and Schanz describing Alaska during the summer months also took on a romantic tinge that undoubtedly encouraged tourism to the region. Glave, for example, encouraged other publications, including rival *Harper's Weekly*, to follow *Leslie's* lead and bring photographers to the territory to capture its wonders, which, he noted, included both wild, rugged land with "fantastic, jagged peaks all snow-clad at the summit," as well as thick forests of spruce, hemlock, willow, poplar, and crab apple trees; rivers teeming with fish; and exotic native villages with "substantially built houses," totem poles, and other carved figurines.[53]

Schanz also used romantic language to describe the landscape. For example, in an article published on September 26, 1891, he recalled several weeks of travel in August 1890 after recovering from his illness:

> The next three weeks presented to us, through the long, dreamy days, the wonderful natural beauties of the upper Yukon palisades; the tiresome monotony of the Yukon flats; the wonderful wild-rose tangles on the site of old Fort Yukon … the frowning bluffs of the lower ramparts with their astounding multiple echoes and their bruin population; the turbulent mouths of the Porcupine and the Tananah [*sic*], and the exciting whirlpools of the lower rapids.[54]

By describing nature's nobility and linking that theme with accounts of their physical adventures, the *Leslie's* reporters were engaging in a literary style commonly used by other nineteenth-century travel writers.[55] Such writing undoubtedly benefited Alaska's nascent tourist industry by promoting the area as an extraordinary, exotic location to visit.[56] Initial tourism forays to the region had only begun in the late 1870s, barely a decade before the *Leslie's* reporters traveled to the territory. Captain George S. Wright is credited with leading a group of tourists up the Stikine River in 1878. Steamship companies that were already supplying the Alaskan fur and fishing trades with goods began adding coastal tours during the summer months in the late 1870s for well-to-do travelers.[57]

Wells and Schanz also noted the new territory's benefit to the broader United States and the nation's manifest destiny. Wells told readers his expertise via his 1890 and 1891 travels led him to foresee the southern half of the territory as becoming a new and important state, while relegating the northern portion of the territory to its native inhabitants. "The north half will remain as it now is, a barren wilderness, the haunt of Arctic animals and of wild men." As with previous writers who examined the American West, Wells saw Alaska's future as linked to white immigration to the region. Anglo-Saxon men, the journalist said, would exploit the territory's rich soil, its mineral wealth, and

By highlighting romantic summer landscapes and exotic native cultures, the *Leslie's* series would contribute to the acceleration of Alaska tourism during the Gilded Age—though glaciers would remain the prime attraction, as for these passengers of the steamer *Topeka*, Sept. 25, 1895, at Muir Glacier (Library of Congress, item cph.3b01942).

its animals. The territory's lakes held "inexhaustible supplies of fish," while vast forests offered "boundless" supplies of timber, ripe for exploitation.[58]

## Reporters' Portrayals of Self and "Other"

Although *Leslie's* Anglo-Saxon journalists constructed images of themselves as self-reliant and embraced the commonly held racial belief of the time that they were at the top of the racial order by virtue of their whiteness, these beliefs were undermined by the reality of their journey. The "explorers" relied heavily on Native Americans to survive. The men they hired knew the landscape and guided them as the journalists "explored."[59] They also helped paddle canoes and rafts through often-treacherous waters, carried the men across freezing rivers, tracked game, and helped the urban journalists to hunt.[60] But in an era of strongly held racial beliefs, the journalists rarely bothered to mention the names of their native guides and only occasionally demonstrated a grudging respect for the men and the native peoples whose villages they visited.[61]

Dominant racial views also led the journalists to provide contradictory narrative accounts of the region's native peoples, portraying them alternatively as exotic, polite, and hospitable, yet also as dirty, lazy, and uncivilized. Such views were commonly held among previous Anglo explorers as well as among the growing number of tourists who visited during the summer months.[62] Tourists and explorers alike wanted exotica, but they also wanted to see the last vestiges of a primitive past that to them was embodied by Alaska's native peoples.[63] Glave's August 9, 1890, account and accompanying sketches provided a window into the lives of Alaska's native peoples via descriptions and anecdotes that depicted finely-created jewelry, hair combs, houses adorned with images of ravens, bears, and whales, and similarly adorned gravesites and totem poles surrounding the village. While such visual artifacts attested to the Chilkat tribe's rich cultural heritage, it was too dissimilar to what Glave expected for him to pronounce it civilized.

The English explorer also regularly pronounced the native people to be lazy, not understanding why they would not serve as porters and guides as he had previously experienced in Africa. That these regions were very different and that winter travel in Alaska could prove deadly were issues the Englishman did not appear to comprehend. Furthermore, the fact that Alaska's native people had become familiar with the value of money especially annoyed Glave. He acknowledged that it "took a lot of haggling" to secure the service of several guides to escort the journalists up the Chilkat River. When strong winds and a seven-knot current began working against the men in their flotilla of boats, Glave angrily recounted that the white men worked hard, "pushing, pulling and towing against a contrary wind," while the Indians did less work. "The Indians have a great aversion to doing any work which they can get others to execute for them, and until we convinced them that we objected to their mode of action they were perfectly satisfied to squat in the canoes and allow the white men to tow them upstream, while they lazily steered the craft and enjoyed their pipes."[64]

Upon their arrival at the Indian village of Klokwan, following a three-day river journey, Glave marveled that the tribe lived in "substantially built houses" made from heavy timber planks, praised the tribe's children as "certainly nice looking," and acknowledged the tribe's hospitality. But he again demonstrated he was disgusted by the community's "filth," including the discarded remains of fish and the grease that native peoples used on their hair and faces to protect themselves from the elements.[65] Glave's disgust was common among late-nineteenth-century Anglo visitors who usually described Alaska's native inhabitants in pejorative terms, a mediated construction that allowed white middle-class travelers and parlor ethnographers to affirm their own racial superiority.[66]

The journalists also noted that white settlers to the territory were quickly changing the native people's way of life. Glave acknowledged tribal children still engaged in traditional pastimes such jumping games and tests of strength, but also played with marbles. The tribe also relied almost exclusively on traders for food, embracing a diet that leaned heavily toward biscuits, salt, and sugar, rather than salmon and other traditional, healthier foods. Most of the members also worked for the Alaska Commercial Company, canning fish and providing furs.[67]

Although Glave's observations of white encroachment struck a melancholy note at times, his ethnographic observations of native villages often took a pejorative tone. He provided detailed descriptions and illustrations of the village's buildings and individual household items, but then acknowledged the cultural differences between Anglo and Indian possessions, calling the totems, masks, cooking pots, dried bear meat, sheepskins, clothes, and snow shoes as a "queer assortment" of items, while proclaiming carved figurines and animal totems as "grotesque."[68]

Noting the degree to which white ways of life had crept into the lives of the tribes they visited, Glave's companions saw the changes as largely positive. Schanz claimed, for example, that many native peoples were beginning to embrace "civilized garments" and furniture obtained through trade. One village chief wore "cowhide boots and tailed coat," and some members of the tribe spoke Russian.[69] Similarly, in an October 1,

INDIAN VILLAGE, HOWKAN, ALASKA.                    COPYRIGHT BY WINTER&POND

1890, article, Wells praised a Reverend Killbuck, a "full-blooded Delaware Indian" who resided at a Moravian Mission on the Kuskokwin River, but only because he had adopted Anglo-Saxon ways. While Wells admitted his surprise at Killbuck's lineage, expecting Russian or Greek Orthodox priests such as those he had met in other Alaskan communities, Killbuck was singled out for praise because he had "a fine education and polished manners ... spoke English with a perfect accent and was a compassionate person." In a back-handed compliment common to the nineteenth century, Wells added: "In nothing save his face—and perchance his name—could one detect aught of the North American red man."[70]

The reporters never suggested the extermination of Alaska's native peoples, as did so many journalists in parts of the American West before them. Indian Affairs Commissioner J.D.C. Atkins made clear in his annual report of 1887 that Alaska's natives were not seen in the same way as tribes on western reservations:

> They are Alaskans, the native people of the land, who know how to support themselves by the resources of the country and the industries naturally arising there from, are ready to engage in any other industries which may be established there and to assimilate the customs of those who come to settle among them, and are anxious to be educated. They are the laboring class, which needs neither corralling nor feeding nor agencies nor any of the machinery which has sprung up on connection with our Indian service....[71]

Advocating assimilation, *Leslie's* journalists noted that the "civilizing" influence of white settlers, and especially white missionaries, would be a necessary factor for native assimilation. Among the reporters, Wells was particularly caustic in his assessment of Russian and Greek orthodox priests who he believed could make greater efforts to improve the lives of native peoples near their missions.[72]

## Accomplishments of Leslie's Expedition

From an exploration standpoint, the 1890–1891 expedition yielded little scientific, ethnographic, or exploratory insight. Wells provided some new information about the Tanana River region, Glave added some new information about the upper Alsek River, and Schanz defined and mapped Lake Clark.[73] The expedition's importance lay in the reporters' abilities to fire their readers' imaginations by providing detailed verbal and visual description of America's enormous territorial acquisition in the Far North. Via their multi-part series, the *Leslie's* correspondents drew upon older images of the West that saw the region as a wild and untamed place—a geographic location that would benefit the nation once tamed by whites, while also making use of romantic imagery that celebrated the territory's natural grandeur.

The journalists' coverage of Alaska did not break new reportorial ground. The series put the dominant Anglo-Saxon culture at the forefront as a civilizing influence, while linking the acquisition of Alaska to the broader issue of manifest destiny. The journalists

*Opposite:* Sketches in the *Leslie's* series offered readers a close look at native cultural practices and living conditions during a time when some communities were beginning to adopt Anglo diets, language, and clothing. Here, Haida children assemble on the front porch of a home in the village of Howkan, Alaska, under a watchful eagle ... and a precariously balanced totem pole (photograph by Winter & Pond, c. 1901, Library of Congress, Item cph.3c072 71).

made clear, however, that despite the region's vast distance from the rest of the continental United States, Alaska's natural resources would prove beneficial to the nation.

Although the series presented an uneven view of the territory's native peoples, a viewpoint born of the *Leslie's* men's pre-existing racial beliefs, the journalists never called for the natives' extermination, as had so many writers before them. Nor did the journalists view Alaska's tribes entirely through the conflicting nineteenth-century stereotypes that saw native peoples as either noble people whose culture had been subsumed to the more dominant white culture or as "savages" who needed to be exterminated. Instead, Alaska's native peoples were largely presented as exotic, hospitable, yet stubborn, a people whose way of life was in transition by the encroachment of white settlement into the territory. Such contradictory stereotypes were, however, commonly expressed by many white explorers and visitors to Alaska who found themselves both repulsed by and attracted to the seemingly exotic lifestyles of Alaska's natives. Like those visitors, the *Leslie's* reporters made no attempt to get to know the territory's Native Americans. They were curiosities to be viewed, not unlike a museum exhibit.

## NOTES

1. An earlier version of this essay was published in *Journalism History*, 42:1, 24–32, DOI: 10.1080/0094 7679.2016.12059139. Reprinted with permission.

2. W. J. Arkell, *Frank Leslie's Illustrated Newspaper*, April 5, 1890, 190; Walter R. Borneman, *Alaska: Saga of a Bold Land* (New York: Perennial, 2004), 133–143; John B. Branson, *The Life and Times of John W. Clark of Nushagaka Alaska, 1846–1896* (Anchorage: National Park Service, 2012), 169.

3. For example, in 1879, James Gordon Bennett Jr. funded an expedition to the North Pole, while other publications sent reporters to Greenland, Japan, China, South America, Turkey, New Zealand, Panama, Jamaica, Siberia, and Egypt, among other "exotic" locales. Some publications even sent reporters into the "rough" sections of New York and London, seeing these as equally dangerous and adventurous trips. For more, see Hampton Sides, *In The Kingdom of Ice: The Grand and Terrible Polar Voyage of the USS Jeannette* (New York: Doubleday, 2014); James MacCauley, *The Past is an Exotic Place: Nineteenth-Century Travel, Adventure and Discovery Journalism* (no city: Forward-Thinking Press, 2011); Barbara M. Freeman, *Kit's Kingdom: The Journalism of Kathleen Blake Coleman* (Don Mills, ON: Oxford University Press, 1989); Gloria T. Hull, ed., *The Works of Alice Dunbar-Nelson*, vol. 3 (New York: Oxford University Press, 1988).

4. Martin Dugard, *Into Africa: The Epic Adventures of Stanley and Livingstone* (New York: Broadway Books, 2003), 279; Alan Moorehead, *The White Nile* (New York: Perennial, 2000), 122–123.

5. Dugard, *Into Africa*, 286.

6. Robert Campbell, *In Darkest Alaska: Travel and Empire along the Inside Passage* (Philadelphia: University of Pennsylvania Press, 2007), 31; Frank Luther Mott, *A History of American Magazines, 1885–1905*, vol. 4 (Cambridge: Harvard University Press, 1957), 96.

7. N. W. Ayer, *N. W. Ayer and Son's American Newspaper Annual* (Philadelphia, 1890), 504; David Reed, *The Popular Magazine in Britain and the United States of America, 1880–1960* (Toronto: University of Toronto Press, 1997), 50–53; Brayton Harris, *Blue and Gray in Black and White: Newspapers in the Civil War* (Dulles, VA: Batsford Brassey, 1999), 12. Harris notes that one issue of *Leslie's*, which featured news of a prize fight, sold 347,000 copies.

8. Campbell, *In Darkest Alaska*, 28–30; *Frank Leslie's Illustrated Newspaper*, April 5, 1890, 190.

9. Melody Webb, *Yukon: The Last Frontier* (Vancouver: University of British Columbia Press, 1993), 116; Branson, *The Life and Times of John W. Clark*, 167. Schanz had worked as an assistant astronomer at the Allegheny Observatory in New York before turning to journalism. Wells had traveled approximately 2,000 miles through the Yukon and Alaska in 1889. For more, see "Will Map Out Alaska," *The Tribune* (Great Falls, MT), March 19, 1890.

10. Webb, *Yukon*, 116.

11. Because virtually all of the articles were headlined "Our Alaska Expedition," this research uses citations that include the date of each article, including on second and subsequent references, to clarify which issues of *Leslie's* is being referenced.

12. For example, see "To Explore Alaska," *Daily Tobacco Leaf-Chronicle* (Clarksville, TN), March 14, 1890; "Will Map Out Alaska" and "Will Explore Alaska," *Daily Morning Astorian*, April 27, 1890.

13. E. H. Wells, "Our Alaska Expedition," *Frank Leslie's Illustrated Newspaper*, July 4, 1891; Schanz provided

details of his illness and recuperation in the September 26, 1891, issue. Schanz, "Our Alaska Expedition," *Frank Leslie's Illustrated Newspaper*, Sept. 26, 1891.

14. Many newspapers covered the story. For a sample of stories, see "Two Explorers Missing," *Pittsburg Dispatch*, Jan. 5, 1891; "Lost in a Wilderness," *New Castle (PA) News*, Jan. 7, 1891; "Trouble Among Alaskan Travellers," *New York Sun*, Dec. 15, 1890; Branson, *The Life and Times of John W. Clark*, 171. See also Alfred S. Johnson, ed., "Alaska," *The Quarterly Register of Current History*, vol. 1 (Detroit: The Evening News Association, 1892), 294. St. Michael was the headquarters for the Alaska Commercial Company and the Western Fur and Trading Company. It held a village, a fort, and warehouses. For more, see Webb, *Yukon*, 67.

15. Michael Gates, *Gold at Fortymile Creek: Early Days in the Yukon* (Vancouver: University of British Columbia Press, 1994), 59; "Terrors of Ice and Snow," *Indianapolis Journal*, May 3, 1891.

16. The quote is attributed to U.S. Senator Henry Cabot Lodge who in 1895 said of America's foreign policy: "From the Rio Grande to the Arctic Ocean there should be one flag and one country." Quoted in Campbell, *In Darkest Alaska*, 20.

17. Webb, *Yukon*, 118.

18. Both were quoted in an editorial in *Leslie's*. See "Adventures in Alaska," *Frank Leslie's Illustrated Newspaper*, June 20, 1891, 331.

19. The June 20, 1891, article focused on Alaska's resources and its possible contribution, as a territory, to the United States. For a scholarly assessment of the role of the American West as central to the national economy in the post-civil war years, see David R. Roediger and Elizabeth D. Esch, *The Production of Difference: Race and the Management of Labor in U.S. History* (New York: Oxford: 2014), 68.

20. Alexander Saxton, *The Rise and Fall of the White Republic: Class Politics and Mass Culture in Nineteenth-Century America* (New York: Verso, 2003), 147; Reginald Horsman, *Race and Manifest Destiny: The Origins of American Racial Anglo-Saxonism* (Cambridge: Harvard University Press, 1981), 83–84. The argument put forth by white writers was a straightforward one: Since Anglo-Saxons were a "superior" race with "superior" ideas, civilization, and culture, white Americans were destined to control the continent. For more, see Shelly Streeby, *American Sensations: Class, Empire and The Production of Popular Culture* (Berkeley: University of California Press, 2002), 170.

21. John Sears, *Sacred Places: American Tourist Attractions in the Nineteenth Century* (New York: Oxford University Press, 1999), 2–8; Marguerite S. Shaffer, *America First: Tourism and National Identity, 1880–1940* (Washington, D. C.: Smithsonian Institution Press, 2001), 3–4.

22. *Ibid.*

23. For a few representative samples, see M. H. Dunlop, *Sixty Miles from Contentment: Traveling the 19th Century American Interior* (New York: Basic Books, 1995); Richard Howard, ed., *Henry James: Collected Travel Writings: Great Britain and America* (New York: Library of America, 1993); Mary Suzanne Schriber, ed., *Telling Travels: Selected Writings by Nineteenth-Century American Women Abroad* (DeKalb: Northern Illinois University Press, 1994); Katrina J. Quinn, "'Across the Continent … And Still the Republic!' Inscribing Nationhood in Samuel Bowles's Newspaper Letters of 1865," *American Journalism* 31, no. 4 (2014): 468–489.

24. Henry Nash Smith's classic work, *Virgin Land*, traces mediated views of the American West throughout the nineteenth century via fiction and non-fiction writers and details how the authors' personal views, social stereotypes, literary conventions, prejudices, politics, and social theories affected their constructed images of the West. See Henry Nash Smith, *Virgin Land: The American West as Symbol and Myth* (Cambridge: Harvard University Press, 2001).

25. Joy S. Kasson notes that William F. "Buffalo Bill" Cody, as well as other showmen, authors, and playwrights, used history, drama, and nostalgia to construct visions of the American West. Joy S. Kasson, *Buffalo Bill's Wild West: Celebrity, Memory, and Popular History* (New York: Hill and Wang, 2000), 20–27, 85.

26. John D. Unruh, Jr., *The Plains Across: The Overland Emigrants and the Trans-Mississippi West, 1840–1860* (Urbana: University of Illinois Press, 1993), 397–399; Smith, *Virgin Land*, 211.

27. David H. Murdoch, *The American West: The Invention of a Myth* (Reno: University of Nevada Press, 2001), 25.

28. Murdoch, *The American West*, 10; Robert P. Porter, the Superintendent of the 1890 U.S. Census, declared that the western part of the United States had so many settlements that "there can hardly be said to be a frontier line." Alaska, therefore, became a new frontier for American citizens. Gerald D. Nash, "The Census of 1890 and the Closing of the Frontier," *Pacific Northwest Quarterly* 71, no. 3 (1980): 98.

29. David Reed, *The Popular Magazine in Britain and the United States of America, 1880–1960* (Toronto: University of Toronto Press, 1997), 54–55.

30. David B. Sachsman and David W. Bulla, eds., *Sensationalism: Murder, Mayhem, Mudslinging, Scandals, and Disasters in 19th-Century Reporting* (New Brunswick, NJ: Transaction Publishers, 2013), xxiv.

31. Paul Sothe Holbo, *Tarnished Expansion: The Alaska Scandal, the Press, and Congress, 1867–1871* (Knoxville: University of Tennessee Press, 1983); Lisa Trimble Actor, "Surveying Seward's Folly: The U.S. Coast Survey in Alaska," *Alaska Journal* 16 (1986): 28–35.

32. "We intend to own this continent," the *Charleston (SC) Daily News* stated. "We have the satisfaction of knowing that when we do go back into the Union, it will be a considerably larger Union than when we left it." "The Russian Treaty," *Charleston (SC) Daily News*, April 12, 1867.

33.  Alaska Department of Fish and Game. "Rivers and Lakes." www.adfg.alaska.gov/index.cfm?adfg=rivers. main.

34.  Joshua Brown, *Beyond the Lines: Pictorial Reporting, Everyday Life, and the Crisis of Gilded Age America* (Berkeley: University of California Press, 2006), 172–173, 234.

35.  Claus M. Naske and Herman E. Slotnick, *Alaska: A History* (Norman: University of Oklahoma Press, 2014), 33–122; Corey Ford, *Where the Sea Breaks Its Back: The Epic Story of Early Naturalist Georg Stellar and the Russian Exploration of Alaska* (Portland, OR: Alaska Northwest Books, 2003).

36.  C. E. S. Wood, "Among the Thlinkits [*sic*] in Alaska," *Century Magazine*, July 1882, 323. The *New-York Times* had sent explorer Frederick Schwatka on an 1886 expedition to climb Mount St. Elias. He gained fame for his 1883 exploration of the Yukon River for the U.S. Army. He produced a popular book, *Along Alaska's Great River*, in 1885, which detailed the 1,300 mile journey, the longest raft journey in recorded history. For more, see Martin Sandler, *Resolute: The Epic Search for the Northwest Passage and John Franklin, and the Discovery of the Queen's Ghost Ship* (New York: Sterling Publishing, 2006), 247–248. For more on journalistic and literary works on Alaska prior to 1890, see Campbell, *In Darkest Alaska*, 18–35.

37.  Murdoch, *The American West*, 10

38.  The articles pertaining to the men's winter explorations can be found in the following issues: Sept. 11, 1891, Sept. 19, 1891, Oct. 3, 1891, Oct. 10, 1891, Oct. 22, 1891, Oct. 31, 1891, Nov. 7, 1891, and Nov. 14, 1891.

39.  Branson, *The Life and Times of John W. Clark*, 168–190. Schanz noted that another census enumerater, W. C. Greenfield, also accompanied them during Schanz's and Clark's 700-mile canoe journey to Nushagak. Schanz, "Our Alaska Expedition," *Frank Leslie's Illustrated Newspaper*, Sept. 26, 1891, 121.

40.  Nadine Muller and Joanne Ella Parsons, "The Male Body in Victorian Literature and Culture," *Nineteenth Century Contexts: An Interdisciplinary Journal* 36, no. 4 (2014): 304. "Adventures in Alaska," *Frank Leslie's Illustrated Newspaper*, June 20, 1891, 331.

41.  Schanz, "Our Alaska Expedition," *Frank Leslie's Illustrated Newspaper*, Sept. 26, 1891, 122.

42.  Schanz, "Our Alaska Expedition," *Frank Leslie's Illustrated Newspaper*, Oct. 10, 1891, 156.

43.  Schanz wrote about his explorations around Nushagak and his eventual "discovery" of Lake Clark in four editions of *Leslie's*: the Oct. 3, Oct. 10, Oct. 31, and Nov. 14, issues of 1891.

44.  Schanz, "Our Alaska Expedition," *Frank Leslie's Illustrated Newspaper*, Nov. 7, 1891, 224. Schanz noted in his Nov. 14, 1891, article that despite the winter hardships, his team had explored three regions, discovered three streams and the territory's second largest lake, settled the source of the Iliamna's water supply, and taken the census of sixteen native villages. "We were satisfied with the record," he stated. Schanz, "Our Alaska Expedition," *Frank Leslie's Illustrated Newspaper*, Nov. 14, 1891, 241.

45.  *Ibid.*

46.  E. H. Wells, "Our Alaska Expedition," *Frank Leslie's Illustrated Newspaper*, June 27, 1891, 335.

47.  Wells, "Our Alaska Expedition," *Frank Leslie's Illustrated Newspaper*, June 27, 1891, 355.

48.  *Ibid.*

49.  Wells, "Our Alaska Expedition," *Frank Leslie's Illustrated Newspaper*, Sept. 19, 1891, 106.

50.  Wells, "Our Alaska Expedition," *Frank Leslie's Illustrated Newspaper*, June 27, 1891, 355.

51.  "Mr. Wells' Statement," *Frank Leslie's Illustrated Newspaper*, June 20, 1891, 340. Schanz made similar statements in a June 20, 1891, article. Sniffing dismissively at "parlor explorers" who gave the public misinformation, Schanz said Alaska was little known and much of what was in print about the territory was untrue. Schanz, "EXPLORING ALASKA!" *Frank Leslie's Illustrated Newspaper*, June 20, 1891, 337.

52.  *Ibid.*

53.  E. J. Glave, "Our Alaska Expedition," *Frank Leslie's Illustrated Newspaper*, July 19, 1890, 507, 510. Also see the Sept. 6, 1890, article by Glave. "Magnificent scenery surrounds us on all sides, bold rugged-peaked mountains line each side of the lake and fall away in forest-clad foothills to the water's edge," he stated. Glave, "Our Alaska Expedition," *Frank Leslie's Illustrated Newspaper*, Sept. 6, 1890, 86.

54.  Schanz, "Our Alaska Expedition," *Frank Leslie's Illustrated Newspaper*, Sept. 26, 1891, 122.

55.  Nash, *Virgin Land*, 211; Monica Rio, *Nature's Noblemen: Transatlantic Masculinities and the Nineteenth Century American West* (New Haven: Yale University Press, 2013), 9; Unruh, Jr., *The Plains Across*, 397; Murdoch, *The American West*, 3; Deborah L. Madsen, *American Exceptionalism* (Jackson, MS: University Press of Mississippi, 1998), 74.

56.  A. B. Schanz, "Exploring Alaska!" *Frank Leslie's Illustrated Newspaper*, June 20, 1891, 337; "Mr. Wells's Statement," *Frank Leslie's Illustrated Newspaper*, June 20, 1891, 337.

57.  Campbell, *In Darkest Alaska*, 80–81.

58.  Wells, "Mr. Wells' Statement"; Schanz, "EXPLORING ALASKA!" 337; Murdoch, *The American West*, 9.

59.  Wells, "Our Alaska Expedition," *Frank Leslie's Illustrated Newspaper*, Sept. 5, 1891, 75. Also see Glave's accounts of Aug. 9, 1890, and Sept. 6, 1890.

60.  The journalists occasionally acknowledged the value of their native guides, but always put themselves, as white men, at the forefront of leadership. Two illustrations demonstrate that the journalists were far from rugged explorers, however. An illustration on page 575 of the August 9, 1890, issue shows Glave being rescued by native guides after a fall down a crevice (one that most likely would have killed him, hence the probability

that the image was exaggerated); and an image on page 289 of the May 30, 1891, issue that shows the white journalists being carried on the backs of native guides during the fording of a river.

61. See the articles of Oct. 31, 1891, and Nov. 7, 1891, for positive views of native peoples.

62. Campbell, *In Darkest Alaska*, 143–183.

63. *Ibid.*, 152.

64. E. J. Glave, "The *Frank Leslie's Newspaper* Alaska Expedition," *Frank Leslie's Illustrated Newspaper*, July 19, 1890, 510.

65. *Ibid.*

66. Webb, *Yukon*.

67. Glave, "The *Frank Leslie's Newspaper* Alaska Expedition."

68. Glave, "The *Frank Leslie's Newspaper* Alaska Expedition." Another article of the same title, that ran June 20, 1891, on p. 332, "Alaska Pictures. Totems," was not written by the men and seems to have been written by an editor, but reflected the "otherness" of the natives and the lack of respect of peoples of color that was common at the time. "A totem is a class of objects which is regarded by a savage with superstitious respect, believing that there exists between him and every member of the class an intimate and peculiarly special relation." Wells' article of October 1, 1890, pronounced the native peoples as friendly, but filthy. "These Mahlemutes have no idea of cleanliness. Bathing is unknown to them." Wells, "Our Alaska Expedition," *Frank Leslie's Illustrated Newspaper*, Oct. 1, 1890, 75. An article by Schanz published October 10, 1891, pejoratively noted that the native men were "too dull" to comprehend the purpose of census questions (Schanz, "Our Alaska Expedition," *Frank Leslie's Illustrated Newspaper*, Oct. 10, 1891, 156). Such views of Alaska's native peoples were common among white visitors to Alaska. See Campbell, *In Darkest Alaska*, 144–147.

69. Schanz, "Our Alaska Expedition," *Frank Leslie's Illustrated Newspaper*, Oct. 31, 1892.

70. Wells, "Our Alaska Expedition," *Frank Leslie's Illustrated Newspaper*, Oct.1, 1890, 75. The journalists held only one native guide consistently in high regard, a middle-aged man known as "Indiank," whose portrait ran in the September 5, 1891, issue of Leslie's. Indiank, whose real name was Duckaskinaw Sinquoquada, had joined the *Leslie's* explorers from the time the men arrived via *The Patterson*, a U.S. Coast Guard and Geodetic Survey ship, at Pyramid Harbor by the mouth of the Chilkat River. Indiank was a veteran guide, having worked with Frederick Schwatka during his explorations of Alaska in 1883. For more on Schwatka's explorations for the U.S. military, see Webb, *Yukon*, 104–106.

71. *Annual Report of the Commissioner of Indian Affairs to the Secretary of the Interior for the Year 1887* (Washington, DC: Government Printing Office, 1887), xix.

72. Wells, "Our Alaska Expedition," *Frank Leslie's Illustrated Newspaper*, Oct. 1, 1890, 75; Webb, *Yukon*, 171–174; Madsen, *American Exceptionalism*, 50 and 55.

73. Webb, *Yukon: The Last Frontier*, 117–118.

# Teresa Howard Dean

*Reporting Tragedies and Triumphs
from the American West*

PAULETTE D. KILMER

From the safety of her desk at the *Chicago Herald* in the fall of 1890, Teresa Howard Dean warned readers about the laziness of the Sioux. With other tribal nations, she referred to them generically as "Indian," portraying them as inferior people united by their worst trait: difference from white Christians.[1] Perhaps, thinking about the Sioux from afar piqued Dean's curiosity. And soon, it would be time to set out for herself, because that winter, hundreds of Sioux would be mercilessly slaughtered at the hands of the U.S. Cavalry in one of the most horrifying massacres in U.S. history, the Battle of Wounded Knee, on December 29, 1890. Dean wanted to join *Herald* reporters Sam Clover and Charles Seymour on site. Setting out in early 1891, Dean didn't know quite what to expect. *Herald* Editor Jimmy Scott gave her a small revolver, a Pullman ticket, and press credentials. Dean donned her warm gray ulster and wool cap, packed her bags, and boarded the night train headed west from Chicago on January 12. She would see for herself the scene of the carnage, one of the most tragic and historically significant encounters of the growing United States and the native peoples of the West.

This essay examines the adventure reportage of Dean, a widely read reporter for the *Chicago Herald* and the *Chicago Inter-Ocean*, from the western plains in that fateful winter of 1891, as well as her subsequent reportage from two of the events that would celebrate America's national and technological stature at the end of the nineteenth century: the World's Columbian Exposition of 1893 and its immediate successor, San Francisco's California Midwinter Exposition of 1894. Unlike other adventure reporters of the Gilded Age, Dean's career was not forged in the saddle or the jungle; instead, inspired by the staggering heartbreak of Wounded Knee and the strangely antithetical, constructed displays of the global exotic at the world expositions of 1893 and 1894, she strove for a glimpse at the sensational human tragedies and triumphs of the day. She sought anecdotes, eyewitness accounts, and striking details, accepting the dangers inherent in traveling alone to get the inside scoop. But when given the opportunity to cross boundaries and transcend common stereotypes, Dean's reporting shows she often preferred fiction to reality.

## An Unlikely Choice for Adventure

Born around 1852, Dean spent her childhood in tomboy pursuits after her parents moved from New York to Appleton, Wisconsin. She came of age as a growing number of women college graduates excelled in jobs considered unladylike. As girls grew up, they emulated suffrage activist Susan B. Anthony, whose life proved a single woman could support herself and earn public approval even as she broke entrenched codes of social respectability. Dean would later acknowledge changing standards in areas such as education and entertainment in her popular writings on women's topics.[2]

In this era of robber barons and social upheaval, women pursued careers, defying gendered expectations. Indeed, Dean, who had studied art at Appleton's Lawrence College, married and gave birth to a son, but when the marriage ended,[3] she closed her prosperous arts studio and stopped freelancing travel pieces for the Appleton *Crescent*.[4] She moved to Chicago circa 1884 and sold pen and crayon sketches until 1889, when she discovered a knack for a different type of sketch: the verbal kind. She began writing weekly items as "Theo" for the *Herald* and as "Sis" for the *Chicago Tribune*. By August 1890, she cut her ties with the *Tribune*, trading her genteel ways for the rowdy life of an editorial-page columnist with the *Chicago Herald*.[5]

As one of the Gilded Age's bold "ladies of the press," she insisted from her first "Snap Shot" that her name appear with her columns and developed a form of human-interest writing that focused on individual experience as the center of her reportage.[6] Employing "great versatility and sympathetic touches" as one of Chicago's best-known reporters, Dean built her reputation on being "bright and good,"[7] writing in a decidedly personal style.

Dean was, at first glance, an unlikely choice for an adventure journalist. The woman who became known for traveling solo through the West, and who later served as a war correspondent, had come to fame by penning a popular beauty book for women titled *How to Be Beautiful: Nature Unmasked: A Book for Every Woman*. Similar to some of her previous women's page columns, the 1889 tome gave advice about bathing, exercising, the importance of corsets, how to develop an agreeable and fascinating personality, and weight loss. Dean encouraged women to drink Claret instead of water as a weight loss technique and provided recipes for cold creams, perfumes, and hair shampoos.[8] But her buoyant style would earn her a place in an 1895 article on American press women that noted Dean's "chatty" columns "have made thousands of readers claim her as their particular friend."[9]

## Peeks Across a Boundary at Pine Ridge

It would be in 1891, following the massacre at Wounded Knee, that Dean launched her search for a more serious journalistic adventure and the opportunity to report on something ultimately more worldly. It was a tense time. In the years following the Civil War, the quickly expanding nation had encroached on much of the Indian territories of the West, bringing tensions with indigenous peoples of the region to the boiling point. Native populations represented a direct challenge to the sovereignty of the nation and the actualization of the manifest destiny doctrine. After decades of tension and outright warfare, the press continued to play its role in constructing Indians as "other" in a lose-lose scenario, depicting those who defended their lands as brutal or savage, while depicting those found to be docile or compliant as lazy or unintelligent. This rhetoric fueled the ideal of American expansionism, justified violence, and provided support for anti–Indian policy in Washington.

By 1889, as the bleak outlook for native sovereignty became more and more certain, desperate communities seized on a spiritualist movement that provided hope. Born in the Paiute nation of Nevada, the Ghost Dance movement promised a ritualistic reunification of the souls of the living and the dead, by which the white invaders would be removed and the overhunted buffalo would return to save the people from starvation.[10] "Indians embraced the Ghost Dance and the last hope of salvation it offered," according to historian Robert M. Utley. "When the miracles failed to occur, the reality of their political subordination could no longer be denied or ignored."[11] Tragically, the ritual raised concern among white settlers, who misinterpreted the ritual as prelude to military attack.[12] As the U.S. Cavalry attempted to disarm the Lakota, a rifle discharged and the soldiers attacked, leaving between 250 and 300 people, including many women and children, dead.

Just two weeks later, Dean was on her way. As the sun rose on Dean's train, Illinois and Iowa were but a dream. Dust swirled everywhere across the open plains. Trees and grass rarely broke the brown monotony. She gasped at the occasional two-room sod houses where white settlers lived in remote, primitive conditions. Switching trains at the depot in Omaha, Dean later wrote, she saw farmers, homesteaders, and relatives of soldiers, who told her they were afraid of the Indians. "The only incentive to life is this fear of being scalped by red men," she said in her *Chicago Herald* dispatch on January 20, 1891.[13]

Like many of the era, Dean espoused racist views of Native Americans, and her widely read reportage helped perpetuate stereotypes. Articles like her "The Noble Red Man: He Has No Respect for Women of His or Any Other Race,"[14] which appeared in many newspapers, reinforced prejudices, even as the author prepared to enter native territory.[15] She also questioned an emerging social stereotype that had gained traction now that most Native Americans had been pacified and forced onto reservations: the image of the so-called "noble savage."[16] In a widely reprinted column titled "The Indian's Gratitude," Dean told readers in February 1891 that many Indians she encountered were unrepentant beggars rather than noble beings who lived in harmony with nature. Dean observed white settlers and travelers handing out cigarettes to Native American men, then claimed the result was that the men repeatedly came back for more tobacco and brought other members of their tribe who desired a smoke. "As beggars they are most supreme. The pride that their admirers trot out as symbols of their nobility never interferes with their pleading for pennies, nickels, dimes, tobacco or any thing else," Dean opined.[17] She interviewed everybody she could before catching a ride the next day on the Army courier wagon.[18]

When Dean arrived at Pine Ridge, she was one of only two female reporters, according to Charles W. Allen, the other being Mrs. Thomas Tibbles, there with her husband, of the *Omaha World-Herald*.[19] Dean found that the male newspaper correspondents covering the story treated her coolly, and only Seymour and George Harriss of the *New York Journal* supported her appearing in a group portrait. After fabricating blood-curdling accounts of their harrowing life on the frontier, the reporters may have dreaded looking silly if a fashionably dressed woman stood casually next to them in a photo.[20] Carolyn

Edy notes that, while the male reporters determined the frontier locale was "no place for a woman," Dean had the last laugh when she later disclosed that the male reporters "embellished, exaggerated, and, in some cases, made up their stories, and they were busier dressing the part and taking photographs of themselves than gathering news."[21]

Dean could not live in the tent with her two male *Herald* colleagues, and so she stayed at the government Indian boarding school, an opportunity to enter, in at least a cursory way, the world of the Sioux.[22] She made friends with the children who followed her. Dean later reported that she was stunned at the chinks in the walls, uncomfortable furniture, and matches so substandard that she heated them in the cooking stove before they would strike.[23] Outside, however, she knew even worse conditions confronted the Sioux as the government had not sent food—and without buffalo, the nation was on the brink of starvation.

Although she arrived after the Wounded Knee Massacre, Dean "furnished the news of the most exciting Indian battles during the campaign of General Nelson A. Miles" for the *Chicago Herald*, writing so vividly others later assumed she had witnessed the tragedy.[24] Edy lists Dean as one of few women who had "'scooped' or otherwise outdone a man in war correspondence" and who subsequently "saw the novelty of their experience as a woman overshadow the content and significance of any news they reported."[25] Questions about her gender surfaced in 1891 and again in 1895, as readers wondered if a woman could write with such fire and passion. Her "terse, graphic style" confused those who thought only male reporters told engaging true stories.[26]

Unable to stay in the tent with male reporters, Teresa Dean stayed at the Pine Ridge School for Indians, where she was appalled by the primitive conditions. Students at government boarding schools were taught English, industrial skills, and Christian principles (photograph by John C.H. Grabill, 1891, Library of Congress, Item cph.30a19793).

At Pine Ridge with General Miles, looking for adventure, "she scoured the country fearlessly on horseback under military escort and sometimes without it for news and impressions."[27] Dean convinced military officers she could handle herself and often took off on horseback alone. In late January, she borrowed a horse from General Miles to accompany a patrol recovering bodies of slain Sioux. Crossing "the treeless rolling prairie to White Horse Creek," Dean felt anxious because some Native American policemen and troop scouts rode behind her.[28] But what she saw upon arrival was not what she expected: the frozen corpses of a mother, her son, and two daughters. In an article published January 28, 1891, Dean admitted, "With a full understanding of the treachery in Indian nature, and that the same thing, and a thousand times worse, had occurred without number to white people, as I stood there and saw those three little children and their mother lying on their faces in the snow, it seemed to me to be nothing else than cold-blooded murder."[29] She watched as Red Hawk, a Sioux policeman with the agency, identified the bodies as his sister and her three children. They had been shot, he said, two days after the hostilities as they hid under a cliff. A broken doll lay beside one of the little girls. Yet Dean still was bound by the limitations of a racist ideology. "I realized," Dean wrote, prompting stark disappointment in the modern reader, "that the soul of a Sioux might possibly in its primitive state have started out on the same road as did the soul of a white man."[30]

After the U.S. government confiscated 7.7 million acres of the sacred Black Hills region of South Dakota from the Sioux tribe, officials in 1889 sent members of the Oglala Lakota to live on the newly established, resource-poor Pine Ridge Reservation (photo: John C. H. Grabil, "A Pretty Group at an Indian Tent," on or near Pine Ridge Reservation, 1891. Library of Congress, Item cph.3a240410).

## Reporting from the White City

Dean's stay on the Pine Ridge Reservation was not a long one, and she returned to Chicago educated but not reformed. She arrived with an Indian war bonnet, a gift from the Oglala Lakota Chief American Horse, which her editor placed atop a bust of Grover Cleveland in the business office.[31] Before long, the *Herald* sent Dean abroad to write human interest pieces from less exotic locations such as London and Paris,[32] continuing her focus on society reporting.[33] Holmes notes that "Many times she called herself a 'story hunter' or a 'cosmopolitan vagabond.'"[34]

Returning to the U.S., Dean would not have to travel far for her next glimpse of exotic cultures as she joined more than 27 million foreign visitors and U.S. citizens who marveled at the wonders of 200 temporary buildings and hundreds of exhibits at the World's Columbian Exposition, held in Chicago from May through October 1893.[35] In homage to the exposition's "White City," a group of fourteen Beaux Arts buildings constructed with a whitewashed mixture of plaster, cement, and fiber, Dean, now writing for Chicago's *Daily Inter Ocean*, titled her regular column "White City Chips."[36] The columns appeared in newspapers as widely dispersed as the Lansing, Minnesota, *Mower County Transcript*; the Burlington, Vermont, *Free Press*; and the Wichita, Kansas, *Daily Eagle*. "Teresa's experiences at the World's Fair were very interesting and worthy of preservation," Moses P. Handy, an *Inter Ocean* correspondent, asserted.[37] Praised as columns of "sparkle and wit," the reportage was reprinted in 1895 as a book, found by a contemporary reviewer to be "spicy and full of life."[38]

Immersing herself in events provided a perceptual stage for unique insights into the experiences of fair attendees. Diana Holmes notes that Dean focused on "the little incidents that 'just happen' on the fringe of the official Exposition spectacle." Much to the delight of the newspapers that ran her sketches, Dean tracked down lively leads by jumping over fences, walking along muddy roads, and consciously ignoring no-trespassing signs, according to Holmes.[39] Her approach to news marked an important form of human-interest reporting that captured the experiences of average citizens. Often penned by women journalists, this reporting established a credible role for the average citizen in modern public space. Besides grabbing the readers' attention, according to historian Alice Fahs, these human-interest stories empowered later generations of journalists to write about people regardless of their social status.[40] Dean shifted her form stylistically so that the words did not reveal her gender, setting as her goal "giving incidents of the days, as they rolled by so rapidly—to be only one of the people, to write my column for them, and from their standpoint."[41]

Capturing the exuberance of the Gilded Age, the lavish exposition, held in commemoration of the 400th anniversary of Christopher Columbus's "discovery" of America, was a future-oriented showcase of remarkable architecture, thrilling amusements, and technological innovation, featuring electric railways and moving walkways, experiments with artificial lightning, Kodaks, the Midway Ferris wheel, and many other more or less practical inventions. The fair also highlighted cultural otherness with constructed tableaux that served as ethnological exhibits, in tune with growing interest in global cultures. Dean reported on displays featuring Native Americans, Chinese, a belly dancer named "Little Egypt," and Buffalo Bill Cody's mixed-race company—all safe and scripted scenes of the exotic, interpreted through a paradigm of American exceptionalism and packaged for mass consumption.

The Chicago exposition of 1893 not only marked the end of the American frontier with the speech of Frederick Jackson Turner, but it heralded a new age of science, technology, and, with its remarkable Beaux-Arts architecture, the city of the future—here seen from the rooftop deck of the Manufactures and Liberal Arts Building, in a photograph by C. D. Arnold (The Art Institute of Chicago, digital ID 198902.E20807).

As a reporter with eastern ideals, Dean was not able to transcend racial assumptions concerning the original inhabitants of the West. Throughout her reportage on the exhibition and despite any human insight she may have gained during her time at Pine Ridge, Dean assessed Native Americans according to their compliance with or divergence from Indian stereotypes promulgated by popular culture. This simplistic dualism directed her, and thus her readers, to reinforce racist ideologies that rested on depiction of Native Americans as good or bad. In fact, Dean's White City Chips columns demonstrate that she preferred artificial presentations of native peoples and cultures to the experience of the real thing on the frontier. As an example, she was perturbed to find that Native Americans at the American Indian village, an exhibit on the Midway next door to the ostrich farm, were too pale to be interesting since they did not don war paint and feathers. She recommended they learn how to look authentic from Chief No Neck and the Sioux performing in Buffalo Bill's exhibition show.[42]

In "What Should Be Done with the American Indian," she described her conversation with Antonio Apache, a native orphan educated at Harvard, who was assisting Professor Putnam in presenting an ethnological exhibit of Plains Indians. Labeled a "good Indian" in Dean's column, Apache explained the mixed fate of educated Indians, who had limited opportunities in white society and, likewise, in native society. Many returned to the reservations trained in professions impossible to practice on the Great Plains. He lamented the loss of Native American life to disease and violence. Dean admitted, "I thought—I thought—I wished that things were different for the Indian."[43] Apache had stayed to work with the professor. "The United States Army can be proud of its way of civilizing an Indian," Dean reflected. "It does not send the Indian back to his tribe after he is educated. It allows him to work out his own salvation. Antonio will civilize even Geronimo if he brings him here."[44]

In multiple columns, Dean relayed anecdotes about other Native Americans appearing at the exhibition—human exhibits not of technology or architecture but of a mythic West that by 1893 was largely relegated to history. Among them was the Lakota warchief Rain-in-the-Face, reputed to have cut out Lieutenant Col. Thomas Custer's heart at Little Big Horn in 1876. Dean ridiculed another woman reporter—an opportunist, she believed—who proposed marriage to the 58-year-old chief. But Rain-in-the-Face had rejected her. He "scorned her fame, money, her," Dean wrote. "Miss Newspaper Woman from Cleveland went away much disgusted and disappointed." Dean scoffed at the Ohio writer who, she said, loved only a sensational story, concluding the groom needed just as much protection from the scheming bride as the crowd did from him scalping them.[45]

In another anecdote, she exhibited sympathy for a man named Chasing Fly, who stayed in his tent with his face hidden to mourn the death of his brother at Standing Rock. A translator relayed the visitors' condolences to him, and Chasing Fly extended his hand to Dean, smiling briefly. She contrasted this individual's docile behavior with the proud warchief. "In his blanket and paint, [Chasing Fly] looked more savage than Rain-in-the Face," Dean observed. "But they say he is a good Indian and never makes any trouble. Rain-in-the-Face pouts. He needs constant attention."[46] In a rare moment of sympathy, Dean urged skeptics to see the human being under the war paint and feathers. But her sympathy had disturbing limitations as she noted that "back of it all (the savage guise) there may be reasoning powers and a just resentment that the red man has not the opportunity to grow a soul, even if one should take root."

Among the most prominent features of the world's fair, and one which highlighted Dean's preference for artificial depictions of race relations, was the extravagant and popular exhibition of Buffalo Bill Cody. Dean had met the military scout, hunter, and show empresario in 1891 in South Dakota. Buffalo Bill had worked happily with Native Americans in his shows, which began just after the Civil War and gelled into a Wild West extravaganza by 1882. Later, Cody helped military leaders establish peace after the massacre on December 29, 1890, near Wounded Knee Creek on the Lakota Pine Ridge Indian Reservation. At the Chicago exhibition, his show spotlighted the history of American Indians from their perspective, and he employed Native Americans as performers. "Indians are quick to learn," he explained, "and I have never had any trouble with those I have taken hold of."[47]

Perhaps one reason Buffalo Bill and his Sioux prospered was because he treated them respectfully. Dean interviewed the living legend in the dining tent. The company, the show's business staff, and the representatives of all nations—U.S. Indians, Mexican and American soldiers, English Lancers from the Prince of Wales's Regiment, the Germans, the French, and the Russian Cossacks—all ate together at long tables. She declared if the Humane Society witnessed the lunch provisions, they would never question "the way Buffalo Bill feeds his Indians or other people entrusted to his care."[48] His lavish exposition ran until the end of October, lasting longer than the world's fair itself.

## Cultural Encounters in California

The World's Exposition was so popular that just a year later, 2.5 million individuals, including Dean, visited the California Midwinter Exposition at Golden Gate Park. From January to July 1894, visitors could see amazing attractions—some hauled directly from Chicago. Like the fair in Chicago, the California Exposition provided another artificial glimpse at the exotic through ethnological exhibits. With buildings and costumed performers of many ethnic backgrounds in residence, scenes included representations of life in colonial French Africa, Japan and the South Seas, an Alaskan Eskimo village, and "Oriental" locations which included Turkish, Greek, Algerian, and Egyptian scenes. Some exhibits were new, as in a Gold Rush exhibit and a gigantic knight made of prunes, symbolizing California's agricultural glories.

Continuing her columns, now titled "Golden Gate Chips," reprinted widely in newspapers across the country, Dean's work drew praise. *The (Phoenix) Arizona Republican* knew it would be a stellar event by the quality of the correspondents sent by eastern newspapers, including Teresa Dean. "The *Chicago Inter Ocean* has sent out a lady who has gained a well-deserved reputation in the journalistic field—Mrs. Teresa Dean Tallman, better known to eastern readers as 'Teresa Dean,'" the paper reported.[49]

ESQUIMAUX VILLAGE—REINDEER AND DOG TEAM.

**Dean and some 2.5 million other visitors admired cultural tableaux featuring Native Americans and other cultural groups in allegedly authentic environments. This facsimile of an "Esquimaux Village" was thus equipped with reindeer and plastered igloos (Library of Congress, Item 90712005).**

Contrary to California's reputation for balmy temperatures, San Francisco weather taught Dean what "chilled to the bone" meant. "It is a dampness so penetrating that nothing, no amount of clothing, checks or blocks its way."[50] She wore her warm coat, mittens, and hat to endure the rain that fell constantly during the first few days. Despite the cold, Dean's curiosity kept her warmly involved in reporting everyday scenes at the fair—like the pretty, smiling gum girl in her dark blue uniform, sailor's hat, and short skirt, who outsold the boys hawking guidebooks. Dean learned to distinguish a fiddle from a violin and paid $1.50 to master the Pacific Coast game, Keno. She took in an aerial view of the grounds from an enclosed car on the Firth Wheel, a smaller version of the Chicago Exposition Ferris Wheel, that rose 150 feet into the air. She and her companion, Jack, spotted the Hawaiian Village from the top and watched hula dancers. Dean decided the women's moves hit "a happy medium ... between the exercises propounded for all women as necessary to perfect health ... [and] the defended and denounced Egyptian dance of the [Chicago fair] Midway."[51]

But Dean's reporting from California included real-life cultural encounters as well. While in San Francisco, Dean ventured into San Francisco's Chinatown to "discover" this important immigrant group for herself. Dean was one of many late nineteenth-century journalists who penned exposés on the lives of immigrants for an anxious, post–War citizenry concerned with tenuous race relations, growing industrialization, mass immigration, and urban ills. Like other journalists, however, Dean's widely reprinted articles promoted racial stereotypes while also reinforcing Anglo-dominant ideologies. The very "otherness" of the Chinese made them both controversial and exotic.[52] Her articles on San Francisco's Chinatown, along with accompanying illustrations, highlighted the exotic nature of the immigrant group, but in an age of broad public anxieties about immigration, Dean's article, which emphasized the Chinese's use of opium, her portrayal of Chinese immigrants as lazy, and her mocking and misunderstanding of Chinese religious beliefs and customs made clear that this immigrant group was the antithesis of Americans.[53] Many of Dean's readers had never met a Chinese immigrant in person and thus learned about them through mediated images—via newspapers and magazines.[54]

Touring Chinatown, moreover, was not boundary-crossing for Dean, who remained decidedly on the periphery of what to her was a very alien culture. Visiting Chinatown's famous opium dens, she described "seven almond eyed Celestials" who "hoarded their piles of gold" and "burned sandalwood punk to keep the devil away." As Dean led readers down the underground tunnels, she claimed that if the sandalwood strategy failed, "I'm sure the combination of the other odors would lay low his Satanic Majesty if he tried to cross the threshold."[55] After taking tea in a restaurant and having the workings of an opium pipe explained to her, Dean and her companions were taken on a tour of Chinese workers' meager basement homes. Dean displayed her ignorance to readers by assuming that the Chinese word for homes was "holes" since the immigrants referred to their dank, tightly confining basement quarters as such.[56]

Dean's pictorial description of Chinatown reflected her Anglo-American readers' cultural norms and social expectations. Her urban adventure through Chinatown, although undoubtedly born of her innate curiosity, was part of the slumming phenomenon, common in the 1880s and 1890s. The phenomenon began in London before spreading to New York and other cities. Middle- and upper-class citizens in both America and England were simultaneously drawn to—and horrified by—their nation's urban ills. Although many wealthy citizens believed that slums were the result of poor citizens'

Dean found the sights, sounds, and smells of San Francisco's Chinatown quite exotic. She visited during a time of mounting anxiety about immigration—not to mention the growing reputation of the district for vice in the form of opium dens, gambling, and prostitution (Library of Congress, Item cph.3b17743).

laziness, vices, or sins, the brief urban tourism movement called slumming was motivated for some by "curiosity, excitement and thrill" while "others were motivated by moral, religious, and altruistic reasons."[57] The "spatial separation" between rich and poor brought on by rapid industrialization and urbanization led both rich and poor to be, as the *New York Times* noted, "as ignorant [of each other] as if they were inhabitants of a strange country."[58]

## *"Entrusted with … the greatest responsibility"*

Unlike many daring and often inspirational adventure journalists, Dean was constrained by boundaries. Unable to transcend intellectual and ideological barriers, Dean held fast to the prejudices of her day despite adventures that brought her into contact with native peoples of the West. She preferred the artificial tableaux of foreign cultures that rendered them harmless spectacles within a panoply of American exceptionalism. Her writing thus reified racial disparities and reinforced ideologies that would lead to racist social practices and legislation. Still, the Native Americans and the Chinese whom Dean visited allowed her to provide readers with vivid portrayals of the exotica that they craved from within their own national borders.

Despite her perceptual limitations, Dean joined the ranks of women who proved themselves credible storytellers in the pages of Gilded Age newspapers. From her first contribution, Dean's signature appeared below her articles, a rare honor for any reporter, and rarer still for women. She zealously shed the old-fashioned expectations of what "ladies" wrote. Instead, she earned praise from the *Indianapolis Sun* as one of the women "entrusted with 'assignments' of the greatest responsibility [who] are invariably doing their work with great credit to themselves and their papers."[59] She helped organize professional associations to advance women writers, including the Illinois Woman's Press Association, founded in 1885. Moreover, Dean, "a staunch and true friend" to her peers, welcomed newcomers into journalism and offered them advice enthusiastically because "she [believed] there is always room for one more competent woman."[60]

The editor of the *Indianapolis Sun* considered this to be Dean's most stellar accomplishment: ownership of her writing career. "It is becoming quite evident that to some extent, at least, woman is the coming man in journalism," the *Sun* editor observed. "And Teresa H. Dean is quite close to the head of the procession."[61]

## NOTES

1. John Coward, *The Newspaper Indian: Native American Identity in the Press, 1820–90* (Champaign: University of Illinois Press, 1999), 26–27.

2. "Gossipy Gleanings," *Troy (NY) Times,* August 14, 1890, p. 2. The roundup of women's interest items reprinted Teresa Dean's call in the *Chicago Herald* for a woman's bicycling costume.

3. Douglas C. Jones, "Teresa Dean: Lady Correspondent Among the Sioux Indians," *Journalism and Mass Communication Quarterly* (1972): 656–662. Jones writes that Dean was once divorced and once widowed. She left Chicago to join the staff of the *Town Topics,* "a New York scandal sheet with an extremely clouded reputation," which has resulted in librarians not preserving that newspaper and much of Dean's work being difficult to access, according to Jones.

4. "Personals," *The Appleton (WI) Crescent,* September 10, 1881, 3.

5. Alice Fahs, *Out on Assignment: Newspaper Women and the Making of Modern Public Space* (Chapel Hill: University of North Carolina Press, 2011), 98–99. For more on the Chicago media in the nineteenth century, see Richard Junger, *Becoming the Second City: Chicago's Mass News Media, 1833–1898* (Urbana: University of Illinois Press, 2010).

6. "Four Women Who Write. They Represent Eastern Newspapers and Will Describe the Fair. Their Journalistic Feats. Mrs. A.V.H. Wakeman, Teresa Dean, Mrs. M.C. Knapp and Miss Colby—Their Personality and Their Plans," *San Francisco Examiner,* February 25, 1894, 16. See also Ishbel Ross, *Ladies of the Press* (New York: Arno, 1974).

7. The report of her studying the Indians appeared in *The (Indianapolis, IN) Sun,* No headline, January 29, 1891. The observations about her character originated in "She Is Bright and Good. Teresa Dean a Representative of the Coming Woman. Author of White City Chips. Her Notes on the World's Fair and Letters from Abroad Gave Here Well Earned Fame—Will Be the Star of the I.W. P. A. Convention," *The (IL) Morning Star,* June 16, 1895.

8. Teresa Dean, *How to be Beautiful: Nature Unmasked: a Book for Every Woman* (Chicago: T. Howard, Publisher, 1889).

9. "Women of the Press," *Defiance Daily Crescent,* March 29, 1895. This article was published in numerous newspapers across the nation.

10. For details on federal policy and personal failures that led to the Sioux Indians starving on their

reservations, see Guy Gibbon, *The Sioux: The Dakota and Lakota Nations* (Malden, MA.: Wiley-Blackwell, 2003), 135–144.

11. For more on the Ghost Dance, see Robert M. Utley, *The Indian Frontier of the American West, 1846–1890* (Albuquerque: University of New Mexico Press, 1989), 261.

12. Utley, *The Indian Frontier of the American West.* Wounded Knee served as a watershed moment, after which "the Sioux resignedly submitted to the reservation system and thus implicitly surrendered the last vestiges of sovereignty to the invader," according to Utley, 261.

13. Jones, "Teresa Dean: Lady Correspondent Among the Sioux Indians," 658.

14. "The Noble Red Man. He Has No Respect for Women of His or Any Other Race. Teresa H. Dean in Chicago Herald," *Indianapolis Journal*, February 2, 1891. For another difficult example of her racist rhetoric, specifically calling the Sioux "reptiles," see "Two Views of Lo." [signed Teresa Dean] *Troy (NY) Times*, January 1, 1891.

15. Coward, *The Newspaper Indian*, 25–28.

16. See S. Elizabeth Bird, ed. *Dressing in Feathers: The Construction of the Indian in American Popular Culture* (New York: Routledge, 2018), 4.

17. "The Indian's Gratitude," *Logansport Reporter*, February 14, 1891.

18. Jones, "Teresa Dean: Lady Correspondent Among the Sioux Indians," 658.

19. Charles W. Allen, *From Fort Laramie to Wounded Knee: In the West That Was* (Lincoln: University of Nebraska Press, 1997), 261 note 1.

20. "He Was A Daring Man. That New York Correspondent. Did He Not Risk His Precious Life by Traveling in Care, Eating in All Sorts of Places and Letting His Whiskers Grow?" [signed Teresa Dean] *Chicago (IL) Herald*, February 5, 1891, 9.

21. Carolyn M. Edy, *The Woman War Correspondent, the U.S. Military, and the Press: 1846–1947* (London: Lexington Books, 2017), 20.

22. Nancy M. Peterson, "The Unwanted Female Reporter at Wounded Knee," *Wild West*, December 2011, pp. 42–48. Also at Historynet at www.historynet.com/ wild-west-december-2011-table-of-contents.htm.

23. Jones, "Teresa Dean: Lady Correspondent Among the Sioux Indians," 659.

24. "The Midwinter Fair. An Interview with Mr. John Armstrong on the Pacific Display," *(Phoenix) Arizona Republican*, February 15, 1894.

25. Edy, *The Woman War Correspondent, the U.S. military, and the Press*, 18.

26. *The (Indianapolis, IN) Sun*, January 29, 1891, 2.

27. "A Woman War Correspondent," (Washington, DC) *Evening Star*, May 21, 1898, 1. Both quotations originate in this source.

28. "Over Wounded Knee. Search for the Body of a Squaw. Red Hawk's Sister and Her Children Found Cold in Death—The Troops Reviewed and the Hospital Visited—An Indian Curiosity." [Signed "Teresa Dean."] *Chicago Herald*, January 28, 1891, 9.

29. *Ibid.*

30. Jones, "Teresa Dean: Lady Correspondent Among the Sioux Indians," 656–662.

31. Marcia Winn, "Teresa Dean's Clippings Given to Medill School," *Chicago Tribune*, July 6, 1941, 9.

32. "At the Graves of the Great, And Amid the Haunts of the Fashionable in Lunnon Town. Snap Shots on Rotten Row—A Visit to Famous St. Paul's and Westminster Abby. An American Hero-Worshiper in England," *San Francisco Morning Call*, August 30, 1891, 14. "State Jottings," *Milwaukee Weekly Wisconsin*, August 21, 1891, p. 6. This news appeared in a paragraph without a headline.

33. "Points about People," *Oshkosh Northwestern*, June 23, 1891, 2. "Personals," *Appleton (WI) Crescent*, September 12, 1891, p. 5.

34. Diana Holmes, David Platton, Loic Artiago, and Jacques Migozzi, eds. *Finding the Plot: Storytelling in Popular Fictions* (Tyne, UK: Cambridge Scholars Publishing, 2014), 142.

35. For details about the Chicago World's Fair, which was also referred to as the Columbian World Exposition or the Chicago Columbian Exposition, see the link at the Chicago Historical Society, "The World's Columbian Exposition," at www.chicagohs.org/history/expo.html.

36. "Who Is Teresa Dean? Queries Respecting the Writer of 'White City Chips.' Many Persons Curious. Ask Whether the Contributor is a Man or a Woman. Some of the Correspondents Reason Cleverly and Hail Teresa as a Sister," *Chicago (IL) Inter Ocean*, November 6, 1893, 7. The quotation subhead and all the quotations in the paragraph appear in this story.

37. "Major Handy's Letter. Facts, Fancies, and Stories with a Sprinkling of Opinions," *(Chicago, IL) Inter Ocean*, February 14, 1894, 6.

38. "Current Literature Writings of Alexander Dumas—Bookbinding Old and New. L. Prang & Co. Art Work. In Unknown Seas—California—Poems of the Farm. Two Years on the Alabama—A Hidden Faith—An Occult Story—Domesticated Animals," *(Chicago, IL) Inter Ocean*, December 7, 1895, 9.

39. Holmes, *Finding the Plot*, 141–142.

40. Fahs, *Out on Assignment*, 98–99.

41. *Ibid.*, 95.

42. "White City Chips. Teresa Dean Sees Queer Things at The Fair. Gondoliers Are Real. And the Board

of Lady Managers Dissolves. Geronimo, the Apache, to Visit the Exposition, Guided by Antonio, the Good Indian," *(Chicago, IL) Inter Ocean*, August 15, 1893, 7.

43.   "What Should Be Done with the American Indian? Plaint of an Apache. Has No Opportunity to Profit by Education. Injustice Which Arises from Ignorance of the Red Man's True Condition." [signed Teresa Dean] *(Chicago, IL) Inter Ocean*, September 15, 1893, 7. The quotations in this paragraph originate in this article.

44.   "White City Chips. Teresa Dean Sees Queer Things at The Fair. *(Chicago, IL) Inter Ocean*, August 15, 1893, 7.

45.   "White City Chips. Teresa Dean Passes a Day on the Midway. Music and Savagery. She Told the Truth and Was Allowed to Talk. Miss Newspaper Woman Seeks Fame and the Hand of Rain-in-the-Face," *(Chicago, IL) Inter Ocean*, October 6, 1893, 7.

46.   *Ibid.*

47.   "Buffalo Bill and the Indians. Danger of More Troubles If They Are Not Treated Right," *Chicago (IL) Herald*, February 5, 1891, 3.

48.   "Men Who Can Ride. Buffalo Bill's Camp of Roughriders of All Nations. Arabs of the Desert. Cavalrymen of the Steppes and Their Chief. Teresa Dean Dines with Colonel Cody and Views His Cossacks and Lancers," *(Chicago, IL) Inter Ocean*, April 20, 1893, 7.

49.   At the time, Dean was married to Dr. W. Lewis Tallman, whom she would divorce in 1896. "The Midwinter Fair. An Interview with Mr. John Armstrong on the Pacific Display," *(Phoenix) Arizona Republican*, February 15, 1894, 3.

50.   "Teresa Dean's Impressions of California's Midwinter Fair. Fracas with the Climate. Amid Fields of Flowers Fur Wraps Are Needed. The Inter Ocean's Special Correspondent Learns a Mysterious Pacific Coast Game," *(Chicago, IL) Inter Ocean*, February 17, 1894, 4.

51.   "'Jack' Has Arrived. Teresa Dean's Midway Companion Joins Her Again. At the Midwinter Fair. Together They Take in the San Francisco Sights. Visit the Hawaiian Village and Witness the Native Hula-Hula Dances." [signed Teresa Dean] *(Chicago, IL) Inter-Ocean*, February 28, 1894, 4.

52.   Mary M. Cronin and William E. Huntzicker, "Popular Chinese Images and 'The Coming Man' of 1870,," *Journalism History* 38, no. 2 (2012): 87.

53.   Andrew Gyory, *Closing the Gate: Race, Politics, and the Chinese Exclusion Act* (Chapel Hill: University of North Carolina Press, 1998), 17–18.

54.   Charles J. McClain, *In Search of Equality: The Chinese Struggle against Discrimination in Nineteenth-Century America* (Berkley: University of California Press, 1969), 9–36; William E. Huntzicker, "Newspaper Representations of China and Chinese Americans," in Frankie Hutton and Barbara Straus Reed, eds., *Outsiders in 19th Century Press History: Multicultural Perspectives* (Bowling Green, OH: Bowling Green State University Popular Press, 1995), 93–114.

55.   "Golden Gate Chips. "Teresa Dean Goes on a Trip Through Chinatown. How Seven Almond Eyed Celestials Hoarded their Piles of Gold—Joss-Houses and Chinese Restaurants," *Worthington (MN) Advance*, April 26, 1894, 6.

56.   *Ibid.*

57.   Andrzej Diniejko, "Slums and Slumming in Late Victorian London," accessed January 31, 2020, www.victorianweb.org/history/slums.html.

58.   *Ibid.*; "Slumming in this Town," *New York Times*, September 14, 1884.

59.   *(Indianapolis, IN) Sun*, No headline. January 29, 1891, 2.

60.   "She Is Bright and Good." *The (IL) Morning Star*, June 16, 1895, 2.

61.   *(Indianapolis, IN) Sun*, No headline. January 29, 1891, 2.

# PART II

# Globetrotters

# Thomas Wallace Knox

*A Celebrity Journalist's Travel
and Adventure in Siberia and China*

William E. Huntzicker

"In the winter of 1865 I met a gentleman who was familiar with most countries of the Old World," Thomas Wallace Knox wrote in *Harper's New Monthly Magazine* in August 1868. "I contemplated a journey to Northern Asia, so I ventured the inquiry:

"'How can I visit Siberia?'

"'Oh,' he said with a smile, 'there are two ways of reaching Siberia: you can go there or you can be sent.'"

This exchange opened Knox's *Harper's* article and set up numerous other articles and books based on his trip to Siberia and other parts of Asia—trips that established Knox as a travel writer, adventurer, and celebrity journalist. Knox also developed a style that combined his first-person narrative with an adventure and a geography lesson.[1] He entered the "eastern gate of Asiatic Russia" and traveled by rivers most of the way to Europe.

His book based on the trip, *Overland Through Asia: Pictures of Siberian, Chinese, and Tatar Life* (1870), opened by quoting an old sailor's view of the shrinking world with the ocean steamer eclipsing seamanship. "More correctly," Knox wrote, "he might have predicted the end of the romance of ocean travel. Steam abridges time and space to such a degree that the world grows rapidly prosaic. Countries once distant and little known are at this day near and familiar. Railways on land and steamships on the ocean, will transport us, at frequent and regular intervals, around the entire globe." Ocean travel no longer depended on helpful breezes, and a hundred-day trip would now involve "a dozen changes of conveyance and a land travel of less than a single week."[2]

With this introduction, Knox expressed his desire to see the shrinking world, to write about places he visited, and to promote travel. *Overland* provided commentary on the places and people he visited. Like his readers, he grew curious about the unexplored areas of the globe. As the growing literature on adventure journalism points out, journalists like Knox filled an increasing demand for travel information in Gilded Age newspapers, magazines, and books.[3]

Knox is best known among historians as the civilian *New York Herald* correspondent court-martialed by Union General William T. Sherman for disobeying military orders. On Civil War battlefields far from his New York base, Knox had honed his reportorial skills, a talent for keen observations, an appreciation of history, and an engaging writing style—skills that would translate nicely into his future career as a travel writer, producing as many as forty-five travel books.[4] Some of these works mixed truth and fiction, as in several richly illustrated volumes aimed at juvenile audiences, with two fictional boys and their uncle setting off on great adventures.[5]

*Overland Through Asia,* Knox's first and most successful travel book after his Civil War memoir, related his personal experiences as an adventurer and included stories of adventures from people he encountered along the way. In keeping with emerging journalistic ethics, he usually identified the sources of his stories, but he also sometimes conflated his own tales with those he borrowed. When Knox encountered it, the Amur (then spelled Amoor) River marked the still-unclear border between Russia and China. He acknowledged that his trip was a follow-up to one made fourteen years earlier by Major Perry McD. Collins,[6] the only other American known to have written about the region. Knox admitted a variety of motives for the trip, not the least of which was to scout a route for a telegraph line:

THOMAS W. KNOX.

**Unlike the light-packing Nellie Bly, Thomas Knox boarded his ship in San Francisco well-accoutered with a trunk, valise, boxes, satchel, bundle of newspapers, an unexplained bouquet, and a dog. "After falling a dozen times upon his side, [the dog] succeeded in learning to keep his feet," Knox remembered of their first day aboard the highly unsteady screw steamer, the *G.S. Wright* (Knox, *Overland through Asia*, Chapter II) (The Miriam and Ira D. Wallach Division of Art, Prints and Photographs, New York Public Library, Item 510d47e2-a801-a3d9-e040-e00a18064a99).**

The journey herein recorded was undertaken partly as a pleasure trip, partly as a journalistic enterprise, and partly in the interest of the company that attempted to carry out the plans of Major Collins to make an electric connection between Europe and the United States by way of Asia and Bering's Straits. In the service of the Russo-American Telegraph Company, it may not be improper to state that the author's official duties were so few, and his pleasures so numerous, as to leave the kindest recollections of the many persons connected with the enterprise.[7]

Portions of the book had already been published in magazines and were so favorably received, Knox claimed, that he was encouraged to write the book, the largest part of which was from "a carefully recorded journal" in print for the first time with illustrations he credited, in part, to an artist of the telegraph expedition and photographer August Hoffman of Irkutsk in eastern Siberia. Few of the pictures are credited, but "in all cases great care has been exercised to represent correctly the costumes of the country." When

Knox veered from his own experiences into those of his sources, he must have relied on illustrations re-created from scenes he never witnessed, though he does not always acknowledge doing so.[8]

One of the author's small illustrations depicts him on board a boat as his entourage embarked on their ocean voyage. Knox, who was over six feet tall, tried to sleep in a bunk under five feet long; his bed extended by breaking a wall into a storage space. "The cabin roof was high enough for the colonel, but too low for me. Under the skylight was the only place below deck where I could stand erect. The sleeping rooms were too short for me, and before I could lie, at full length in my berth, it was necessary to pull away a partition near my head. The space thus gained was taken from a closet containing a few trifles, such as jugs of whiskey, and cans of powder. Fortunately no fire reached the combustibles at any time, or this book might not have appeared."[9]

The author assumed the Gilded Age idea of progress and, as he traveled west across Asia, he also assumed an implicit manifest destiny, somewhat like that in the development of the American West. (Later, we'll see that he criticized Russians for the same assumptions.) Knox traveled across previously unmapped, but not unexplored, territory. In Asia, Knox often depended on servants, but sometimes took them for granted without mentioning them, except incidentally when helpful to an anecdote. He usually had a local traveling companion, and when he arrived at a remote village, he was often treated as a celebrity. Occasionally, an entire village would come to the river to greet him and his party. To help his readers, he offered comparisons to people and places they might recognize.

OVER SIX FEET.

Traveling by horse, foot, stagecoach, or ship, adventure journalists often found themselves sacrificing comfort for content, as did the tall Thomas Knox in his steamer sleeping compartment (Wikisource contributors, *Overland Through Asia* by Knox, Thomas Wallace.djvu/41, *Wikisource*).

## A Master Storyteller

Readers of Knox's *Overland* tales of the Russian Empire were led by a master story-teller whose adventures brought those distant communities to life with intimately personal experiences and observations. When Knox and his companions approached the Russian village of Petrovsky, he was told the river had washed away close to four hundred feet of shoreline in the previous three years, leaving a single row of houses and a narrow street separating them from the water. Nonetheless, "[t]he whole population, men, women, and children, turned out to meet us. The day was cool and the men were generally in their sheepskin coats. The women wore gowns of coarse cloth of different colors, and each had a shawl over her head. Some wore coats of sheepskin like those of the men, and several were barefooted. Two women walked into the river and stood with utter nonchalance where the water was fifteen inches deep. I immersed my thermometer and found it indicated 51°."[10]

In the town, he was "nearly overturned by a small hog running between my legs. The brute, with a dozen of his companions, had pretty much his own way at Petrovsky, and after this introduction I was careful about my steps. These hogs are modelled something like blockade runners: with great length, narrow beam, and light draft. They are capable of high speed, and would make excellent time if pursued by a bull-dog or pursuing a swill-bucket." Strangely, the accompanying illustration shows the author not being "overturned" but appearing to trip over the pig.[11]

With an hour to spare in the village, Knox and his traveling companion improvised a hunting trip where birds had been spotted. "It proved in every sense a wild-goose chase, as the birds flew away before we were in shooting distance. Not wishing to return empty-handed we purchased two geese a few hundred yards from the village, and assumed an air of great dignity as we approached the boat. We subsequently ascertained that the same geese were offered to the steward for half the price we paid."[12]

While not necessarily adventurous, anecdotes like his pig ambush and wild-goose chase added authority to Knox's travel reporting by lending an air of self-deprecating honesty to the journalist, and connected him to his readers back home. Describing Petropavlovsk, for example, Knox invited his readers to draw on common American images. "Take a log village in the backwoods of Michigan or Minnesota," he suggested, "and transport it to a quiet spot by a well sheltered harbor of Lilliputian size. Cover the roofs of some buildings with iron, shingles or boards from other regions. Cover the balance with thatch of long grass, and erect chimneys that just peer above the ridge poles. Scatter these buildings on a hillside next [to] the water; arrange three-fourths of them in a single street, and leave the rest to drop wherever they like. Of course those in the higgledy-piggledy position must be of the poorest class, but you can make a few exceptions. Whitewash the inner walls of half the buildings, and use paper or cloth to hide the nakedness of the other half."[13] Following these steps, Knox proposed, would give the reader "a fair counterfeit" of the Russian village.

Knox often conveyed his observations by retelling conversations and anecdotes. In one instance, he recalled his first view of China. "While I was arranging my toilet the steward pointed out of the cabin window and uttered the single word 'Kitie'—emphasizing the last syllable. I looked where he directed and had my first view of the Chinese empire. 'Kitie' is the Russian name of China, and is identical with the Cathay of Marco Polo and other early travelers." Knox could see little difference between the two sides of the Ussuri (then spelled Ousuree) River which separated Russia and China in some places. "[T]here were trees and bushes, grass and sand, just as on the opposite shore. In the region immediately above the Ousuree there are no mountains visible from the river, but only the low banks on either hand covered with trees and bushes. Here and there were open spaces appearing as if cleared for cultivation." With an occasional sand bar and low islands, "the resemblance to the lower Mississippi was almost perfect."[14]

This passage continued with his most harrowing adventure story, which also illustrates his storytelling technique. Like tales around a campfire, this adventure, like many of Knox's stories, began with an anecdote that sets up a horrible worst-case scenario—this one beginning with a traveling companion's fleeting glimpse of a tiger on the Chinese side of the river. Knox, who had never seen a tiger in the wild, could not see it with either an opera glass or a rifle scope, but his companions "retired to the cabin and made a theoretical combat with the animal until dinner time."[15]

Among the passengers with tiger stories was a man headed to a Cossack post along the river, and Knox recounted it for his readers back home. "I was out (said he) on a survey that we were making on behalf of the government to establish the boundary between Russia and China." The only settlements along the river then were native villages about thirty or forty miles apart. "At one village we were warned that a large tiger had within a month killed two men and attacked a third, who was saved only by the sudden and unexpected appearance of a party of friends. We prepared our rifles and pistols, to avoid

Just as Knox was curious to see the residents of Russian villages along the river, so too were they to see the broad-shouldered American. "The peasants always came to the bank where we stopped, no matter what the hour," Knox wrote from the Amoor ("Peasants on the Ussuri River, at Iman?" by William Henry Jackson, Oct. 12, 1895, Library of Congress, Item 20047081 21).

the possibility of their missing fire in case of an encounter with the man-stealing beast. Rather reluctantly some of the natives consented to serve us as guides to the next village." Although "the natives were almost universally kind to us," their reluctance "showed the great fear they entertained of the tiger."[16]

While camped on the Ussuri about ten miles from a village, the story continued, the group prepared breakfast while a native waded into a nearby pond to spear salmon. After taking three or four salmon in just twenty minutes, he returned to camp, and, as the man climbed the river bank with his catch, the tiger "darted from the underbrush" and sprang upon the man as a cat would a mouse. His companions were astonished and momentarily struck motionless. "The unfortunate man did not struggle with the beast, and as the latter did not stop to do more than seize him, I suspected that the fright and suddenness of the attack had caused a fainting fit. I and my Russian companion seized our rifles, and the natives their spears, and started in pursuit."[17]

Hoping to catch the beast before he could consume his prey, the storyteller and his companions had tracked the tiger by following drips of the victim's blood. "I freely and gladly admit that I have never had my nerves more unstrung than on that occasion, though I have been in much greater peril." The narrator and his companion were good shots but no match for the tiger. "Just as we were beating around a little clump of bushes, fifteen or twenty yards across, my companion on the other side shouted: 'Look out; the tiger is preparing to spring upon you.' Instantly I cocked my rifle and fired into the bushes; they were so dense that I could hardly discern the outline of the beast, who had me in full view, and was crouching preparatory to making a leap." The narrator then called on his companion to shoot, which he did. As the tiger leaped toward him, the man shot it in the breast and his companion hit him from the other side. Still the tiger sprang and landed on his foot, causing him to be lame for months and scarred for life.

"We found the remains of the poor native somewhat mutilated, though less so than I expected. There was no trace of suffering upon his features, and I was confirmed in my theory that he fainted the moment he was seized, and was not conscious afterward." His friends buried the body where they found it, piled logs above the grave and observed "certain pagan rites, to secure the repose of the deceased." The tiger, the anecdote concluded, "was one of the largest of his kind. I had his skin carefully removed, and sent it with my official report to St. Petersburg. A Chinese mandarin who met me near Lake Hinka offered me a high price for the skin, but I declined his offer, in order to show our Emperor what his Siberian possessions contained." Even though the story concluded with the narrator's reference to "our Emperor," it's easy for the reader, in the midst of the adventure complete with an illustration, to lose track of who's narrating the story—in this case a passenger headed to a Cossack outpost.[18]

## Into Siberia and the Chinese Empire

The traveler seeking Siberia, Knox wrote, passes through clouds of dust or pools of mud, depending on the weather. He meets long trains of carts drawn by mules, oxen, or ponies—most of them carrying produce to the Imperial city. Knox enumerated his own harrowing experiences, contending with ice floes on the river, rickety wagons on extremely rough and narrow roads, obnoxious horses and mules, and packs of wolves known to attack people.

"The warmth of the garment atones for its cumbersome character," Knox wrote of his dehar, "and its gigantic size is fully intentional. The length protects the feet and legs, the high collar warms the head, and the great width of the dehar allows it to be well wrapped about the body. The long sleeves cover the hands and preserve fingers from frost bites. Taken as a whole it is a mental discomfort but a physical good, and may be considered a necessary nuisance of winter travel in Siberia" (Wikisource contributors, *Overland Through Asia* by Knox, Thomas Wallace. djvu/12, *Wikisource*).

Knox provided fascinating detail about the newly developing region and its many challenges, including transportation, weather, and cultural and language differences. He described Siberia's growing diversity, partly the result of becoming a penal colony for Russia and a place of refuge for Poles, other internal ethnic groups, and those at war with Russia. In gestures to his sponsor, Knox occasionally noted places that could benefit from better communication and a telegraph line, also suggesting difficulties or advantages of building roads and stringing wires in different places. As an explorer, he scouted the potential for future development and the availability of natural resources. "Up to the present time," he reported, "no coal has been mined along the Amoor, though enough is known to exist. The cheapness and abundance of wood will render coal of little importance for many years to come." A smelting establishment, Knox proposed, could draw iron ore, coal, copper, and silver from various regions.[19] Despite this focus on development, Knox also noted the beauty of the landscape, finding the colors of the cliffs, hills, ravines, islands, and occasional meadows and forests were such that "no pen can picture."[20]

As his party continued up the river, Knox found himself retracing the steps of the earlier Collins expedition, and facing some of the same hazards. At one tumultuous region of the river, at a point where Collins' boats were nearly capsized in an eddy, Knox noted, "When our steamer struck this rapid it required all the strength of our engines to carry us through."[21] When exploring the shoreline, even under normal conditions, trails were difficult. "Animals with pack-saddles, swaying under heavy burdens, swell the caravans, and numerous equestrians, either bestriding their steeds, or sitting sidewise in apparent carelessness, are constantly encountered," Knox reported. "Now and then an unruly mule causes a commotion in the crowd by a vigorous use of his heels, and a watchful observer may see an unfortunate native sprawling on the ground in consequence of approaching too near one of the hybrid beasts. Chinese mules will kick as readily as their American cousins; and I can say from experience, that their hoofs are neither soft nor delicate."[22]

To supplement his own adventures, Knox reported observations of places he did not visit. Chinese cities were all very much alike, he wrote. "None of them have wide streets, except in the foreign quarters, and none of them are clean; in their abundance of dirt they can even excel New York, and it would be worth the while for the rulers of the American metropolis to visit China and see how filthy a city can be made without half trying."[23] Ancient greatness and modern filth were two ways Knox described the capital city, Beijing. Its architecture, he claimed, provided testimony to the "glorious history of the Celestial empire," showing that the Chinese, even hundreds of years earlier, "were no mean architects; its walls could resist any of the ordinary appliances of war before the invention of artillery, and even the tombs of its rulers are monuments of skill and patience that awaken the admiration of every beholder. Throughout China Pekin* is reverentially regarded, and in many localities the man who has visited it is regarded as a hero."[24]

Knox described the exotic cultural practices of Beijing's many residents, including "a liberal assemblage of peddlers, jugglers, beggars, donkey drivers, merchants, idlers, and all the other professions and non-professions that go to make up a population."[25] Like many adventurers of the Gilded Age, Knox was fascinated by the familiar and

---

*Pekin was Knox's term for Peking or Beijing; he also occasionally used Cathay, an outdated name for China. Knox used the term Orient to refer to the area we call the Middle East today.

unfamiliar culinary tastes of the people, and entertained his American readers with colorful descriptions:

> The peddlers have fruit and other edibles, not omitting an occasional string of rats suspended from bamboo poles, and attached to cards on which the prices, and sometimes the excellent qualities of the rodents, are set forth. It is proper to remark that the Chinese are greatly slandered on the rat question. As a people they are not given to eating these little animals; it is only among the poorer classes that they are tolerated, and then only because they are the cheapest food that can be obtained. I was always suspicious when the Chinese urged me to partake of little meat pies and dumplings, whose components I could only guess at, and when the things were forced upon me I proclaimed a great fondness for stewed duck and chicken, which were manifestly all right. But I frankly admit that I do not believe they would have inveigled me into swallowing articles to which the European mind is prejudiced, and my aversion arose from a general repugnance to hash in all forms—a repugnance which had its origin in American hotels and restaurants.[26]

Any American visitor to China would be aware of the appeal of other exotic curiosities, expressed in a way that does not threaten the readers and may, in fact, reinforce their stereotypes. Among gender issues, Chinese foot-binding apparently interested American readers. Visitors in southern China rarely saw "the famous small-footed women" in public. "The odious custom of compressing the feet is much less common at Pekin than in the southern provinces," Knox wrote. The ruling dynasty had always opposed and had issued several edicts against foot-binding, he said. "The jealousy of the men and the idleness and vanity of the women have served to continue the custom. Every Chinese who can afford it will have at least one small-footed wife, and she is maintained in the most perfect indolence. For a woman to have a small foot is to show that she is of high birth and rich family, and she would consider herself dishonored if her parents failed to compress her feet."[27]

When criticized for foot binding, the Chinese compared it to compressing the waist in America and Europe. "We like women with small feet and you like them with small waists. What is the difference?" Knox explained the difference, in rather graphic detail: "The compression is begun when a girl is six years old, and is accomplished with strong bandages. The great toe is pressed beneath the others, and these are bent under, so that the foot takes the shape of a closed fist. The bandages are drawn tighter every month, and in a couple of years the foot has assumed the desired shape and ceased to grow." He noted that the process often led to disease and immobility. "To have the finger-nails very long is also a mark of aristocracy," he wrote. "Sometimes the ladies enclose their nails in silver cases, which are very convenient for cleansing the ears of their owner or tearing out the eyes of somebody else."[28]

Knox reported that the Chinese loved to gamble and Beijing had "a fair number" of gamblers and gambling houses. "Gambling is a passion with the Chinese, and they indulge it to a greater extent than any other people in the world. It is a scourge in China, and the cause of a great deal of the poverty and degradation that one sees there. There are various games, like throwing dice, and drawing sticks from a pile, and there is hardly a poor wretch of a laborer who will not risk the chance of paying double for his dinner on the remote possibility of getting it for nothing." Rich and poor alike were addicted, Knox wrote, even if they lost their money, houses, land, wives, children, and even themselves.[29]

The Chinese were also noted for torture, and their methods of punishment could fill a separate volume, Knox wrote. "Punishment is one of the fine arts, and a man who can skin another elegantly is entitled to rank as an artist. The bastinado and floggings are common, and then they have huge shears, like those used in tin shops, for snipping off feet and arms, very much as a gardener would cut off the stem of a rose." Several years earlier, the governor had ordered nearly all the people of a village tried, imprisoned, tortured, and whipped to stop a rash of robberies. The robberies ended.[30]

Dusty in dry weather and muddy when wet, Beijing streets did not welcome travel, and, unlike the growing trends among middle-class Americans and Europeans, Knox wrote, "A Chinese never travels for pleasure, and he does not understand the spirit that leads tourists from one end of the world to the other in search of adventure." For recreation, he sits down, smokes his pipes, and thinks about his ancestors. "He never rides, walks, dances, or takes the least exercise for pleasure alone. It is business and nothing else that controls his movements."[31]

Beijing, furthermore, was not conducive to sight-seeing. "It is not easy to go about Pekin," he wrote, "It is a city of magnificent distances, and the sights which one wants to see are far apart." Streets had deep ruts that made riding uncomfortable, and the cabs were little carts without springs and just large enough for two persons of medium size.[32] Knox described the parks, shrines, temples, and an emperor's summer palace that "bore the relation to Pekin that Versailles does to Paris." He wrote in past tense, he explained, because the city had been ravaged by the English and French forces during the Opium War, and all the largest and best of the buildings were plundered or burned. Knox criticized the British and French for the destruction: "The cost of this palace amounted to millions of dollars, and the blow was severely felt by the Chinese government. The park is still worth a visit, but less so than before the destruction of the palace."[33]

Even as he defended China against the unfair attacks by the West, Knox celebrated the arrival of free trade with the broader world, which would work to China's advantage. "Probably there is no people in the world that can be called a nation of shop-keepers more justly than the Chinese; thousands upon thousands of them are engaged in petty trade, and the competition is very keen." Increased trade and modern technology had begun to transform the society. "Foreign systems of banking and insurance have been adopted, and work successfully." But he noted the Chinese had their own economic successes, "a mode of banking long before the European nations possessed much knowledge of financial matters; and it is claimed that the first circulating-notes and bills-of-credit ever issued had their origin during a monetary pressure at Pekin."[34]

Chinese merchants, Knox said, also understood the importance of reliable and speedy communication and transportation; railways would follow the steamboat, and telegraph wires would provide instantaneous communication to replace dispatch-boats a few times a week. Knox, whose trip was underwritten by a telegraph company, said the Chinese did not understand how the telegraph worked, but they made liberal use of it, especially those groups who traded or worked in other countries, like the United States.

In a joke or a bit of sarcasm that is difficult for modern readers, he ridiculed "pigeon-English" as difficult to learn as well as to translate and simplify for the telegraph. "It is just as difficult for a Chinese to learn pigeon-English as it would be to learn pure and honest English, and it is about as intelligible as Greek or Sanscrit to a newly-arrived foreigner. In Shanghae or Hong Kong, say to your Chinese ma-foo, who claims to speak English, 'Bring me a glass of water,' and he will not understand you. Repeat your order in those words, and he stands dumb and uncomprehending, as though you had spoken the dialect of the moon. But if you say, 'You go me catchee bring one piecee glass water; savey,' and his tawny face beams intelligence as he obeys the order.'"[35]

Respect for ancestors was a prominent feature of Chinese culture that attracted attention from the West. Families around Beijing created private burial grounds, sometimes in cooperatives with other families, but each had a private spot, often in a grove of trees they would make as private as possible. People who lived in "a miserable hovel" still could look forward to "a commodious tomb beneath pretty shade trees," Knox wrote. "The tender regard for the dead is an admirable trait in the Chinese character, and springs, no doubt, from that filial piety which is so deeply engraved on the Oriental mind." Coffins were occasionally displayed in the home. Of course, such coffins were finely ornamented to reflect the owner's circumstances. "Whenever the Chinese sell ground for building purposes they always stipulate for the removal of the bones of their ancestors for many generations. The bones are carefully dug up and put in earthen jars, when they are sealed up, labeled, and put away in a comfortable room, as if they were so many pots of pickles and fruits. Every respectable family in China has a liberal supply of potted ancestors on hand, but would not part with them at any price."[36]

While devoted to the past, Chinese were also curious about technology. With "a river-system unsurpassed by that of any other nation of the world," for example, China welcomed steamships, which could surpass the indigenous junks, strongly influenced by controlling currents and winds. An early steamboat operator described the reception of his vessel. "Our propeller was quite beneath the water, and so far as outward appearance went there was no visible power to move us." The steamboat attracted attention. "Chinamen are generally slow to manifest astonishment, and not easily frightened, but their excitement on that occasion was hardly within bounds. Men, women, and children ran to see the monster, and after gazing a few moments a fair proportion of them took to their heels for safety. Dogs barked and yelped on all the notes of the chromatic scale, occasional boats' crews jumped to the shore, and those who stuck to their oars did their best to get out of our way." Within a few years, the river supported many competing fast steamboat lines and stimulated the growth of foreign banking and insurance interests.[37]

After devoting many pages to his descriptions of city life in China, especially in Beijing, Knox admitted that he did not even go there on this adventure. "It was my original intention to make a journey from Kiachta to Pekin and back again," he wrote, "but the lateness of the season prevented me. I did not wish to be caught in the desert of Gobi in winter." Instead, as he proceeded across Asia, he interviewed other travelers and carefully reported their experiences.[38]

A Russian gentleman, for example, told of getting lost in the Gobi Desert and losing all sense of direction and notion of where he was, demonstrating that "it is quite easy for a stranger to be lost in the Mongolian desert beyond all hope of finding his way again." While suffering from hunger and thirst, he was haunted by thoughts of wild beasts devouring him. Then his pony ran away. After days of suffering, he was approached by two Mongol horsemen who were leading his fugitive pony. "The Mongols are a strong, hardy, and generally good-natured race, possessing the spirit of perseverance quite as much as the Chinese. They have the free manners of all nomadic people, and are noted for unvarying hospitality to visitors." But they "have no great friendship for the Chinese inhabitants, who are principally engaged in traffic and the various occupations connected with the transport of goods." A few Russians live there and they may have designs on Mongolia whenever the opportunity offers. "In the spirit of annexation and extension of territory the Russians can fairly claim equal rank with ourselves. I forget their phrase for 'manifest destiny,' and possibly they may not be willing that I should give it," Knox wrote.

"The Chinese and Russian settlers live in houses, and there are temples and other permanent buildings, but the Mongols live generally in yourts, which they prefer to more extensive structures."[39]

Besides relating Russian expansion to manifest destiny in the American West, Knox also compared emancipation of slaves in the United States and of serfs in Russia. He described immigrants and refugees as well as the political exiles who had been sent to Siberia. Some communities had accommodated all of these groups. A telegraph would be useful here, he reported. "Couriers have passed from Kiachta to Pekin in ten or twelve days; but the rough road and abominable carts make them feel at their journey's end about as if rolled through a patent clothes wringer. A mail is carried twice a month each way by the Russians. Several schemes have been proposed for a trans-Mongolian telegraph, but thus far the Chinese government has refused to permit its construction."[40]

Knox wrapped up his *Overland* trip by passing through the Ural Mountains amidst life-threatening blizzards and wild beasts. His travelogue described farm land, mining, and industry, and speculated about the country's potential. He said he avoided discussing politics but, if he did, he could discuss as freely as in New York. "A mosque and a church,

CONCENTRATED ENERGIES.

**"About midnight the yemshick [driver] exhibited his skill by driving into a mudhole where there was solid ground on both sides," Knox wrote from the road near Chita. He and his Cossack companion found a board with which to lift the front end of the carriage. Knox's role was to motivate the horses to pull: "I attributed no small part of the success to the effect of American horse-vocabulary upon Russian quadrupeds" (Chapter XXIII) (Wikisource contributors, *Overland Through Asia* by Knox, Thomas Wallace.djvu/295, *Wikisource*).**

side by side, symbolized the harmony between Tartar and Russian."[41] As he crossed from Asia to Europe, Knox said he did not notice much difference, even as he stood with a foot on each continent, fulfilling a childhood dream. After traveling among wide-ranging cultural and language groups, he expressed astonishment at the amount of business one could conduct with but limited capital of words.

## Bringing Cultural Observations Home

With his first-hand experience as an adventure journalist in Asia, Knox sought to establish himself as an authority on Chinese culture in his later publications. Although he offered descriptions of Beijing without actually going there, Knox gave a more genuine view of Chinese life when he explored Chinatown in San Francisco for a series published by *Frank Leslie's Illustrated Newspaper.* Joseph Becker, one of *Leslie's* most trusted and prolific illustrators, provided the pictures. The series, called "The Coming Man," took more of an anthropological look at the community and described daily life to readers who may not have understood it—all at a time when immigration of Chinese was becoming controversial as Chinese workers were being imported to build the Transcontinental Railroad. While Knox's detail-driven style of reporting informed readers about the Chinese and their lives in urban America, Becker's thirty accompanying illustrations were, as always, the selling point in *Leslie's.*[42]

Knox later visited New York City's Chinatown for an account that was published in 1897, a year following his death. Unlike the San Francisco series, the New York account forwarded an agenda from Gilded Age reformers who needed to demonstrate that the squalor of the city needed fixing. The book's primary author, Helen Stuart Campbell, was a missionary and social reformer who wrote about poverty and helped create the academic study of home economics. The third author, Thomas F. Byrnes, was an Irish-born American police officer and head of the New York City detective department. Prominent theologian Lyman Abbott provided an introduction.

A publisher's preface stated that "Col. Thomas W. Knox was assigned the task of delineating phases of city life that a trained journalist of many years' experience in New York is more familiar with than almost any other person. To the advantages of his facile pen and quick observation, born of long newspaper work, are added those of a lifetime spent in the great city and perfect familiarity with many features of metropolitan life which he so well describes."[43] The publisher acknowledged support from a list of organizations, including the Children's Aid Society, the Society for the Prevention of Cruelty to Children, and various missions, asylums, and charities.

Knox delivered a Chinatown consistent with the book's premise with a heavy emphasis on opium use and gambling. "Nearly every Chinaman in Mott Street—and in the whole of New York for that matter—is fond of fan-tan and other gambling games, and nearly every Chinaman smokes opium. The whole race seems to be devoted to gambling, and the most of the work of the police with them is to break up their gambling-houses and their opium-dens. It's very difficult to break up their gambling-places, though, for the reason that they will rarely betray their comrades, and they never allow a white man to play at their games."[44]

Some of Knox's anecdotes occasionally tied personal stories to local social, economic, and cultural values. In one of his stories in *The Talking Handkerchief,* he tells of a young couple forced to elope to marry across the cultural barriers in Russia, where some families valued their status and titles more than land and wealth. A young Russian woman had to run away with her lover to avoid an arranged marriage, and Knox related the dramatic escape. In his travelogue along the Amur, however, he told a similar story of a proposed arranged marriage and dramatic escape and pursuit by soldiers. In this case, however, the story came to a tragic end.[45]

In a short book called *John; or, Our Chinese Relations: A Study of Our Emigration and Commercial Intercourse with the Celestial Empire* in 1879, he compared China's significant influence on North America with William the Conqueror's invasion of England in 1066, which led to constitutional government and creation of the British empire.[46] "By a similar line of reasoning," Knox wrote,

> we owe all that we possess to-day, as a nation, to the moon-eyed Celestials who a century ago cultivated the tea-plant on the sloping hillsides of antipodal China. From China came tea; from tea came the odious tea-tax which was levied by England upon her American colonies, from the tea-tax came the historic 'Boston Tea-party'; from the Boston Tea-party and other defiant incidents came the war of the Revolution; from the war came our independence; from our independence came the present greatness and glory of the nation known as the United States. If the eagle on our national coat of arms should desire a resting-place for his feet, a tea-chest might form a pedestal not altogether inappropriate.[47]

The basis for *John; or, Our Chinese Relations* was, in part, a six-hundred-mile trip up the Yang-Tse, the great river that was "a magnificent water-way, and enabled the foreigner to carry his flag into the heart of the empire. American and English steamers stem its muddy current, and find it without a rival save in the western hemisphere." It was like the Mississippi at Memphis or Cairo, Illinois, but none could match its volume of commerce, he wrote.[48]

Despite acknowledging the ongoing connection of China with the U.S., Knox revealed a condescending attitude in his use of the name John, even though the term "John Chinaman" permeated nineteenth-century newspaper writing. In *The Talking Handkerchief*, Knox wrote: "I sent for John, my servant. John was not his Christian name; in fact he was a 'heathen Chinee,' and there was nothing Christian about him, in name or anything else. I always made it a rule to name my servant 'John,' without the least regard to the outlandish appellation he bore on entering my service. It saved an effort of the memory, and efforts of that sort are worth something in China, where you have half a world between you and your native land."[49]

In the beginning of this narrative, Knox also explained his use of the first-person pronoun: "One of the tales that was told me in China I will here repeat; for convenience of narration I will give it in the first person singular, and singular enough it is to the American who has never seen Asia." He then related in the first person the story of a man kidnapped by pirates who was able to send information to an oncoming British steamer by sending messages in signal code from the portal in his locked room using a handkerchief. "His rescue was a surprise to everyone on board."[50]

In these narratives, Knox blurred the line between fact and fiction while claiming to provide educational geography lessons. "A wise man once declared that it was an excellent provision of Providence to make great rivers run by large cities, he might have mentioned another curiosity of nature, that the cities at the mouths of great rivers, are generally seaports. The rivers and seaports of China have been very useful to commerce and greatly facilitated the work of extending trade to foreign countries."[51]

## Advice to Travelers from the Great Storyteller

In addition to relating his own travels, Knox advised readers how to prepare for their own adventures in an 1888 book, *How to Travel: Hints, Advice, and Suggestions to Travelers by Land and Sea All Over the World.* He suggested, for example, that his readers be patient and polite with authorities, choose honesty as a best policy, and recognize that smuggling is as illegal as burglary. A traveler without conscience, he proposed, should travel just after a new administration has taken office and has removed experienced people in consular offices and replaced them with newer ones. He also advised that his readers carry passports "in case of trouble with the authorities." In one way, he wrote, a passport was like a gun: "An old frontiersman once said of the revolver which he habitually carried, 'You don't need it often; perhaps may never need it at all, but when you do want it you want it awful bad, I tell you.'" Of course, Knox recommended buying his book and carrying it on the trip along with other, more specific travel guides.[52]

As an adventure journalist, Knox placed his readers in front-row seats as he and they explored unmapped territory in the rivers that separated Russia from China. At the same time, travel exposed them to new people and places—a patriotic act, in his view:

> If you have been reared in the belief that your own country, or your own state, town, or hamlet, contains all that is good in the world, whether of moral excellence, mental development, or mechanical skill, you must prepare to eradicate that belief at an early date…. To an observant and thoughtful individual the invariable effect of travel is to teach respect for the opinions, the faith, or the ways of others, and to convince him that other civilizations than his own are worthy of consideration. At the same time the traveler will find his love for his native land as strong as ever and his admiration for his own institutions as warm as on the day of his departure. An old traveler once said: 'I have found good among every people, and even where there was much to condemn there was much to admire. I have never returned from a journey without an increased respect for the countries I have visited and a greater regard for my own land than ever before. The intelligent traveler will certainly be a true patriot.'[53]

Good advice, but Thomas W. Knox did not always live up to this goal. As a reporter, he advocated facts but integrated fictional tales into his stories. As an adventurer, he experienced foreign nations through the lens of his own culture. But he successfully introduced his readers to relatively unexplored lands and people with the wit and wisdom of a true celebrity journalist.

### Notes

1. Thomas W. Knox, "To and Upon the Amoor River," *Harper's New Monthly Magazine* XXXVII, no. CCXIX, August 1868, 289–307. Knox's account continues at "Traveling in Siberia," *Harper's New Monthly Magazine* no. CCXX. September 1868, 449–466.

2. Thomas W. Knox, *Overland Through Asia: Pictures of Siberian, Chinese, and Tartar Life* (Hartford, CT: American Publishing Company, 1870), 19. The edition used here was from Echo Library, 2011. Notes that follow will provide the page number from this edition and chapter number to make it easier to find the relevant passage in the various editions. This text is available through several online sources, and some are based on scans of earlier editions. Pdf and text versions are available at ia801009.us.archive.org/6/items/overland-througha01knox/overlandthrougha01knox.pdf As a result, some page numbers are not consistent. Some online portals have links to Knox publications, including onlinebooks.library.upenn.edu/webbin/book/lookupname?key=Knox%2c%20Thomas%20Wallace%2c%201835%2d1896.

3. See, for example, Lee Jolliffe, guest editor, *Adventure Journalists in the Gilded Age*, a special issue of *Journalism History* 42, no. 1 (2016), especially the editor's note by Lee Jolliffe.

4. Knox's Civil War memoir is Thomas W. Knox, *Camp-Fire and Cotton-Field* (New York: Blelock and

Company, 1865). See also John F. Marszalek, *Sherman's Other War: The General and the Civil War Press* (Memphis, TN: Memphis State University Press, 1981); John A. Haymond, "Laws of War: The Trial of Thomas Knox," *Quarterly Journal of Military History* 29, no. 4 (2017): 13–16; and William E. Huntzicker, *The Popular Press, 1833–1865* (Westport, CN: Greenwood Press, 1999), Chapters 7 and 8.

5. Knox's 20-volume *The Boy Travelers* series included titles such as *Adventures of Two Youths in a Journey to Japan & China* (1879), *Adventures of Two Youths in a Journey to Egypt and the Holy Land* (1882), and *The Boy Travelers in the Congo: Adventures of Two Youths in a Journey with Henry M. Stanley "Through the Dark Continent"* (1887). Some illustrations in these volumes seem to be drawn directly from Knox's 1870 Asian adventure.

6. *Memorial of Perry McD. Collins*, No. 12, v. 40 of Ignatius Donnelly Library Pamphlet Collection, Minnesota Historical Society, 1864.

7. Knox, *Overland Through Asia*, second paragraph of the Preface, p. 5.

8. *Ibid.* Knox noted that portions had been published in *Harper's, Putnam's, The Atlantic, The Galaxy, Overland*, and *Frank Leslie's Illustrated Newspaper*.

9. Knox, *Overland Through Asia*, Chapter II, 30–31.

10. *Ibid.*, Chapter XV, 171.

11. *Ibid.*

12. *Ibid.*, Chapter XV, 172.

13. *Ibid.*, Chapter III, 43–44.

14. *Ibid.*, Chapter XV, 170–171.

15. *Ibid.*, Chapter XV, 179.

16. *Ibid.*, Chapter XV, 180.

17. *Ibid.*, Chapter XV, 180–181.

18. *Ibid.*, Chapter XV, 181–183.

19. *Ibid.*, Chapter XX, 233.

20. *Ibid.*, Chapter XX, 232.

21. *Ibid.*

22. *Ibid.*, Chapter XXXI, 352.

23. *Ibid.*, Chapter XXX, 336.

24. *Ibid.*

25. *Ibid.*, Chapter XXX, 338.

26. *Ibid.*

27. *Ibid.*, Chapter XXX, 341.

28. *Ibid.*, Chapter XXX, 341–342.

29. *Ibid.*, Chapter XXX, 342–343.

30. *Ibid.*, Chapter XXX, 344.

31. *Ibid.*, Chapter XXX, 345–346.

32. *Ibid.*, Chapter XXX, 345.

33. *Ibid.*, Chapter XXX, 348.

34. *Ibid.*, Chapter XXIX, 331–332.

35. *Ibid.*, Chapter XXIX, 334.

36. *Ibid.*, Chapter XXX, 348–350.

37. *Ibid.*, Chapter XXIX, 330–331.

38. *Ibid.*, Chapter XXXI, 351.

39. *Ibid.*, Chapter XXXII, 362–368.

40. *Ibid.*, Chapter XXXII, 368–369.

41. *Ibid.*, Chapter LI, 591–592.

42. Indeed, the engravings in the nation's illustrated newspapers had always been the draw. An intrigued public had so liked pictorial reporting that sales of illustrated newspapers and magazines frequently exceeded 100,000 copies during the Civil War. See Mary M. Cronin and William E. Huntzicker, "Popular Chinese Images and 'The Coming Man' of 1870: Racial Representations of Chinese," *Journalism History* 38:2 (2012): 86–99.

43. *Darkness and Daylight; or, Lights and shadows of New York life; a pictorial record of personal experiences by day and night in the great metropolis* (Hartford, CT: A. D. Worthington and Company, 1891).

44. *Darkness and daylight*, 552.

45. Thomas W. Knox, *The Talking Handkerchief and Other Stories* (Akron, OH: Saalfield Publishing, 1900), 251–257; and *Overland Through Asia*, Chapter XLIV, 402–406.

46. Thomas W. Knox, *John; or, Our Chinese relations: a study of our emigration and commercial intercourse with the celestial empire.* (New York: Harper & Brothers, 1879), 10–14. Also available as a pdf at hdl.handle.net/2027/uc2.ark:/

47. Knox, *John; or, Our Chinese Relations*, 10–14.

48. *Ibid.*, 17–18.

49. Knox, *The Talking Handkerchief*, 12.

50. *Ibid.*, 10.

51. Knox, *John; or, Our Chinese Relations,* pp. 17–18.

52. Thomas W. Knox, *How to Travel: Hints, Advice, and Suggestions to Travelers by Land and Sea All Over the World* (New York: G. P. Putnam's Sons, 1888): 16–17.

53. *Ibid.*, 16–17.

# "Burning of the Clipper Ship *Hornet* at Sea" and Other Reports from Hawaii

## Mark Twain's Adventure Reporting from the Sandwich Islands

JENNIFER E. MOORE

In January of 1866, Samuel L. Clemens wrote to his mother and sister, "I don't know what to write—my life is so uneventful. I wish I was back there piloting up & down the river again."[1] Better known by his nom de plume, Mark Twain, the young reporter was feeling restless. His earlier life as a riverboat pilot on the Mississippi had been far more exciting than sitting about in a newspaper office, waiting for stories to break. Having just enjoyed modest success and unexpected national attention for his tale "Jim Smiley and His Jumping Frog," Twain was still unsatisfied.[2] Sharing his surprise at the sketch's success, Twain was aghast that *this* was the writing that would deliver his biggest readership to date, saying the story was a "villainous" and "backwards" tale.[3] Twain had been working in northern California for a little over a year, and it is clear from reading his letter to family that he was already in search of a new adventure.[4]

In the letter's postscript, Twain mentioned the big break that would soon diminish his melancholy. Describing the first trip of the steamship *Ajax* from San Francisco to the Hawaiian Islands, known then as the Sandwich Islands, Twain told his mother and sister that the passengers were "the cream of the town—gentleman & ladies both, & a splendid brass band."[5] He expressed regret that he was unable to accept an invitation to join the steamer's inaugural voyage: "But I am so sorry now. If the *Ajax* were back I would go—quick!—and throw up the correspondence." Twain stayed behind to fulfill his obligation as the San Francisco correspondent for the Virginia City, Nevada, *Territorial Enterprise*.[6] But a few weeks later, Twain would grab his chance to set sail aboard the *Ajax* for an adventure and reporting experience that proved to be life-changing.

Through the connections he made as a reporter for the short-lived San Francisco newspaper *The Californian*, Twain persuaded the owners of the *Sacramento Union* to hire him as a correspondent.[7] His new employer commissioned Twain to write about travel to the Sandwich Islands on the *Ajax's* second voyage in March 1866. Using the sharp observational skills that would later become his hallmark, Twain detailed his four-month travel experience traversing the Islands in a constant flow of stories mailed to California and soon picked up by newspapers nationwide. Readers learned about the foreign land and its unfamiliar local customs through the letters, describing his roving adventures, often on horseback. He related experiences with the local food culture, the beautiful and partially inhabited landscape, his visits with indigenous populations and missionary settlers, and a wealth of commentary on new and emerging trade opportunities. In short, Twain's letters suggested he was having the time of his life.

These stories established Twain as an adventure journalist, a post–Civil War era hero who writes and seeks assignments to explore little-known and often faraway places. Writing for a newspaper or other periodical, these journalists were at work telling exciting and dramatic stories as the nation rebuilt after the war years.[8] In the case of Twain's reporting, readers learned about the cultural and economic particularities of the Sandwich Islands through the eyes of a "tireless sightseer."[9] Twain's reports, published as "letters," were filled with details that put his literary skills on display. His ability to weave together stories of adventure with commercial and domestic interests showed his talent as a storyteller that would only improve over time.

While Twain made his name as a reporter in the Sandwich Islands in 1866, his many perambulations around the globe—to India, the Alps, and more, crossing the Atlantic twenty-nine times—served as the basis for future stories and books. Photography by Mathew Brady, 1871 (Library of Congress, Item cwpbh.04761).

As an independent territory, the Sandwich Islands were of great interest to armchair adventure-seekers, but also to the business community. The proprietors of the *Sacramento Union* likely felt that Twain would attract an audience considering his success with "Jim Smiley and His Jumping Frog." Likewise, The California Steam Navigation Company that owned the *Ajax* undoubtedly did not turn down an opportunity to host a journalist on board as they were building a clientele for a regular route between San Francisco and Hawaii.[10]

As both a "means and an object of his visit,"[11] the collection of letters Twain wrote for the *Union* about his experience traveling by sea on a steamship and his four-month stay on the Islands was transformative. He left California as a regionally known journalist who'd had a taste of national fame and returned as an international celebrity. The Sandwich Island series helped launch his career as a sought-after lecturer and would later be included in early editions of his first book, *The Innocents Abroad*. As a literary figure and humorist—arguably most well-known for his two novels with "adventure" in their titles—Twain is an excellent candidate to be added to the ranks of adventure journalists.[12]

## Journalism After the War

The post-war years were the perfect time for a journalist to set sail for lands unknown. The technological, cultural, and economic forces at play during the U.S. Civil War had advanced the news industry and helped transition newspapers from political affiliates to capitalistic enterprises. If the partisan press arguably helped set the stage for the Civil War before 1861, newspaper proprietors in the post-war era performed similar roles to attract the burgeoning middle class as well as advertisers in post-war America.[13] Reconstruction, economic growth, the rise of scientific reason, advances in technology, and reform movements shifted how Americans understood their world.[14] These changes also influenced the expansion of the press, making newspapers a part of the daily social fabric of previously excluded working- and middle-class citizens.[15] To maintain and increase readership, editors and publishers needed to be creative. One way to attract readers was through adventure writing.[16]

Using the adventure journalism genre as a lens to study Twain's correspondence from the Sandwich Islands for the *Sacramento Union* offers an opportunity to understand this historical movement in a new way. Part participant observation and part travel writing, Twain's twenty-five letters, completed between April and November 1866, are quintessential adventure journalism that succeeded in "capturing the public eye, selling newspapers, and building reputations."[17] Archival materials, including Twain's personal letters to family and associates, the Sandwich Islands letters, responses to Twain's correspondence, and the rich and deep research from others about Twain and his adventures as a journalist inform this essay. While it is well established that Twain's early career as a journalist helped launch his literary career, here we add a new layer to Twain's place in nineteenth-century newspaper and journalism history.

## Newspapers in California and the West

For adventure-seekers like Twain, California was a magnet. Fortune hunters and entrepreneurs alike were attracted to what would become the thirty-first state in mid–nineteenth-century America.[18] Twain was among many who migrated West in search of a new way of life. The rush for gold would attract thousands, and California newspapers were a part of the information and communication revolution that corresponded to the population growth.[19]

San Francisco's first newspaper, the *California Star*, began publication in 1847. Proprietor Samuel Brannon's success can be partly attributed to advertising and promoting the gold rush to fortune-seekers back East.[20] However, unlike the established printing industry in the East, the news business in California had some catching up to do. Press culture had been slow to develop under both Spanish and Mexican rule, with only one printing press and no newspapers in the territory.[21] But once the gold explorers arrived, the printing business exploded. "No country under the sun can show so large a proportion of what are termed 'newspaper men.' Our cities have broken out in newspapers. Every surge of popular excitement has been capped with a printed sheet," one writer at the time observed.[22]

The newspaper industry in California did not have the political heritage of its eastern counterparts. Rather, Far West papers sprang up to support and promote the explosion of mining when gold was discovered in 1848.[23] Frank Luther Mott explains how San

Francisco suddenly became a city as the "rush of adventurers" help spur the growth of newspapers.[24] By 1853 there were at least twelve daily papers in California, including the *Sacramento Union*, where Twain's letters from the Sandwich Islands were published.[25] When it began in 1851, the *Union*—both a daily and a weekly at various times—served a population somewhat isolated but eager for news and information. The *Union* built its reputation by emphasizing that it was not aligned with a political party, "independent, above suspicion, trusted by the people. It came to be known as something more than a newspaper—an institution," according to Twain scholar Walter Frear.[26] When Twain arrived in northern California in 1864, the *Union* was the largest circulating newspaper in the state.[27] Editors at the *New-York Tribune* ranked the *Union* among the best of California's ninety or so newspapers.[28] Until shutting down in 1994, the *Union* was the longest-running daily newspaper west of the Mississippi River.

The daily version of the *Union* in the 1860s was an eight-page publication and more than two feet in width. Its length fluctuated between four and eight pages when Twain's letters became a regular feature between April and November of 1866. The *Union* was filled with as much advertising as it had news, reflecting overall trends in the business where newspapers were "a servant of business rather than of politics," as press historian Gerald Baldasty explains.[29] Despite being advertising-supported, *Union* proprietors were committed to the public they served. Publishers James Anthony and Paul Morrill shared a "love of journalism, high moral standards, and a sincere desire to promote public welfare."[30]

## Expanding U.S. Influence Across the Pacific

While it would be nearly a century before Hawaii would become the fiftieth U.S. state, the transformation of the island into a Western holding was underway in the mid–nineteenth century. Strategically, Hawaii, with its eight-island cluster, was rich with natural resources and was used by both European and American seafarers as a place to refuel and refresh. As an 1816 article explained, "American vessels … frequently stop at the Sandwich Islands for refreshments and repairs, and the restoration of health to their crews, generally impaired by fatigue to the boisterous passage round Cape Horn."[31]

The Sandwich Islands received their name from Captain James Cook, who named the Islands after one of his primary backers, John Montague, the Earl of Sandwich, who led the Board of Admiralty.[32] Cook's "discovery" of the Sandwich Islands in 1778 was a friendly encounter, but he would be killed and cannibalized by hostile inhabitants on his third visit in 1779.[33] Readers of Twain's Sandwich Islands correspondence would be familiar with the legend of Captain Cook and mythology surrounding Cook's death, as well as his important contributions to mapping the South Pacific that would allow European and American explorers to develop commercial interests globally.[34] In 1849, the "United States and Hawaii concluded a treaty of friendship that served as the basis of official relations between the parties."[35]

## Twain and His Journey to the Sandwich Islands

Long before his success as an internationally known lecturer, humorist and writer, Mark Twain was an itinerate journalist. A biographer describes Twain as "alternately idle and desperately industrious" while struggling to make a living in the West.[36] Twain was working as a journalist at a time when "reporting became a more highly esteemed and more highly rewarded occupation," explains historian Michael Schudson.[37] Like many in the profession, Twain was introduced to the occupation when he worked as a printer's apprentice after his father's death when Twain was eleven.[38] He would later work for his older brother, Orion, who had bought their hometown newspaper *The Hannibal Journal*, where Twain would write for the first time.[39] If not born an adventurer, Twain's desire for new experiences and travel was likely enabled by his training as a Mississippi steamboat pilot—a job that served him well later in his literary career. When the Civil War disrupted traffic and commerce on the Mississippi River in 1861, Twain found himself out of work.[40] In reflections published later in life, Twain suggested that he was never happier than when he was piloting on the river.[41] One must wonder—if the South had not seceded and sparked the U.S. Civil War, would Samuel L. Clemens have remained a steamboat pilot and never entered the storytelling profession?

Persuaded by hometown friends, Twain briefly volunteered for the Confederacy, but he never fired a shot.[42] In an effort to remain neutral on the war, Twain decided to follow Orion to the territory of Nevada. In *Roughing It,* Twain admitted he coveted his brother's "distinction and financial splendor" as the appointed secretary of the Nevada Territory.[43] Motivated by both envy and the desire for adventure, Twain soon found company in the saloons and newspaper offices in the region.[44] He started writing for local press, and that work would jumpstart his career as a journalist, prompting him to experiment with several pen names until Mark Twain stuck.[45]

By early June 1864, Twain was working in San Francisco, after leaving behind both a journalism job and his brother in Nevada.[46] His first reporting job was with the *San Francisco Morning Call,* and his work was reprinted early on in the *Alta California*, also in San Francisco.[47] Prior to his Sandwich Islands assignment with the *Sacramento Union*, he was settled and happily earning $50 a month to compose a weekly article for the *Californian* under the editorship of Bret Harte.[48] But the busy Twain did not entirely break his ties with the Nevada press. He also continued to write, now as the San Francisco correspondent, for Joe Goodman at the *Territorial Enterprise* in Virginia City, Nevada.[49]

There are conflicting accounts about why Twain left San Francisco to live in a cabin on Jackass Hill and Angel's Camp during the winter of 1864 to 1865. One source explains that he "had gone to avoid the police."[50] Another says he accompanied a friend on the run from authorities; others report he went to dabble in pocket mining.[51] Nonetheless, biographers all agree that the time he spent on Jackass Hill was a boon to his career; this is where he first heard the story that led him to write "Jim Smiley and His Jumping Frog." Published in New York's *The Saturday Press* in 1865, the humorous tale was an immediate success and republished shortly thereafter in the *Californian* and other periodicals across the country. Introducing Twain to a national audience,[52] the short story was later reproduced with the alternate title, "The Celebrated Jumping Frog of Calaveras County," and periodically presented on stage by Twain himself through his years as a lecturer and performer.[53]

Twain's newly found fame likely led to an invitation to join the inaugural voyage of the *Ajax* from San Francisco to the Sandwich Islands in January 1866, but he turned it down. Writing to his mother and sister that same month, he expressed regret for losing a chance to travel abroad: "I got an invitation, but I could not accept it, because there would be no one to write my correspondence while I was gone." Twain was writing a letter a week for the *Territorial Enterprise*, likely his primary source of regular income at the time.[54]

The letters that Twain wrote to his mother and sister indicate that Twain then conceived of a plan to join *Ajax*'s second voyage and write about the Sandwich Islands for the *Union*. It was an opportunity for a new adventure while making some money at the same time.[55] It is also likely that Charles H. Webb, the former Civil War correspondent and San Francisco–based writer who would edit a future version of "Jumping Frog," recommended Twain to the publishers of the *Union*.[56] Perhaps Twain was also feeling hamstrung and lacked the motivation to work on a book-length project that he had mentioned to a fellow reporter.[57] Writing about the Sandwich Islands would give him a chance at a real adventure by traveling the open seas and visiting a tropical land known by few.[58]

The opportunity to be a passenger on a new steamship bound for a territory of great

**After brief service to the Union Army during the U.S. Civil War, the two-year-old steamer *Ajax* became the first steamer to regularly haul freight and God-fearing (vomiting) passengers between San Francisco and Hawaii. Twain sailed on its second Sandwich Islands voyage. Photograph: Honolulu Steamer Ajax, Greenwich Street Wharf, San Francisco, 1865 (The Miriam and Ira D. Wallach Division of Art, Prints and Photographs: New York Public Library, ID G89F403_013F).**

interest to post-war Americans was a strategically shrewd story to pitch, as well. At the time, the Sandwich Islands were independent and maintained diplomatic and commercial relationships with both Britain and the United States. The islands' location was useful for international shipping interests, providing a good stopping point for many oceanic routes. Twain's successful proposal to write about the islands and his ocean journey led to a series of opportunities that created the literary giant he would become. As a journalist-turned-lecturer, the twenty-five letters he wrote for the *Sacramento Union* led to what Twain described later in his life as his "debut as a literary person."[59]

Traveling and writing about the Sandwich Islands provided the 31-year-old with a new adventure that could satisfy his wanderlust and provide an income through his storytelling skills.[60] In a letter to his family two days before his departure on March 7, 1866, Twain wrote, "I am to remain there a month & ransack the islands, the great cataracts & the volcanoes completely, & write twenty or thirty letters to the *Sacramento Union*—for which they pay me as much money as I would get if I staid at home."[61] He spent a good deal of his adventure traveling around the islands on horseback. In a letter to W.C. and W.W. Kimball, fellow passengers on the *Ajax,* Twain described his horse's best attributes: "His strong suit is grace & personal comeliness, rather than velocity."[62]

It is clear from both his personal correspondence and autobiographic writing that Twain understood news was as much a business as it was a democratizing mode of mass communication. The letters he wrote for the *Union* reflect a storyteller's understanding of his audience and what would help sell newspapers. Reflecting on his professional life in an essay for *The Century Magazine* in 1900, Twain recalled his desire to explore the islands and how the publishers "listened to me and gave me the opportunity" despite the fact that "there was but slender likelihood that it could profit them in any way."[63] Remembering them fondly, Twain described the *Sacramento Union* owners as "lovable and well-beloved men."[64]

As America's cherished humorist, Mark Twain was prone to hyperbole, a distinctive characteristic of his comic genius. Keeping in mind his penchant for exaggeration, a careful reading of his letters for the *Union* reveals a roving reporter who had a keen eye for detail, and prose seemingly sprinkled with embellishment for storytelling effect. Twain's reportorial observations also reveal personal attitudes of the author that accompany his extensive descriptions of a land not familiar to most Americans.[65] An individual bound to his place in history, Twain played on the exotic and racial prejudices of the day to write about native Hawaiians' traditions and customs to his audience back home.[66]

## *"Several Effects of the Turbulent Sea"*

Right from the first installment of the Sandwich Island letters, published April 16, 1866, *Sacramento Union* readers found vivid descriptions of both the joys and tribulations of Twain's voyage aboard the *Ajax*. Twain reported leaving on Wednesday, March 7, and his first letter is dated March 18. Twain included descriptions of the crew, Captain Godfrey, livestock and other cargo as he detailed the first day of his journey from San Francisco to Honolulu. He described some of the passengers, including three "old ship captains (and) whalers." Consulting his notes, he described in detail how he observed Captain Godfrey's ability to stay upright as the ship lurched back and forth on the choppy sea. Meanwhile, some of the passengers were not so lucky. Never one to gloss over the unglamorous realities of sea travel, Twain painted a vivid description of the seasick passengers:

I found twenty-two passengers leaning over the bulwarks vomiting and remarking, "Oh, my God!" and then vomiting again. Brown was there, ever kind and thoughtful, passing from one to another and saying, "That's all right—that's all right, you know—it'll clean you out like a jug, and then you won't feel so ornery and smell so ridiculous."[67]

The passenger named "Brown," it turns out, was a recurring fictitious character in Twain's Sandwich Island letters and future writings as well. Journalists at the time were not beholden to notions of objectivity in their reporting, so perhaps Twain used Brown to help personify what he felt like he could say better through a character. Nonetheless, the message was clear: a steamship cruise was challenging and certainly not for the faint-hearted.

Though Twain's first letter, dated March 18, would take nearly a month before appearing on page five of the eight-paged *Union*, his second letter would be published the next day, April 17, on page two. Letter three was on page one, beating out Boston, New York, and other correspondents for the front-page spot. Over the course of the twenty-five-letter run, Twain's correspondence would appear on the front page ten times and on page two seven times, particularly after his front-page exclusive about the survivors of the *Hornet* shipwreck with the headline, "Burning of the Clipper Ship *Hornet* at Sea. Detailed account of the Sufferings of Officers and Crew, as given by the Third Officer and Members of the Crew."[68] Reflecting on his reporting years later, Twain disclosed that it was a story that almost didn't happen. Laid up with his own injuries, Twain had been carried by stretcher to the hospital where the fifteen survivors of the shipwreck were being treated.

Fusing personal experience with timely reporting, the adventure writer did not neglect to also talk about America's strategic interest in the Sandwich Islands, suggesting great opportunities for American commercial interests. Twain wrote about the whaling industry, duties paid on molasses and sugar imports, and the potential for expanded trade with the islands—all within reach thanks to advances in steamer ship transportation.[69] Speedier and more reliable ships like the state-of-the-art *Ajax* offered more profitable trade opportunities than did the slower and less-reliable clipper sailing ships.[70] Twain would have been engaging his audience in a broader conversation about labor and American progress in a post-slavery society. His observations about the shipping industry and opportunities to expand U.S. commercial interest reflected the burgeoning U.S. industrial economy and a corresponding reimagining of what it meant to be an American in relation to the social change that accompanied a post–Civil War economy.[71] And who but *the* American, as Twain would come to be known later in his career, was more capable of commenting on nationalistic ambitions abroad?

His second and third correspondence for the *Union* would continue providing details of the journey, with an explanation of the "nor'west swell" that had caused the nauseating turbulent waters, a dossier on Captain Godfrey, details about the *Ajax*, and a "caution to romantic young people" on what it would take to be a sailor aboard the vessel.[72] What's revealed in these letters and is visible throughout the series is the reporting

*Opposite*: This sailing card for the *Hornet* alerted potential shippers that "the ships of this line sail more promptly and regularly than those of any other between New York and San Francisco." Its 107 days to the Pacific Coast was considered speedy in the years before the Trans-Continental Railroad reduced that time to less than a week (G.F. Nesbitt & Co., printer, *Westward by Sea: A Maritime Perspective on American Expansion, 1820–1890*, Library of Congress, Westward by Sea Collection).

Twain completed to accompany his first-hand accounts of his adventure abroad. For example, he shared statistics compiled by a San Francisco broker about trade between the U.S. and the Islands. On one hand, Twain highlighted the strategic importance of the Sandwich Islands, but he also wrote persuasively to advocate for U.S. expansion into the independent nation. With transportation improvements and a desire to expand U.S. interests, Hawaii offered a post-war opportunity to increase American influence abroad: "let the Islands be populated with Americans. To accomplish the latter, a steamer is indispensable."[73] The series of correspondence built a persuasive case to advocate for the United States to increase trade with the Islands.

While Twain was mindful of his audience and wrote about business interests, he seems to have understood his role as a journalist and not as a propagandist. In what would be his last letter, Twain commented in the final paragraph, "It is at very long intervals that I mention in a letter matters which properly pertain to the advertising columns, but in this case it seems to me that to leave out the fact that there is a neat, roomy, well furnished and well kept hotel at the volcano, would be to remain silent upon a point of the very highest importance to any one who might desire to visit the place."[74]

Twain's early cultural excursions included an afternoon spent at a Saturday marketplace in Honolulu. He wrote about the "natives" with deep description and curiosity. "The girls put on all the finery they can scare up on a Saturday afternoon…," some dressing in "flowing red" robes that "nearly put your eyes out."[75] At the market he was introduced to poi, the "chief article of food among the natives." Describing poi as a floury paste served in open bowls, his comic and stomach-turning description of how it was eaten serves as a stark contrast to Victorian eating manners that most of his audience likely observed:

> The forefinger is thrust into the mess and stirred quickly round several times and drawn as quickly out, thickly coated, just as if it were poulticed…. Many a different finger goes into the same bowl and many a different kind of dirt and shade and quality of flavor is added to the virtues of its contents. One tall gentleman, with nothing in the world on but a soiled and greasy shirt, thrust in his finger and tested the poi, shook his head, scratched it with the useful finger, made another test….[76]

This unflattering image of a native Hawaiian would eventually catch the attention of local journalists who were critical of some of Twain's reporting. Copies of the *Union* would begin to arrive on the Islands as Twain was planning his departure back to California.[77] Local journalists also accused Twain of stealing a copy of *History of the Sandwich Islands* from a local mission library and plagiarizing its content. But, as one scholar aptly put it, these criticisms were akin to "tossing pebbles at a tiger."[78] Twain returned fire and toyed with one opponent: "If he cannot tell when I am writing seriously and when I am burlesquing—if he sits down solemnly and takes one of my palpable burlesques and read it with a funeral aspect, and swallows it as petrified truth—how am I going to help?"[79]

One letter that likely offended local readers was Twain's recounting of a visit to the Hawaiian legislature. In letter number twelve, dated May 23 and published on June 20, 1866, Twain wrote as if he were surprised to find local politicians to be civilized. He painted a vivid picture of the physicality of His Royal Highness M. Kekuanaoa, as if describing chattel, calling him an "erect, strongly built, massive featured, white-haired, swarthy old gentleman of eighty years or thereabouts." Twain went on to communicate surprise at Kekuanaoa's transformation to a statesman from what he imagines would have been his primitive childhood during the reign of Hawaii's first ruler, Kamehameha I, at the turn of the century. Quoting his inner dialogue, Twain proposed, "This man, naked as the day he was born, and war club and spear in hand … has worshiped wooden images on his bended knees; has seen hundreds of his race offered up in heathen temples and sacrifices to hideous idols…." The politician's transformation, in Twain's mind, was remarkable: "—and now look at him: an educated Christian; neatly and handsomely dressed; a high-minded, elegant gentleman … a man practiced in holding the reins of an enlightened government."[80] But while he was complimentary of the legislative body's efforts to Westernize, he deemed Hawaiian politicians to be comparable to others around the world: "The mental caliber of the Legislative Assembly is up to the average of such bodies the world over—and I wish it were a compliment to say it, but it is hardly so."[81]

The most widely read of Twain's Hawaii correspondence was his exclusive interview series with survivors from the *Hornet,* the clipper ship that burned at sea. Relating the story of fifteen men who were adrift on the Pacific for more than a month until reaching the island's shores on June 15,[82] the story occupied half of the *Union's* July 19 front page. Twain described a harrowing forty-three days. Detailing their rationing routine, Twain explained how they managed to catch birds and flying fish for food, and reported that toward the end of their ordeal "the poor wretches had been cutting their old boots into small pieces and eating them. They would also pound wet rags to a sort of pulp and eat them."[83]

His reporting on the burning of the *Hornet* and recounting stories from survivors was a windfall for both Twain and his employer. His fifteenth letter from Hawaii was the first complete account of the *Hornet's* demise at sea to reach American shores, and his report was reprinted widely. Describing how the crew watched their ship burn to the waterline, Twain wrote, "All night long the thirty-one unfortunates sat in their frail boats and watched their gallant ship burn; and felt as men feel when they see a tired friend perish and are powerless to help him."[84] Less than half the people who escaped the ship survived their ordeal in the lifeboats. While Twain was indeed building his regional recognition and growing his national standing, the *Hornet* story was his first major scoop.[85]

In a 1900 article for *The Century Magazine*, Twain retold the story of his reporting on the *Hornet*, which he found nearly as harrowing as the shipwrecked crew he interviewed. He was in bed and "unable to walk" due to saddle boils caused by a difficult ride by horseback.[86] Anson Burlingame, a U.S. diplomat who happened to stop over in Hawaii on his way to serve as the U.S. minister to China, had helped arrange for Twain to be transported by a stretcher to the hospital to interview the fifteen survivors.[87] Twain reflected that, without Burlingame's help, it was a story he probably would not have been able to write. In his autobiography, Twain described how he managed to beat the competition:

> I took no dinner, for there was no time to spare if I would beat the other correspondents. I spent four hours arranging the notes in their proper order, then wrote all night and beyond it; with this result: that I had a very long and detailed account of the "Hornet" episode ready at nine in the morning, while the other correspondents of the San Francisco journals had nothing but a brief outline report—for they didn't sit up.[88]

## "The Vision of Hell and Its Angels"

Twain's final letter—dated June 3 but not published until November 16—told a story of his visit to the Kilauea volcano. Twain wrote this correspondence and the previous seven letters after he returned to San Francisco in June, but that did not prevent the journalist from sharing many details.[89] "I suppose no man ever saw Niagara for the first time without being disappointed," he began. Filling the rest of his opening paragraph with metaphor, Twain prepared his readers to share in his initial disappointment seeing the volcano. "It is a comfort to me to know that I fully expected to be disappointed, however, and so, in one sense at least, I was not disappointed," he wrote.[90] Despite claiming disappointment, however, Twain's vivid and detailed description of the volcano says otherwise.

The hook in Twain's last dispatch set his readers up for an uncertain journey. By using his imaginary friend, Mr. Brown, to help narrate his adventure, Twain took readers on an intimate tour of the volcano. To evoke a sense of "being there," Twain used local references for his readers to grasp what he was seeing. He described lava streams that looked like "a colossal railroad map of the State of Massachusetts done in chain lighting on a midnight sky."[91] When he and Brown spotted a house at the volcano's edge, he explained how it appeared "like a marten box under the eaves of a cathedral!" in relation

With a hotel sitting at the rim of the Kilauea crater, Twain wasn't the only visitor to make his way up the 4,000-foot mountain. But unlike the imaginary Mr. Brown or these visitors in 1896, Twain was completely unimpressed (Library of Congress, Item 1s12157).

to what he estimated to be a three-mile wide volcanic crater.[92] He continued giving readers a sense of distance traveled: "…we spurred up the animals and trotted along the brink of the crater for about the distance it is from the Lick House, in San Francisco, to the Mission, and then found ourselves at the Volcano house."[93]

He spared little detail when describing his observations of the active volcano. In one passage, he and Brown took in quite a sight:

> Here and there were gleaming holes twenty feet in diameter, broken in the dark crust, and in them the melted lava—the color a dazzling white just tinged with yellow—was boiling and surging furiously; and from the holes branched numberless bright torrents in many directions, like the 'spokes' of a lady's fan, and kept a tolerably straight course for a while and then swept round in huge rainbow curves, or make a long succession of sharp worm-fence angles, which looked precisely like the fiercest jagged lighting.

If Twain was indeed disappointed by his journey to Kilauea, the correspondence he wrote likely did not disappoint his audience.

## "In Prison Again"

When Twain returned San Francisco, even as he still had a few letters to complete for the *Union*, biographers note that he was already scheming to find another adventure.[94] It is clear from his personal notebook that living abroad and relaying his adventures kept his spirit alive. On August 13, the day he landed in California, he referred to his return home as returning to prison: "The city seems so cramped and so dreary with toil and care and business anxiety. God help me, I wish I were at sea again."[95]

Reflecting on her family's employment of Twain to write correspondence for the *Union*, Mary Josephine Anthony, one of the owners' daughters, remarked in a letter to a friend that Twain was paid $50 per letter and put his employers on the hook for paying his way back to the States because he had spent all of his earnings while in Hawaii.[96] While it is not entirely clear what was left in his bank account after his work for the *Union* was over, Twain scholars agree that the public lecture about his Sandwich Island trip was scheduled because he needed the cash.[97]

Through his network of friends in the newspaper business, Twain planned his first public lecture in part to help finance a book-length manuscript he had hoped to publish based on his letters from the Sandwich Islands. But it turned out that Twain was just as talented a public speaker as he was an adventure journalist. From his first public lecture, it was clear that Twain knew how to play to his audience. He cleverly marketed the lecture with handbills and newspaper advertisements that suggested an evening of humor and intrigue. The tantalizing words "Doors open at 7 o'clock. The trouble begins at 8 o'clock" anchored the bottom of the advertisements. Admittedly, he was overwhelmed at first with stage fright, but soon found an enthusiastic audience responded fervently to his storytelling style. The reviews were quite favorable and helped propel his lecture tour to cities across the country. While he would not write that book-length manuscript on the Sandwich Islands, the letters would make an appearance in early editions of *Roughing It*, first published in 1872, where the prose reflects a more polished and experienced storyteller.[98]

Twain's visit to Hawaii and his Sandwich Island reporting remained a highlight of his life, both personally and professionally. Arguably his most well-known biographer,

Albert Bigelow Paine, succinctly explained, "Mark Twain immediately fell in love with Hawaii and remained in love with it his life long."[99] By placing Twain's 1866 Sandwich Islands correspondence for the *Sacramento Union* in the broader context of the newspaper business in post-war America, it becomes evident that Twain was writing with a sense of calculated purpose and adventure. Twain wrote to multiple audiences, using hyperbole, metaphor, and eye-witness reporting to skillfully communicate stories about the exotic, exciting, and unknown to an eager audience. He also knew his audiences well enough to write about the emerging business opportunities that awaited industrious post-war entrepreneurs.

One Twain biographer sums up Twain's career as an assemblage of the industrious American in his era: "He was a humorist, novelist, story-story writer, social historian, dramatist, journalist, occasional lecturer and frequent dinner speaker, inventor, entrepreneur, all-night raconteur and billiard player, lavish host, and devoted family man."[100] Perhaps "adventure journalist" is implied in this inventory of Twain's talents; his industrious and adventurous spirit begets all of those aforementioned attributes.

## NOTES

1. Samuel Langhorn Clemens (hereafter SCL) to Jane Lampton Clemens and Pamela A. Moffett, January 20, 1866, San Francisco, Calif. (*UCCL 00094*); www.marktwainproject.org/xtf/view?docId=letters/UCCL00094.xml;style=letter;brand=mtp .

2. Mark Twain, "Jim Smiley and His Jumping Frog," *The Saturday Press*, November 18, 1865.

3. SCL, January 20, 1866.

4. Roy Morris, *American Vandal* (Cambridge, MA: Harvard University Press, 2015), 6; SLC to Orion Clemens, 26 May 1864, Virginia City, NV (UCCL 00082), www.marktwainproject.org.

5. Morris, *American Vandal*, 6.

6. Walter Francis Frear, *Mark Twain and Hawaii* (Chicago: Lakeside Press, 1947), 83.

7. SLC to Jane Lampton Clemens and Pamela A. Moffett, March 5, 1866, San Francisco, Calif. (UCCL 00096), n. 1. www.marktwainproject.org.

8. Lee Jolliffe, "Adventurer Journalists in the Gilded Age," *Journalism History* 42, no. 1 (2016): 3.

9. *Mark Twain's Letters from Hawaii*, ed. A. Grover Day (New York: Appleton-Century, 1966), vi.

10. James E. Caron, *Mark Twain, Unsanctified Newspaper Reporter* (Columbia: University of Missouri Press, 2008), 283–285.

11. Frear, *Mark Twain and Hawaii*, 93.

12. Those titles are *The Adventures of Tom Sawyer* and *Adventures of Huckleberry Finn*.

13. For an explanation of the news business after the war, see David B. Sachsman, "Introduction," in *After the War: The Press in a Changing America, 1865–1900* (New Brunswick, NJ: Transaction Publishers, 2017), xv–xxxii.

14. Alan Trachtenberg, *The Incorporation of America: Culture and Society in the Gilded Age* (New York: Hill and Wang/Macmillan, 2007), 103–105.

15. For example, see Gerald J. Baldasty, *The Commercialization of News in the Nineteenth Century* (Madison: University of Wisconsin Press: 1992); Thomas B. Connery, *Journalism and Realism: Rendering American Life* (Evanston, IL: Northwestern University Press, 2011); Hazel Dicken-Garcia, *Journalistic Standards in Nineteenth-Century America* (Madison: University of Wisconsin Press, 1989); William Huntzicker, *The Popular Press, 1833–1865* (Westport, CT: Greenwood Press, 1999); Paul Starr, *The Creation of the Media: Political Origins of Modern Communications* (New York: Basic Books/ Hachette, 2005).

16. Jolliffe, "Adventurer Journalists," 2–3.

17. Jolliffe, "Adventurer Journalists," 3.

18. Dorothy Gile Firebaugh, "'The Sacramento Union': Voice of California, 1851–75," *Journalism Quarterly* 30, no. 3 (1953): 321–330.

19. Richard Thomas Stillson, *Spreading the Word: A History of Information in the California Gold Rush* (Lincoln: University of Nebraska Press, 2006), 119.

20. Stillson, *Spreading the Word*, 131.

21. *Ibid.*

22. Firebaugh, "'The Sacramento Union,'" quoting Douglas C. McMurtrie, ed., *A History of California Newspapers* (New York: Plandome Press, 1927), vi–viii.

23. Frank Luther Mott, *American Journalism: A History of Newspapers in the United States Through 250 Years, 1690–1940* (New York: Macmillan, 1941), 290, and Firebaugh, "'The Sacramento Union,'" 321.

24. Mott, *American Journalism*, 290.

25. Firebaugh, "'The Sacramento Union,'" 321.

26. Frear, *Mark Twain and Hawaii*, 94.

27. Firebaugh, "'The Sacramento Union,'" 323.

28. *Ibid.*

29. Baldasty, *The Commercialization of News in the Nineteenth Century*, 37.

30. Firebaugh, "'The Sacramento Union,'"322.

31. "Sandwich Islands," *The North-American Review and Miscellaneous Journal* 3, no. 7, May 1816, 42–43.

32. "Sandwich Islands," *North-American Review*, 48.

33. For a history of Captain James Cook and his explorations, see Martin Dugard, *Farther Than Any Man: The Rise and Fall of Captain James Cook* (New York: Atria/ Simon & Schuster, 2001).

34. *Ibid.*

35. U.S. Department of State. Accessed July 11, 2017. 2001–2009.state.gov/r/pa/ho/time/gp/17661.htm.

36. Justin Kaplan, *Mr. Clemens and Mark Twain: A Biography* (New York: Simon and Schuster, 1966).

37. Michael Schudson, *Discovering the News: A Social History of American Newspapers* (New York: Basic Books, 1978), 68.

38. Carlynn Trout, "Samuel Langhorne Clemens," *Historic Missourians* (St. Louis: State Historical Society of Missouri, undated); shsmo.org/historicmissourians/name/c/clemens/index.html.

39. Harold Bloom, ed., *Mark Twain: Bloom's Modern Critical Views* (Philadelphia: Chelsea House Publishers, 2003), 14.

40. Frederick William Lorch, *The Trouble Begins at Eight: Mark Twain's Lecture Tours* (Ames: Iowa State University Press, 1968), 9.

41. For example, see Bloom, *Mark Twain*, 23.

42. Lorch, *The Trouble Begins at Eight*, 9; Roy Morris, *American Vandal*, 4–5.

43. *Roughing It*, 3.

44. Lorch, *The Trouble Begins at Eight*, 11.

45. James E. Caron, *Mark Twain, Unsanctified Newspaper Reporter: Mark Twain and His Circle Series* (Columbia: University of Missouri Press, 2008).

46. Caron, *Mark Twain, Unsanctified Newspaper Reporter*, 164.

47. Caron, *Mark Twain, Unsanctified Newspaper Reporter*, 163–164.

48. Margaret Duckett, *Mark Twain and Bret Harte* (Norman: University of Oklahoma Press, 1964), 24.

49. Lorch, *The Trouble Begins at Eight*, 23.

50. Frear, *Mark Twain and Hawaii*, 4.

51. Lorch, *The Trouble Begins at Eight*, 23.

52. Margaret Duckett, *Mark Twain and Bret Harte*, 8–9.

53. Morris, *American Vandal*, 146.

54. SLC to Jane Lampton Clemens and Pamela A. Moffett, January 20, 1866, San Francisco, Calif. (*UCCL 00094*). www.marktwainproject.org.

55. *Ibid.*; Lorch, *The Trouble Begins at Eight*, 23–24.

56. Caron, *Mark Twain, Unsanctified Newspaper Reporter*.

57. In a letter to his mother and sister in January 1866, Twain included a newspaper clipping that read, "The San Francisco Examiner says: 'That rare humorist, 'Mark Twain,' whose fame is rapidly expanding all over the country, informs us that he has commenced the work of writing a book." That book, likely his book on the Mississippi, would not manifest for years to come. From SLC to Jane Lampton Clemens and Pamela A. Moffett, 20 Jan 1866, San Francisco, Calif. (*UCCL 00094*), n. 8. www.marktwainproject.org.

58. Frear, *Mark Twain and Hawaii*, 83–84.

59. Mark Twain, "My Debut as a Literary Person," *The Century Illustrated Monthly Magazine* 59, Nov 1899, 77.

60. Frear, *Mark Twain and Hawaii*, 4.

61. SLC to Jane Lampton Clemens and Pamela A. Moffett, March 5, 1866, San Francisco, Calif. (UCCL 00096). www.marktwainproject.org.

62. SLC to W. C. Kimball and W. W. Kimball, April 26, 1866, Maui, Hawaii (*UCCL 00098*). www.marktwainproject.org.

63. Twain, "My Debut as a Literary Person," 77.

64. *Ibid.*

65. Day, *Mark Twain's Letters from Hawaii*, vii–viii.

66. *Ibid.*

67. "Letter from Honolulu," *Sacramento Daily Union*, April 16, 1866.

68. "California Digital Newspaper Collection," *California Digital Newspaper Collection*, accessed July 20, 2017, cdnc.ucr.edu/.

69. "Letter from Honolulu," *Sacramento Daily Union*, April 17, 1866.

70. *Ibid.*
71. Eric Foner, *The Story of American Freedom* (New York: W. W. Norton & Company, 1999), 117–118.
72. "Letter from Honolulu," *Sacramento Daily Union*, April 17, 1866.
73. *Ibid.*
74. "Letter from Honolulu," *Sacramento Daily Union*, November 16, 1866.
75. "Letter from Honolulu," *Sacramento Daily Union*, May 21, 1866.
76. *Ibid.*
77. Mark Twain, *Letters From the Sandwich Islands: Written for the "Sacramento Union,"* ed. G. Ezra Dane (Stanford, CA: Stanford University Press, 1938), 215–217.
78. *Ibid.*, 216.
79. *Daily Hawaiian Herald*, October 17, 1866, in Twain letters edited by Dane, 217.
80. "Letter from Honolulu," *Sacramento Daily Union*, June 20, 1866.
81. *Ibid.*
82. Day, *Mark Twain's Letters from Hawaii*, x; SLC to Jane Lampton Clemens and Pamela A. Moffett, June 27, 1866, Honolulu, Hawaii (UCCL 00103). www.marktwainproject.org.
83. "Letter from Honolulu," *Sacramento Daily Union*, July 19, 1866.
84. *Ibid.*
85. David Zmijewski, "'Hornet': Mark Twain's Interpretations of a Perilous Journey," *The Hawaiian Journal of History* 33 (1999): 55.
86. *My Debut as a Literary Person*, 77; Day, *Mark Twain's Letters from Hawaii*, ix.
87. *My Debut as a Literary Person*, 77; Day, *Mark Twain's Letters from Hawaii*, ix–x.
88. *Autobiography of Mark Twain,* ed. Harriet Elinor Smith et. al. (Berkeley: University of California Press, 2010), 128–129 in Gary Scharnhorst, "Mark Twain Reports the 'Hornet' Disaster," *American Literary Realism* 47, no. 3 (2015): 272.
89. Day, *Mark Twain's Letters from Hawaii*, x.
90. "Letter from Honolulu," *Sacramento Daily Union*, November 16, 1866.
91. *Ibid.*
92. *Ibid.*
93. *Ibid.*
94. Lorch, *The Trouble Begins at Eight,* 24.
95. Lorch, *The Trouble Begins at Eight,* quoting Albert Bigelow Paine, ed., *Mark Twain's Notebook,* 29.
96. SLC to Jane Lampton Clemens and Pamela A. Moffett, June 27, 1866, Honolulu, Hawaii (UCCL 00103). www.marktwainproject.org.
97. Day, *Mark Twain's Letters from Hawaii*, xi.
98. Day, *Mark Twain's Letters from Hawaii*, x–xi.
99. Quoted in Frear, *Mark Twain and Hawaii*, 87.
100. Kaplan, *Mr. Clemens and Mark Twain*, 175.

# "The First Bold Adventure in the Cause of Humanity"

*Henry Morton Stanley's Adventure*
*Journalism in Africa*

JAMES E. MUELLER

About four months into his second trek across Africa—this time to find the source of the Nile River—Henry Morton Stanley's expedition was in trouble. He had lost about 125 men out of an original force of 300 to "dysentery, famine, heart disease, desertion and war," the latter against the Watura tribe, which had vigorously contested his crossing of their territory. Even Stanley's British bulldog, somewhat unimaginatively named "Bull," was killed, but not before, as Stanley wrote proudly, he "had seized one of the Watura by the leg and given him a taste of the power of the English canines of his breed." But now on March 1, 1875, with the Watura defeated, Stanley faced a more disagreeable task—writing up some stories for the *Herald*.[1]

As he camped on the shores of Lake Victoria, Stanley was eager to put together the four sections of his boat, the *Lady Alice,* named after the fiancée he had left back home. He and his men had hauled it from Zanzibar and would use it to become the first to chart the entire lake. "It is with great pride and pleasure I think of our success in conveying such a large boat safely through the hundreds of miles of jungle which we traversed, and just now I feel as though the entire wealth of the universe could not bribe me to turn back from my work. Indeed, it is with the utmost impatience that I think of the task of writing my letters before starting upon the more pleasant work of exploring, but I remember the precept, 'Duty before pleasure.'"[2]

And Stanley could dutifully crank out the prose when he had to. He was a fast and prolific writer, producing his two-volume, 1,092-page book about his second African trip, *Through the Dark Continent,* in a remarkable eighty days when he returned to London.[3] In the field, Stanley wrote lengthy dispatches that would sometimes fill a whole page of the *Herald.* The conditions did not bother the work-obsessed Stanley, who had first learned adventure reporting as a correspondent for the *Missouri* (St. Louis) *Democrat* covering life in the American West, including an 1867 Indian war. Whether in America or Africa, Stanley had the knack for bringing his readers with him to the wild parts of the world, making himself the center of his stories, and conveying his feelings of terror, joy, or amazement at the things he experienced.

Stanley's reporting epitomized a new style of journalism that was responding to the public's need for escapism amid the disruption of industrialization. Historian Ted Smythe pointed out that "[p]eople needed and sought entertainment to break their humdrum, ten-hour-a-day, six-day workweek."[4] In fact, Stanley's reporting of his two expeditions into central Africa would be some of the best examples of adventure journalism of the Gilded Age.

## The Creation of Henry Morton Stanley

Like the best writers, Stanley had spent years honing his craft. He was born John Rowlands in 1841 in Wales. His father never acknowledged him, and his mother's family abandoned him to be raised in a workhouse for the poor. As a teenager, he worked his way to America on a ship, arriving in New Orleans. Stanley claimed years later that he was befriended by a wealthy merchant named Henry Stanley and adopted that man's name.[5]

Enlisting in the Confederate Army during the Civil War, Stanley was captured at Shiloh—his very first battle. He switched sides while a POW, but was discharged (or deserted, depending upon whose account you believe) before seeing combat again. After about two years working as a deckhand and later as a law clerk, Stanley joined the Union Navy, writing some stories about his ship's actions and submitting them to New York newspapers. He tried to get a full-time reporting job, but New York editors told him to first get experience in "the provincial press," so he headed to St. Louis.[6]

Stanley initially got a job as an "occasional"—a part-time reporter—for the *Missouri Democrat,* but his work covering stories in the West and then the Missouri Legislature earned him a full-time job. His assignments were to cover the West, the Indians, and specifically General Winfield Scott Hancock's 1867 Expedition in Kansas, which has come to be known as "Hancock's War."[7] Stanley's vivid writing featured the dramatic first-person style that would become his trademark.

Stanley believed he was ready to try New York again, and he approached *New York Herald* owner James Gordon Bennett Jr. for a job. Though Bennett would not hire Stanley as a full-time reporter, he agreed to his proposal to cover Great Britain's 1868 war with Abyssinia (present-day Ethiopia) as a stringer, a reporter paid by the published word. From Africa, Stanley provided the best coverage of the Abyssinian war, scooping more experienced reporters and winning him a full-time job with Bennett as a foreign correspondent.[8]

Yet Stanley remained beset by a lack of confidence. After years of struggle, he was determined to show his success in Abyssinia was not a fluke. "I must keep a sharp lookout that my second coup shall be as much a success as my first," Stanley wrote in his journal.[9] And indeed it was, and more. Stanley's coup was his 1872 story about finding missionary/explorer Dr. David Livingstone in central Africa for the *New York Herald*—a feat the paper bragged was "the first bold adventure in the cause of humanity, civilization and science."[10] It was a remarkable example of exploration and a new style of journalism in the adventure mode. Stanley battled disease, hostile tribes, and dangerous animals on a year-long, 700-mile journey from the eastern coast to reach a village called Ujiji near Lake Tanganyika, where he heard he would find the missing doctor.

Livingstone's servants came to Stanley's caravan before they reached the village. Stanley's men fired their guns in the air in celebration as a crowed swelled around them and accompanied them to the village. "As we advanced the crowd became larger and more mingled with the chief Arabs, and the noise of firing and shouting became deafening," Stanley wrote. "Suddenly the firing and hubbub ceased; the van of the expedition had halted." Stanley saw a pale, gray-headed white man in the middle of a knot of Arabs. He knew it was Livingstone, a man whose book on Africa he had read as a boy and who was the object of his long search. Stanley wanted to run up and shake his hand, but, he wrote, "False pride and the presence of the grave-looking Arab dignitaries of Ujiji restrained me and suggested me to say, with a shake of the hand, 'Dr. Livingstone, I presume?' 'Yes,' was the answer, with a kind smile."[11]

Stanley's formal greeting became immediately famous and a symbol of Anglo-Saxon tough reserve or silly self-consciousness, depending upon one's point of view. Dance hall comedians put it in skits, and in modern times it is the stuff of legend. To cite a few examples, both Big Band leader Artie Shaw and the rock band the Moody Blues used it as the title of a song, and the children's television show *Sesame Street* used the meeting as the basis of

**Abandoned by his mother, educated in an abusive workhouse, emigrating to New Orleans as a teenager, and then enlisting in both the Confederate and the Union armies in the U.S. Civil War, Henry Morton Stanley was always on the run. As a journalist, he found adventure in the American West, the Ottoman Empire, Ethiopia, Spain, and the Middle East before heading to Africa in 1871 (photograph by London Stereoscopic & Photographic Company, Wellcome Library, London, Wellcome Images).**

a skit with the characters Bert and Ernie.[12] Historian Edward Berenson wrote that the iconic phrase is one of a handful like "four score and seven years ago," "Let them eat cake," and "Give me liberty or give me death" that have endured and "distill certain great moments of the past."[13] Berenson argued that the ordinariness of Stanley's greeting gave nineteenth-century readers the sense they were witnessing an event in a place that had previously been mysterious and unknown. "This new cultural force possessed the ability to bring even those places most distant and least familiar to Europeans and Americans into the realm of everyday knowledge and rapid communication," Berenson wrote. "His dispatches made the globe seem much smaller than it had ever been."[14]

Stanley's reporting was also new because he created the story. He went out and found Livingstone rather than waiting on the coast for news of the missionary to come to him. The act of seeking—exploring the environment—is a natural human drive, according to recent psychological research, and Stanley's seeking Livingstone stirred that emotion in readers. Stanley's writing style was much more vivid than readers were used to,

The phrase "Dr. Livingstone, I presume" would forever embarrass reporter Henry Morton Stanley, whose treks in Africa were far more serious than the suddenly popular phrase would have suggested. "Stanley Meets Livingstone," 1872 (Library of Congress, Item ppmsca.186 47).

and he made liberal use of the first person, writing unabashedly from his own point of view. Stanley used the conventions of adventure stories, persuading the readers to identify with the hero—him.[15] Stanley was a surrogate for readers, taking them along on his expeditions by building the narrative around his experience. In this way, Stanley was a forerunner of modern writers like Hunter Thompson and Joan Didion.

## Finding Livingstone

The story that made Stanley internationally famous solved a mystery that had enthralled the public—the disappearance of Livingstone. The famous missionary/explorer, born in 1813 in Scotland, was a medical doctor who had made several well-publicized expeditions to Africa to evangelize and explore the continent. Livingstone's goal had been to find trade routes and open Africa to European commerce, which he believed would end the slave trade. In 1865, he had left England for another expedition, and in December 1866 some of his men abandoned him, returning to Zanzibar with the claim that he was dead. Subsequent letters from Livingstone were delivered in 1867 and 1868, suggesting he was still alive, but there were only vague rumors of his whereabouts after that.[16]

Stanley credited his publisher Bennett with the idea of searching for Livingstone and making it a great newspaper saga. But Tim Jeal, who wrote the newest and most definitive biography of Stanley, argues that Stanley had been following Livingstone's career since he was a boy and had conceived of the story as early as 1866. Jeal speculated that Stanley "gave" the story idea to Bennett and never wanted to take credit because he depended on the publisher for future work and because he did not want anyone to think he was looking for the missionary in order to advance his career.[17]

At any rate, Stanley had received Bennett's blessing and arrived in Zanzibar in January 1871. There still had been no news of Livingstone, so he gathered supplies, animals, and a crew of more than 100 men, assembled at Bagamoyo on the African mainland, and began his trek on March 21, 1871. His first story was published on December 22, 1871, detailing the beginning of the search. It was the only story he sent for about six months as the caravan struggled through the wilderness. Stanley found Livingstone on November 10, but because of the distance to travel back to a city with a telegraph, the first news of the meeting and a summary of Stanley's adventure was not published in the *Herald* until July the next year. The *Herald* boasted that Stanley's reports were an exciting narrative. "As mere relations of personal courage and perseverance amid exciting and trying situations these letters will be read with deep interest and pride by the American people, and will be found of sufficient value to reach, without the lapse of a letter, every country where civilization is more than a name. On this ground alone they will be prized, and will bear out the olden aphorism that 'truth is stranger than fiction.'"[18]

What made Stanley's stories so prized? From the first sentence of his first story, Stanley addressed the reader directly, talking to the *Herald* publisher and readers as if they were a unified community living vicariously through his trip:

> Your expedition, sent out under me, has arrived in Unyanymbe. Were you living in Zanzibar or on the East African coast you would have a much better idea what the above few words meant than you have now. You would know, without any explanation, that it had travelled 525 and a half miles, and if you heard that we had travelled that great distance within eighty-two days—a little under three months—you would at once know that we had marched it in a very short time; but since you and your readers live in America I must return to the island of Zanzibar, close to the coast of East Africa, whence we started, and give you a brief summary of the incidents and misfortunes which befell us throughout the march.[19]

Stanley shared with the reader his innermost thoughts as he reacted to misfortunes. Getting ready for the expedition in Bagamoyo was worse than two months at Sing Sing prison, he wrote. "It was work all day, thinking all night; not an hour could I call my own," he wrote. "It was a steady grind on body and brain this work of starting." If he'd had to stay any longer he would have killed himself by sticking his head in a barrel of sand, "which I thought to be a most easy death, and one I gratuitously recommend to all would-be suicides."[20]

Stanley wrote the above somewhat early in the trip, but much more stress than all-night planning sessions lay ahead. At one point his way was blocked by a war between an African tribe and Arab traders in which several of his own men were killed. Sick on and off with malaria, Stanley waited in Unyanyembe for two months as he tried to figure out a way to continue his journey. The locals told him he would never be able to continue until the war was over—which could take years—and his men began to rebel. No one knew where Livingstone was, and Stanley began to wonder if the tale of the good doctor was just a myth. Stanley's story conveyed a sense of madness at the frustration: "I wish I could write as fast as the thoughts crowd my mind. Then what a wild chaotic and incoherent letter you would have! But my pen is stiff, the paper is abominable, and before a sentence is framed the troubled mind gets somewhat calmer. I am spiteful, I candidly confess, just now; I am cynical—I do not care who knows it. Fever has made me so." The whining and cowardice of his men and the lying of the Arab traders was too much: "The rock daily, hourly growing larger and more formidable against which the ship of the expedition must split—so says everybody, and what everybody says must be true—makes me fierce and savage-hearted. Yet I say that the day after to-morrow every man Jack of us who can walk will march."[21]

Stanley's fierce drive to succeed permeated all his stories, including his first one, which ended with a promise: "Until I hear more of him or see the long absent old man face to face I bid you a farewell; but wherever he is be sure I shall not give up the chase. If alive you shall hear what he has to say; if dead I will find and bring his bones to you."[22]

Stanley also shared his happy feelings with readers, and his happiest time was when he found Livingstone: "Only two months gone, and what a change in my feelings! But two months ago, what peevish, fretful soul was mine! What a hopeless prospect presented itself before your correspondent!" His men had been deserting, and he had been called mad to think he would find Livingstone. But everything changed when he succeeded. "Wonderful, is it not, that such a thing should be, when the seers had foretold that it would be otherwise—that all my schemes, that all my determination would avail me nothing?"[23] It is significant that although Stanley provided some details about Livingstone's activities, the story was framed from Stanley's point of view. Angry, frustrated, or despairing depending upon the state of his search, Stanley is overjoyed when he has found the missionary. Livingstone, while the object of the search, is always of secondary importance to the adventure of finding him.

And Stanley provided plenty of details about the adventure. The most dramatic tale involved a mutiny among his men, who wanted to extend a three-day rest halt for another day. After marching only three miles, the men stopped without orders. Stanley saw his guide and another man sitting on an ant hill off the trail, holding their guns suspiciously. Stanley knew the rest of his men were watching to see if he could keep control of the expedition. He pointed his shotgun at the men, telling them to come back or he "would blow them to pieces." They walked back toward Stanley, but the guide smiled, pointed his gun at Stanley, and asked what he wanted. At the same time the other conspirator tried to sneak behind Stanley. Keeping his shotgun steady, Stanley threatened to shoot them both, telling his guide to "lower his gun if he did not wish to receive the contents of mine in his head." The tense standoff ended when one of Stanley's loyal men knocked the gun out of the guide's hand. The two mutineers asked for forgiveness, and Stanley, who was usually free with the whip on malcontents, decided to let them go without punishment. He later second-guessed himself, wondering whether he should have punished them. But as always with Stanley, the story came first. Stanley finally decided that if he had punished them, all of his men would have deserted, and the search for Livingstone would have ended there and then, "which would have been as unwelcome to the *Herald* as unhappy for myself."[24]

If he was not battling his men, Stanley was fighting nature, including crocodiles, which he called "cruel as death." Crossing the Malagarasi River in present-day Tanzania, while Stanley's men rode in boats, they had to let their donkeys swim across. One donkey "had barely reached the middle of the river when a crocodile, darting beneath, seized him by the neck and dragged him under, after several frantic but ineffectual endeavors to draw him ashore. A sadness stole over all after witnessing this scene, and as the shades of night had now drawn around us, and had tinged the river to a black, dismal color, it was with a feeling of relief that the fatal river was crossed, that we all set foot ashore."[25]

The animals were dangerous, but so was the terrain. Stanley described a surreal river as broad as the Hudson in New York, but covered by plants and grasses so thickly interwoven that they formed a natural bridge. The natives used it, but Stanley was skeptical, especially since he had heard the tale of an Arab caravan of about forty men and a donkey that had taken a wrong step and disappeared. He could see the grass waving around his men as they crossed, sinking about a foot into the water. A donkey broke through the bridge, and it took ten men to pull him out. "I expected every minute to see them suddenly sink out of sight."[26]

Disease, too, was an ever-present danger, and Stanley sounded like Edgar Allan Poe when he described what he endured from a case of malaria. "(T)he brain becomes crowded with strange fancies, which sometimes assume most hideous shapes," he wrote. "Before the darkened vision float in a seething atmosphere figures of created and uncreated, possible and impossible figures, which are metamorphosed every instant into stranger shapes and designs, growing every instant more confused, more complicated, hideous and terrible until the sufferer, unable to bear longer the distracting scene, with an effort opens his eyes and dissolves it, only to glide again unconsciously into another dreamland, where a similar unreal inferno is dioramically revealed."[27]

Stanley also gave his readers evocative portraits of some of the Africans he met, describing their dress, manners, and language, which were exotic to his readers. One chief would not let Stanley's men in his village or trade for food because he had never seen a white man before and was suspicious. Stanley gave the chief a substantial gift of cloth—quite prized in central Africa—that persuaded the chief to visit the explorer's camp with gifts of food and native beer:

> I at once advanced and invited the Chief to my tent, which had undergone some alterations, that I might honor him as much as lay in my power. Ma-manyara was a tall, stalwart man, with a very pleasing face. He carried in his hand a couple of spears, and, with the exception of a well-worn barsati (cloth) around his loins, he was naked. Three of his principal men and himself were invited to seat themselves on my Persian carpet. They began to admire it excessively, and asked if it came from my country? Where was my country? Was it large? How many days to it? Was I a king? Had I many soldiers? Were questions quickly asked, and as quickly answered, and the ice being broken, the chief being equally candid as I was myself, he grasped my fore and middle fingers and vowed we were friends.[28]

Stanley then opened his medicine chest and gave the chief and his men each a teaspoonful of brandy, which they declared "wonderful." Then they all got a sniff of his ammonia bottle. "Smelling of the ammonia bottle was a thing all must have; but some were fearful, owing to the effects produced on each man's eyes and the facial contortions which followed the olfactory effort. The Chief smelt three or four times, after which he declared his headache vanished and that I must be a great and good white man. Suffice it that I made myself so popular with Ma-manyara and his people that they will not forget me in a hurry."[29]

In scenes like these Stanley used a light touch of humor to make himself appear likeable and forge a connection with readers. Yet he also revealed his own ruthlessness in achieving his goals, baring his faults to the readers so that it seemed as if he had such an intimate relationship with them that no knowledge was out-of-bounds.

Stanley drove himself hard, and he expected the same from his men. Stanley flogged deserters and then bound their necks with a slave chain lent to him by Sheik bin Nasib, one of the powerful Arabs who lived in the area. Stanley wrote the men deserved such treatment because they were the same sort who deserted from the Union Army during the Civil War. "(T)hese men were as much bounty jumpers as our refractory roughs during the war, who pocketed their thousands and then coolly deserted. These men, imitating their white prototypes, had received double pay of cloth and double rations." They deserted, he believed, because they thought they could take advantage of Stanley like they had with previous missionaries to the country. But Stanley found his harsh methods kept his crew together. "I will never travel in Africa again without a good long chain."[30]

For Stanley, the ends justified the means in finding the heroic missionary. Stanley even suggested the hand of "Providence" in their meeting. It had been hard to find Livingstone in the great lands of central Africa, and both of their expeditions had met unforeseen delays of just the right amount of time that allowed them to come together at Ujiji. "It was as if we were marching to meet together at an appointed rendezvous—the one from the west, the other from the east."[31]

The *Herald*'s American readers, who were barely five years removed their own bloody war to end slavery, doubtless could see the hand of God in Livingstone's work to end the African slave trade and Stanley's efforts to rescue him. To twenty-first century readers, tales of whipping and slave chains may seem unconscionable. But Stanley presented his violent acts in the context of the American Civil War, pointing out that Livingstone had named a lake after Lincoln. "This was done from the vivid impression produced on his mind by hearing a portion of his inauguration speech read from an English pulpit, which related the causes that induced him to issue his emancipation proclamation, by which memorable deed 4,000,000 of slaves were forever freed. To the memory of the man whose labors in behalf of the negro race deserved the commendation of all good men Livingstone has contributed a monument more durable than brass or stone."[32]

At any rate, the trek certainly made Stanley's reputation. Bennett, who had been less than enthusiastic about the expedition in the beginning, acknowledged as much, congratulating Stanley in a telegram: "You are now famous as Livingstone having discovered the discoverer."[33] Others were not so kind. A few newspapers claimed Stanley had faked letters from Livingstone, and the Royal Geographical Society initially snubbed him with faint praise before finally awarding him its Gold Medal. But Queen Victoria granted Stanley an audience and gave him a gold snuff box decorated with rubies and diamonds.[34] Stanley was vindicated, but for the peripatetic reporter, the question, as always, was "What next?"

## Searching for the Source of the Nile

Stanley wrote a book about the Livingstone expedition, which became a "runaway bestseller," and launched a lecture tour. But the reporter was irritated by the role reversal of being covered by what he called "the scavenger-beetles of the press" who published "vulgar, even hideous nonsense (and) untruths."[35] He wrote an adventure novel based on his experiences, but he longed to go back to Africa. When he had finished the Livingstone expedition, he felt profoundly sad, writing in his diary, "My dark friends who had travelled over so many hundreds of miles, and shared so many dangers with me, were gone and I was left alone. How many of their friendly faces shall I see again?"[36] He wanted to go back to work with Livingstone, who had continued to explore central Africa, but Bennett sent Stanley instead to Madrid and then to West Africa to cover a colonial war. Livingstone died in 1874, increasing Stanley's desire to finish the missionary's exploration. Stanley persuaded London's *Daily Telegraph* and Bennett to split the costs of a grand expedition to find the source of the Nile. He left Zanzibar with an expedition of about 230 people on November 17, 1874, intending to circumnavigate Lake Victoria, Lake Tanganyika, Lake Albert, and then follow the Lualaba River to its source, determining the connection, if any, of the lakes to each other, and to find the source of the Nile River.[37]

The *Herald* editorialized that Stanley's work was more than just ordinary reporting. "(I)t is a pleasant thing to see the journalism of England and America laboring hand in hand to solve the problem of this mysterious and wonderful land and an American correspondent carrying the flags of the two nations into the hidden regions of an unknown continent."[38]

Stanley took his readers into the unknown with him, describing the terror of being surrounded and outnumbered by hostile natives. After days of walking through rough country, Stanley's expedition camped near a village of about 3,000 people. The people were surly and suspicious, although Stanley was able to trade cloth for milk, eggs, and chickens for his hungry crew. He continued to trade with visitors, including a shaman who wanted beads as a gift to show they were brothers. "Half an hour afterward the war cry of the Waturu was heard resounding through each of the 200 villages of the valley of the Leewumbu," wrote Stanley, who as he did when covering the Indian wars used phonetic spellings to let the reader better imagine the scene. "The war cry was similar to that of the Wagogo, and phonetically it might be spelt 'Hehu, A Hehu,' the latter syllables drawn out in a prolonged cry, thrilling and loud." About 100 warriors gathered on the outskirts of camp, dressed in their fighting costumes decorated with eagle feathers and zebra manes. As the warriors' numbers increased and surrounded the camp, one of Stanley's men who had been collecting firewood straggled back with a spear wound and his nose crushed by a knobstick. His companion had been killed with a dozen spears in his back.

Stanley ordered 60 men to deploy in front of the camp while the rest cut bushes and made a fence, and they fashioned sections of their boat, the *Lady Alice*, into a fortress in the middle of camp for a last-ditch defense. Stanley's men beat back the attack, and he then went on the offensive, ordering four detachments to go in different directions to seize cattle and burn villages. "Long before noon it was clearly seen that the savages had had enough of war and were demoralized, and our people returned through the now silent and blackened valley without molestation." But Stanley had lost 125 of his own men, whom he could not replace. "What name will you give such a loss when you cannot recruit your numbers, where every man that dies is a loss that cannot be repaired; when your work, which is to last years, is but beginning; where each morning you say to yourself, 'This may be your last?'"[39]

Stanley came closer to his last day as he found himself fighting an assortment of cannibal tribes that pursued his expedition. While canoeing down the Lualaba River, a series of waterfalls forced the expedition to come ashore repeatedly to cut a path through the forest and drag the canoes to the next navigable part of the river. "The savages seemed to think that we had no resource left but to surrender and be eaten at their leisure," Stanley wrote. But half his men would fortify each camp site and beat back the cannibals while others hacked a path through the forest. This went on for 24 days before they passed all the waterfalls. Then cannibals pursued them in a running fight on the river and finally blocked them with about 50 canoes, including a "monster" that had 80 crewmen and a platform on the bow holding 10 spearmen. Stanley's canoes lined up together, awaiting the attack.

"We had no time even to breathe a short prayer or to think of indulging in a sentimental farewell to the murderous cannibalistic world in which we found ourselves," he wrote. "The enemy, in full confidence of victory, was on us, and the big monster as it shot past us launched a spear—the first. We waited no longer; they came to fight. The cruel faces, the loudly triumphant drums, the deafening horns, the launched spears, the swaying bodies, all proved it; and every gun in our little fleet angrily gave response to our foes. We were in a second almost surrounded, and clouds of spears hurtled and hissed for a short time—say 10 minutes." Stanley's superior firepower broke their charge, and he and his men chased them back to shore, and then in a frenzy, pursued them into their village, where his men looted some ivory as "prize money."[40]

Although Stanley breathlessly recounted his fights with hostile tribes, his writings also showed his respect for Africa's people and their culture. In a story about the mapping of Lake Tanganyika, Stanley told the story of the creation of the lake through traditional African folktales, which he explained are "the mother of history." One Wajiji tale claimed the area once had been a dry plain, but one family owned a secret fountain that was home to a delicious fish. When the husband went on a trip, he warned his wife not to show the fountain to anyone. But the adulterous woman showed it to her lover as soon as her husband left. Her paramour put his hand in the water, which suddenly caused a gigantic flood that created the lake. "Within a few days the husband, returning from Uvinza, approached Ujiji, and saw to his astonishment a large lake where once a plain and many towns stood, and he knew than that his wife had revealed the secret of the mysterious fountain and that punishment had fallen upon her and her neighbors because of her sin."[41]

Stanley, like his hero Livingstone, hated the enslavement of Africans, a sentiment he repeated often in his stories. "Nothing would have pleased me better than to have been commissioned by some government to hang all such wretches wherever found," Stanley wrote of slave traders.[42] Although Stanley's main purpose was exploration, he tried to convince his readers to pressure the European powers to end the slave trade. He started one story "I promise you not to indulge my personal feelings, but to be cool, precise and literal, believing that the letter will have more effect than if it contained merely vituperations and objurgations against the slave traders." Stanley explained that the Arab slave traders and the African tribes that enslaved other Africans picked on the weakest tribes. By the time the captives reached the slave markets, Stanley's chilling narrative explained, they were too starved and dispirited to even cry:

> Their voices have quite lost the manly ring; they are mere whines and moans of desperately sick folk. Scarcely one is able to stand upright; the back represents an unstrung bow, with something of the serrated appearance of a crocodile's chine. Every part of their frames shows the havoc of hunger, which has made them lean, wretched and infirm creatures. Just here I could, if I might, launch into vigorous abuse of the authors of these crimes, and they deserve a thousandfold more denunciation than can be invented by me or by any humane soul in Europe; but I have promised to be cool, precise and literal. Yet I may say that all the Satanic host protects them, for it must be assuredly owing the deep wiles of hell and its habitants that the people of a small island like Zanzibar are permitted to commit crimes such as no European State understands.

Stanley urged the readers to pray with him that England would "rescue inland Africa, and to check these wholesale murders of inoffensive tribes in the interior of the sad continent."[43]

Stanley unofficially adopted Kalulu, or Ndugu M'Hali, during his first trip to Africa. In *Through the Dark Continent*, Stanley recalls how the child was killed when he and four others were swept over a waterfall in a canoe. Kalulu was only 12 years old (photograph by London Stereoscopic & Photographic Company, 1872, Smithsonian Institution, Item SIL28–277–01).

The *Herald* proudly editorialized that its correspondent had brought eyewitness testimony to the world of the horrors of the slave trade, "which still flourishes in Central Africa like a poisonous plant that overgrows and destroys all it touches." The *Herald* argued that Stanley's exploration would lead to commercial development and civilization that would in turn lead to the end of slavery: "If the only result of Stanley's journeys was the exposure of the slave trade, which is connived at by great European commercial nations, it would be a praiseworthy achievement worthy of the days of chivalry. But Stanley has accomplished more than this by opening to the world a territory so vast and varied in character as to tempt enterprises that of themselves annihilate the illegitimate trade in human beings."[44]

Stanley admitted he was no missionary like Livingstone, but he tried to share Christianity where he could, including with an African king in Uganda named Mtesa. Stanley was impressed by Mtesa's country, his court, and his personality. "As soon as Mtesa began to speak," he recalled, "I became captivated by his manner, for there was much of the polish of a true gentleman about it—it was at once amiable, graceful and friendly. It assured me that in Mtesa I had found a friend, a generous King, and an intelligent ruler." Mtesa was a Muslim, but Stanley persuaded him to study Christianity. "He has caused the ten commandments of Moses to be written on a board for his daily perusal, as Mtesa can read Arabic, as well as the Lord's Prayer and the golden commandment of our Savior, 'Thou shalt love they neighbor as thyself.'" Stanley urged missionaries to come to Africa to build homes, improve agriculture, and fight disease. Mtesa had assured Stanley he would welcome such aid.[45]

But Stanley was an explorer, and after visiting with Mtesa, he was off again to chart central Africa's waterways. He shared his amazement at the terrain of Africa, which he described as "either remarkably or savagely beautiful." Standing on a hill, gazing at the scenery, he found the countryside beautiful and explicitly guided his readers' attention across the view: "Look closer and analyze all this, that you may find how deceptive is distance. The grasses are coarse and high and thick. They form a miniature copy of an African forest. Their spear-like blades wound like knives and their points like needles; the reeds are tall and tough as bamboo; in those pretty looking bushes are thorns—truly the thorns are hooks of steel; the crown of that yonder low hill with such a gentle slope is all but inaccessible."[46]

Yet the grandeur of the forest was at times overwhelming for Stanley. Once, while he was cutting some cane, he felt himself inexplicably drawn to stop his work and look upward at the gigantic trees:

> I gradually felt myself affected more strongly than can be described at the deathly stillness, in the middle of which appeared those majestic, lofty, naked and gray figures, like so many silent apparitions. I looked at them with the same feeling I have often felt in looking at very ancient ruins; for these were also venerable monuments, witnesses of the ancientness of time, all the more impressive because I alone was thus surrounded by them.
>
> Looked I above or around, north or south, east or west, I saw only the silent gray shafts of these majestic trees. The atmosphere seemed weighted with an eloquent, though dumb, history, wherein I read, heard, saw and inhaled the record of lost years and lands. For the time I dropped all remembrance of self and identity—all perception of other scenes and reposes.[47]

Stanley realized the trees were centuries old, and had grown unaffected by all of the human struggles of the past. He fancied they said to him: "What art thou but a brief accident, slight as the dead leaves under thy feet? Go and tell your kind you have seen silence!"[48]

At other times, the silence would be broken by strange, hoarse cries. Stanley thought they might be gorillas or chimpanzees, but he could not tell because he could not see them. Also unseen were a tribe of "terribly vicious dwarfs, striped like zebras, who deal certain death with poisoned arrows." Stanley heard they were anywhere from thirty inches to four feet tall. "They are said to be exceedingly fond of meat, all creatures furnishing them with the means of existence, from an elephant to a rat. They are more attached to the pursuit of the elephant than any other, probably because of the abundance of meat those animals supply. Their weapons are poisoned arrows, whose deadly effect is so feared by the Wanguana that they have renounced all intention to molest them any more." Still the inquisitive Stanley vowed, "While in the new region to which I am bound I shall endeavor to obtain a personal knowledge of the sokos (gorillas) and the dwarfs."[49]

Stanley insisted on seeing things for himself before he wrote his stories because he did not want to use the excuse for any mistakes that he was merely quoting someone else, especially when the natives were prone to exaggeration of things like distance.[50] He filled his copy with details like barometer and temperature readings, the history of previous explorations, and the origins of African names, like "Tanganyika," which he found came from "Kitanga" for lake and "Nika" for plain.[51] Stanley wrote he was obligated to provide these seemingly "trite details" because his readers needed them to have a "thorough comprehension" of the subject.[52]

Stanley's sense of duty pushed him onward, overcoming warfare, disease, and, ultimately, starvation. Near the end of the expedition, Stanley and his people had been without food for days when they arrived at a small village, Nsanda, of about fifty people. There was not enough food for Stanley's group, so he sent some men ahead to beg any Europeans at Boma to send supplies. Stanley's people were so overjoyed when they got the food that they began chanting a spontaneous song of thanks. Stanley went to his tent so they would not see him cry. He wrote the rescuers that "(I)t will be the study of my life to remember my feelings of gratefulness when I first caught sight of your supplies, and my poor, faithful and brave people cried out, 'Master, we are saved; food is coming.'"[53]

The *Herald* marveled at the feat he had accomplished, claiming that it was more difficult than fifty Indian campaigns, because the danger was constant for Stanley, while Indian campaigns were marked by breaks in combat and the return of the troops to the shelter of forts. "One long, bloody, exhausting, life-wasting struggle was waged by the exploring party from the start to the finish of that journey. When the savages retired hunger and fatigue took their places and surrounded camps and canoe without cessation," the newspaper wrote. "From being an adventurous advance for the benefit of geographical science the movement became a perilous retreat of famine-stricken men toward a far distant point of safety and relief over a route wholly unknown as to its difficulties and natural perils, and through the midst of cannibals who harassed the travelers at every opportunity." It was, the *Herald* announced, the "greatest geographical success on modern record."[54]

## A Place in the History of Exploration and of Journalism

While the expedition to find Livingstone had made Stanley famous, the trek across the continent to find the source of the Nile gained him "a foremost position among African pioneer explorers, not only of the nineteenth century, but of all time."[55]

Stanley would return to Africa for two major projects, one of which ruined his historical reputation because he helped King Leopold II of Belgium establish what became the harsh Congo Free State. He served one term in Parliament and died in 1904 at the age of 63, weakened by the rough life of his explorations.

Stanley has since become a symbol for the evils of Western colonialism even though he denounced the slave trade and personally tried to fight the exploitation of the Congolese to the point that Leopold refused to make him Governor-General of the colony.[56] Stanley thought he was helping Africans by bringing Western civilization and was working to end the slave trade. Though shocking in the twenty-first century, his harsh methods were similar to those of other explorers or missionaries of the time; he just wrote about them honestly and dramatically.[57]

Despite his success as a writer, Stanley found it tedious. The very first lines of the first story from his expedition to find the source of the Nile tells readers what he thought of writing. He had just returned from a scouting mission of the Rufiji River before starting his caravan across Africa. "As I sit down to the table and take up the writing implements to record my experiences of the last few weeks a wish darts to my mind—that the art of writing was never invented. It is true. Writing to me is such a labor at this moment."[58]

Yet Stanley's writing about exploration sparkled with his sense of boyish adventure. During his search for the source of the Nile, Stanley ended one story by telling his readers he had not yet decided which route to follow. "And the prospect of entering any one of them causes me to quiver with delight, though merely anticipating what lies ahead 'Shall I search for the head of the Alexandra Nile, or shall I continue along the right bank of the Lualaba?' is a proposition which agitates the silent hours of night with me."[59] He held nothing back: his frustration, his rage, and ultimately his joy at finding Livingstone and later the source of the Nile. His commonplace greeting to Livingstone seems real because it was so ordinary and fit the adventurous correspondent personality Stanley had crafted. That personality captivated readers and took them with him across Africa in the excitement of what they might see next.

## NOTES

1. Henry M. Stanley, "Henry M. Stanley," *New York Herald*, October 11, 1875. The story was dated March 1, 1875, but because of the difficulty of getting the dispatches to a city with a telegraph, Stanley's stories appeared in print months after they were written.

2. *Ibid.*

3. Tim Jeal, *Stanley: The Impossible Life of Africa's Greatest Explorer* (London: Faber and Faber, 2007), 221.

4. Ted Smythe, "The Reporter, 1880–1890: Working Conditons and Their Influence on the News," *Journalism History* 7, no. 1 (Spring 1980): 72.

5. Stanley biographers disagree on the depth of his connection to the merchant, some arguing they never actually met while others claim the merchant was a pseudo father. Jeal, *Stanley: Impossible Life* (35–37), argues convincingly in the most recent major biography of Stanley that he made up the relationship and was actually befriended by a merchant named James Speake.

6. John Bierman, *Dark Safari: Life Behind the Legend of Henry Morton Stanley* (Austin: University of Texas Press, 1993), 37–41; Frank McLynn, *Stanley: The Making of an African Explorer* (Chelsea, MI: Scarborough House, 1990), 48–49.

7. Bierman, *Dark Safari*, 38–46; James Mueller, "Stanley Before Livingstone: Henry Morton Stanley's Coverage of Hancock's War against the Plains Tribes in 1867," *Journalism History* 42, no. 1 (April 2016): 5–14.

8. McLynn, *Stanley: The Making*, 67; Oliver Knight, *Following the Indian Wars: The Story of the Newspaper Correspondents Among the Indian Campaigners* (Norman: University of Oklahoma Press, 1993), 68; Henry M. Stanley, *The Autobiography of Sir Henry M. Stanley: The Making of a 19th Century Explorer* (Santa Barbara, CA: The Narrative Press, 2001), 234–235; Alan Gallop, *Mr. Stanley, I Presume? The Life and Explorations of Henry Morton Stanley* (Stroud, England: Sutton Publishing, 2004), 88–89.

9. Martin Dugard, *Into Africa: The Epic Adventures of Stanley & Livingstone* (New York: Broadway Books, 2004), 74.

10. "Our African Exploring Expedition," *New York Herald,* December 23, 1871.

11. Henry Morton Stanley, "Livingstone," *New York Herald,* September 20, 1872. Stanley did not receive a byline for some of his stories although his name was mentioned in the secondary headlines.

12. Clare Pettitt, *Dr. Livingstone, I Presume? Missionaries, Journalists, Explorers, and Empire* (Cambridge, MA: Harvard University Press, 2007), 13–17.

13. Edward Berneson, *Heroes of Empire: Five Charismatic Men and the Conquest of Africa* (Berkeley: University of California Press, 2011), 22.

14. *Ibid.*, 24.

15. *Ibid.*, 17, 25, 27, 46.

16. Byron Farwell, *The Man Who Presumed: A Biography of Henry M. Stanley* (New York: W. W. Norton and Company, 1989), 51–52, 58–59.

17. Jeal, *Stanley: Impossible Life,* 65–66, 500; Berenson, *Heroes of Empire,* 32–33.

18. "Letters from the 'Herald' Expedition to Africa," *New York Herald,* July 15, 1872.

19. "Dr. Livingstone," *New York Herald,* December 22, 1871.

20. *Ibid.,* "Dr. Livingstone," *New York Herald,* December 22, 1871.

21. August 9, 1872.

22. "Dr. Livingstone," *New York Herald,* December 22, 1871.

23. "The Road to Ujiji," *New York Herald,* August 10, 1872.

24. *Ibid.*

25. *Ibid.*

26. *Ibid.*

27. *Ibid.*

28. *Ibid.*

29. *Ibid.*

30. *Ibid.*

31. "Livingstone's Nile," *New York Herald,* August 15, 1872.

32. *Ibid.*

33. Jeal, *Stanley: Impossible Life,* 133.

34. *Ibid.,* 138–142.

35. *Ibid.,* 144, 147.

36. *Ibid.*

37. *Ibid.,* 164–165.

38. "Mr. Stanley's Expedition," *New York Herald,* December 2, 1874.

39. Henry M. Stanley, "Henry M. Stanley," *New York Herald,* October 11, 1875.

40. Henry M. Stanley, "Lualaba—Congo," *New York Herald,* November 24, 1877.

41. Henry M. Stanley, "Stanley," *New York Herald,* March 26, 1877.

42. Henry M. Stanley, "Stanley," *New York Herald,* November 29, 1875.

43. Henry M. Stanley, "Stanley's Letters," *New York Herald,* October 10, 1877.

44. "Stanley's Letters from Nyangwe," *New York Herald,* October 10, 1877.

45. Henry M. Stanley, "Religion at Court," *New York Herald,* November 29, 1875.

46. Henry M. Stanley, "Stanley's Letters," *New York Herald,* October 10, 1877.

47. *Ibid.*

48. *Ibid.*

49. H. M. S., "Stanley's Letters," *New York Herald,* October 9, 1877; Henry M. Stanley, "Stanley's Letters," *New York Herald,* October 10, 1877.

50. Henry M. Stanley, "Stanley," *New York Herald,* March 27, 1877.

51. Henry M. Stanley, "Henry M. Stanley," *New York Herald,* October 11, 1875; Henry M. Stanley, "Stanley," *New York Herald,* March 26, 1877.

52. Henry M. Stanley, "Stanley," *New York Herald,* March 27, 1877.

53. H. M. Stanley, "Stanley's Explorations," *New York Herald,* October 12, 1877.

54. "Stanley's Letters—Unveiling the Mysteries of Equatorial Africa," *New York Herald,* October 9, 1877.

55. E. G. Ravenstein, "Henry M. Stanley," *GJ* 24 (1904): 104.

56. Jeal, *Stanley: Impossible Life,* 287–288.

57. *Ibid.,* 224.

58. Henry M. Stanley, "Africa," *New York Herald,* December 2, 1874.

59. Henry M. Stanley, "Stanley," *New York Herald,* March 27, 1877.

# To Better See the World

*The Adventure Journalism of Eliza Ruhamah Scidmore*

James E. Mueller

When reporter Eliza Ruhamah Scidmore arrived at the Hotel Nederland in Batavia in the Dutch East Indies,[1] she was astounded at the dress, or rather lack of it, by the patrons. Men wore pajamas and slippers, and women wore sarongs or a skirt and jacket, and—horrors for the last year of the nineteenth century—exposed their ankles to view.

"It is a dishabille beyond all burlesque pantomime, and only shipwreck on a desert island would seem sufficient excuse for women being seen in such an ungraceful, unbecoming attire—an undress that reveals every defect while concealing beauty, that no loveliness can overcome, and that has neither color nor grace nor picturesqueness to recommend it," she wrote in her book about Java in 1899. The hotel rooms opened onto a garden court, and the guests lounged in front of their rooms staring at Scidmore and her companions. "Men in pajamas thrust their bare feet out bravely, puffing clouds of rank Sumatra tobacco smoke as they stared at the new arrivals; women rocked and stared as if we were the unusual spectacle, and not they; and children sprawled on the cement flooring, in only the most intimate undergarments of civilized children."[2]

Scidmore had seen even more dishabille in Japan, and included in her book on that country at least a half dozen anecdotes about the natives' unconcern with public nudity. In one inn, her room had been off a corridor that led to the public bath. She kept her door open because the room was so small and close, and she was repaid with an eyeful. "Gentlemen with their clothes on their arms went back and forth before our door as if before the life class of an art school," she wrote in her most famous travel book, *Jinrikisha Days in Japan*. Traveling down the road near Otsu, she saw a woman taking a bath on her doorstep while calmly watching the road and the passersby. Scidmore was amazed at the sparse clothing of her jinrikisha runners, who would take off their sole garment while resting and sit cooling off in the open covered only by their tattoos.[3]

Why Scidmore's focus on casual dress? Perhaps it was a way of titillating her Victorian-era readers in the United States. She certainly knew how to engage her audience. Scidmore (pronounced Sid-more) was the first woman to serve on the National Geographic Society's Board of Directors and has been credited with helping to modernize the society's magazine through the use of photographs.[4] But maybe her coverage of uncoverage was a reflection, too, of Scidmore's intensely private personality, a trait that came across in her writing. Unlike other adventure journalists of the period, she rarely used the first person or made herself the center of the story. She alluded to her various traveling companions, but told the readers almost nothing about them. Such a person might naturally be astonished by people who bared themselves, literally, to the world.

Publishing hundreds of articles and more than a half dozen books on her global adventures, Scidmore instead was the consummate reporter, recording scientific facts about natural phenomena like the glaciers of Alaska, or relaying the history and legends of Japanese shrines, or describing the unusual—both good and bad—food that she ate. A reflection of the global and scientific curiosity of the age, Scidmore craved knowledge about exotic people and environments and nurtured that excitement in her readers. Unlike post–Civil War adventure journalists like Henry Morton Stanley, though, Scidmore was primarily an observer rather than a participant, and her career, which lasted from 1876 to the 1920s, can be seen as a forerunner of the professionalized journalism that developed in the twentieth century.

Scidmore's *Alaska, Its Southern Coast and the Sitkan Archipelago*, published in 1885, was an assemblage of letters appearing in the *St. Louis Globe-Democrat* and the *New York Times*, intended to enrich the experience of future travelers to the region (photograph c. 1895, The Miriam and Ira D. Wallach Division of Art, Prints and Photographs, New York Public Library, ID 3939822).

## "Daydreams … of other countries"

Scidmore was born in the Midwest[5] in 1856 and moved with her family to Washington, DC, where her mother ran a boarding house and claimed to know every president from Lincoln to William Howard Taft. With relatives in the newspaper business and a taste of Washington society, she got the writing bug herself at a young age. Attending Oberlin College in Ohio for a year, she wrote her first major newspaper story about the 1876 Centennial for the *National Republican* in Washington. Scidmore began her journalism career as many nineteenth century women reporters did, writing for the society pages. But this was merely prelude. Scidmore once told an interviewer that she was born with a sense of wanderlust and that "My daydreams were always of other countries."[6] So now, with income from columns published in a number of newspapers, including the *New-York Times*, and a brother serving in the U.S. diplomatic corps in eastern

Asia, Scidmore had enough money and the wherewithal to pursue her travel dreams, ultimately visiting places such as England, Ireland, and Italy in Europe; Java, China, Korea, and Japan in the Far East; and Russia and India in central Asia.[7]

Publishing accounts of her trips regularly and widely, Scidmore's most famous Gilded Age adventures were to Alaska in 1883–84; to Japan on multiple occasions beginning in the 1880s; and, in the 1890s, to Java, an island of present-day Indonesia.[8] Unlike reporters who explored areas relatively untouched by Western civilization, such as Africa and the Arctic, Scidmore traveled in places offering many of the comforts to which she was accustomed. But her timing was impeccable, reaching these remote destinations just as her own nation was turning toward a new role on a global stage. Sailing for Alaska in 1883, for example, she noted that the recent Russian possession was less well-known than the Congo, and claimed that more Americans had traveled to the Alps than had seen Alaska's mountain ranges. Similarly, she went to Japan at a time when that country was undergoing a series of dramatic changes on the political, economic, and cultural fronts during the Meiji period of the late nineteenth century. It had only recently been opened to Westerners, and Americans as well as Europeans were obsessed with Japanese art and culture in the "Japonisme" movement. Less familiar still was the island of Java, characterized by tropical rainforests and legendary wildlife, a region experiencing a period of population growth under Dutch colonial rule in the late nineteenth century. Scidmore was one of the few popular nineteenth century writers to personally visit and describe what had been a truly wild Javanese landscape just decades earlier.[9] Her goal was not so much to take readers on a wild adventure as to teach them about other cultures and to show them that they, too, could travel to exotic places.[10]

Though adventure writing was a far cry from her start in journalism, Scidmore was a pioneering woman reporter in what was overwhelmingly a man's profession. Indeed, crossing boundaries into some of the world's most unfamiliar regions—unfamiliar, that is, to her American readers—must have held a particular allure, and made the inquisitive Scidmore a perfect Gilded Age traveling companion to her many devoted readers. It is no wonder that she was so successful at this style of writing—her stories about Alaska inspired so much travel to that state that she is credited with helping to launch its cruise ship industry—because she was at heart a tourist herself, wanting to see everything she could see.

## A Working Tourist Along the Shores of Alaska

Scidmore decided to tour Alaska after reading naturalist John Muir's newspaper accounts of his own travels to the territory. Purchased from Russia in 1867, a deal widely known as "Seward's Folly," after U.S. Secretary of State William Seward, who brokered the deal, Alaska was still a frontier, largely unknown to the American public, with the discovery of gold still 13 years in the future at the time of Scidmore's trip. Notably, traveling by boat along the coast in 1883 and 1884, she and her companions were the first tourists to sail in Glacier Bay. But Scidmore was a working tourist. She got up every morning with a breakfast of coffee and rolls, and spent the day observing what she later told an interviewer was "a watercolor country." She would then write about what she'd seen and learned. Her stories were published in the *St. Louis Globe-Democrat*, the *New York Times*, and *Harper's Weekly*, and ultimately collected in *Alaska: Its Southern Coast and the Sitkan*

*Archipelago*, in 1885. Impressed, a book reviewer called Scidmore "one of the best women correspondents in the country."[11] *Alaska* was revised and republished twice, the second as part of a series of guidebooks for tourists, yet it was considered scientific enough to be used as a resource for naturalists.[12]

Scidmore's Alaska reporting set a pattern for the rest of her widely traveled writing career. She chose not to glamourize her adventures but to give her readers a true picture of what they could see and do by addressing the landscape, culture, food, religion, horticulture, art, and fashion of every country she visited. She immersed herself in her subjects, learning everything she could and describing it for her readers with the detail of a sightseeing guidebook and the storytelling of a history text. Her works were sprinkled with the humor of a weary traveler, with just enough adventure to make the reader interested but not too scared to make the same journey.

Seven years before *Leslie's* would send its group of journalists to the "almost undiscovered country,"[13] Scidmore provided her readers exhilarating tales of life aboard a ship navigating through dangerous glacial waters, as when John Carroll, the captain of Scidmore's vessel, the *Idaho*, took his passengers to an unsurveyed part of Glacier Bay to see a monstrous glacier, so massive that the huge chunks of ice it dropped in the water allegedly rattled teacups in houses thirty miles away. The purveyor of that tale, an Alaska pioneer named Dick Willoughby, told Scidmore and her companions that they were brave ladies to make such a trip. "We received this with some laughter," Scidmore wrote, "and expressed entire confidence in the captain and pilot, who had penetrated glacial fastnesses and unknown waters before." Scidmore recounted the dangers of the Arctic adventure as the ship approached an ice field through which Captain Carroll had to steer. "We steamed slowly down the inlet, and out into Glacier Bay, stopping, backing, and going at half speed to avoid the floating ice all around us, that occasionally was ground and crunched up by the paddle-wheels with a most uncomfortable sound. With each thump from the ice, and the recurrence of the noise in the paddle-box, and then the sight of some red slats floating off on the water, Dick Willoughby's concern was remembered."[14]

Yet in the very next paragraph, Scidmore described an onboard birthday party for an 8-year-old passenger, striking an unlikely but incisive narrative contrast of adventure and tourism. One of the young friends who helped blow out the birthday candles wished he would be able to celebrate many more birthdays in Glacier Bay. The adults, apparently unconcerned at the damaged paddlewheel, cheered.[15] But Scidmore, remembering the danger, constructed the captain as a hero, daring to face the dangers of an icy frontier:

> It takes a daring and skillful navigator to carry a ship through that dangerous reach, and it is something fine to watch Captain Carroll, when he puts extra men at the wheel and sends his big steamer plunging and flying through the rapids. The yard-arms almost touch the trees on the precipitous shores, and the bow heads to all points of the compass in turn, as the 'salt, storm-fighting old captain' stands on the bridge with his hands run deep in his great-coat pockets, and drops an occasional 'Stab'ord a bit!' 'Hard a stab'bord!' or 'Port your helm!' down the trap-door to the men at the wheel.[16]

People took second place to experience, culture, and landscape in Scidmore's work. The private Scidmore seemed reluctant to use her writing to create portraits of the people she encountered. Carroll, the captain of the *Idaho*, who befriended Scidmore and even named a glacier after her, was dismissed with a pedestrian description of a few unimaginative paragraphs. "Captain Carroll, for so many years in command of the mail steamer on this Alaska route, is a genius in his own way, and a character, a typical sea captain, a fine navigator, and a bold and daring commander, whose skill and experience have carried his ships through the thousand dangers of the Alaska coast. He is a strict disciplinarian, whose authority is supreme, and the etiquette of the bridge and quarterdeck is severely maintained." Children loved him, and he was a great raconteur, but his stories, like the salt air, were impossible to repeat, she wrote.[17]

Though Alaska was still a frontier, she traveled with modern accommodations on ship, and rarely ventured far ashore. "One dreads to get to land again and end the easy, idle wandering through the long archipelago," she wrote of her Alaska travels. "A voyage is but one protracted marine picnic and an unbroken succession of memorable days."[18] Nevertheless, she and other adventurous passengers endeavored to explore the terrain first-hand by taking small boats from the ship. When the boats had to anchor twenty feet from shore, the sailors carried the women through the shallow water to land. "The burly captain picked out the slightest young girl and carried her ashore like a doll," Scidmore wrote, "but the second officer, deceived by the hollow eyes of one tall woman, lifted her up gallantly, floundered for a while in the mud and the awful surprise of her weight, and then bearer and burden took a headlong plunge."[19] Once successfully established on the beach, Scidmore walked on the glacier and its detritus of rocks, minerals, and mud.

As she would on many occasions throughout her travels, Scidmore paused long enough from the dangers of her adventure to revel in the awesome beauty of the scenery. In heavily descriptive passages that brought these landscapes into resolution for her readers, Scidmore adopted a narrative approach that allowed them to see the scene as it unfolded before her:

> Of all scenes and natural objects, nothing could be grander and more impressive than the first view up the inlet, with the front of the great glacier, the slope of the glacial field, and the background of the lofty mountains united in one picture. Mount Crillon and Mount Fairweather stood as sentries across the bay, showing their summits fifteen thousand feet in the air, clear cut as silhouettes against the sky, and the stillness of the air was broken only by faint, metallic tinkling sounds, and the ice floes ground together, and the waters washed up under the honeycombed edges of the floating bergs. Steaming slowly up the inlet, the bold, cliff-like front of the glacier grew in height as we approached it, and there was a sense of awe as the ship drew near enough for us to hear the strange, continual rumbling of the subterranean or subglacial waters, and see the avalanches of ice that, breaking from the front, rushed down into the sea with tremendous crashes and roars.[20]

Scidmore's writing was equally evocative when she described the feel of being in what for her readers would be unusual places. She thought the Wrangell Narrows in Alaska would have been worthy inspiration for a Romantic poet like William Blake—and indeed adopted a poetic voice to convey the experience. "Leaving Fort Wrangell in the afternoon," she wrote, "it was an enchanting trip up that narrow channel of deep waters, rippling between bold island shores and parallel mountain walls. Besides the clear, emerald tide, reflecting every tree and rock, there was the beauty of foaming cataracts leaping down the sides of snow-capped mountains, and the grandeur of great glaciers pushing down through sharp ravines, and dropping miniature icebergs into the water." She could see three glaciers on one side of the narrows, with the largest one, Patterson Glacier, extending back forty miles from the shore. "Under the shadow of a cloud the glacier was a dirty and uneven snow field, but touched by the last light of the sun it was a frozen lake of wonderland, shimmering with silvery lights, and showing a pale ethereal green, and deep, pure blue, in all the rifts and crevasses in its icy front."[21]

"It is a straggling, peaceful sort of a town, edging along shore at the foot of high mountains, and sheltered from the surge and turmoil of the ocean by a sea-wall of rocky, pine-covered islands," Scidmore wrote of Sitka, an area settled more than 10,000 years ago by the Tlingits (Irma and Paul Milstein Division of United States History, Local History and Genealogy, New York Public Library, ID 1629196).

Landscape was not the only subject to receive extensive attention in Scidmore's *Alaska* reporting. Though the territory was still a frontier and trading outpost to mainland Americans, it was home to native Alaskans, including Tlingits and Aleuts. Visiting coastal towns and villages gave the inquisitive Scidmore an opportunity to observe social customs up close. As a pioneering woman reporter, Scidmore was particularly aware of the way women were treated compared with men. Scidmore wrote with bemusement that native women in Alaska had great power and more rights than Indian women on the Great Plains and in some cases more than American women. She noted that Alaskan women typically steered the canoe when they sailed with their husbands. "Often she paddles steadily, while the man bales out the water with a wooden scoop."[22] The culture of the Sitka (pronounced Sheet'ka), who lived in southeastern Alaska, provided that when a chief died, his wives would go to his next heir unless they could purchase their freedom. "Curiously with this subjection of the women," she wrote, "it is they who are the family autocrats and tyrants, giving the casting-vote in domestic councils, and overriding the male decisions in the most high-handed manner. Henpecked is too small a word to describe the way in which they bully their lords." Scidmore complained that the savvy women sometimes interfered with deals she had made to buy souvenirs from their husbands. "Woman's rights, and her sphere and influence, have reached a development among the Sitkans, that would astonish the suffrage leaders of Wyoming and Washington Territory," she wrote. "They are all keen, sharp traders, and if the women object to the final price offered for their furs at the Sitka stores, they get into their canoes, and paddle up to Juneau, or down to Wrangell, and even across the border to the British trading posts. They take no account of time or travel, and a journey of a thousand miles is justified to them, if they only get another yard of calico in exchange for their furs."[23]

To illustrate the complex gender-based power structures, Scidmore used narrative anecdotes. A woman known as Mrs. Tom had amassed a fortune through shrewd trading. "Mrs. Tom is a character, a celebrity, and a person of great authority among her Siwash neighbors, and wields a greater power and influence among her people, than all the war chiefs and medicine-men put together," Scidmore wrote. Rumor had it that on one of her trading journeys Mrs. Tom bought a handsome young slave at a bargain price. "The slave was considerably her junior, but in time her fancy overlooked that discrepancy, and after a few sentimental journeys in the long canoe she duly made him Mr. Tom, thus proving that the human heart beats the same in Siwash town as in the Grand Duchy of Gerolstein." Scidmore admitted that this juicy bit of gossip was denied by some, who claimed Mr. Tom was a chief in his own right. "Any one would prefer the first and more romantic biography, but, anyway, Mr. Tom is a smooth-faced, boyish-looking man, and evidently well trained and managed by his spouse."[24]

A second anecdote illustrated Scidmore's observation that Alaskan men had to assert their power through sly rhetorical asides. Adopting the practice of native families to use animals like crows, bears, eagles, and whales as a sort family crest to decorate totem poles or other artwork, one chief explained his family lineage to Scidmore. "In his queer idiom, he tells one, 'I am a Crow, but my wife is a whale'; and as Mrs. John is of generous build, there is lurking sarcasm in his statement."[25]

Scidmore was less amused by the culinary practices of the native Alaskans, expressing revulsion at their unfamiliar fare. She wrote that the Sitka Indians were expert hunters and fishermen, but they rarely ate game or choice salmon, instead selling them at market. "It takes away a civilized appetite to see them eat the cakes of black seaweed, the sticks and branches covered with the herring roe that they whip from the surface of the water at certain seasons, and the dried salmon eggs that they are so particularly fond of," she wrote. "They eat almost anything that lives in the sea, and the octopus, or devil-fish, is a dainty that ranks with seal flippers for a feast. Clams of enormous size, found on the beaches through the islands, and mussels are other staple dishes."[26] When it came to exotic fare, Scidmore was satisfied to remain a distant observer.

## Adventure in Japan

Of all her exotic destinations, Japan held the greatest appeal for Scidmore, and she visited several times beginning in the 1880s. Scidmore found English-language newspapers, excellent hotels, and great food available in large Japanese cities. "Both living and travelling are delightfully easy in Japan, and no hardships are encountered in the ports or on the great routes of travel," she wrote enthusiastically.[27]

Although she often traveled in comfort, Japan was the scene of one of Scidmore's most vivid and dangerous adventures, the treacherous ascent of Mount Fuji, which she described in an extended narrative. When she arrived at the village of Subishiri at the base of the Holy Mountain, she thought the village seemed to be in a perpetual party of welcome for the 30,000 or so pilgrims who came each year from all over the world to hike the mountain trail.[28] But when she got up at four o'clock in the morning to start her own pilgrimage, the thought of climbing Japan's tallest volcano at more than 12,000 feet as daunting. Scidmore and her female companions planned to ride kagos—small baskets slung from a pole carried by two men. While Japanese travelers would sit on their heels and found it comfortable, Westerners like Scidmore, who were usually larger, found the conveyance not only uncomfortable but stomach-churning from the constant sway-ing. On top of that, Scidmore wrote, the Westerner typically felt guilty for being carried by men the size of 10-year-old American boys. Nevertheless, the kago was the standard transportation for women up to the point called, fittingly, Umagayeshi, or Turn Back Horse, where kagos and horses had to stop, and from which travelers proceeded on foot. Scidmore and her companions packed eight pairs of straw sandals to tie onto their boots as protection from the jagged, sole-destroying volcanic cinders on the path.

Each woman was assigned three guides, one to carry her pack and two to push and pull her up the harrowing mountain trail. "Aided still further by tall bamboo staffs, we were literally hauled and boosted up the mountain, with only the personal responsibil-ity of lifting our feet out of the ashes." After a hike (or haul) of about four miles, they emerged from a dense forest to behold the summit of Mount Fuji and a clear path, with houses, leading to the top. From this point, Scidmore wrote, "There are no dizzy preci-pices, no dangerous rocks, no hand-over-hand struggles, nor narrow ledges, nor patches of slippery stone—only a steadily ascending cinder path to tread. Above the forest line, nothing interrupts the wide views in every direction, and the goal is in plain sight."

Her optimism turned to desperation, however, when a sudden storm hit, wrap-ping her group in fog that obscured their surroundings. The rain came hard. Cascades of water rushed down the hardened lava tracks. "Glancing along the sloping lava-track," she wrote, "we saw a foaming crest of water descending from those sunny uplands, and had

Scidmore did not enjoy her rides in the kago, a contraption in which the rider is suspended in a swaying basket between two men. This circa 1890 kago, carried by four men, was apparently an upgraded model (Library of Congress, Item cph.3g14284).

barely time to cross its path before the roaring stream came on and cut off retreat." After two hours of hard climbing they made it to a one-room shelter made of logs and huge lava blocks. The doors were bolted shut against the storm, so Scidmore and the other 41 people huddled inside were nearly blinded by smoke from a fireplace sunk in the middle of the floor. They slept on mattresses on the hard, cold floor while the storm shook the cabin, and the one lamp hanging from the ceiling cast a weird light on the drenched hikers. "The shriek and roar and mad rushes of wind were terrifying, and we were by no means certain that the little stone box would hold together until morning," she wrote. The cabin held firm, but served as the hikers' prison for what Scidmore called three "endless" days and nights, the storm roaring and shaking the cabin like a ship in a hurricane. Scidmore and her companions put their feet in the ashes of the fireplace to get warm while they put handkerchiefs over their eyes to keep out the smoke.

On the third morning, the storm broke, and Scidmore and the other hikers climbed slowly to the summit. The view, she wrote, was worth the wait. But she barely had time to enjoy it before another storm rose up, blowing sheets of rain on the hikers. She rushed through the temple on the summit, obtained a certificate of ascent from the priest, then slipped, plunged, and rolled down the mountain with the help of her guides, stopping to argue about her bill with the landlord of the cabin shelter. Her soaked dress became too heavy, so she hung it as an offering to Fuji-san, and replaced it with a red Navajo blanket. Looking back up at Mount Fuji as she continued her travels, Scidmore reflected that although Mount Rainier was more beautiful, the Japanese reverence for Fuji made it more special than the American mountain. "We have not the people instinct with love of poetry and nature; we have not the race-refinement, and the race-traditions, that would make of it another Fuji, invested with the light of dream and legend, dear and near to every heart."[29]

Like her reporting from Alaska, Scidmore's extensive writing from Japan provided readers not only with adventure but also with comprehensive descriptions of the country's culture and institutions. She devoted a chapter of *Jinrikisha Days* to the Japanese theater and dutifully reported how the plays were written, how the actors were paid, and how the theater had developed historically, fitting into Japanese society. She managed to visit backstage with Danjiro, one the most famous Japanese actors of the day, and met some other unnamed actor at a tea. Like Captain Carroll from her Alaskan expedition, the great Danjiro received but a thin portrait. Although she had an interpreter, she relayed no dialogue, preferring to describe their actions. "Nothing could be more scornful and indifferent that Danjiro's treatment of the high-priced visitors to his dressing room," she wrote. "Fulsome flattery, if offered with the florid and elaborate Japanese forms, will mollify him, and the old fellow—eighth idolized Danjiro in succession—will finally offer tea, present a hair-pin to a lady, or write an autograph on a fan in his most captivating stage daimio (lord) manner."[30]

Scidmore also reported on the evolving nature of gender relations in Japan. During one of her visits, she visited a mountain temple that featured a platform from which husbands had once hurled wives who they suspected were unfaithful. If the wife survived the 150-foot drop onto the jagged rocks, she was assumed innocent. In other traditions, Japanese wives had been forbidden to entertain in mixed companies, and geishas had been the most educated women in the society. But Scidmore found those attitudes were changing, noting in her extensive description of the Imperial family that the emperor and empress were setting an example by trying to "harmonize the Occidental, chivalrous

After violent storms delayed their ascent, Scidmore and her companions found the view worth the wait. "As the clouds lifted, we could see for miles down the wet and glistening mountain to a broad, green plain, sparkling with flashing diamonds of lakes, and gaze down a sheer ten thousand feet to the level of the sea. It was a view worth the three days of waiting" (*Jinrickisha Days*, pg. 185, photograph by Herbert G. Ponting, c. 1905, Library of Congress, Item cph.3b168 50).

ideas of deference to women with the unflattering estimate of the Orient." Shockingly for the time, they rode side-by-side in a state carriage. "When, that night, he offered his arm to lead her to a twin arm-chair in the state dining hall, a new era was begun in Japanese history," Scidmore wrote, noting the political implications of the act. Furthermore, the empress adapted Western dress for ceremonies, allowing her to stand rather than sit or kneel as had been the earlier custom. The adaption of restrictive Western dress, Scidmore wrote drily, was "conduct little short of heroic for one accustomed to the loose, simple, and comfortable garments of her country."[31]

For an American dining abroad, Japanese food itself was part of the cultural adventure. In Kyoto, located in the Kansai district on Honshu, Scidmore attended a dinner arranged by a club of merchants that featured performances by geishas and multiple courses including salads, omelets, soups, jellies, and meats punctuated by sake toasts. "Did I not possess the ocular proof of a fan and a few souvenirs I could believe the fete which I saw to have been but a midsummer night's dream," she wrote. The dream became a disturbing reality, however, when she saw the pièce de résistance, "a magnificent carp, still breathing, and with his scales shining as if just drawn from the water." The master of ceremonies turned the tray with the quivering fish so that all the diners could get a good look. It was, Scidmore explained, an old tradition that foreigners usually did not get to see. "Morsels of the fish were presently lifted from its back and passed to the company," she wrote. "To us, the performance was a kind of cannibalism possessing a horrible fascination, but the epicures uttered sounds expressive of appreciation as they lingered over the delicious morsels. A sudden jar or turning of the tray made the carp writhe, and left upon us a sense of guilty consent and connivance that lasted for days."[32]

## In Search of Adventure in Java

Java, like Japan, offered many modern conveniences, although Scidmore did find the tropical climate oppressive and hard to get used to when she first arrived.[33] Still, she sought adventure, never refusing daring or strenuous activities. Scidmore had heard plenty of fantastic stories, like the one about a man who fell asleep in a Javanese rice field and woke up feeling a great sense of wetness on his knee. He looked down and saw a nonpoisonous snake had swallowed his leg to the knee. "All travel, though, is only such disillusionment and disappointment, and he who would believe and enjoy such blood-curdling things should stay by his own fireside," Scidmore wrote. "The disillusioned traveler has but to choose, on his return, whether he will truthfully dispel others' fondest illusions, or, joining that nameless club of so many returned travelers, continue to clothe the more distant parts of the world with the glamour of imagination."[34] Scidmore had also heard stories about huge tigers, cobras, and pythons in Java, and wanted to see a wild animal, at least from the train—she had heard a story of a locomotive surprising a tiger on the tracks—but a Dutch resident told her she would only see wild animals in the zoo.[35] In fact, Scidmore's adventure reporting from even the wild areas of Indonesia proved relatively tame, and highlighted the role of reporting in dispelling inaccurate or exaggerated representations of remote destinations.

As part of her regular cultural exploration, Scidmore took her readers on an adventure through the Javanese cultural landscape, but this time, she found the local cuisine quite delightful. She loved sampling the fruits she discovered in Java, devoting more than a half dozen pages of her book to their look, smell, and taste. She bought fresh fruit throughout her trip, keeping on hand her favorites. She thought the red rambutan was worth buying for its beauty alone, looking like a green chestnut bur with spines tinted a deep rose. The jamboa, or roseapple, was also lovely, with shades of snow white and rosepink making it look delicious. "One bites into the fine, crisp, succulent pulp, and tastes exactly nothing, and never forgives the beautiful, rose-tinted, watery blank for its deluding," she wrote. She enjoyed cutting apart the Chinese gooseberry, which split into triangular sections that made for a pleasant "after-dinner amusement." The mangosteen, however, was best. "It is a delight enough to the eye alone to cut the thick, fibrous rind, bisect the perfect sphere at the equator line, and see the round ball of 'perfumed snow' resting intact in its rose-lined cup. The five white segments separate easily, and may be lifted whole with a fork, and they melt on the tongue with a touch of tart and a touch of sweet; one moment a memory of the juiciest, most fragrant apple, at another a remembrance of the smoothest cream ice, the most exquisite and delicately flavored fruit-acid known—all the delights of nature's laboratory condensed in that ball of neige parfumee."[36]

Just as she had marveled at the icy frontier landscape of Alaska, Scidmore could also evocatively capture the heat and mystery of the Javanese jungle. Scidmore, always an early riser, found the gray dawn cast a peculiar light on the temple at Boro Boedor, giving it an eerie sense of mystery. Sunset, too, created an uneasy feeling. Pitch darkness quickly followed the sunset, and the lamps drew huge moths and flying beetles. Villagers who came to pay homage seemed to appear suddenly out of the darkness. They would stand motionless next to the grim stone images of the giant pyramid:

> Then lizards 'chuck-chucked,' and ran over the walls; and the invisible gecko, gasping, called, it seemed to me, '*Becky! Becky! Becky! Becky! Becky! Becky!*' and Rebecca answered never to those breathless, exhausted, appealing cries, always six times repeated, slowly over and over again, by the fatigued soul doomed to a lizard's form in its last incarnation. There was infinite mystery and witchery in the darkness and sounds of the tropic night—sudden calls of birds, and always the stiff rustling, rustling of the cocoa-palms, and the softer sounds of the other trees, the shadows of which made inky blackness about the (hostel); while out over the temple the open sky, full of huge, yellow, steadily glowing stars, shed radiance sufficient for one to distinguish the mass and lines of the great pyramid.[37]

Near the end of her trip, she climbed Mount Papandayan, a hike that took her through tangled bushes and thick bamboo grass. Her guide, who was always troublesome—he had once eaten all the sandwiches that had been packed for their day—tried to convince her to turn around. When she insisted on proceeding, he tried to scare her, remembering that she and her companions were always on the lookout for huge snakes. "Slanga! Slanga! (snakes) always live in dis kind of grass," he said with a mournful look on his face. "Very well," Scidmore replied. "That's just what we want to find. Be sure you tell us as soon as you step on one or see it moving." They never saw a snake on the climb, and on the summit only what she described as "the murky, blue, misty horizon of the rainy season."[38]

Later that night, after she had retired to her comfortable room off a garden overlooked by an iron bust of Mozart, she heard the bamboo chairs on her porch overturned and being dragged around. "'The snake!—at last!' was the first thought and cry; and as the thrashing continued, it was evident that a whole den of pythons must be contorting outside. 'A tiger' and we peered through a crack in the lattice door and saw our Tissak Malaya basket scattered in sections over the garden path, and monkeys capering off with our store of Boro Boedor cocoanut-palm sugar. And this petty larceny of the garden monkeys was our only adventure with wild beasts in the tropics!"[39]

## Finding Much to Admire

Scidmore acknowledged the limitations of her Western perspectives to thoroughly understand the communities she encountered in her travels. She did not abandon Western values in her assessment of those cultures, making judgments and using terminology that sound especially harsh to twenty-first century readers. As an outsider in the reported environment, she made generalizations about the people she observed, perhaps about their hygiene, intelligence, or habits. For example, on her arrival in Java, she was surprised to find modern conveniences and not "the screaming heathen of all other Asiatic ports."[40] Though these paradigms were not unusual in the context of nineteenth century journalism, Scidmore also subjected her own Western culture to criticism and found many things on her travels that she thought were better than in America. On the political front, she asserted that the United States and other Western powers had bullied and treated Japan shamefully in treaty negotiations; that in Alaska, the United States had not provided enough funds for education for the natives; and that Dutch rule had been brutal toward the Indonesians.[41]

"Steam jets roared and hissed from all parts of the quaking solfatara, and from the rumblings and strange underground noises one could understand the native legends of chained giants groaning inside of the mountain, and their name for the Papandayang, 'The Forge'" (*Java: The Garden of the East*, 319) (photograph by Ohannes Kurkdjian, before 1903, Leiden University Library, Southeast Asian and Caribbean Images, KITLV 75176, CCBY license).

Though her writing largely supports the notions of American exceptionalism, Scidmore found much to admire, particularly in Japan, praising many things from its military to the courtesy of its citizens. In passages written some fifty years before Pearl Harbor, Scidmore was unintentionally prescient about the difficulty the United States would experience were it ever to find itself at war with Japan. Noting the Japanese victories against China in recent incursions, she wrote, "In the relief of the legations and the occupation of Peking (Beijing) has proved her soldiers first in valor, discipline, equipment, and in the humanity to the conquered, and there was abundantly displayed that high passion of patriotism which the Japanese possess in greater degree than any other people."[42] The Japanese navy, she asserted, put the U.S. Pacific fleet to shame, and their army was among the best in the world, taking a little of the best practices from the top militaries of Europe. "There is a military genius in the people, and the spirit of the old samurai has leavened the nation, making the natty soldiers of to-day worthy of the traditions of the past."[43]

She also found the Japanese education system much the equal of America's, and Japanese children more gentle than their American peers. American adults to Scidmore seemed more impetuous and pushy than the Japanese, and less able to appreciate beauty. During the plum festival, she noticed the Japanese would admire the trees in a reverent, thoughtful manner. "It is a place for poesy and daydreams, but the foreign visitor dedicates it to luncheon, table-talk, and material satisfactions, and, perhaps, the warm sun and air, and the mild fragrance of the plum-blossoms aid and abet the insatiable picnic appetite."[44]

While Scidmore had been enamored of Japan almost from the beginning of her travels, Java took longer to grow on her. But on one stroll around a temple she felt a great sense of peace seeing the piles of tempting fruit for sale and the native babies sprawled contentedly on the warm, brown earth, eating watermelon. She acknowledged the allure of crossing boundaries, dispensing with Western structures of space, knowledge, and identity. "There was such an easy, enviable tropical calm of abundant living and leisure in the Lilliput village under Brobdingnag trees that I longed to fling away my 'Fergusson' (guidebook), let slip life's one golden, glowing, scorching opportunity to be informed on ninth-century Brahmanic temples, and, putting off all starched and unnecessary garments of white civilization, join that lifelong, happy-go-lucky, care-free picnic party under the kanari-trees of Brambanam."[45]

## Bringing the World Home

Though the private Scidmore would never adopt the casual dress that so shocked her on her travels, she brought more than just the stories of her adventures when she returned to the U.S.; she brought an insight and even an appreciation for distant cultures and a vision that would transcend national boundaries. But more than just a reporter on the exotic in remote locations, Scidmore brought a different legacy of those climes to blossom in her native city. In fact, it was Scidmore who most actively advocated for the planting of cherry trees in Washington, DC, beginning after her return from Japan in 1885. She wanted the capital to have the beauty of the cherry blossom festivals she had loved in Japan, but it was not easy to get the government to cooperate. She badgered officials on and off for 24 years before finally convincing First Lady Helen Taft to include it in her beautification plan for the city.[46] Scidmore brought her world adventures home in another way as well, serving as an accomplished photographer for *National Geographic*. Her images depicted people and places of her travel, providing a complement to the rhetorical pictures of her travels.[47]

Scidmore moved to Geneva in 1922, where she became a great advocate for world peace and the League of Nations.[48] She died in 1928 after a bout with appendicitis, succumbing to the complications that followed, perhaps exacerbated by her impatience with the medical treatment. A cousin who was with her said she fought remedies, which she felt were slow and "disarranging to all my plans."[49] Scidmore asked her family to burn her letters upon her death, making this most private of journalists a difficult subject for other writers. She left a letter with the American consulate that, fittingly for her desire for anonymity, directed there be no funeral, and that her body be cremated and the ashes disposed in the "most seemly way." The ashes were buried with her brother and mother in the Japanese city of Yokohama, on Tokyo Bay.[50]

Despite Scidmore's very visible impact on the foliage of the nation's capital, it was her writing in the nineteenth century that is perhaps her greatest legacy. As Isabel C. McLean noted in a profile of Scidmore's Alaska reporting, "We have forgotten the importance of a well-turned descriptive phrase before the advent of color photography."[51] Scidmore's descriptions spurred interest in the places she traveled, and that was good enough for her. As she wrote in the introduction to *Jinrikisha Days*: "The book will have attained its object if it helps the tourist to see better the Japan that is unchanging, and if it gives the stay-at-home reader a greater interest in those fascinating people and their lovely home."[52]

## NOTES

1.  Batavia is now Jakarta, Indonesia.
2.  Eliza Ruhamah Scidmore, *Java, The Garden of the East* (New York: The Century Co., 1899), 25–26. Some of the book was published earlier in *Century Magazine*.
3.  Eliza Ruhamah Scidmore, *Jinrikisha Days in Japan* (New York: Harper and Brothers Publishers, 1902), 203, 218, 253–4. A jinrikisha is more commonly now called a rickshaw.
4.  Diana Parsell, "From Early 'Lady Writer,' Washington Cherry Blossoms and National Geographic Legacy," January 16, 2018, blog.nationalgeographic.org/2018/01/16/from-early-geographic-lady-writer-d-c-cherry-blossoms-and-tsunami/.
5.  Sources disagree on whether she was born in Iowa or Wisconsin. She most likely was born in Clinton, Iowa, and attended a private school in Madison, Wisconsin, while her family lived in Washington, DC. See Isabel, C. McLean, "Eliza Ruhamah Scidmore," *Alaska Journal* 7, no. 4, (1977) 238, for a brief account of her early years.
6.  Nina Strochlic, "The Woman who shaped National Geographic," February 2017, www.nationalgeographic.com/magazine/plus/lost-and-found/woman-shaped-national-geographic-eliza-scidmore.
7.  Strochlic, "The Woman who Shaped National Geographic."
8.  Scidmore's trip to India was just as colorfully recounted in a 1903 book, *Winter India,* in which she noted that "despite its color and picturesqueness," and her expectations that the country would be "melancholy and depressing," she found it "so absorbingly interesting, so packed with problems, so replete with miracles accomplished by alien rule, so ripe with possibilities, that one soon overlooked the unnecessary hardships and discomforts of travel…" Like Scidmore's other collected works, *Winter India* is available on Google Books.
9.  The few previous books about Java were primarily scientific and colonial administrative accounts of the island, such as *Java; or, how to Manage a Colony,* published by an English-Indian explorer, J.W.B. Money, in 1861. See Jennifer Speake, *Literature of Travel and Exploration: G to P* (Taylor & Francis, 2003), 646–48.
10.  Scidmore, *Jinrikisha*, iii–iv; *Java*, viii.
11.  *Ibid.*
12.  McLean, 239–240.
13.  W. J. Arkell, *Frank Leslie's Illustrated Newspaper*, April 5, 1890, 190. See Chapter 5.
14.  *Ibid.*, 82–83.
15.  *Ibid.*, 83.
16.  *Ibid.*, 128.
17.  Scidmore, *Alaska*, 153–154.
18.  Scidmore, *Alaska,* 153.
19.  Scidmore, *Alaska*, 48.
20.  Eliza Ruhamah Scidmore, *Alaska: Its Southern Coast and Sitken Archipelago* (Boston: D. Lothrop and Company, 1885), 76–78.
21.  *Ibid.*, 46.
22.  *Ibid.*, 27–28.
23.  *Ibid.*, 99–100.
24.  *Ibid.*, 96–97.
25.  *Ibid.*, 146.
26.  *Ibid.*, 99.
27.  *Ibid.*, 22.
28.  The account of the climb comes from Scidmore, *Jinrikisha*, 162, 165, 178–187.
29.  *Ibid.*, 189.
30.  *Ibid.*, 109–111.
31.  *Ibid.*, 86, 90, 114, 120–123, 229.
32.  *Ibid.*, 300–303.
33.  Scidmore, *Java*, 324.
34.  *Ibid.*, 166.
35.  *Ibid.*, 165.
36.  *Ibid.*, 80–88.
37.  *Ibid.*, 211–212.
38.  *Ibid.*, 319–320.
39.  *Ibid.*, 323.
40.  *Ibid.*, 1–2.
41.  Scidmore, *Jinrikisha*, 360; Scidmore *Alaska*, 125; Scidmore, *Java*, 41.
42.  Scidmore, *Jinrikisha*, v.
43.  *Ibid.*, 36–45.
44.  *Ibid.*, 54, 57, 33.
45.  Scidmore, *Java*, 220.
46.  "Eliza Scidmore's Faithful Pursuit of a Dream," www.nps.gov/articles/scidmore.htm; Jennifer

Pocock, "Beyond the Cherry Trees: The Life and Times of Eliza Scidmore," www.nationalgeographic.com/travel/intelligent-travel/2012/03/27/beyond-the-cherry-trees-the-life-and-times-of-eliza-scidmore.

47. See Strochlic, "The Woman who shaped *National Geographic*."
48. "Miss Eliza Scidmore Dies in Geneva at 72," *New York Times,* November 4, 1928.
49. "The Woman who shaped *National Geographic*."
50. "Miss Eliza Scidmore Dies."
51. McLean, 239.
52. Scidmore, *Jinrikisha*, iv.

# "Mr. Bennett's Expedition"

## *The* New York Herald's
## *Arctic Adventure*

### CROMPTON BURTON

"Doctor Livingstone, I presume?"[1]

With those dramatic words published July 2, 1872, *New York Herald* correspondent Henry Morton Stanley's search for explorer David Livingstone reached its celebrated climax not just in the jungles of Africa, but in the pages of the newspaper that had sponsored his epic journey. A creation of entrepreneurial publisher James Gordon Bennett Jr. the safari to the dark continent[2] was nothing short of an elaborate invention of news and headlines designed to boost circulation and in this, the scheme proved a spectacular success.

However, not every promotional project Bennett conceived ended with such unqualified gratification. The next initiative intended to fuel his readers' fascination with faraway places via descriptive letters and breathless specials, the ill-fated *Jeannette* expedition in search of the North Pole, produced decidedly different results. Indeed, the outcome of the *Herald*'s flawed foray to the frozen reaches of the Arctic went well beyond mere exploitation and commercialization to include daunting hardship, starvation, and death to the majority of the ship's company, including the newspaper's own correspondent.

Recent works such as Hampton Sides' best-selling narrative, *In the Kingdom of the Ice*, and the Library of Congress' online exhibition, *Shared Frontiers*, have drawn heavily upon *Herald* accounts to refresh the story of the *Jeannette* expedition for contemporary readers. Yet, these thoughtful studies have stopped short of capturing the stupendous lengths to which publishers such as Bennett were prepared to go in not only hatching and sustaining promotional circulation schemes, but maintaining them long after propriety and good taste suggested the last telegraph message, self-serving editorial, or decked headline be written. Indeed, a micro-study of the *Herald*'s decade-long investment in the *Jeannette* expedition saga reveals the creation of circumstances from which the final outcome in the frigid wilderness of the Arctic proved almost predictable; a tragedy some forty years in the making, born of the sensational human-interest predispositions of the penny press, advanced by the most "public promotion of the myth of the explorer," and ultimately sustained by Gilded Age ideals of manliness and the struggle against the elements so closely attended by all of the excesses and scandal of the times.[3]

It cannot be surprising that James Gordon Bennett Jr. proved to be the architect of the *Jeannette* sensation that came to dominate headlines, gave rise to commemorative songs, poems, bestsellers, monuments, and works of art, and sold hundreds of thousands of editions of his *New York Herald*. How could it be otherwise given that he took his cue from a master, his father, who founded the journal in 1835? The senior's *Herald* was imaginative and innovative, and he a tireless gatherer of news as well as a shameless purveyor of sensational copy filled with tales of lurid crimes, runaway avarice, and ruined reputations. So profitable and powerful was the combination that by the time the younger and largely untrained namesake stepped forward at the age of twenty-six to take control of the newspaper at the close of the Civil War, he might well have been tempted to leave the management of the newspaper to the capable staff put in place by his father prior to retirement.

But Bennett Jr., or "the Commodore," as he came to be called, was most certainly not one to be upstaged in the running of his influential inheritance. He proved more engaged and attentive than anyone might have predicted, once upbraiding a group of executives, "I am the only reader of this paper. I am the only one to be pleased. If I want it to be turned upside down, it must be turned upside down."[4] Bennett developed an intuitive sense of the public taste in journalism like his father and became adept at delivering on his audience's expectation—even if that meant manufacturing the news to suit. In the process, his demands of his staff were simply and easily articulated. "Never spare expense or space when the news justifies it," he once admonished a new managing editor. "Whenever there is an important piece of news I want the *Herald* to have the fullest and best account of it."[5]

Remaining true to the notion of scoops no matter the cost, either in financial or, as events would prove, human terms as well, Bennett mimicked his father's tactic of sending correspondents to the scene of unfolding events. It was his belief that the geographical or cultural backdrops against which the action was taking place could be of equal or perhaps even greater interest to his readers than descriptions of the events themselves. As Arctic scholar Beau Riffenburgh observes, "It was a logical progression … for Bennett to send correspondents as members of expeditions, and then to organize and send the expeditions himself. In that way, Bennett himself could simply create the popular desire for information and then satisfy it with exclusive reports."[6]

Encouraged by the sensation of the Stanley-Livingstone story and well aware of the powerful pull on the public imagination of the North Pole, Bennett took less than a year to turn his attention from the miasmic swamps of equatorial Africa to the newspaper's next theater of drama and wonder, the trackless ice pack of the Arctic. He was keenly aware of just how much readers had relished tales of the lost expedition of Sir John Franklin and had rejoiced in the accomplishments of the country's first rival to the British monopoly seeking to navigate the Northwest Passage, Elisha Kent Kane.[7]

Lieutenant George Washington De Long of the United States Navy was of the very same mind. A promising young officer with northern notions of his own, he sought an audience from Bennett to discuss financial backing for a new expedition. He secured a meeting with the *Herald*'s publisher in January 1874 but nothing immediately came of the conversation. De Long quickly became embroiled in a court-martial resulting from the grounding of his ship in the Florida Strait. For his part, Bennett chose to invest in a failed bid to navigate the Northwest Passage and a second expedition to Greenland, neither of which boosted sales to expectation.

Exiled from high society in New York by scandal,[8] Bennett fled to Europe but never

Known for professional as well as personal extravagances, James Gordon Bennett Jr. thought it would be a good idea to send reporters to the Arctic in a used wooden gunboat. Not coincidentally, the phrase "Gordon Bennett" came to be used as an expression of outrage and disbelief in the United Kingdom (Houghton Library, TCS 1.2292, Harvard Theatre Collection, Harvard University).

lost his determination to underwrite an Arctic expedition, nor did he fall out of touch with De Long. In March 1877, the quixotic publisher visited renowned geographer August Petermann at his home in Germany, coming away from the visit convinced that the most promising route north was actually to be found via the Bering Strait as a "thermometric gateway" to the open water of a polar sea. It was a scenario made for the *Herald*, its news-making mastermind, and its daring correspondents, suggesting that "The solution to the Arctic Question awaited those bold and resourceful enough to attack it from a different direction."[9]

## "Bold and Resourceful Enough"

In the early summer of 1878, Bennett purchased the British steamer *Pandora* for the voyage to the Arctic. De Long took extended leave to oversee her refitting. Thus committed, the *Herald* began to build its readers' anticipation for their next great adventure. Buried deep within telegraphic news on July 5, a modest item noted the rechristening of James Gordon Bennett Jr.'s steamer as the *Jeannette* in honor of his sister. The ceremony in Le Havre was attended by the Commodore, De Long, Stanley, and a host of other Americans, and the brief article served as the perfect prelude to present Petermann's theories in detail and their not-so-subtle justification of the *Herald*'s pressing ahead with preparations for the expedition.

On July 15 under the headline, "The Next Great Discoveries to Be Made in the North," Bennett and his editors set the project's agenda in an updated interview with the professor. Unable to rely upon the publisher's inadequate notes from the March meeting, a *Herald* correspondent was sent back to Germany returning with the desired carte blanche in quotes. "I would not dwell too much on science, as that will come in its time," offered Petermann. "Of course, all that can be done for science will be so much gained, but the main thing now is to find new coasts, and new lands, and the Pole. Everything is secondary to that."[10]

Unfettered by serious scientific considerations, Bennett and De Long moved forward rapidly and the *Herald* was there every column inch of the way. When Petermann passed away in the fall, "Under the Northern Lights" carried details of the journal's efforts to secure his notes, charts, and papers for the reference of De Long. Two days after Christmas, the *Jeannette* arrived at San Francisco for further refitting, and, by "special dispatch," the newspaper highlighted the ship's seakeeping qualities boasting, "the *Jeannette* will prove equal to the difficulties of navigation in the far north when she steams ahead with her bowsprit pointing toward the Pole."[11]

In February 1879, Bennett and his editors reprised an invaluable element of the Stanley-Livingstone success story by running the first in a series of articles on the missing Swedish expedition of Adolf Erik Nordenskjöld.[12] Seeking to navigate the Northeast Passage, his ship, the *Vega*, was icebound and beyond communication. What better than positioning the *Herald,* De Long, and his expedition as potential saviors? On February 3, the newspaper's headlines read, "Nordenskjold's Fate, The Position of the Swedish Arctic Expedition Considered Perilous" and the clincher, "The American Arctic Steamer *Jeannette* Relied on to Afford Assistance." Bennett now had not only his Stanley, but as events would prove, the first of two Livingstones as well.[13]

Still, he did not yet have the Stars and Stripes. Bennett and his commander greatly desired official sanction for the expedition by the United States Government. Leveraging the influence of the *Herald* in Washington, Bennett soon enlisted Secretary of the Navy, Richard Wigginton Thompson, to shepherd a bill through Congress guaranteeing official sanction and, in the exchange, ensuring Bennett's exclusive access to all the news and drama. The U.S. Arctic Expedition, as it was now known, was coming together better than Bennett and De Long had originally planned.

And so was De Long's crew. Names that would become well-known to readers in the months and years to come were beginning to appear on the ship's muster roll in the spring of 1879 and among the first was Jerome J. Collins, signed aboard as scientist and photographer as well as the *New York Herald*'s correspondent upon Bennett's personal recommendation. Collins was the chief meteorologist for the *Herald*'s weather bureau and initially De Long was enthusiastic, writing of his shipmate, "He has a large fund of general information and will make a name for himself in the Arctic, I am sure." Another officer, navigator John Danenhower, was not so certain, describing Collins as a dilettante "who knows a little bit about everything in general and not a great deal about anything in particular." Most ominous of all, De Long and Collins suffered a serious falling out in the run-up to the *Jeannette*'s sailing date, with the correspondent taking offense at remarks made by the commander that seemingly marginalized the reporter's role in the upcoming expedition.[14]

The De Long-Collins feud, skyrocketing refit costs, and Bennett's growing disinterest in the project manifesting itself in his evasion of urgent requests to see the expedition off proved just so much backstory to the steady stream of optimistic reports from the *Herald*'s West Coast correspondent. By May, telegraph dispatches to New York updated readers on the *Jeannette*'s readiness, successful completion of sea trials, and De Long and his officers being feted by the California Academy of Sciences. In full promotional stride, Bennett's newspaper brought interest in the upcoming departure of the *Jeannette* to fever pitch the first week of July 1879.

There was plenty of help. Newspapers from around the country joined in the collective well-wishing. Polar perspectives poured in from Rochester, Philadelphia, and Washington, each dutifully reprinted in the *Herald*, building an impressive library of third-party endorsements for the "intelligent liberality of Mr. Bennett" and the "route Mr. Bennett has selected," along with the mission of "Mr. Bennett's expedition."[15]

## *"Off to the Pole"*

At last, the day of the *Jeannette*'s departure arrived and on July 8, 1879, San Francisco provided a sensational send-off meticulously reported in the *Herald*'s edition of the next day. "Off to the Pole" and "Ten Thousand People Cheer the Gallant Explorers" headlined coverage that also included a detailed map "illustrating Previous Expeditions to the North Pole via Behring Strait, the Voyage of Nordenskjold and the Highest Points Reached by Explorers since 1728." Especially gratifying for the expedition's absentee

*Opposite*: The officers of the *Jeannette* would become famous. They included experienced Arctic sailors, an engineer, a navigator, a surgeon, a carpenter, and scientists. Crew members included hunters, firemen, a machinist, sixteen seamen, and two cooks recruited from San Francisco's Chinatown (Raymond L. Newcomb, *Our Lost Explorers*, Frontispiece. 1882, University of Washington, Freshwater and Marine Image Bank, Item 46626).

OFFICERS OF THE
Jeannette Arctic Expedition.

COPYRIGHT SECURED 1882, AMERICAN PUBLISHING COMPANY

ARTOTYPE, E. BIERSTADT, N. Y.

patron and his enterprising staffers was the July 10 edition, in which most of the *Herald*'s New York competitors' items were reprinted paying homage to the country's top story if not its creator. The *Tribune*, the *World*, the *Evening Post*, the *Graphic*, and the *Mail* all offered up heroic platitudes perfectly fit for the occasion with one marked exception. Missing from the *Herald*'s festival of farewells was the *New York Times*. Its modest item from page five, while factual, lacked the necessary dash, ending as it did with the laconic description of the *Jeannette*'s taking leave, stating simply, "she steamed seaward."[16]

Burdened with provisions and fuel for a full three years, the *Jeannette* nosed to the north ever so slowly, making calls at Unalaska, St. Michael, and St. Lawrence Bay. From each isolated trading post, Collins industriously supplied the *Herald* with the Arctic equivalent of Stanley's African travelogue. As was the newspaper's custom, each dispatch was announced in a separate item in bold type, alerting readers the latest from the expedition had been received by telegraph and was featured in greater detail elsewhere in the journal.

Collins's copy played to the imagination and sense of adventure of his audience rather than its scientific curiosity. Vignettes of life in the Arctic captured images of drunken Aleuts playing pipe organs, greedy whiskey traders preying upon innocent natives, duck hunts, local marriage and courtship rituals, and lonely fur company agents and their families making merry by hosting dances. Leaving nothing to chance, the *Herald* confirmed the need for such reportage because "so little is known by the majority of our citizens of our far Northwestern Territory of Alaska." Relying upon Collins and his portrayals of "pioneers of civilization" and their "copper-hued charges," the *Herald*'s readership furthered its education with every updated edition of the newspaper.[17]

All too quickly, however, the "breezy" letters from the journal's correspondent came to an abrupt end. In the October 17, 1879, edition, Collins closed his letter with a sentimental sketch of an Aleut husband bidding his new bride farewell as he shipped aboard the *Jeannette* as a guide. The reporter also recognized the time had come to say his own goodbye, writing, "Feeling that we have the sympathy of all we left at home we go North trusting in God's protection and our good fortune. Farewell."[18] The editors back home in New York picked up on the hint of the ship's departure from civilization and severing of communication noting, "As the dark Arctic winter settles down upon the little band of explorers we may, therefore, cherish the hope that they have escaped the battle of the icy sea and are now in winter shelter."[19]

What the *Herald*'s editors and readers did not know was that even as they learned of the expedition's final departure for the Pole in mid–October, the *Jeannette* had already been "nipped" by the ice floes and entrapped in the pack several weeks earlier, well short of its hoped-for winter harbor. Beyond a few scattered sightings reported by whalers returning to San Francisco and the long-delayed delivery of some assorted letters, nothing further would be heard or seen of the expedition for the next two years. A lesser newspaper than the *Herald* might have been content to go as dark and silent as the northern night descending upon the expedition, but Bennett's staff was no ordinary team of journalists. Over the next twenty-six months, the story of the *Jeannette* was only infrequently absent from the columns of the journal.[20]

Prepared for just such an eventuality, Bennett's savvy staff sought relevant items to maintain audience interest in Arctic exploration and, by association, the *Jeannette*. In December, announcing the release of a book on the Arctic voyages of ill-fated explorer Charles Francis Hall, the *Herald* took the opportunity to proclaim De Long "master of the situation" and in no danger. Showing tireless enterprise, the *Herald* closed 1879 with an extensive feature dedicated to describing how previous expeditions had passed the Christmas holiday while similarly isolated and adrift in the polar pack. In the spirit of the season, the article closed, "With no uneasiness for their safety, but with many earnest desires for their success, let the friends of our Arctic heroes wish them to-day a right merry Christmas."[21]

Cheery as the salutation may have been, nobody had heard from the *Jeannette* and nothing had been seen of her for months. However, in the absence of hard news, the *Herald* was undeterred and conjecture and speculation from ranks of experts became the pemmican and biscuit of the American public anxiously awaiting word from the Arctic. High-ranking Navy officers held forth on the probable position or disposition of De Long and his party of explorers throughout most of 1880. Thus prompted, the Secretary of the Navy himself attached no credit to rumors of distress. One Arctic veteran stated flatly, "In none of these suppositions do any grounds seem to exist for serious apprehensions for Captain De Long and his crew; for if the vessel is lost the crew are very likely to be saved, but news from them cannot yet have reached us." That voice of authority was from none other than A.E. Nordenskjöld, the man De Long had been dispatched to rescue, who had passed out of sight of the *Jeannette* on his way southward, clear of the pack before it closed in for the winter.[22]

Nordenskjöld's grim mention of no word yet expected did little to mollify the press or the public. On January 30, 1881, with still no news of the *Jeannette*, the *Herald* featured an item in which it was announced that the U.S. Navy was costing out a relief effort for the consideration of Congress. When the paper's correspondent pressed for details, the response provided by Commodore Jeffers, chief of the Bureau of Ordnance, was ominous: "We expected to have to go in search of the *Jeannette* when she went away, and that an expedition will be fitted out you need have no doubt."[23]

## Dual Missions of Mercy

With Senate committees recommending funding for a relief effort and boards studying the logistics of sending another ship north, not to mention reports being authored and filed, the *Herald* was never wanting for new developments in the *Jeannette* story during the spring of 1881. The search for De Long and his company was on in earnest. While the first tentative journey of the USS *Corwin* yielded not a clue as to the whereabouts of the U.S. Arctic Expedition, its failure produced even more strident efforts from the government to mount not one but two relief cruises. The USS *Alliance* would search from the Atlantic side and the USS *Rodgers* from the Pacific.

The pace of preparations was agonizingly slow. By early June, neither ship was away, inviting a restless press to snipe. The *New York Truth*, never on board with Bennett or his profiting at the expense of taxpayer-funded rescue operations, thundered away at the *Herald*. "If the *Jeannette* expedition is a failure, and the men who manned it starving, they have had time to die twenty-four times over while the Rodgers has been preparing to go to her relief," declared the *Truth*. "The humane thing to do would have been for James Gordon Bennett to prepare, victual and send off at a moment's notice a vessel to save those whom he consigned to an almost certain death in the rotten little tub he named after his sister. But no, the Government must pay for his criminal blunder."[24]

Later, the *Truth* would be joined by a chorus of criticism, but for the moment Bennett and the *Herald* owned not just the story of the *Jeannette*, but the rapt attention of a national audience held captive by dramatic events unfolding that summer of 1881. Displaying a special skill for turning concern and question over the expedition to advantage, Bennett and the *Herald* made certain to assign reporters to accompany both the *Alliance* and the *Rodgers* on their dual missions of mercy. Each seized the opportunity to assume the role Collins was to have played, providing descriptive travelogues interspersed with updates on the progress of the search.

From the *Alliance* came narratives of howling gales, cruel Icelandic winter, and scrumptious shipboard seafood feasts. But it was from William Henry Gilder aboard *Rodgers* that the *Herald* readers received their true allowance of Arctic fare. Described by Riffenburgh as a polar reporter of rare ability able to establish easy relationships with his readers, Gilder succeeded so well because he "never lost his innocence, his fresh vision, his inquiring attitude." His description of a walrus hunt in August 1881 was published more than two months later, even as the *Rodgers* continued to seek any sign of the missing expedition. In his account, Gilder demonstrated a keen eye for the detail so totally in tune with an American audience unable to get enough of the *Jeannette* story.[25]

Gilder proved more than a valuable voice of adventure for the *Herald*. In the weeks to come, he exhibited an ability to improvise and take the initiative, rendering him one of the most resourceful correspondents Bennett's newspaper ever employed. His role in breaking the story of the final fate of the U.S. Arctic Expedition remains one of the most breathtaking examples of sensational reportage of the Gilded Age, rivaling even Stanley for its dramatic delivery under the most trying of conditions.

But it was not Gilder's dispatch that brought the telegraph to life in the *Herald*'s London office early on the morning of December 22, 1881. The message came from the expedition's engineer, George Melville. Sent almost twelve hours earlier from eastern Siberia, the contents were electrifying. "Jeannette was crushed by the ice in latitude 77 degrees 15 min. north, longitude 157 degrees east," read the telegram. "Boats and sleds made a good retreat to fifty miles northwest of the Lena River, where the three boats became separated in a gale." There was further word one boat was feared lost at sea and that the two others had made landfall though only one group was confirmed safe.[26]

Melville sent three telegrams in all, one to the *Herald*, one to the Navy Department, and a third to the U.S. Minister in St. Petersburg. The story he had to tell was an incredible tale of determination and endurance. He and his crew completed an epic retreat across the ice after the ship went down, navigated a howling storm before making landfall, and marched out of the wilderness to find rescue. It was beyond anything Bennett or his correspondents might have conjured on their most creative day and coverage in the newspaper's next edition was beyond anything yet published.

Next to two large maps tracing the track of the *Jeannette* and its survivors were no fewer than fourteen decked headlines. "Lost in the Arctic" and "Three Months of Suffering" were prominently featured along with "Two Boatloads Landed in Pitiable Condition" and "Boat No. 2 Missing." Absent much that was fresh besides the brief content of Melville's dispatch, extensive background material was presented along with great play given to the expert opinions of everyone from the man on the street in Brooklyn to officialdom in Washington. Fourteen more decked headlines greeted readers in the next edition even though the *Herald* still had little in the way of new information to share. Instead, short biographies of some of the ship's officers accompanied mention of intense interest in their hometowns.[27]

In an effort to reach land, the crew of the *Jeannette* boarded three boats bound for the Lena Delta on the northern coast of Siberia. Separated in a storm, two of the boats made landfall, with the third presumed lost. It was the second week of September 1881, already more than two years after their July 8, 1879, departure from San Francisco ("Wading Ashore" by George T. Andrew, from *The Voyage of the Jeannette, Volume II*, p. 759, edited by Emma DeLong, 1884, Naval History and Heritage Command, Item nh-92142).

## *"How mighty is the press!"*

Throughout Christmas week, the *Herald*'s reports remained decidedly more hopeful than accurate when not dishing up a hefty helping of self-promotion. Asked to share his thoughts on the news from Russia, Admiral Phillip H. Cooper prefaced his remarks with the kind of copy Bennett's best pitch man might have been hard pressed to deliver. "The *Herald* is everywhere," offered Cooper. "I have been in all parts of the world, and in the most remote region I have never failed to meet a *Herald* man. They seem indigenous to all climes."[28]

Indeed, after what some called "fashionable foraging for sensation" and following further critique from the *Truth* asking if perhaps even the sponsoring newspaper wasn't "working" the story "just a little too much," Bennett's intuition prompted him to send reinforcements to Siberia early in January. Not having heard from the *Rodgers* or Gilder and becoming apprehensive over implications of misconduct and negligence by De Long and his officers appearing in letters to the paper and in fresh dispatches finally coming over the wire, he assigned veteran European correspondent John P. Jackson to "write up" the *Jeannette* story and protect *Herald* interests. Already in St. Petersburg seeking the requisite travel documents, Jackson immediately set out for Irkutsk, where he intended to intercept the expedition's survivors and telegraph appropriate narratives home to New York.[29]

During Jackson's three-week journey east with artist M.A. Larsen of the *London Illustrated News*, he filed imaginative feature stories at every available stop with liberal doses of wolves, blizzards, and Cossacks filling his dispatches. But more importantly, he *received* telegraphed instructions from Bennett that included a stern warning "not to air soiled linen." Upon arrival in Irkutsk, the reach of the *Herald* and its publisher was further confirmed with another telegram addressed to Jackson, this one from the Navy Department, which granted permission to "open De Long's and Collins's papers, if found, and forward any matter for Bennett and the *Herald*." Control of the story remained firmly in the hands of the newspaper that had set the disaster in motion.[30]

And what a print property the U.S. Arctic Expedition remained throughout the spring of 1882. By then, Melville had filed a report detailing a frantic but unsuccessful search in the *Lena Delta* for De Long's missing party of survivors, but it was not Melville's missive that dominated the *Herald*'s April 19 edition. "Burned in the Ice" and "How the *Rodgers* Was Destroyed in Lutke Harbor" headlined the paper with the "startling piece of intelligence" that the search vessel had itself been destroyed and sunk in November with Gilder bravely volunteering to carry word of the mishap to the outside world. Miraculously encountering Jackson after "Bringing the News through the Deserts of North Siberia" and completing "A Remarkable Journey," Gilder's sledge trip over the tundra placed not one, but two *Herald* correspondents at the center of the *Jeannette* story. The *Oakland (CA) Evening Tribune* expressed what many must have been wondering at when it proclaimed, "It is entirely fit and appropriate that a *Herald* reporter from the *Rodgers* should travel hundreds of miles through incredible dangers to meet another who had come over thousands almost as bad to tell the sad tale of destruction. How mighty is the press!"[31]

And now, it was *Jeannette* survivor John Danenhower's turn to tell his story. The first installment of his interview with Jackson was published on April 26. Primarily a summary of the ship's trials in the ice and review of observations confirming the absence of any thermal currents opening a path to the Pole, his opening account was straightforward and forthright, the report one might have expected from an officer in the U.S. Navy. Chapter Two of the Danenhower narrative ran May 2, 1882, and carried his recollections forward to the date upon which the *Jeannette* was finally crushed in the ice and the crew forced to abandon ship.[32]

The serialization of the Danenhower interview was pure gold for Bennett and the *Herald*, but its final two sections were pure dynamite even with Jackson's filtering of the most volatile versions of events. In the May 3 and May 5 editions, Danenhower abandoned the esprit du corps that had characterized his first responses and openly questioned his captain's leadership, bristled at what he felt was unfair treatment from Melville, and wondered aloud why the engineer delayed in searching for De Long when time was of the essence. Operating from the precept that conflict is news, Bennett's editors ran with the corrosive copy rather than suppress it.

Even as *Herald* readers digested these startling revelations, more dispatches hummed over the wire to the newspaper's offices later that same evening. From Melville arrived the terse announcement, "I have found Lieutenant De Long and his party; all dead." He added, "All the books and papers have also been found." With still one boat missing, Melville signed off declaring he would continue the search.[33]

When the *Herald*'s May 6 edition was published with the rules printed in black for the first time since the death of President James Garfield, there was much greater detail included in the journal's columns on the death of the expedition's commander than was contained in the previous evening's few lines from the *Jeannette*'s engineer. Those specifics did not come from Melville. Incredibly, they came from Gilder. Somehow, he had intercepted Melville's courier in the vast wasteland of Siberia, cajoled the Cossack to open his sealed dispatches, discovered news of De Long's death, used the information to draft his own narrative of the *Jeannette* disaster, placed both sets of dispatches back in the pouch, and hurried the courier on his way to Irkutsk where both were transmitted, Melville's news to the Navy Department and Gilder's special to the offices of the *New York Herald*.

## *The Scent of Scandal*

Reaction was swift in the days that followed. As was to be expected, the *Herald* mourned its "gallant men" and Lieutenant George Washington De Long as "a Christian, a gentlemen, a hero" and one who "will have distinction unparalleled in Arctic annals." The *Chicago Tribune* saw things differently, topping its decked headlines on May 6 with "Arctic Horrors" and "Yesterday's Dispatches from Siberia Laden with Death and Despair." Even more disturbing were references such as "De Long Put Melville in Command When He Should Have Appointed Danenhower" and "Melville Lost Weeks of Precious Time in Opening the Search."[34]

*The Saturday Review* went farther calling out armchair adventurers like Bennett. "The moral is—that these private adventure explorations in circumstances so dangerous as those of Arctic travel are mistakes, unless the adventurer goes himself," read the editorial. The critique of private sponsorship for exploration continued with a sketch of expedition commanders compelled to reach beyond realistic limits to deliver sensational results for their sponsors. "He feels himself bound to give his owner a run for his money; he is reluctant to quit the quest without something solid and sounding, likely to satisfy the non-expert mind."[35]

The strong scent of scandal was in the wind, but if Bennett saw a storm warning, he also saw sensational sales ahead for his own *New York Herald*. Ignoring the momentary closure brought by news of De Long's death, Bennett and his managing editor, Harold T. Flynn, applied the true test of their newspaper's coverage and ownership of a story. "The instant you see a sensation is dead, drop it and start in on something new," was the Commodore's creed in determining when to cut losses and move on. Everything about the *Jeannette* story was telling him there was plenty of life left in the *Herald*'s Arctic adventure.[36]

Jackson and Gilder certainly thought so. Both correspondents relentlessly chased Melville in the Siberian snows anxious to invoke telegraphed permission from the Navy Department to examine any papers found on the bodies of De Long or his party. Eventually, Jackson caught up with a wary Melville who had advised his fellow survivors to remain silent in front of the reporter and "avoid useless talk." "Men might talk too much … say things they were not prepared to swear to," was the engineer's advice. The meeting had more the feeling of a confrontation than a rescue with Melville remembering the *Herald* man's pompous demands that he turn over De Long's and Collins's log books and journals on Bennett's orders.

When refused, Jackson set out for the burial site of De Long and his company where he exhumed the bodies and rifled the remains in search of any additional documents. He found none and Melville was livid upon learning of Jackson's actions. "Had I supposed it was the intention of this ghoul-like party to break open the cairn-tomb, I would certainly

The thirteen survivors of the *Jeannette* are pictured in Yakutsk, Russia, on December 27, 1881. Left to right, back row: Newcomb, Noros, Wilson, Tong Sing, Anequin, Leach. Middle: Melville, Danenhower. Front: Lauderback, Bartlett, Coles, Nindermann, Mansen. Only Melville would return to the Arctic, on a rescue mission in 1884 (photograph by A. Petrov, University of Wisconsin–Milwaukee Libraries, Digital ID pr001507).

have accompanied them, and prevented such a desecration," recalled Melville. "But, I never dreamed that a person born in a Christian land would so far forget the respect due to our honored dead as to violate their sacred resting-place for the purpose of concocting a sensational story, and making sketches, or out of idle curiosity."[37]

What Melville could not have known was that Jackson, for all his bluster and zeal, was truly acting upon Bennett's orders, but it mattered less now that the story of the U.S. Arctic Expedition was hitting much closer to home. Even as Bennett and the *Herald* defensively extolled the virtues of the explorers and pledged financial support for the families of the lost, Danenhower arrived in New York at the end of May. While he stopped short of totally recanting his accusations of misconduct, he did "wish it to be understood that these officers fulfilled their whole duty in every particular—a fact which he declares will clearly appear in the investigation that of course will take place."[38]

Investigation? Daunting as such a prospect may have been for Bennett, he was not unaware of the potential boost in circulation that would come from the *Jeannette* story developing into an extended courtroom drama. As a steady stream of sensational reports and specials from Melville, Gilder, and Jackson continued to find their way from Siberia into the pages of the *Herald* in June, July, August, and September, clamor for a court of inquiry grew. Most vocal were the two brothers of Jerome Collins, the newspaper's lost correspondent. After consulting with Danenhower, it was their contention that there was no question their brother and De Long's entire party might have been saved had Melville acted more decisively. Their outrage was made complete upon learning that stories of their brother's arrest for insubordination and prevention from carrying out his scientific work were corroborated. In their conversation, Danenhower termed Collins's service aboard *Jeannette* "merely a hell in the Arctic for three years," and said that in Collins's place, he "would have gone over the side."[39]

Upon his arriving home, Melville not only learned that President Chester Arthur had approved a joint resolution instructing the Secretary of the Navy to convene an inquiry into the loss of the steamer *Jeannette*, but that arrangements were being made to transport her dead home to the United States. Clearly, there was more mileage to be found in the story of "Mr. Bennett's Expedition." The Navy Department hearings opened on October 5 with an immediate directive that all business be conducted with "open doors" with the final report being forwarded to Secretary Chandler who, in turn, would send along the findings to Congress.[40]

Open the doors may have been for testimony, but behind closed ones Chandler, Melville, and De Long's widow, Emma, were determined to avoid tarnishing reputations and met for pre-inquiry strategy sessions. The actual proceedings began with an exhaustive examination of the *Jeannette*'s seaworthiness and fitness for Arctic voyaging before Danenhower began his lengthy deposition in mid–October. Day after day, for more than a dozen grueling sessions, the ship's navigator covered much the same ground as in his previously published interview, but in significantly greater detail. The *Herald* borrowed liberally from the inquiry's official transcript to once again fill the newspaper's columns with dramatic installments. Melville followed with his own expanded version of events and was not excused until the end of November with his testimony running to more than 400 pages.

In the end, Danenhower flirted with second-guessing De Long and Melville, and even toyed with shining a brighter spotlight on the Collins subplot. But he was no match for Bennett, Chandler, Melville, Emma De Long, and a host of witnesses who declined the invitation to forever tinge the legacy of the expedition with the remembrance of petty feuds and grudges. Despite bitter protests from Collins's family, on February 19, 1883, the *Herald* and its publisher stood exonerated by the Navy's report and its Congressional approval. Under six decked headlines, the verbatim presentation of the report read more like a jury verdict than journal article. The *Jeannette* was sound, the expedition managed appropriately, the loss of the ship unavoidable, and the "general conduct of the personnel of the expedition seems to have been a marvel of cheerfulness, good fellowship and mutual forbearance; while the constancy and endurance with which they met the hardships and dangers that beset them entitle them to great praise."[41]

Absolved, but far from unscathed, the *Herald* came in for yet another round of criticism in the pages of its competition. For months, rival newspapers had peppered the Commodore and his journal. The *New York Times* termed the expedition outcome a "criminal waste of money" and a "reckless risk of life." The *San Diego Sun* declared, "It is beyond question that the expedition was arranged solely for purposes of personal notoriety." And, the *Kansas City Star* added, "The *Jeannette* Expedition was a pretty good advertisement for the *New York Herald*, but a little severe upon the poor fellows who miserably perished." With the Navy Department's acquittal of the *Herald*, howls began anew with many editorial writers sharing the view of the *Boston Herald* that Arctic exploration was "senseless" and finding the North Pole would ultimately prove nothing short of an "empty honor."[42]

If rival journals sought the final word on the tragic outcome of the expedition, they sorely underestimated Bennett and his newspaper. Throughout 1883 stories continued to surface in the *Herald* on the return of the last survivors, an addendum to the Navy Department report, the publication of Emma De Long's book, and honors for those who helped the survivors in Siberia.

For all that, however, it was the article of December 22 that truly transitioned the story from its adventure travelogue and courtroom proceedings to one final and dramatic chapter. "The remains of Commander De Long and his comrades of the ill-fated *Jeannette* expedition, have arrived here," read the cable from Irkutsk. And so began a macabre funeral pageant that not only featured the *Herald*'s day-by-day monitoring of the cortege's progress across the steppes of Russia to Moscow and then on to Hamburg for embarkation on the steamer *Frisia*, but extensive coverage of arrangements in New York to receive the honored dead.[43]

Anyone in danger of losing track of the mournful procession's progress had only to refer to the *Herald*'s issue of February 7, 1884, to remain clear on the details of the epic effort to bring De Long and his comrades home. A huge map dominated page three, chronicling not only the reindeer and horse sledge legs of the journey, but also the railroad connections in place as well as the vast distances traveled. A footnote ensured that every reader understood the delays in the "table of time" were the result of "stoppages and demonstrations by the people and officials in Moscow and Berlin, as set forth in the *Herald*'s special cable despatches [*sic*]."[44]

Finally, on February 20, the *Frisia* docked in New York delivering her sad and somber cargo, triggering yet another round of print prostration from the hometown journal. On February 21, even as plans were completed for the grand funeral march of the next day, the newspaper celebrated its returned "stout hearted fellows" and laid not the last wreath of words at the feet of the fallen explorers. "Had they returned alive they would have been the heroes of the hour, and all young enthusiasts would have cheered them," editorialized the *Herald*. "But when to-morrow, with closed eyes and mute lips, they pass through the reverent throng that will fill Broadway, every man who in his own daily life, however humble and obscure, is combating misfortunes from which he can see no release will be stronger and better as he realizes how heartily humanity honors noble endurance."[45]

The morning edition of February 22 overflowed with details of the upcoming celebration of the newspaper's Arctic heroes, including a diagram of the order in which the hearses would proceed up Broadway to City Hall Park. The pending pageant of grief and glorification took center stage. Under a cloudless sky and to the tolling of bells and booming of cannon, Lieutenant Commander George Washington De Long and his six comrades were paraded before thousands of mourning New Yorkers. Rules turned dark once again, the *Herald* of the next day, February 23, 1884, missed not a single, sensational detail in its moment-to-moment account of the funeral's choreography with subsequent editions of February 24 and 25 proclaiming "Rest at Last" and "Death Did Not Mean Failure."[46]

"Rest at last" there may have been for the victims of the *Jeannette* expedition, but not for their story. Throughout much of 1884, a second inquiry in the form of a Congressional Investigating Committee demanded by the Collins family moved forward even though energetically discredited by the *Herald* as unnecessary. It revealed little that was new and there was scant surprise when in February 1885, De Long was once again exonerated of any blame in the disaster. Final addenda materialized in the form of dispatches from Siberia upon the occasion of the United States government bestowing gifts upon those who had assisted the survivors, but Bennett and his editors finally realized it was time to move on. The saga of the U.S. Arctic Expedition in the pages of the *New York Herald* gradually faded from the headlines more than five years after first electrifying them with the *Jeannette*'s departure from San Francisco.

## A Complicated Legacy

James Gordon Bennett Jr. never lost his fascination with the Arctic. He continued to invest in coverage of the quest for the North Pole, including his purchase of Dr. Frederick Cook's tale of reaching the top of the world in 1909 for $25,000. Robert Peary's counter claim was the property of the rival *New York Times* and the competing journals staged an epic copyright and circulation war over ownership of one last northern narrative.

By the time the National Geographic Society endorsed Peary's version of events, Bennett had already turned much of his attention to the flagging finances of his newspaper. Seeking to reverse the effects of his own profligate spending and mitigate the impact of multiple missteps on the business side, the Commodore managed to navigate the turmoil of the Great War, but it was a losing battle. Shortly after his death in 1918, the *Herald* was sold to Frank A. Munsey who merged it with the *Tribune* in 1924. The one-time circulation powerhouse and swashbuckling source of Stanley and Livingstone and the U.S. Arctic Expedition was no more.

The legacy of the *Jeannette* and George Washington De Long is a paradoxical one at best. On the one hand, the ship's almost immediate entrapment in the ice, while effectively disproving Petermann's theory of an open polar sea, prevented much else of significance from being added to the body of science surrounding the polar region. The modest mapping of the Siberian coast did yield a measure of discovery, but the *Jeannette*'s two-year uncontrollable drift rendered reaching the North Pole an impossibility. And with only thirteen of the thirty-three-man crew returning alive from the Arctic adventure, by most accounts the cost of "Mr. Bennett's expedition" was dear indeed and the outcome a tragic failure.

Or was it? By other measures, Bennett's return on investment had been remarkable. For well over a thousand days, the expedition generated headline after headline and article after article, driving sales of the *Herald* ever upward, reaching their zenith in 1885 with a circulation of 190,500. The adventure-courtroom drama-pageant evolution of the story was wildly successful thanks to the innovative journalistic methods applied to covering it. Embedded correspondents, interviews, the use of images, extensive backstories, telegraph and Atlantic cable technology, and expert opinion substituting for hard news were all instrumental in extending the life of the *Jeannette* saga. Many of these practices or modern variations of them remain in use today as fundamental elements of press coverage for breaking news and events.

If puzzling over the lasting legacy of the U.S. Arctic Expedition represents something of a conundrum, the same cannot be said of the absolute clarity with which the *New York Herald*'s Arctic adventure and its publisher's purpose were viewed in its day. Something of a joke at the time was the notion that when the North Pole was finally reached, a "Scotchman will be found perched on the top of it; but Scotchman or not, he will be a newspaper correspondent." This obvious reference to Bennett and his family ancestry was amusing, but the note on reporters amazingly prescient.[47]

A review of Gilder's book, *Ice Pack and Tundra: An Account of the Search for the "Jeannette" and a Sledge Journey through Siberia*, is particularly helpful in making sense of the enduring elements of the U.S. Arctic Expedition and its legacy, at least from a journalistic perspective. Published in the *British Quarterly Review* in 1883, the piece highlights a fundamental shift in the relationship between the press and its subject(s) in which "newspaper correspondents have recently taken a due share of the perils and dangers of Arctic adventure, and have favoured [*sic*] us with detailed and effective records which we should otherwise have missed."[48]

Such was the signature of Bennett and his corps of correspondents in bringing home fascinating tales of heroes, adventure, and discovery at the height of the Gilded Age. Few of his competitors were able to grasp the formula that transformed the pages of the newspaper into something more like *Robinson Crusoe* or *Treasure Island* than a journal of the daily news. Fewer still could leverage either the financial or reportorial assets to operationalize the one immutable truth that fueled the *Herald*'s domination at the newsstand not just for months and years in the early 1880s, but for decades.

The Livingstones and De Longs of the period, while gifted with bravery and fortitude, were not men blessed with the "power of vivid description." It was left to newspapers such as the *Herald* and reporters the likes of Stanley, Collins, Gilder, and Jackson to serve as "the link between the actor and the great public," satisfying the readership's insatiable appetite for adventure and fueling the financial formulas of publishers willing to not only capture the news, but manufacture it to ensure exclusivity and competitive advantage at any cost.[49]

## Notes

1. *New York Herald*, July 2, 1872.
2. Africa was so called in the nineteenth century to indicate it was unknown and unmapped by European explorers. Stanley himself would later popularize the term in his 1878 book about his expeditions there, *Through the Dark Continent*.
3. Beau Riffenburgh, *The Myth of the Explorer: The Press, Sensationalism, and Geographical Discovery* (New York: Oxford University Press, 1994), 2.
4. Richard Kluger with the assistance of Phyllis Kluger, *The Paper: The Life and Death of the New York Herald Tribune* (New York: Alfred A. Knopf, 1986), 142.
5. *Ibid.*, 145.
6. Beau Riffenburgh, "James Gordon Bennett, the *New York Herald*, and the Arctic," *Polar Record* 27 (1991): 11.
7. An experienced ship captain and Arctic explorer, Franklin's fourth trip to the polar region in 1845 was lost when the ships became icebound. Multiple expeditions, even as recently as 2014, were launched to investigate the fate of the expedition. Kane, a well-known American Arctic explorer, was among those searching for Franklin.
8. Fond of the high life and prone to unpredictable behaviors, Bennett departed New York for Europe when his engagement to Caroline May was ended in 1877.
9. Michael F. Robinson, *The Coldest Crucible: Arctic Exploration and American Culture* (Chicago: University of Chicago Press, 2006), 87; Leonard F. Guttridge, *Icebound: The Jeannette Expedition's Quest for the North Pole* (Lincoln, NE: iUniverse, Inc., 2006), 25.
10. *New York Herald*, July 15, 1878.
11. *New York Herald*, November 15, 1878; *New York Herald*, December 28, 1878.
12. Arctic explorer Nordenskjöld led the first successful crossing of the Northeast Passage in 1878–79.
13. *New York Herald*, February 3, 1879.
14. *Ibid.*, 122; Guttridge, *Icebound*, 73–74.

15. *New York Herald*, July 9, 1879.

16. *New York Herald*, July 10, 1879; *New York Times*, July 9, 1879.

17. *New York Herald*, October 13, 1879.

18. *Ibid.*; *New York Herald*, October 17, 1879.

19. *New York Herald*, October 27, 1879.

20. Hampton Sides, *In the Kingdom of the Ice: The Grand and Terrible Polar Voyage of the* USS *Jeannette* (New York: Penguin Random House, 2015), 153.

21. *New York Herald*, December 24, 1879. Charles Francis Hall (c. 1821–71) died under mysterious circumstances—suspected arsenic poisoning—on a *Polaris* expedition in 1871. See Chauncey C. Loomis, *Weird and Tragic Shores: The Story of Charles Francis Hall, Explorer* (New York: Random House, 2000).

22. *New York Herald*, November 16, 1880.

23. *New York Herald*, January 30, 1881.

24. *New York Truth*, June 5, 1881.

25. Riffenburgh, *Myth of the Explorer*, 86; *New York Herald*, November 17, 1881.

26. Sides, *In the Kingdom of the Ice*, 374.

27. *New York Herald*, December 21, 1881.

28. *New York Herald*, December 22, 1881.

29. Guttridge, *Icebound*, 248; *New York Truth*, December 25, 1881; and George W. Melville, *In the Lena Delta: A Narrative of the Search for Lieut.-Commander DeLong and his Companions Followed by An Account of the Greely Relief Expedition and A Proposed Method of Reaching the North Pole* (Boston: Houghton, Mifflin and Company, 1884), 369.

30. Guttridge, *Icebound*, 246.

31. *New York Herald*, April 19, 1882; *New York Herald*, April 29, 1882.

32. *New York Herald*, April 26, 1882; *New York Herald*, May 2, 1882.

33. *New York Herald*, May 6, 1882.

34. *New York Herald*, May 6, 1882, and May 7, 1882; *Chicago Tribune*, May 6, 1882.

35. "The Jeannette," *The Saturday Review of Politics, Literature, Science, and Art* 53 (May, 1882), 595–596.

36. Kluger, *The Paper*, 145.

37. Writing to his publisher in 1883, Jackson denied any voyeuristic motives in the visit to the grave, but rather confirmed his desire to retrieve any papers from De Long or Collins that would prove to be of value or interest to Bennet and the *Herald*. See Melville, *In the Lena Delta*, 370, and Guttridge, *Icebound*, 259.

38. *New York Herald*, May 29, 1882.

39. Guttridge, *Icebound,* 261.

40. *New York Herald*, October 6, 1882.

41. *New York Herald*, February 19, 1883.

42. It should be noted that not all newspapers shared the view that the *Herald*'s sponsorship of the U.S. Arctic Expedition was without merit. The *Canton Repository, Cincinnati Commercial Tribune*, and *Philadelphia Inquirer*, among others, all offered support for Bennett and the *Herald*. Please see *New York Times*, December 24, 1881, *San Diego Sun*, May 10, 1882, and *Kansas City Star*, May 8, 1882. See also *Canton Repository*, May 11, 1882, *Cincinnati Commercial Tribune*, May 10, 1882, *Philadelphia Inquirer*, May 22, 1882, and *Boston Herald*, February 24, 1883.

43. *New York Herald*, December 22, 1883.

44. *New York Herald*, February 7, 1884.

45. *New York Herald*, February 21, 1884.

46. *New York Herald*, February 24 and February 25, 1884.

47. "Ice Pack and Tundra: An Account of the Search for the '*Jeannette*' and a Sledge Journey through Siberia," *British Quarterly Review* 78 (1883): 196.

48. *Ibid.*

49. *Ibid.*

# "Alive, but wiser from our experience"

## Nellie Bly's Adventure Reporting from Mexico and Around the World

### Jack Breslin
### *and* Katrina J. Quinn

Founded in 1863, New York City's Woodlawn Cemetery has scores of famous people eternally resting in its four hundred acres. The National Historic Landmark's guide map lists eighty celebrated individuals from eight categories of fame, and at the top of the list of seven famous writers is Nellie Bly, described as a "pioneer in investigative reporting."[1] Her grave is in the Honeysuckle Lot at the cemetery's western boundary,[2] where the headstones are more modest than the impressive mausoleums, sculptures, and monuments for wealthier deceased, including her publisher at the *New York World*, Joseph Pulitzer. And a few sections away from Pulitzer's grand monument rests a woman whose missed steamship connection could have radically changed Bly's fame—her unanticipated competitor in the race around the world, Elizabeth Bisland. Bly's grave is easy to miss. It was not properly marked until 1978, when the New York Press Club erected a simple granite headstone "in honor of a famous news reporter." Rather ironic for the most famous woman in the world besides Queen Victoria at one time.

Bly's journalistic feats, however, are the stuff of legend, memorialized in dozens of books, songs, documentaries, a TV movie, an amusement park, and even a board game, preserving her memory in popular culture. But who really was Elizabeth Cochrane Seaman, better known to the world as Nellie Bly?[3] This essay analyzes two of Bly's reporting trips—her 1886 sojourn in Mexico and her 1889–90 race around the world—to argue that Bly was not only a "famous news reporter" but indeed an adventure journalist, one who, to paraphrase Lee Jolliffe, set out to find adventure, placed herself on-stage as a player in events, and reported back to the periodical press about those events.[4] Coming of age in an era of adventure journalism, when newspapers increasingly sent reporters to the far corners of the globe, Bly reported on people, places, and events even as she was at the heart of the adventure. While her writing style was at times unsophisticated, Bly's detailed reporting demonstrates an eye for news, a responsibility to the reader, and an adventurous, sometimes daring spirit to pursue stories where few women of her time dared to venture.

## Emergence of a Reporter

Elizabeth Jane Cochran (1864–1922) was born in tiny Cochran's Mills, Pennsylvania, a town named for her father, Judge Michael Cochran. Following Cochran's sudden death when Bly was six years old, a family quarrel over his estate left her mother and children destitute. Although her mother remarried, the marriage ended in divorce, with some biographers crediting this unsettled childhood for Bly's self-reliant nature and adventurous spirit. After attending the nearby Indiana (Pennsylvania) Normal School for one semester, Elizabeth relocated with her mother to Pittsburgh in 1880, following two of her brothers, and added an "e" to her last name to become Elizabeth Cochrane.[5]

After several years in Pittsburgh, a local newspaper column radically changed her poor prospects. In several columns titled "Quiet Observations," regularly published in the *Pittsburg Dispatch*, author Erasmus Wilson criticized young women with aspirations outside the traditional Victorian female sphere at home as a wife and mother. An irate Cochrane wrote a feisty reply defending young women, which she signed "Little Orphan Girl." Though poorly composed, the letter prompted Wilson to publicly inquire into the identity of the writer.[6] Rather than respond by mail, Cochrane went to the newspaper's office and met its managing editor, George Madden, who invited her to write an article on the "women's sphere." Impressed, Madden hired her in 1885, and created her byline, "Nellie Bly," inspired by the Stephen Foster song "Nelly Bly." In addition to soft-news features about women's interests typically assigned to female reporters, a crusading Bly reported on local women's working conditions and their struggles to climb out of poverty.

## Opportunity Strikes for an Adventure South of the Border

Just nine months into her budding newspaper career, the 21-year-old Bly decided to set off for a tour of Mexico, promising to send descriptive stories back to the *Dispatch*. Bly and her mother traveled south of the border from February to June 1886, during which time she produced a series of letters for the *Dispatch*, later collected as a generously named book, *Six Months in Mexico*, in 1888. The narrative structure mirrors similar adventure journalism collections, beginning with a ritualistic departure and a crossing of boundaries, participation of the author as a central figure, detailed adventures to significant and obscure sites, and an interpretation of the adventure for readers back home.

The trip was conceived as an opportunity for meaningful reporting. In the first of the book's thirty-seven chapters, the reporter revealed that an adventurous spirit and journalistic ambition prompted the extended expedition, which would include travel through historic, unfamiliar urban, native, and exotic environmental settings. "Only a few months previous I had become a newspaper woman," she wrote. "I was too impatient to work along at the usual duties assigned women on newspapers, so I conceived the idea of going away as a correspondent."[7] The trip took her through El Paso to Mexico City by train; into the poorest neighborhoods of Mexico City on foot; off on horseback for a 30-mile ride to Chapultepec castle, site of recent battles between Mexico and its northern neighbor; by boat to see the floating gardens at La Viga; and to the cities of Cholula, Puebla, Cordoba, Orizaba, and Guadalupe by train.

Like other adventure journalists of her day, Bly adopted a binary narrative approach that fused subjective experiential content and objective reportorial material.[8] While Bly's Mexico adventure letters included focused reporting on economics, social issues, and culture, then, they also featured the author as the main character and focalizer of the story. Her early columns, for example, included some typical homesick tourist complaints, such as constricted food options and a Spartan hotel room, "so miserable—like a prisoner's cell—that I began to wish I was at home."[9] In a later example, during her trip by horse to Chapultepec, the reader learns not only of the history and repurposing of the great estate, but also how Bly's party took off-road detours through fields, bounded over ditches, trotted past a native village, and finally scraped through a field of thorny agave or pulque plants, from which they emerged "alive, but wiser from our experience."[10]

The author's point of view was established promptly in the first column, as Bly discussed her emotional reaction to the anticipated journey. The column acknowledged a sense of youthful wonder when, after departing on a wintry night, she quickly found herself "in the lap of summer.... [I]t seemed like a dream."[11] She revealed an awareness of transition as the train crossed geographic and cultural boundaries, noting symbolic artifacts such as "the first real, live cowboy I saw on the plains." He and his companions "wore immense sombreros, huge spurs, and had lassos hanging to the side of their saddles."[12] Despite her wanderlust, she worried how the Mexican cowboys would respond to her impetuous wave. "From the thrilling and wicked stories I had read, I fancied they might begin shooting at me as quickly as anything else," she wrote. But as she would attest on multiple occasions throughout her trip in Mexico, the reality was quite different from

While the Castle of Chapultepec sits "as a crown or guard to the vast valley beneath," wild agave is seen growing in the foreground. "It ran its sharp prongs into the legs of the men, endeavored to pull the skirts off the women, and played spurs on the horses; but we finally emerged ... alive, but wiser from our experience" (photograph by William Henry Jackson, 1884–85, Library of Congress, Item cph.3c07863).

common stereotypes, as the men returned her greeting by lifting their sombreros "in a manner not excelled by a New York exquisite...."[13]

Boundaries thus reveal a meeting of cultures and a confrontation with the foreign and exotic, known previously to Bly only through stories and stereotypes. She described El Paso, Texas, as a "progressive, lively, American town" in contrast to El Paso del Norte, Mexico, which was "as far back in the Middle Ages, and as slow as it was when the first adobe hut was executed in 1680."[14] She illustrated the meeting of cultures by explaining how modern houses abutted ancient dwellings, and painted cultural disparities for her readers with broad strokes, using a rhetorical "there" to indicate intellectual distance between the observer and the observed:

> One can hardly believe that Americanism is separated from them [residents of El Paso del Norte] only by a stream. If they were thousands of miles apart they could not be more unlike. There smallpox holds undisputed sway in the dirty streets, and, in the name of religion, vaccination is denounced; there Mexican convict-soldiers are flogged until the American's heart burns to wipe out the whole colony; there *fiestas* and Sundays are celebrated by the most inhuman cock-fights and bull-fights, and monte games of all descriptions.[15]

A juxtaposition of a morally and socially antiquated Mexico and a modern Americanism, represented by superior infrastructure and refined civic practices, would set an observational paradigm that shaped Bly's early encounters with a foreign people and culture. As if to say the evolution of society was a foregone conclusion, Bly noted active resistance to new practices among the residents of the Mexican town, with Americans and Americanness symbols of cultural change and technological modernity. "The old town seems to look with proud contempt on civilization and progress," she asserted with mild scorn, "and the little *padre* preaches against free schools and tells his poor, ignorant followers to beware of the hurry and worry of the Americans—to live as their grand- and great-grandfathers did."[16] Bly was predisposed to observe the deficient, unfamiliar, and inhospitable in the early days of the trip, her commentary saturated with images of darkness and confinement: a prison, the dim light of lanterns, a cramped berth aboard a train in the darkness, and disappointment upon a first glance at a stark desert landscape.[17]

The paradigm gradually shifted, however, as her physical and psychological immersion in Mexico continued. Aboard the train, for example, Bly interrupted her landscape lament with a sudden rhetorical shift: "But the weather! It was simply perfect, and we soon forgot little annoyances in our enjoyment of it." The transformation continued as the journey progressed. "As we got further South the land grew more interesting," she explained.[18] The paradigmatic evolution was gradual, but palpable, as she pivoted from superficial criticism to engagement. After "[h]ucksters and beggars" greeted her train at a station, instead of escaping the space as she had at a previous stop, Bly was willing to make purchases, including "flowers, native fruit, eggs, goat milk, and strange Mexican food," the last including the pear cacti, found to have "a very cool and pleasing taste." The passage is particularly notable because the consumption of an unfamiliar food marked a distinct reversal from a previous, desperate longing for a familiar packed lunch.[19]

After arriving at Mexico City, Bly acknowledged and even praised what she at times found to be admirable social and cultural practices on the part of the Mexican citizenry. In fact, overtly confronting stereotypes of Mexicans was a recurring feature of Bly's reporting. "The Mexicans are certainly misrepresented, most wrongfully so," she insisted. "They are not lazy, but just the opposite. From early dawn until late at night they can be seen filling their different occupations."[20] At various times during her expedition, she positively reported on the sanitary habits of the "Indians" in Mexico City and Cordoba, the productivity of Mexican workers and servants, the public order and dignity of social intercourse, and the propriety of Mexican habits and manners.[21] She directly called on readers to reconsider widespread stereotypes, for example, by describing people in their cultural context and drawing comparisons of meaningful import. "Those who call the Mexicans 'greasers,' and think them a dumb, ignorant class, should see the paseo on Sunday," she exclaimed, describing the carriages, horses, and attire of those out for a Sunday ride in the city. "Pittsburg [sic], on this line, is nowhere in comparison."[22] During a visit to church, Bly admired the integration of economic classes in worship:

> Pews are unknown, and on the bare floor the millionaire is seen beside the poverty-stricken Indian; the superbly clad lady side by side with an uncombed, half naked Mexican woman. No distinction, no difference. There they kneel and offer their prayers of penitence and thanks, unmindful of rank or condition. No dividing the poor from the rich, but all with uniform thought and purpose go down on their knees to their God.[23]

The passage highlighted Bly's externality to the scene and her investigative role as a reporter, but also a growing ability to reflect on and even criticize American cultural assumptions. She called on her readers to reconsider, in an age of expansionism, the purported value of intervention and conversion: "How a missionary, after one sight like this, can wish to convert them into a faith where dress and money bring attention and front pews, and where the dirty beggar is ousted by the janitor and indignantly scorned down by those in affluence, is incomprehensible."[24]

People-watching was one of Bly's priorities in her adventure in Mexico. "In Mexico, as in all other countries," she wrote, "the average tourist rushes to the cathedrals and places of historic note, wholly unmindful of the most intensely interesting feature the country contains—the people."[25] She described a variety of people in a variety of settings, from the women in the streets of Mexico City, who always seemed to have one or more babies suspended in their *rebozos*, to families bathing and laundering in the waters of La Viga, to the honest and industrious *aquadores*, to the men and women out for a stroll on a Sunday afternoon.[26] At La Viga, Bly and her mother admired the vendors and craftsmen, who "look at us with a pleasant smile, and we answer their cheerful salutes with a happy feeling."[27] Yet like other reform-minded journalists of her age, she did not turn a blind eye to the stark inequalities of urban life. Bly displayed a veteran journalist's eye for detail as she described individuals of various classes, and particularly the most destitute as they crouched homeless in the dusty streets. She described the urban poor as "not a clean, inviting crowd.... Their lives are as dark as their skins and hair, and are invaded by no hope that through effort their lives may amount to something.... Their living is scarcely worth such a title. They merely exist."[28] Her reporting was full of narrative snapshots, as of a homeless boy carrying a dying baby, to illustrate the bleak human landscape.[29]

The reader was never far from Bly's adventure, as she explicitly framed many of her experiences and observation for her American audience. Like other adventure reporters encountering unfamiliar landscapes and cultures, Bly recognized a responsibility to interpret her experience for her readers back home, most of whom would never see the land south of the border for themselves, and used descriptive language—sometimes verging on the poetic—to do so. "How much I would like to paint the beauties of Mexico in colors so faithful that the people in the States could see what they are losing by not coming here," she wrote.[30] In a remarkable extended passage characterized by direct address of the reader, Bly embraced an epistolary mode, a voice that speaks to the reader

"Speaking of honesty they say the aquadores, or water-carriers, are the most honest fellows in the city. They have a company, and if any one is even suspected of stealing he is prohibited from selling any more water. At intervals all over the city are large basins and fountains where they get their water" (Bly. *Six Months in Mexico*, 71; photo by William Henry Jackson, 1884–85, Library of Congress, Item det.4a28139).

as though she were writing a familiar letter and not a newspaper column addressed to thousands:

> How I would like to show you the green valley where the heat of summer and blast of winter never dare approach; where every foot of ground recalls wonderful historical events, extinct races of men and animals, and civilization older by far than the pyramids. Then would I take

you from the table-land to the mountain, where we descend into deep canons that compare in their strange beauty with any in the world.... Then would I lead you to the edge of some bluff that outrivals the Palisades—and let you look down the dizzy heights 500 feet to the green meadows, the blooming orchards, the acres of pulque plant, the little homes that nestle at the foot of this strange wall. Then further up into the mountains you could see glaciers, grander, it is claimed, than any found in the Alps. Here are buried cities older than Pompeii, sculptures thousands of years old, hieroglyphics for the wise to study, and everywhere the picturesque people in their garb and manners of centuries ago—and all this within a day's travel from the city. Surely in all the world there is none other such wonderful natural museum.

The power of the passage lies in the author's invitation to join her, directing the reader's imagination along with her on a fanciful trip, drawing word pictures with sensory shading, and tugging on the memories and knowledge of the readers to populate these images in comparison to more familiar landscapes of Europe.

Auditory details were embedded in Bly's reporting and further sharpened the linguistic resolution of the adventure for the readers. Bly was attracted by the "musical sound of a strange language"[31] and incorporated Spanish words in her columns to authentically represent the reported environment. Unique cultural artifacts such as the *serape* and *rebozo*, each denoting a piece of clothing with cultural significance, were introduced early with italic type and a description of how each was worn and used.[32] Bly also included the pronunciation and translation of a number of unfamiliar Spanish place names, such as the region *Chihuahua*, which was phonetically deconstructed in a footnote, and Casa de Mata and El Molino del Rey, each presented with an English translation.[33] As Bly's residency in Mexico continued, the reader can see a deeper integration with her linguistic milieu through presentation of dialogue. Ready to ride a horse to Chapultepec, for example, Bly's Mexican guide asked, "*Vamos?*' (Let us go)" to which Bly replied, "'*Con mucho gusto*' (with much pleasure)."[34]

Sensory detail in the reporting enhanced the rhetorical tapestry as Bly placed experiential components of her adventure center-stage. Pulque, she told her readers, "has a peculiar sour-milkish taste, and smells exactly like hop yeast." Mescal, meanwhile, a rum derived from pulque, she explained, was "a lovely brown, golden color, and very pleasant to the taste"—and fortunately did not result in a hangover.[35] From the train, she directed the readers' eyes from magnificent landscapes in the distance, "truly the most beauteous sight in Mexico," to the bull fight arena, describing in lively detail the colors of the painted fence, arrangement and construction of multiple levels of seating, and the positions of band-stands, "filled with brilliantly uniformed musicians."[36] Bull fights function as a metonymic symbol of Mexican cultural foreign-ness in the text. She thus introduced the various players in the drama—including a judge, a citizen, and a bugler in a central box; clowns; the competitors, including "'El Capitan' or matador," *capeadores*, *picadors*, and *lazadores*—as well as their weapons—*banderillas*, swords, *capas*, *picas*, and *lassos*. To this she added descriptions of the eager crowd and its cries of "'El toro! El toro!' (The bull! the bull!)."[37]

While Bly's earliest letters from Mexico grappled with expectations governed by stereotypes, subsequent columns demonstrated how the adventure changed the adventurer. As the trip continued, the reader can observe Bly growing in confidence and resourcefulness. Early in the trip, for example, she relied on train personnel and other figures to dictate her movements—where to stay, when to rise or return, and what to pack. During an excursion to Jalapa, Bly accepted the assistance of a fellow passenger in securing a hotel

Bly described the poor of Mexico City as "not a clean, inviting crowd…. Their lives are as dark as their skins and hair, and are invaded by no hope that through effort their lives may amount to something…. Their living is scarcely worth such a title. They merely exist" (Bly. *Six Months in Mexico*, 20; photo by William Henry Jackson, 1884–85, Library of Congress, Item det.4a27170).

room. When the owner attempted to charge her double the initial rate, the issue was settled by the Frenchman, with Bly swearing that in the future, she would "not drink a glass of water until I knew the price. I had no intention of allowing a Yankee girl to be cheated by a Mexican, man or woman."[38] It was an intentional process of education for the future world traveler, and she was true to her word, refusing to pay extra to a hotel clerk at a subsequent stop, and arguing with a man who seized her luggage in an effort to secure a tip. Bly remembered her former experience and, "wishing to profit thereby," grabbed the man's shirt and demanded "Cuanto?" After snatching her bag back and some quick negotiations in Spanish, a new price was determined, and Bly congratulated herself for saving "ninety-three and three-quarter cents."[39]

Bly's letters also provide evidence of an evolving observational paradigm. As the trip continued, Bly was more apt to criticize Americans and American culture and manners. She shared examples of crude behavior by American tourists and settlers, who were "more than offensive, they are insulting in their actions and language toward the natives, and endeavor to run things." She found that although she had been warned about and initially anticipated crime and violence in Mexico City, "the women—I am sorry to say it—are safer here than on our streets, where it is supposed everybody has the advantage of education and civilization."[40] She applauded the kindness and manners of Mexican policemen and even rowdy crowds, "far surpassing the same class of people in the States; they possess a never-failing kindness and gentleness for one another…."[41]

Bly also displayed evolving perspectives on Mexican culture. In her first visit to a bull fight, for example, Bly reacted with horror and pity at the gruesome assault on the animals, and bestowed graphic content upon her readers. After being gored by the bulls, she acknowledged, "the poor horses are seldom killed instantly. When wounded so that it is impossible for them to walk, they are dragged from the ring and left in a vacant field, where they die that night or the following day, as the Mexicans do not consider them worth a bullet." When a bull was fatally stabbed by a matador, she drew a sympathetic picture of its fate, explaining, "he often staggers along the fence, as though in hopes of finding an exit. The cruel spectators are not satisfied that he is dying, and allow him some little mercy, but stab his wounded flesh, tear open his death wound, twist his tail, do all in their power to enhance his sufferings until he falls dead."[42] In contrast, she later attended an Easter Sunday bull fight, which she declared to be "excellent," noting its intricate choreography, despite the obvious pain and suffering on the part of several of the animals.[43] At another bull fight in Puebla, she offered no words of pity for the bull, killed at once by a daring swordsman, but instead praised the fighters for the carefully scripted exhibition: "It was simply magnificent, and so exciting that everybody was standing on their feet yelling lustily at every new move."[44]

Bly's later columns veered away from immersive, author-centered writing to focus more directly on political reporting, adopting a decidedly more critical and reportorial tone. She openly criticized Presidents Manuel Gonzales and Porfirio Díaz, whom she called "a tyrannical czar," for their roles in suppressing opposition and widespread corruption.[45] In subsequent letters, she reported that the newspapers were a particular target of government suppression, citing police punishment of the press for "so-called libelous items" and incidents of innocent editors being sent to jail. "The Mexican papers never publish one word against government officials," she wrote, "and the people who are at their mercy dare not breathe one word against them…."[46] She wrote that Mexicans "have not the slightest respect in the world" for the country's newspapers and "have nothing but contempt" for press freedom. In subsidizing the press, the government avoided attacks, "so they circulate [lies] among foreigners misrepresenting all Mexican affairs, and putting everything in a false light."[47]

Another column provided a lengthy exposé on the Mexican military, including soldiers from the countryside, known as *rurales*. Bly set up the story by establishing a context of ideological perspective: "El mexicano thinks it would be one of the pleasantest, as well as one of the easiest, things in the world to whip the 'Gringoes,' while the latter, with their heads a little swelled, perhaps, imagine otherwise, and scoff at the idea of the 'Greasers' winning even one battle in the event of war." While the use of racist epithets may offend modern readers, and may contribute to perceptions that she herself was racist,[48] the presentation of those terms in quotation marks in this passage signals a shift of attribution from herself to others in the environment. The letter goes on to discuss the numbers of soldiers; their origin, be it "from mountain, valley, town, and city"; their pay and attire; character; and purpose. She acknowledged the extreme hardships of military life, as well as severe discipline imposed on slackers and deserters. Referring back to the hypothetical contest of Mexican and American forces, Bly concludes for her American readers that "solid, unvarnished facts will prove to the most headstrong that the advantage is mostly on the other side."[49]

Bly's role as a reporter for an American periodical contributed to the precarious nature of her adventure, with some of her columns, first published in the *Pittsburg Dispatch*, printed elsewhere as exchange stories and ultimately reaching the eyes of Mexican authorities. Wanting to avoid being jailed for her criticisms, Bly quickly headed back across the Rio Grande. The departure explains why her later letters abandon the immersive and personal components of the earlier reportage to adopt a more objective, reportorial stance that was also more critical of Mexicans and Mexican practices. "I had some regard for my health, and a Mexican jail is the least desirable abode on the face of the earth," she wrote, "so some care was exercised in the selection of topics while we were inside their gates."[50] In addition to critical pieces on Mexican politics and the press, these later columns include legends, recipes, a re-telling of some material concerning Mexican manners, and more—but clearly, the adventure had come to an end.

## Around the World

Bly returned to the *Dispatch*, but not for long, as one day the 22-year-old famously left a simple note for her editor: "I'm off for New York. Look out for me. BLY." When she arrived in New York in 1887, America's publishing capital was the perfect place for an aspiring reporter—except, perhaps, for a young *female* journalist in the male newspaper world.[51] For several frustrating months, while still sending stories back to the *Dispatch*, Bly created a variety of ruses to get meetings with local publishers, finally landing in the office of Colonel John Cockerill, managing editor of Pulitzer's *World*, one of the leading daily journals. Challenging Bly to prove what she could do, Cockerill approved an idea for her to pose as a deranged Cuban immigrant so she could report from the infamous asylum on Blackwell's Island. The resulting story was reprinted in newspapers from coast to coast, prompting reform in treatment of the mentally ill and boosting its author to national fame.[52]

Though Bly's career would be studded with a number of stunts and investigations, she is best remembered for her famous seventy-two-day "race" around the globe. Some credit Pulitzer, Cockerill, and other editors for the sensational imitation of the fictional adventurer Phileas Fogg in Jules Verne's 1873 classic novel *Around the World in Eighty Days*. But in her later book on the journey, *Around the World in Seventy-Two Days*, Bly took credit for the idea on the first page.[53] She faced initial opposition from her editors since such a rigorous and dangerous journey would surely be risky for a male reporter and even more so for an unaccompanied woman. Indeed, the 1889–90 trip would not have been conceivable had it not been for her adventures in Mexico three years earlier, which taught her how to endure the hardships of travel, proved her ability to navigate unfamiliar surroundings, and boosted the self-confidence necessary to speak and assert her will. These lessons had an immediate payoff, for when her editors finally agreed to the trip, Bly had only a day and a half to order her custom-made travel wardrobe, buy her steamship ticket across the Atlantic Ocean to England, and pack her only luggage: a chamois-skin bag for paper money and a leather grip satchel handbag for everything else.

Bly's itinerary is familiar but presents a litany of exotic nineteenth-century destinations. Departing on the Hamburg-America steamship liner *Augusta Victoria* from Hoboken, New Jersey, on Thursday, November 14, she arrived at Southampton, England, seven days later, crossed the English Channel to Bologna, France, and boarded a train for a 179.5-mile detour to Amiens, where she interviewed *Around the World* author Jules Verne. Swiftly departing for Calais by train, Bly took the India mail train south through France, along the Adriatic Sea, to Brindisi, Italy. There she boarded the Peninsular and Oriental Line steamship *Victoria* to cross the Mediterranean for Egypt, after sending a cable to *The World* on her progress—a page one story the following day.[54] Passing through the Suez Canal from Port Said, Egypt, she made a short visit ashore in Aden, on the Arabian Peninsula, proceeded to Colombo, Ceylon,[55] and then boarded the Peninsular and

Bly was an experienced traveler and clearly an efficient packer by the time she returned from her famous journey in 1890 (Library of Congress, Item cph.3b07664).

Oriental Line steamship *Oriental* for Hong Kong via Penang, Malaysia, and Singapore, where she bought a pet monkey and through which she passed 33 days after departing New York.[56] After crossing the South China Sea, she arrived in Hong Kong, spent five days in Canton, China, over Christmas, and, after sailing to Yokohama, Japan, departed for San Francisco. She rode by train across the continent and arrived in Jersey City on January 25, 1890.

Unlike her longer adventure in Mexico, Bly's world trip was governed not by investigation and reporting but by timeline. The precision of this temporal landscape was established with *The World*'s account that Bly had departed "Thursday November 14, 1889 at 9.40.30 o'clock."[57] Bly's narrative is spotted with references to time—time displayed on a clock, the time spent waiting, time spent rushing, timetables for boats and trains, the urging of a coachman or captain to make good time. The adventure reporting is thus focused explicitly on the physical movement of the reporter and her ability to efficiently navigate the reported space. The journey included its hazards, and Bly admitted to misgivings. "Intense heat, bitter cold, terrible storms, shipwrecks, fevers, all such agreeable topics had been drummed into me until I felt much as I imagine one would feel if shut in a cave of midnight darkness and told that all sorts of horrors were waiting to gobble one up."[58] She encountered the regular retinue of discomforts associated with foreign travel, including cold dinners, bad weather, and sea-sickness. Encountering a monsoon in the South China Sea, however, Bly's fears centered not on drowning but on potential temporal losses. "All the worry in the world cannot change it one way or the other," she considered, but "if the ship does not go down, I only waste so much time."[59]

A variable sense of motion and velocity in Bly's reporting governs the narrative pace, with the methods of transport an important part of the adventure. Like her ramblings in Mexico, Bly's around-the-world adventure was facilitated by a variety of conveyances, including steamship, tugboat, train, carriage, row boat, catamaran, wagon, bullock hackery,[60] "jinricksha,"[61] sampan,[62] gharry,[63] sedan chair, steam launch, and a phaeton drawn by ponies.[64] With the greatest distances covered by water, the *ship* construct emerges as a collaborator in the adventure, with its departures, difficulties, and delays not only controlling the agenda but also playing an important rhetorical role. When moving forward, the boat is a sanctuary, and the sea a refuge, providing a sense of serenity and protection for the adventurer. Leaving Colombo after several days ashore, Bly "found it a great relief to be again on the sweet, blue sea, out of sight of land, and free from the tussle and worry and bustle for life which we are daily, hourly even, forced to gaze upon on land…."[65] In recalling a moment aboard the *Powan*, en route for Canton, Bly was moved to a rare moment of lyricism, exclaiming, "Let me rest rocked gently by the rolling sea, in a nest of velvety darkness, my only light the soft twinkling of the myriads of stars in the quiet sky above; my music, the round of the kissing waters, cooling the brain and easing the pulse; my companionship, dreaming my own dreams. Give me that and I have happiness in its perfection."[66] The boat also carried the reporter into—yet through—moments of true danger, as during the monsoon en route to Hong Kong. Despite her malaise, Bly recalled her great awe at the power of nature and the interface of the vessel with the massive storm. "The terrible swell of the sea during the Monsoon was the most beautiful thing I ever saw," she wrote. "I would sit breathless on deck watching the bow of the ship standing upright on a wave then dash headlong down as if intending to carry us to the bottom."[67]

Even while they carried her to new environments and discoveries, conveyances simultaneously constricted Bly's field of vision. During the early phases of the trip, Bly was aware of how constant displacement compromised the depth of her observations and understanding. From a carriage heading toward London, she was whisked past symbolic landmarks and acknowledged that she "felt that I was taking what might be called a bird's-eye view of London." She compared herself to other travelers who had "taken views in the same rapid way of America, and afterwards gone home and written books about America, Americans, and Americanisms," still clearly uninformed.[68] In England and elsewhere, especially during the early phases of her trip, Bly's peripheral vision was restricted not only by the speed of her forward motion but also by physical and environmental impediments such as fog—both in a physical sense, as landscapes were shrouded in fog, and in a figurative sense, as the exhausted traveler was lulled to sleep by the movement of the train.[69] From the train in France she noted some "high and picturesque mountains," but also exclaimed, "I might have seen more while traveling through France if the car windows had been clean."[70] Crossing into Italy, she was impatient to see what she anticipated to be a beautiful landscape, "but though I pressed my face close to the frosty window pane bleak night denied me even one glimpse of sunny Italy and its dusky people. I went to bed early." When day arrived, fog again obscured her view, until it lifted momentarily just at sunset to reveal bright sailboats on the sea.[71]

At several ports, the itinerary did allow for a tour ashore, and the departure from the ship allowed the reporter a closer look at unfamiliar peoples, cultures, and environments. When time was short, Bly made these forays more in the mode of a tourist than of an investigative journalist. Bly described her brief tour of Port Said, Egypt, for example, as a series of typical tourist amusements: window-shopping, gambling, and buying a souvenir hat. Strolling around the city, she observed people begging in the street; but unlike the sympathy she felt for the poor of Mexico City, she experienced a sense of disgust, described with a candor that is challenging for modern readers.[72] During longer stays in locations such as Colombo, Hong Kong, Canton, and Yokahama, Bly had occasion to expand the compass of her investigation by visiting cultural, religious, and environmental sites. With a five-day wait for her next steamer, Bly took advantage of her time in Colombo, for example, by visiting a variety of sites such as nearby mountains, temples, botanical gardens, and an opera, which she described in her book at great length.[73]

Despite the greater number of sites visited, Bly still relied on the visual and thus the superficial or symbolic aspects of these cultures for understanding—the "bird's-eye view," in some sense, that she had regretted in London. While she found the bay at Hong Kong beautiful and festive, for example, she then perceived the city to be dirty to such an extent that she was not able to see beyond the surface. "The town seemed in a state of untidiness," she wrote. "[T]he road was dirty, the mobs of natives we met were filthy, the houses were dirty, the numberless boats lying along the wharf, which invariably were crowded with dirty people, were dirty, our carriers were dirty fellows...."[74]

Her reporting also highlighted sensational particulars that would have shocked the traveler and enticed the readers. While dispensing with stereotypes related to her personal safety in China, her visit to Canton still resonated with violent images, including a visit to an execution ground still wet with the blood of eleven beheadings conducted the previous day. Her guide, Ah Cum, explained other gruesome methods of execution that took place there, such as the bamboo punishment, by which an individual is slowly impaled with bamboo spikes, and the particular sentence for women, who were bound to a cross and cut to pieces.[75]

Another sensational element of the reporting at many stops was an intimate concern with the exotic physicality of men and women. Bly was continually aware of appearances, and regularly noted handsome and well-dressed men, both in Mexico and around the world. But she was just as quick to describe the physical appearance of individuals she met or observed in remote ports of call, such as women in burkas and naked men wrestling an alligator at Port Said, or the emaciated build and leathery skin of an oarsman. There is often a sensuality in Bly's careful descriptions of individuals' bodies, hair, and attire, particularly of women. In Aden, she described "black people of many different tribes" walking along a road, but paid exacting attention to "a number of women … who walked proudly along, their brown, bare feet stepping lightly on the smooth road…. To me the sight of these perfect, bronze-like women, with a graceful drapery of thin silk wound about the waist, falling to the knees, and a corner taken up the back and brought across the bust, was most bewitching. On their bare, perfectly modeled arms were heavy bracelets, around the wrist and muscle…."[76] Bly provided a similarly sensual account of geisha dancers in Japan, noting that "They powder their faces and have a way of reddening their under lip just at the tip that gives them a most tempting look. The lips look like two luxurious cherries." When the music began, "these bits of beauty begin the dance. With a grace, simply enchanting, they twirl their little fans, sway their dainty bodies in a hundred different poses, each one more intoxicating than the other, all the while looking so childish and shy, with an innocent smile lurking about their lips, dimpling their soft cheeks, and their black eyes twinkling with the pleasure of the dance." After the performance, the girls returned the attention by closely examining Bly's dress, jewelry, and hair. "They said I was very sweet, and urged me to come again," she wrote, "and in honor of the custom of my land—the Japanese never kiss—they pressed their soft, pouting lips to mine in parting."[77]

The episode with the geisha dancers in Japan was a rare moment of intimacy with foreign people and cultures on this around-the-world trip—and yet, formalized by ritual, it illustrates the reporter's continued externality. While the journey surely opened windows to faraway locales, Bly remained very much on the periphery, dancing along the border of the cultures, histories, stories, languages, and peoples who inhabited those places. Once the *Oceanic* with its famous passenger entered San Francisco Bay on the morning of November 21, however, Bly would no longer be on the outside looking in. A tug whisked her and her monkey past the quarantine doctor to a train that had been chartered by her employer. Despite a record-breaking trip across the continent, Bly was no longer an observer in the wings, but now embraced by her country, reconnected with her readers, and indeed "home again."[78]

## *The Legacy of Bly's Gilded Age Adventure Reporting*

Beating her original estimate by three days and Fogg by eight days, Bly traveled 21,740 miles around the world in seventy-two days, six hours, and eleven minutes, arriving in Jersey City, New Jersey, at 3:51 p.m., January 25, 1890, "the best-known and most widely talked-of woman on earth today," *The World* proclaimed.[79] Bly instantly became an advertiser's dream as one of the first global celebrities. She was besieged with offers of commercial endorsements, personal appearances, and book contracts, as a front-page graphic in *The World* had predicted.[80] Her admirers named a hotel, an express train, a

PRESENTING THE GLOBE-GIRDLER A GOLDEN GLOBE.                    THE ARRIVAL IN PHILADELPHIA.

AROUND THE WORLD IN SEVENTY-TWO DAYS AND SIX HOURS—RECEPTION OF NELLIE BLY AT JERSEY CITY ON THE COMPLETION OF HER JOURNEY—From Sketches by C Bunnell.—[See Page 7.]

**No longer on the outside looking in, Bly was very much at the center of the action when she arrived "home again," as depicted in this woodcut in *Frank Leslie's Illustrated Newspaper*, Feb. 8, 1890 (from a sketch by C. Bunnell, Library of Congress, Item 99613984).**

musical comedy song, and a race horse after her, among other honors. *The World* featured a board game based on her trip, after holding a "guessing match" for the closest estimate of her exact traveling time.

The grand adventure at an end, Bly did not sit still. After a short respite at her Manhattan home, she published a popular account of her trip, *Nellie Bly's Book: Around the World in Seventy-Two Days,* and launched a forty-city lecture tour.[81] She worked briefly for the *Times-Herald* in Chicago, married a wealthy industrialist named Robert Livingston Seaman, and later took over his business as it fell into bankruptcy.[82] After his death, she moved to Europe and during World War I became one of the first female war correspondents, taking significant personal risks to report from the Eastern European theater.[83] She returned to the U.S. in 1919 but died of pneumonia on January 27, 1922, at age 57.

Perhaps the best-remembered of all the adventure journalists of the Gilded Age, Nellie Bly exemplified the spirit of those who set out to bring the world to the doorsteps of American readers. Unlike some of the other adventure reporters who penetrated the unknown with a sense of domination or superiority, however, Nellie Bly set out as an unassuming and largely untried observer and witness, responding authentically to her surroundings, carried along by trains and boats, at the mercy of storms and ship captains, subject to haps and mishaps. Her stupendous journey seemed not so impossible of an adventure because she was much like her readers.

Bly's physical presence in these remote locations created a sense of connectivity, an epistemological coherence of the global stage, a sense of conquest. Though not political, the conquest was of distances, time, and nature, and very much in tune with and engaging the scientific impulse of the era. For Nellie Bly, the adventure *was* the story. Not possessed by some overriding mission, as in to recover Dr. Livingstone, discover the final American frontier, or track down the crew of the *Jeannette*, Bly was determined just to complete the adventure—to emerge "alive, but wiser" from the "experience."[84] And while some reporters may have been more eloquent or faced greater dangers, in the collective psyche of the nation, none would capture the essence of Gilded Age adventure journalism better than Nellie Bly.

## NOTES

1. "Guide Map to the Woodlawn Cemetery: A National Historic Landmark'—no date, page numbers or copyright. website: www.thewoodlwncemetery.org.

2. Bly's grave lies in section 19, along with many victims of the 1918 influenza epidemic, prompting references to it as a "pauper's grave." Also in Woodlawn Cemetery is a monument commemorating Lt. Commander George Washington De Long (1844–81), who perished in the *Jeannette* disaster. See Chapter 10.

3. Several scholarly biographies and other works provide important profiles of Bly. The title of Brooke Kroeger's 1994 seminal biography—*Nellie Bly: Daredevil, Reporter, Feminist*—describes Bly's expansive legacy (New York: Times Books/Random House). Alexandra Lapierre and Christel Mouchard's 2007 *Women Travelers: A Century of Trailblazing Adventures 1850–1950* featured a chapter on Bly's round-the-world exploit among thirty-one women travelers (New York: Flammarion/Rizzoli), 3, 130–135. Calling Bly "this woman who was afraid of nothing" and "a great figure in American journalism," Mouchard defended Bly's legacy as an adventurous journalist. See Mouchard, *Women Travelers*, 132. In her 2013 book chapter "Nellie Bly: Flying in the Face of Tradition," Dianne Bragg credited Bly as "a mother of a revolution" who inspired generations of female journalists, despite the sensationalist style of her investigative reporting, which was motivated by her "mission" to get a story no matter what the cost. See Bragg, "Nellie Bly: Flying in the Face of Tradition" in David B. Sachsman and David W. Bulla, eds. *Sensationalism: Murder, Mayhem, Mudslinging, Scandals and Disasters in 19th Century Reporting* (New Brunswick, NJ: Transaction Publishers, 2013).

4. Lee Jolliffe, "Adventurer Journalists in the Gilded Age." *Journalism History* 42:1 (2016), 3.

5. Biographical details were collected from Bly's original works, biographies and commentaries referenced above and throughout. See especially Kroeger, *Nellie Bly: Daredevil, Reporter, Feminist*, and Jason Marks, *Around the World in 72 Days: The Race Between Pulitzer's Nelly Bly and Cosmopolitan's Elizabeth Bisland* (New York: Gemittarius Press, 1993).

6. *Pittsburg Dispatch*, January 17, 1885.

7. Nellie Bly, *Six Months in Mexico* (New York: American Publishers Corporation, 1888), 3. Page references are to this original edition.

8. The use of letters to convey news is as old as newspapers themselves, but the integration of objective reportage and personal experience emerged as an early form of epistolary journalism in the nineteenth century. For more on epistolary journalism, see Katrina J. Quinn, "Reconsidering the Public Letter in Epistolary Theory: The Case of Samuel Bowles (1865)," *The CEA Critic* 77, no. 1 (2015): 97–119. For more on the narrative structure of undercover reporting, see Katrina J. Quinn, "Narratologies of Autodiegetic Undercover Reportage: Albert Deane Richardson's 'The Secret Service,'" *JNT: Journal of Narrative Theory* 49, no. 1 (2019): 1–26.

9. Bly, *Six Months in Mexico*, 3, 17.

10. *Ibid.*, 33–34. Pulque, a traditional alcoholic beverage, is derived from the maguey plant, a prickly succulent that can grow up to twenty feet in diameter.

11. *Ibid.*, 5.

12. *Ibid.*, 6.

13. *Ibid.*

14. *Ibid.*, 9.

15. *Ibid.*, 10.

16. *Ibid.*, 10.

17. *Ibid.*, 9–11.

18. *Ibid.*, 12.

19. *Ibid.*, 13.

20. *Ibid.*, 20.

21. *Ibid.*, 13, 127, 22, 23, 25, 190.
22. *Ibid.*, 29.
23. *Ibid.*, 26.
24. *Ibid.*
25. *Ibid.*, 18.
26. *Ibid.*, 26–31, 71.
27. *Ibid.*, 83.
28. *Ibid.*, 18–19.
29. *Ibid.*, 22.
30. *Ibid.*, 56.
31. *Ibid.*, 40.
32. *Ibid.*, 17.
33. *Ibid.*, 16, 34.
34. *Ibid.*, 32.
35. *Ibid.*, 188.
36. *Ibid.*, 41.
37. *Ibid.*, 42.
38. *Ibid.*, 118–121.
39. *Ibid.*, 123.
40. *Ibid.*, 70–71.
41. *Ibid.*, 96.
42. *Ibid.*, 44–45.
43. *Ibid.*, 105.
44. *Ibid.*, 148.
45. *Ibid.*, 151 and again on 160.
46. *Ibid.*, 151.
47. *Ibid.*, 299–300.
48. See, for example, Alice Gregory, "Nellie Bly's Lessons in Writing What You Want To," *New Yorker*, May 14, 2014, www.newyorker.com/books/page-turner/nellie-blys-lessons-in-writing-what-you-want-to, who calls Bly's writing "casually racist."
49. *Ibid.*, 156–59.
50. *Ibid.*, 300.
51. According to the 1880 census, only 288, or 2 percent, of 12,308 American journalists were women. See Matthew Goodman, *Eighty Days: Nelly Bly and Elizabeth Bisland's History-Making Race Around the World* (New York: Ballantine Books, 2013), 8.
52. So famous was this series that it was republished as a book (Nellie Bly, *Ten Days in a Mad-House* [New York: Munro, 1887]) and is still popular today, appearing online in several places, notably as a facsimile edition at University of Pennsylvania Digital Library's "A Celebration of Women Writers," at digital.library.upenn.edu/women/bly/madhouse/madhouse.html.
53. Nellie Bly, *Around the World in Seventy-Two Days* (London: Bretano's; New York: Pictorial Weeklies, 1890); here, citations are to the more readily available *Around the World in Seventy-Two Days* (Adelaide, South Australia: eBooks@Adelaide, 2014), in this instance, to ch. 1.
54. "Nellie Bly Heard From….," The World, November 26, 1889.
55. Modern-day Sri Lanka.
56. Goodman, *Eighty Days*, 225.
57. Nellie Bly, *Around the World in Seventy-Two Days*, citing The World, December 4, 1889.
58. Bly, *Around the World in Seventy-Two Days* (2014), ch. 2.
59. *Ibid.*, ch. 11. Despite the weather, the *Oriental* landed in Hong Kong two days ahead of schedule. "From Jersey Back to Jersey," The World, January 26, 1890. It was upon arrival in Hong Kong that Bly learned the news that everyone following her journey already knew, that a reporter named Elizabeth Bisland, on assignment for *Cosmopolitan Magazine,* was heading in the other direction ("The Story of A Tour," The World, January 25, 1890).
60. Bly describes this vehicle as "a very small springless cart on two wheels with a front seat for the driver." Bly and her companion sat on a rear-facing back seat with their feet hanging off. She describes the bullock as "a strange, modest-looking little animal with a hump on its back and crooked horns on its head," which moved more quickly than she expected based on its appearance (Bly, *Around the World in Seventy-Two Days*, 2014, ch. 9).
61. More often spelled *jinrikisha,* Bly first saw and rode in this human-drawn wagon in Colombo (*Ibid.*).
62. Bly rode to shore at Colombo in a sampan, or flat boat with oars (Bly, *Around the World in Seventy-Two Days*, 2014, ch. 10).
63. A "light wagon with latticed windows and comfortable seating room for four ... drawn by a pretty spotten Malay pony ..." (*Ibid.*).
64. A light, open-aired carriage (Bly, *Around the World in Seventy-Two Days*, 2014, ch. 12).

65. *Ibid.*, ch. 10.

66. *Ibid.*, ch. 13.

67. *Ibid.*, ch. 11.

68. *Ibid.*, ch. 3.

69. *Ibid.*

70. *Ibid.*, ch. 5.

71. *Ibid.*

72. "The majority of these beggars presented such repulsive forms of misery that in place of appealing to my sympathetic nature, as is generally the case, they had a hardening effect on me. They seemed to thrust their deformities in our faces in order to compel us to give money to buy their absence from our sight" (*Ibid.*, ch. 7).

73. "From Jersey Back to Jersey," *The World*, January 26, 1890. See Bly, *Around the World in Seventy-Two Days* (2014), ch. 9.

74. Bly, *Around the World in Seventy-Two Days* (2014), ch. 12.

75. *Ibid.*, ch. 12.

76. *Ibid.*, ch. 8.

77. *Ibid.*, ch. 15.

78. *Ibid.*, ch. 17.

79. Goodman, *Eighty Days*, 336.

80. "Will It Come to This?," *The World*, January 15, 1889.

81. Goodman, *Eighty Days*, 336–7; Kroeger, *Nellie Bly: Daredevil*, 182.

82. "Mr. and Mrs. Nellie Bly," *The World*, April 21, 1895.

83. "Female war correspondents of World War I: Mapping a thinly researched field in the history of journalism," *ECREA 6th European Communication Conference—Mediated (Dis)Continuities: Contesting Pasts, Presents and Futures*, November 9–12, 2016, Prague, Czech Republic.

84. Bly, *Six Months in Mexico*, 33–34.

# Afterword

## Lee Jolliffe

The closing of the American frontier, announced in 1890 by the U.S. Census Bureau, might have quieted the voices of adventure journalists who so often had been beckoned to the "empty" lands of the American West. Discovery and settlement of the U.S. mainland were accomplished, along with surveying and protection of the greatest natural treasures of the nation. The grandeur of Yellowstone and Yosemite became protected national lands, Yellowstone in 1872 and Yosemite in 1890. John Muir had established the Sierra Club in 1892 to protect the Sierra Mountain Ranges. But now the U.S. frontier was declared "closed." Adventure reporters had essentially finished with the task of bringing that wilderness into American homes. Improved transportation brought middle-class travelers to Yellowstone, Yosemite, and wild locales that were once the province of nomads: indigenous peoples, hardy frontiersmen, and rambling adventurers.

Adventure reporters, though, had made their mark on the West. Crossing the prairies and trekking the mountains, they had placed themselves onstage and reported as characters inside the story of westward expansion. From that stage, they framed what would become the prevailing narratives we would embrace as a nation. Narrative frames including "cowboys and Indians" and "heroic pioneers" became shared ways of viewing western settlement by Euro-Americans. Tales that contributed to an American nationalism told of a Wild West—a sprawling land of rodeos, cattle drives, sod-busting, and land-clearing. A nation's ideas of itself and its newest lands had been shaped by adventure reporters who captured in newsprint the "danger, risk, or struggle" in locations remote, dangerous, exotic, and wild.[1] Their exploits aligned with the desire of Euro-Americans to take and claim ownership of this land, sustaining the notion of manifest destiny.

Even globally, the adventuring genre had become so commonplace that Thomas Knox lamented that even in the most rural parts of Siberia, one might trip over other adventure journalists, as the steamship and the ever-expanding web of telegraph lines made the world smaller.[2] He was right. In 1882, two New York Herald representatives, George Melville and William Gilder, met up by sheer accident in eastern Siberia as both men raced to report the fate of the lost crew of the Jeanette. Adventure journalists were rather thick on the ground, even in Siberia, by 1900.[3]

But as the Gilded Age drew toward its end, so too did the high-circulation "yellow press" newspapers that had been the financiers of adventure reporting. In a last ditch effort to preserve their high circulations, these papers turned to reporting on battles of the Spanish-American War, reporting from the decks of ships in the Philippines and the burned sugar cane fields in Cuba.[4] One-time adventure journalist Stephen Crane would become a controversial war reporter, first in Cuba and then writing dispatches from caves in Greece during the Greco-Turkish War.[5] Meanwhile, back home, a new type of reporting was coming to the fore in newspapers and many magazines; this new style featured investigative exposes known as a whole by the name "muckraking." In the tradition of Nellie Bly, these individuals would challenge Americans' understanding of modern life with exposés on urban slums, as in the groundbreaking photojournalism of Jacob Riis (1849–1914), a police reporter for the *New-York Tribune*, *New York Evening Post* and *New York Sun*; on white mob violence by Ida B. Wells (1862–1931); and on child labor and sweatshops by Florence Kelley (1859–1932).[6]

Travel writing itself continued as it had before and during the adventure reporting period, but these travel works were chiefly of types not considered strictly *adventure journalism* in the rubric of this book. First were the entrepreneurial travel writers, literary-minded individuals who set out on their own adventures and wrote books independently to help finance their wanderlust. Joshua Slocum and his *Sailing Alone Around the World* in 1900 would be one example of the self-contained, literary travel writer.[7] Second were the documentarians, who traveled—often under U.S. government auspices—to survey, chart, and photograph the new lands of remote mountain, desert, and polar regions, much in the tradition of Civil War photographer Timothy H. O'Sullivan, who had made stunning photographs of the American West earlier in the century.[8] Another travel writing strand came from writers who were at heart teachers. Their pedagogical works were published in many magazines that served in large part as nineteenth-century America's adult education system. One prolific teacher-writer was William Woodville Rockhill, a U.S. ambassador who wrote articles and books about Tibet, western China, and Mongolia; his biographer Kenneth Wimmel calls Rockhill a "scholar-diplomat."[9]

These travel writers would continue to publish their colorful works, war reporters would send battle news, and muckrakers would investigate corporate abuses. But what would become of adventure journalism and its authors, those Gilded Age circulation-building explorers "who seek out or are sent out to find adventure, place themselves on-stage as players in events, and report back to the periodical press about the events they witness and generally participate in"?[10]

A fanciful person might say that an 1897 house party, thrown by Alexander Graham Bell at his home near Baddeck, Nova Scotia, saved adventure journalism. At the least, the gathering set into motion a series of events that would preserve the legacy of the Gilded Age adventure journalists and secure their place in the public imagination into the twentieth century. It started innocently enough. Bell's daughter Elsie would meet and eventually marry a youth invited to that house party, Gilbert Hovey Grosvenor. Bell had observed Grosvenor with interest himself, recognizing a promising young intellect. So early the following year, after Bell reluctantly agreed to lead his father-in-law's ailing National Geographic Society,[11] he sought out young Grosvenor to be an editor for the Society's magazine, a dry publication that was "dreadfully scientific, suitable for diffusing geographic knowledge among those who already had it, and scaring off the rest...."[12] Fortunately for the dull newsletter, Grosvenor agreed to create a re-envisioned *National Geographic Magazine* that would adopt a more accessible writing style, borrowed from the adventure journalists. The move would heighten the Society's allure and extend membership beyond scientists and into the general public.[13]

Bell and his *National Geographic* colleagues would capitalize on the success of the daily press's adventure reporting by co-opting the reporter-explorer figure and in addition, with better planning and financial resources, attract reputable explorers and naturalists to lead expeditions. Unlike previous generations of Gilded Age readers, however, *Geographic* subscribers would take on a new role in the adventures funded by their memberships. Readers' engagement via membership gave them a vested interest in the Society and its publication, especially once that publication added photographs and rich description to its pages at the turn of the century.

Bell and Grosvenor also redefined the nature of the organization. While retaining the interest in mapmaking and topography espoused by the 1888 founders of the Society, the new generation broadened the concept of "geography" to encompass the flora, fauna, and peoples of the lands being explored. The reach of the publication would be global, yet its contents would be engaging and accessible to the ordinary people who were now invited to join the Society. Grosvenor would later write that "Dr. Bell's idea of membership in a society, not merely subscription to a magazine, was sound and a great initial asset."[14]

In the first decade of the twentieth century, Grosvenor's *National Geographic Magazine* used a mix of contents that included the first-person narratives popularized by adventure journalists. *Geographic* also expanded the authorship of periodical adventure writing to include more women reporters and photographers, of particular note, Eliza Scidmore and Harriet Chalmers Adams. Scidmore is featured in this book as James Mueller follows her travels and tales to Alaska, Japan, and Java.[15] Harriet Chalmers Adams, whose career fell after the turn of the century, would travel the entire South American continent, Asia, and the South Pacific, writing for *Geographic*, before becoming a battlefront correspondent for *Harper's* during World War I.[16]

Gradually, the cachet of heading up National Geographic Society expeditions, with their world-wide recognition and superior funding, drew growing participation of serious explorers. Though first-person accounts by reporters would continue to win audiences throughout the new century, at least in the new and rapidly growing *National Geographic*, the foregrounded adventures of scientists often left journalists in the wings to write the copy.[17]

The shift in protagonist at the magazine, from journalist to scientist or explorer, led to a profound shift in the framing of foreign lands in these stories. While the adventure journalists of the Gilded Age reported on a personal experience and observations within an unfamiliar territory or culture, scientific explorers were separated from what they observed by a clinical distance. Solidly positioned as "other," as "exotic" and "different," observed people became the butterflies on a pin, to be studied, so that the individuality of people in foreign lands was traded for descriptions of their collective habits. Inclusion of photographs, made more print-worthy by ever-advancing printing technologies, added to the distance rather than bridging it, presenting their subjects as objects of study, minimizing their names, roles, and speech—those elements highlighted, for instance, in *Frank Leslie's* Alaska expedition stories.[18] Photographs placed readers in the position of art critics, with exotic content becoming the studied art in place of the engravings made from the grandiose landscape paintings of Gilded Age artists like Albert Bierstadt, who had prospered by painting the American West.[19]

Outside the pages of a burgeoning *National Geographic* and its expeditions, adventure journalists and their first-person, heroic individualist accounts also maintained a solid media presence in the twentieth century, adopting new technologies and new

Labeled "America's greatest woman explorer" by the *New York Times*, Harriet Chalmers Adams (1875–1937) was also a reporter, traveling extensively through South America, the Caribbean, Europe, and Asia. Her work was carried by numerous publications, especially *Harper's Magazine* and *National Geographic* (Library of Congress, Item cph.3b43526).

mediums. Norwegian Thor Heyerdahl's midcentury account of his *Kon-Tiki* voyage, across the Pacific Ocean on a handmade raft, would become an instant classic and give rise to multiple films and even a museum.[20] Journalist Edward R. Murrow would pioneer environmental sound in radio by walking the streets during the London Blitz and flying along on parachute drops over Europe, broadcasting all the while. In the 1960s, the inimitable Marlin Perkins would take to television to share his explorations with a generation of viewers on "Mutual of Omaha's Wild Kingdom"—though it was inevitably Perkins' assistant, Jim Fowler, who became the hero when the moment came to wrestle an anaconda, while Marlin stood by and said, "Wow, look at the size of that snake that's grabbed Jim."[21] Jim always seemed to be the one left hanging from the back of the vehicle when it was time to flee a furious elephant in the men's trundling Mini-Moke.[22] Though the medium had changed, Perkins and Fowler were quintessential adventure reporters: brave, industrious, and self-sacrificing, portraying themselves as ordinary people who crossed boundaries into the wild and unfamiliar, inviting viewers to witness their experiences—whether heroic or comic.

By the twenty-first century, adventure journalism had spawned programs and magazines that focused their entire contents on the "how-to" of adventuring. Broadcast media have regularly featured the journalist-on-the-road formula, from Charles Kuralt's quarter century of *On the Road* reporting to Anthony Bourdain's multiple series on The Food Network, the Travel Channel, and CNN. New magazines and social media sites enable audiences to seek out their own adventures in exotic locations and challenging terrains. Among the leaders in this genre, *Outside* magazine focuses on "Travel: Adventure, Escapes, Destinations," while *Backpacker* embraces adventure with its regular sections on "Skills" and "Survival." In this media niche, Gilded Age adventure journalism has evolved into a new genre that speaks to an adventuring audience rather than the armchair travelers of previous eras.

Looking back, that 1897 house party hosted by Alexander Graham Bell takes on surprising importance when one considers how the refashioned *National Geographic Magazine* bridged the gap between adventure journalism of the Gilded Age and its progeny: the radio programs, magazines, television shows, video documentaries, and of course the onslaught of digital content that have brought adventure reporting to twentieth and twenty-first century American readers. As they continue to open doors, spark inquiry, and motivate discovery, whether they be home or abroad, journalists continue to be found on the hunt for the next great adventure.

## Notes

1. See Quinn's essay "Adventure Reporting from America's Western Rails and Trails, 1860–1880."

2. See Huntzicker's essay "Thomas Wallace Knox: A Celebrity Journalist's Travel and Adventure in Siberia and China."

3. See Burton's essay "'Mr. Bennett's Expedition': The *New York Herald*'s Arctic Adventure."

4. Stephen A. Banning, "John McCutcheon's Asian Adventure: A nineteenth-century adventure journalist covers the Battle for Manila Bay from the Inside." *Journalism History* 42, no. 1 (Spring 2016): 33–42.

5. Joe Marren, "Activism and Indifference: Stephen Crane and the Reportage of His Career." *Journalism History* 42, no. 1 (Spring 2016): 43–50.

6. See Breslin and Quinn's essay "'Alive, but wiser from our experience': Nellie Bly's Adventure Reporting from Mexico and Around the World"; "Nellie Bly a Prisoner: She has herself arrested to gain entrance to a station-house," *New York World*, February 24, 1889.

7. Joshua Slocum, *Sailing Alone Around the World* (New York: Century Co., 1900).

8. Smithsonian Museum of American Art, "Framing the West: The Survey Photographs of Timothy H. O'Sullivan," exhibit mounted February 12, 2010—May 8, 2010, www.americanart.si.edu/exhibitions/osullivan.

9. Kenneth Wimmel, *William Woodville Rockhill: Scholar-Diplomat of The Tibetan Highlands* (Hong Kong: Orchid Press, 2010).

10. Lee Jolliffe, "Adventurer Journalists in the Gilded Age." *Journalism History* 42, no. 1 (Spring 2016): 3.

11. Alexander Bell's father-in-law, Gardener Greene Hubbard, had founded the Society in 1888, but had died before being able to make it successful. See Howard S. Abramson, *National Geographic: Behind America's Lens on the World* (New York: Crown, 1987), chapter 4.

12. Anne Chamberlin, "Two Cheers for the National Geographic," *Esquire*, December 1963, 206.

13. Gilbert H. Grosvenor, *The National Geographic and Its Magazine* (Washington, DC: National Geographic Society, 1957). Grosvenor would be the magazine's first full-time employee but did not become its editor-in-chief until 1903. In December of 1904, Grosvenor would make a momentous decision. Faced with a "hole" in the publication meant for content that did not materialize, Grosvenor featured full-page photographs from Tibet in the January 1905 issue. The furor was great, but not greater than the increase in attention and subscriptions, and photographs thereafter took pride of place in the magazine.

14. *Ibid.*

15. See Mueller's essay "To Better See the World: The Adventure Journalism of Eliza Ruhamah Scidmore."

16. *LiveScience* Staff, "Eight Unsung Women Explorers," *LiveScience*, April 29, 2012, www.livescience.com/-31380-unsung-women-explorers.html.

17. *National Geographic Magazine* writer-explorer Harriet Chalmers Adams, for instance, wrote in both genres—as protagonist herself and as reporter covering a third party's explorations—in the early years of the twentieth century, as Grosvenor built the modern version of the magazine. See Kathryn Davis, "Harriet Chalmers Adams: Remembering an American Geographer," *The Californian Geographer* 49 (2009): 51–70; especially note the bibliography of Adams' writings at the end of the article.

18. For a recent study of the "distancing" effects of this type of travel reporting, see Catherine A. Lutz and

Jane L. Collins, *Reading National Geographic* (Chicago and London: University of Chicago Press, 1993). For content on Leslie, see chapter 1.

19. John F. Sears, *Sacred Places: American Tourist Attractions in the Nineteenth Century* (New York: Oxford University Press, 1989).

20. Thor Heyerdal, *Kon-Tiki: Across the Pacific by Raft* (originally published in Norway in 1948 as *The Kon-Tiki Expedition: By Raft Across the South Seas*), trans. F. H. Lyon (Chicago: Rand McNally, 1950). The voyage was made into feature-length films in 1950 and 2012. The Kon-Tiki Museum is located in Oslo, Norway.

21. Dave Zelio, "'Jim Will Tackle the Anaconda....': Jim Fowler Still at Home in Wild Kingdom," *Greensboro (NC) News & Record*, October 30, 1993, www.greensboro.com/jim-will-tackle-the-anaconda-jim-fowler-s-still-at/article_50970a51-de3d-5959-96f2-691f9623784d.html.

22. See highlights at "Memorable Moments in the Wild Kingdom," www.youtube.com/watch?v=zbJXzwURIRw.

# Bibliography

Abramson, Howard S. *'National Geographic': Behind America's Lens on the World* (New York: Crown, 1987).

Actor, Lisa Trimble. "Surveying Seward's Folly: The U.S. Coast Survey in Alaska," *Alaska Journal* 16 (1986): 28–35.

"Alaska." *The Quarterly Register of Current History.* Edited by Alfred S. Johnson, vol. 1 (Detroit: Evening News Association, 1892).

Allen, Charles W. *From Fort Laramie to Wounded Knee: In the West That Was* (Lincoln: University of Nebraska Press, 1997).

Allyn, Joseph Pratt. *The Arizona of Joseph Pratt Allyn: Letters from a Pioneer Judge: Observations and Travels, and Travels, 1863–1866.* Edited by John Nicolson (Tucson: University of Arizona Press, 1974).

Ambrose, Stephen E. *Nothing Like It in the World: The Men Who Built the Transcontinental Railroad, 1863–1869* (New York: Touchstone, 2000).

Anderson, Benedict. *Imagined Communities: Reflections on the Origin and Spread of Nationalism* (New York: Verso, 1983).

Aron, Cindy S. *Working at Play: A History of Vacations in the United States* (New York: Oxford University Press, 1999).

Baldasty, Gerald J. *The Commercialization of News in the Nineteenth Century* (Madison: University of Wisconsin Press, 1992).

Barnhurst, Kevin G., and John Nerone. "Civil Picturing vs. Realistic Photojournalism: The Regime of Illustrated News, 1865–1901," *Design Issues* 16, no. 1 (2000): 61–64.

Beattie, Owen, and John Geiger. *Frozen in Time: The Fate of the Franklin Expedition* (Vancouver, BC: Greystone, 2014).

Bederman, Gail. *Manliness and Civilization: A Cultural History of Gender and Race in the United States, 1880–1917* (Chicago: University of Chicago Press, 1995).

Berkove, Lawrence I., ed. *The Sagebrush Anthology: Literature from the Silver Age of the Old West* (Columbia: University of Missouri Press, 2006).

Berneson, Edward. *Heroes of Empire: Five Charismatic Men and the Conquest of Africa* (Berkeley: University of California Press, 2011).

Bierman, John. *Dark Safari: Life Behind the Legend of Henry Morton Stanley* (Austin: University of Texas Press, 1993).

Bird, S. Elizabeth, ed. *Dressing in Feathers: The Construction of the Indian in American Popular Culture* (New York: Routledge, 2018).

Bloom, Harold, ed. *Mark Twain: Bloom's Modern Critical Views* (Philadelphia: Chelsea House Publishers, 2003).

Bly, Nellie. *Around the World in Seventy-Two Days* (London: Bretano's; New York: Pictorial Weeklies, 1890).

_____. *Six Months in Mexico* (New York: American Publishers Corporation, 1888).

_____. *Ten Days in a Mad-House* (New York: Munro, 1887); facsimile edition at University of Pennsylvania Digital Library's "A Celebration of Women Writers," digital.library.upenn.edu/women/bly/madhouse/madhouse.html.

Bolles, Albert S. "Mines and Mining, and Oil." In *Industrial History of the United States, from the Earliest Settlements to the Present Time: Being a Complete Survey of American Industries [...]"* (Norwich, CT: Henry Bill, 1889), Book IV, 667–780.

Boorstin, Daniel J. *The Image: A Guide to Pseudo-events in America* (New York: Harper, 1962).

Boswell, James. *The Journal of a Tour to the Hebrides* (London: Henry Baldwin, 1785).

Boucicault, Dion. "At the Goethe Society," *North American Review* 148, no. 388 (March 1889): 335–343.

Bowles, Samuel. *Across the Continent: A Summer's Journey to the Rocky Mountains, the Mormons, and the Pacific States, with Speaker Colfax* (Springfield, MA: Bowles, 1865).

_____. *Our New West: Records of Travel Between the Mississippi River and the Pacific Ocean* (Hartford, CT: Hartford, 1869).

_____. *The Pacific Railroad—Open, How to Go, What to See: Guide for Travel to and Through Western America* (Boston: Fields, Osgood, & Co., 1869).

_____. *The Parks and Mountains of Colorado: A Summer Vacation in the Switzerland of America, 1868* (Springfield, MA: Bowles, 1869).

Boyer, Paul. *Urban Masses and Moral Order in America, 1820–1920* (Cambridge: Harvard University Press, 1978).

Boyton, Paul. *The Story of Paul Boyton—Voyages on All the Great Rivers of the World, Paddling Twenty-Five Thousand Miles in a Rubber Dress* (Milwaukee: Riverside Printing, 1892).

Brackenridge, Henry Marie. *Views of Louisiana, Together with a Journal of a Voyage Up the Missouri River, in 1811* (Pittsburgh: Cramer, Spear and Richbaum, 1814).

Bragg, Dianne. "Nellie Bly: Flying in the Face of Tradition." In *Sensationalism: Murder, Mayhem, Mudslinging, Scandals and Disasters in 19th Century Reporting*. Edited by David B. Sachsman and David W. Bulla (New Brunswick, NJ: Transaction Publishers, 2013).

Branson, John B. *The Life and Times of John W. Clark of Nushagaka Alaska, 1846–1896* (Anchorage: National Park Service, 2012).

Brown, Joshua. *Beyond the Lines: Pictorial Reporting, Everyday Life, and the Crisis of Gilded Age America* (Berkeley and Los Angeles: University of California Press, 2006).

Browne, J. Ross. *Adventures in the Apache Country: A Tour Through Arizona and Sonora, with Notes on the Silver Regions of Nevada, Illustrated by the Author* (New York: Harper & Brothers, 1869).

Burton, Sir Richard F. *First Footsteps in East Africa; Or, an Exploration of Harar* (London: Longman, Brown, Green, and Longmans, 1856).

_____. *Personal Narrative of a Pilgrimage to El-Medinah and Meccah.* 3 vols. (London: Longman, Brown, Green, and Longmans, 1855–56).

Campbell, Helen Stuart, Thomas W. Knox, and Thomas F. Byrnes. *Darkness and Daylight; Or, Lights and Shadows of New York Life; a Pictorial Record of Personal Experiences by Day and Night in the Great Metropolis.* with an introduction by Lyman Abbott (Hartford, CT: A. D. Worthington, 1891).

Campbell, Robert. *In Darkest Alaska: Travel and Empire Along the Inside Passage* (Philadelphia: University of Pennsylvania Press, 2007).

Caron, James E. *Mark Twain, Unsanctified Newspaper Reporter* (Columbia: University of Missouri Press, 2008).

Catlin, George. *Letters and Notes on the Manners, Customs and Conditions of the North American Indians, 1844.* Edited by Peter Matthiessen (New York: Penguin, 1989).

Cavendish, Richard. "Birth of Celia Fiennes," *History Today* 62, no. 6 (2012): unpaginated. www.historytoday.com/richard-cavendish/birth-celia-fiennes.

Chamberlin, Anne. "Two Cheers for the National Geographic," *Esquire*. December 1963, 300.

Clapp, Elizabeth J. *A Notorious Woman: Anne Royall in Jacksonian America* (Charlottesville: University of Virginia Press, 2016).

Collins, Jane, and Catherine Lutz. "Becoming America's Lens on the World: *National Geographic* in the Twentieth Century," *South Atlantic Quarterly* 91, no. 1 (1992): 161–191.

Collins, Perry McD. *Memorial of Perry McD. Collins.* [Ignatius Donnelly Library Pamphlet Collection.] v. 40, no. 12 (1864), Minnesota Historical Society.

Commissioner of Indian Affairs. *Annual Report of the Commissioner of Indian Affairs to the Secretary of the Interior for the Year 1887* (Washington, DC: Government Printing Office, 1887).

Connery, Thomas B. *Journalism and Realism: Rendering American Life* (Evanston, IL: Northwestern University Press, 2011).

Coward, John. *The Newspaper Indian: Native American Identity in the Press, 1820–90* (Champaign: University of Illinois Press, 1999).

Creelman, James. *On the Great Highway: The Wanderings and Adventures of a Special Correspondent* (Boston: Lothrop, Shepard, 1901).

Cronin, Mary M., and William E. Huntzicker. "Popular Chinese Images and 'The Coming Man' of 1870: Racial Representations of Chinese," *Journalism History* 38, no. 2 (2012): 86–99.

Culler, Jonathan. "The Semiotics of Tourism." In *Framing the Sign: Criticism and Its Institutions* (Norman: University of Oklahoma Press, 1988), 153–167.

Cummings, Amos J. *Frolicking Bears, Wet Vultures, and Other Oddities: A New York City Journalist in Nineteenth-Century Florida.* Edited by Jerald T. Milanich (Gainesville: University Press of Florida, 2005).

_____. *A Remarkable Curiosity: Dispatches from a New York City Journalist's 1873 Railroad Trip Across the American West.* Edited by Jerald T. Milanich (Boulder: University Press of Colorado, 2008).

Curti, Merle. *The Roots of American Loyalty* (New York: Russell & Russell, 1967).

da Pisa, Rustichello. *The Travels of Marco Polo.* c. 1300. Trans by William Marsden (New York: AMS Press, 1968).

Davis, Kathryn. "Harriet Chalmers Adams: Remembering an American Geographer," *The Californian Geographer* 49 (2009): 51–70.

Defoe, Daniel. *A Tour Thro' the Whole Island of Great Britain*. 4 vols. (London: Brown, Osborne, Hitch, and Hawes: 1762).

Dicken-Garcia, Hazel. *Journalistic Standards in Nineteenth-Century America* (Madison: University of Wisconsin Press, 1989).

Dickens, Charles. *American Notes for General Circulation* (London: Chapman and Hall, 1842).

_____. *Pictures from Italy* (London: Bradbury & Evans, 1846).

Diniejko, Andrzej. "Slums and Slumming in Late-Victorian London," www.victorianweb.org/history/slums.html.

Duara, Prasenjit. "Historicizing National Identity, or Who Imagines What and When." In *Becoming National: A Reader*. Edited by Geoff Eley and Ronald Grigor Suny (New York: Oxford University Press, 1996), 151–178.

Duckett, Margaret. *Mark Twain and Bret Harte* (Norman: University of Oklahoma Press, 1964).

Dugard, Martin. *Farther Than Any Man: The Rise and Fall of Captain James Cook* (New York: Atria/Simon & Schuster, 2001).

_____. *Into Africa: The Epic Adventures of Stanley and Livingstone* (New York: Broadway, 2003).

Dunlop, M. H. *Sixty Miles from Contentment: Traveling the 19th Century American Interior* (New York: Basic, 1995).

Dwyer, Richard A., and Richard E. Lingenfelter. *Dan De Quille: The Washoe Giant* (Reno: University of Nevada Press, 1990).

_____ and _____, eds. *Lying on the Eastern Slope: James Townsend's Comic Journalism on the Mining Frontier* (Miami: Florida International University Press, 1984).

Edy, Carolyn M. *The Woman War Correspondent, the U.S. Military, and the Press: 1846–1947* (London: Lexington, 2017).

Egerton, Douglas R. *The Wars of Reconstruction: The Brief, Violent History of America's Most Progressive Era* (New York: Bloomsbury, 2014).

Eley, Geoff, and Ronald Grigor Suny. "From the Moment of Social History to the Work of Cultural Representation." In *Becoming National: A Reader* (New York: Oxford University Press, 1996), 3–38.

_____ and _____, eds. *Becoming National: A Reader* (New York: Oxford University Press, 1996).

Eschner, Kat. "See 17th-Century England Through the Eyes of One of the First Modern Travel Writers: Celia Fiennes Traveled and Wrote About Her Adventures—including a Bit of Life Advice," Smithsonianmag.com, June 7, 2017, www.smithsonianmag.com/smart-news/see-1600s-england-through-eyes-one-first-travel-writers-180963536/ .

Fahs, Alice. *Out on Assignment: Newspaper Women and the Making of Modern Public Space* (Chapel Hill: University of North Carolina Press, 2011).

Faragher, John Mack, ed. *Rereading Frederick Jackson Turner: The Significance of the Frontier in American History" and Other Essays* (New Haven: Yale University Press, 1994).

Farwell, Byron, *The Man Who Presumed: A Biography of Henry M. Stanley* (New York: W.W. Norton, 1989).

Firebaugh, Dorothy Gile. "'The Sacramento Union': Voice of California, 1851–75," *Journalism Quarterly* 30, no. 3 (1953): 321–330.

Floyd, Janet. *Claims and Speculations: Mining and Writing in the Gilded Age* (Albuquerque: University of New Mexico Press, 2012).

_____. "The Feeling of 'Silverland': Sagebrush Journalism in Virginia City's 'Flush Times,'" *Media History* 19, no. 3 (2013): 257–269.

Foner, Eric, *The Story of American Freedom* (New York: W. W. Norton, 1999).

Foner, Phillip S. *The Great Labor Uprising of 1877* (New York: Pathfinder, 1977).

Ford, Corey. *Where the Sea Breaks Its Back: The Epic Story of Early Naturalist Georg Stellar and the Russian Exploration of Alaska* (Portland: Alaska Northwest Books, 2003).

Forestier, Auber. "More About California: An Expedition Underground," *Saturday Evening Post*. June 11, 1870.

Frear, Walter Francis. *Mark Twain and Hawaii* (Chicago: Lakeside, 1947).

Freeman, Barbara M. *Kit's Kingdom: The Journalism of Kathleen Blake Coleman* (Don Mills, ON: Oxford University Press, 1989).

Frothingham, O. B. "Voices of Power," *Atlantic Monthly* 53, February 1884, 176–182.

Gallop, Alan, *Mr. Stanley, I Presume? the Life and Explorations of Henry Morton Stanley* (Stroud, England: Sutton, 2004).

Gates, Michael. *Gold at Fortymile Creek: Early Days in the Yukon* (Vancouver: University of British Columbia Press, 1994).

Gellner, Ernest. *Nations and Nationalism* (Ithaca: Cornell University Press, 1983).

Gibbon, Guy. *The Sioux: The Dakota and Lakota Nations* (Malden, MA: Wiley-Blackwell, 2003).

Gillette, William. *Retreat from Reconstruction, 1869–1879* (Baton Rouge: Louisiana State University Press, 1979).

Gmelch, Sharon Bohn, ed. *Tourists and Tourism: A Reader* (Long Grove, IL: Waveland Press, 2010).

Goodman, Matthew, *Eighty Days: Nelly Bly and Elizabeth Bisland's History-Making Race Around the World* (New York: Ballantine, 2013).

Greeley, Horace. *An Overland Journey, from New York to San Francisco, in the Summer of 1859* (New York: C. M. Saxton, Barker &, 1860).

\_\_\_\_\_. *Recollections of a Busy Life* (New York: J. B. Ford, 1868).

Greene, Carol Marie, *Letters Home: Newspaper Travel Writing of Kate Field, Mary Elizabeth McGarth Blake, and Grace Greenwood* (PhD diss., Indiana U of Pennsylvania, 2001).

Greenwood, Grace. *Haps and Mishaps of a Tour in Europe* (Boston: Ticknor, Reed, and Fields, 1854).

\_\_\_\_\_. *New Life in New Lands: Notes of Travel* (New York: J. B. Ford, 1873).

Gregory, Alice. "Nellie Bly's Lessons in Writing What You Want To," *New Yorker*. May 14, 2014, www.newyorker.com/books/page-turner/nellie-blys-lessons-in-writing-what-you-want-to .

Grosvenor, Gilbert H. *The National Geographic and Its Magazine* (Washington, D.C.: National Geographic Society, 1957).

Guttridge, Leonard F. *Icebound: The Jeannette Expedition's Quest for the North Pole* (Lincoln, NE: iUniverse, 2006).

Gutzlaff, Karl. *Journal of Three Voyages Along the Coast of China in 1831, 1832, and 1833* (London: T. Ward, 1840).

Gyory, Andrew. *Closing the Gate: Race, Politics, and the Chinese Exclusion Act* (Chapel Hill: University of North Carolina Press, 1998).

Hakluyt, Richard, ed. *Divers Voyages Touching the Discoverie of America and the Ilands Adjacent Unto the Same, Made First of All by Our Englishmen and Afterwards by the Frenchmen and Britons: With Two Mappes Annexed Hereunto* (London: Richards, 1852).

Hall, Stuart. "The Spectacle of the 'Other,'" in *Representation: Cultural Representations and Signifying Practices. Edited by* Stuart Hall (London: Sage, 1997), 223–277.

Hanna, Archibald, Jr. "The Genteel Explorers; Or, When the Covered Wagon Became a Pullman Palace Car," *Yale University Library Gazette* 54, no. 2 (1979): 68–78.

Harris, Brayton. *Blue and Gray in Black and White: Newspapers in the Civil War* (Dulles, VA: Batsford Brassey, 1999).

Harrison, William. *Burton and Speke* (New York: St. Martin's Press, 1982).

Hawkins, Stephanie L. *American Iconographic: National Geographic, Global Culture and the Visual Imagination* (Charlottesville: University of Virginia Press, 2010).

Haymond, John A. *The Infamous Dakota War Trials of 1862: Revenge, Military Law, and the Judgment of History* (Jefferson, NC: McFarland, 2016).

\_\_\_\_\_. "Laws of War: The Trial of Thomas Knox," *Quarterly Journal of Military History* (2017): 13–16.

Herbert, Sir Thomas. *A Relation of Some Yeares Travaile, Begunne Anno 1626.…* (London: Stansby and Bloome, 1634), at staffblogs.le.ac.uk/specialcollections/2015/01/07/17th-century-adventures-in-travel-writing/ and a later edition. *Some Years Travels Into Divers Parts of Africa and Asia the Great Describing More Particularly the Empires of Persia and Industan: Interwoven with Such Remarkable Occurrences as Hapned in These Parts During These Later Times* (London: A. Crook, 1665).

Herne, Vickie. *Adam's Task: Calling Animals by Name* (New York: Knopf, 1986).

Heyerdahl, Thor. *Kon-Tiki: Across the Pacific by Raft* (originally published in Norway in 1948 as *The Kon-Tiki Expedition: By Raft Across the South Seas*), translated by F. H. Lyon (Chicago: Rand McNally, 1950).

Hobsbawm, E. J. *Nations and Nationalism Since 1780* (New York: Cambridge University Press, 1990).

Hofstadter, Richard. *Social Darwinism in American Thought* (Boston: Beacon, 1983).

Holbo, Paul Sothe. *Tarnished Expansion: The Alaska Scandal, the Press, and Congress, 1867–1871* (Knoxville: University of Tennessee Press, 1983).

Holmes, Diana, David Platton, Loic Artiago, and Jacques Migozzi, eds. *Finding the Plot: Storytelling in Popular Fictions* (Tyne, UK: Cambridge Scholars Publishing, 2014).

Hoogenboom, Ari. *Rutherford B. Hayes: Warrior and President* (Lawrence: University Press of Kansas, 1995).

Horsman, Reginald. *Race and Manifest Destiny: The Origins of American Racial Anglo-Saxonism* (Cambridge: Harvard University Press, 1981).

Hostetler, Michael J. "Henry Cabot Lodge and the Rhetorical Trajectory." In *The Rhetoric of American Exceptionalism: Critical Essays. Edited by* Jason A. Edwards and David Weiss (Jefferson, NC: McFarland, 2011), 118–131.

Howard, Richard, ed. *Henry James: Collected Travel Writings: Great Britain and America* (New York: Library of America, 1993).

Hull, Gloria T., ed. *The Works of Alice Dunbar-Nelson*. vol. 3 (New York: Oxford University Press, 1988).

Huntzicker, William E. "Newspaper Representations of China and Chinese Americans." In *Outsiders in 19th Century Press History: Multicultural Perspectives*, edited by Frankie Hutton and Barbara Straus Reed (Bowling Green, OH: Bowling Green State University Popular Press, 1995).

\_\_\_\_\_ "Picturing the News: Frank Leslie and the Origins of American Pictorial Journalism." In *The Civil War and the Press. Edited by* David B. Sachsman, S. Kittrell Rushing, and Debra Reddin van Tuyll (New Brunswick, NJ: Transaction Publishers, 2000), 309–324.

\_\_\_\_\_. *The Popular Press, 1833–1865* (Westport, CT: Greenwood, 1999).

Imbarrato, Susan Clair. *Traveling Women: Narrative Visions of Early America* (Columbus: Ohio University Press, 2006).

Ingersoll, Lurton Dunham. *The Life of Horace Greeley* (Chicago: Union Publishing Company, 1873).

Jeal, Tim. *Stanley: The Impossible Life of Africa's Greatest Explorer* (New Haven: Yale University Press, 2008).

Johnson, Samuel. *A Journey to the Western Islands of Scotland* (Dublin, Ireland: Thomas Walker, 1775).

Johnston, Andrew Scott. *Mercury and the Making of California: Mining, Landscape, and Race, 1840–1890* (Boulder: University Press of Colorado, 2013).

Jolliffe, Lee. "Adventurer Journalists in the Gilded Age," *Journalism History* 42, no. 1 (2016): 2–4.

_____. Journalists of the 19th Century (special issue), *Journalism History* 42, no. 1 (2016).

Jones, Douglas C. "Teresa Dean: Lady Correspondent Among the Sioux Indians," *Journalism and Mass Communication Quarterly* (1972): 656–662.

Jones, John Winter, ed. *Divers Voyages Touching the Discovery of America and the Islands Adjacent* (London: Hakluyt Society, 1850).

Junger, Richard. *Becoming the Second City: Chicago's Mass News Media, 1833–1898* (Urbana: University of Illinois Press, 2010).

Kaplan, Amy. *The Social Construction of American Realism* (Chicago: University of Chicago Press, 1992).

Kaplan, Justin. *Mr. Clemens and Mark Twain: A Biography* (New York: Simon & Schuster, 1966).

Kasson, Joy S. *Buffalo Bill's Wild West: Celebrity, Memory, and Popular History* (New York: Hill and Wang, 2000).

King, Clarence, *Mountaineering in the Sierra Nevada, 1872*. Edited and with Preface by Francis P. Farquhar, 1935 (Lincoln: University of Nebraska Press, 1997).

Knight, Oliver. *Following the Indian Wars: The Story of the Newspaper Correspondents Among the Indian Campaigners* (Norman: University of Oklahoma Press, 1993).

Knox, Thomas W. *Camp-Fire and Cotton-Field* (New York: Blelock, 1865).

_____. *How to Travel: Hints, Advice, and Suggestions to Travelers by Land and Sea All Over the World* (New York: G. P. Putnam's Sons, 1888).

_____. *John; Or, Our Chinese Relations: A Study of Our Emigration and Commercial Intercourse with the Celestial Empire* (New York: Harper & Brothers, 1879).

_____. *Overland Through Asia: Pictures of Siberian, Chinese, and Tartar Life* (Hartford, CN: American, 1870).

_____. *The Talking Handkerchief and Other Stories* (Akron, OH: Saalfield, 1900).

Korte, Barbara. *English Travel Writing: From Pilgrimages to Postcolonial Explorations*. trans. Catherine Matthias (New York: Palgrave Macmillan, 2000).

Kroeger, Brooke. *Nellie Bly: Daredevil, Reporter, Feminist* (New York: Times Books/Random House), 1994.

Lapierre, Alexandra, and Christel Mouchard. *Women Travelers: A Century of Trailblazing Adventures 1850–1950* (New York: Flammarion/Rizzoli, 2007).

Lawson, Melinda. *Patriot Fires: Forging a New American Nationalism in the Civil War North* (Lawrence: University Press of Kansas, 2002).

Lee, Erika. *At America's Gates: Chinese Immigration During the Exclusion Era, 1882–1943* (Chapel Hill: University of North Carolina Press, 2003).

Leslie, Miriam. *California: A Pleasure Trip from Gotham to the Golden Gate, April, May, June 1877* (New York: G. W. Carleton & Co, 1877).

Liebersohn, Harry. "Recent Works on Travel Writing," *Journal of Modern History* 68, no. 3 (1996): 617–628.

Linn, William Alexander. *Horace Greeley: Founder and Editor of the "New York Tribune"* (New York: D. Appleton, 1912).

Lorch, Frederick William. *The Trouble Begins at Eight: Mark Twain's Lecture Tours* (Ames: Iowa State University Press, 1968).

Ludlow, Fitz Hugh. *The Heart of the Continent: A Record of Travel Across the Plains and in Oregon, with an Examination of the Mormon Principle* (New York: Hurd and Houghton, 1870).

Lutz, Catherine A., and Jane L. Collins. *Reading National Geographic* (Chicago and London: University of Chicago Press, 1993).

Lyon, Peter. "The Fearless Frogman," *American Heritage Magazine* 11 no. 3 (April 1960): 37–39, 92–93.

Lyons, Chuck. "The Bank Crowd and Silver Kings Made a Fortune from the Comstock," *Wild West Magazine*. April 2015, republished at www.historynet.com/the-bank-crowd-and-silver-kings-made-a-fortune-from-the-comstock.htm.

MacCauley, James. *The Past Is an Exotic Place: Nineteenth-Century Travel, Adventure and Discovery Journalism* (no city: Forward-Thinking Press, 2011).

Madsen, Deborah L. *American Exceptionalism* (Jackson: University Press of Mississippi, 1998).

Marks, Jason. *Around the World in 72 Days: The Race Between Pulitzer's Nellie Bly and Cosmopolitan's Elizabeth Bisland* (New York: Gemittarius, 1993).

McClain, Charles J. *In Search of Equality: The Chinese Struggle Against Discrimination in Nineteenth-Century America* (Berkley: University of California Press, 1969).

McLean, Isabel C. "Eliza Ruhamah Scidmore," *Alaska Journal* 7, no. 3: (1977): 238–243.

McLynn, Frank. *Stanley: The Making of an African Explorer* (Chelsea, MI: Scarborough House, 1990).

McMurtrie, Douglas C., ed. *A History of California Newspapers* (New York: Plandpme, 1927).

Melton, Jeffrey Alan. *Mark Twain, Travel Books, and Tourism: The Tide of a Great Popular Movement* (Tuscaloosa: University of Alabama Press, 2002).

Melville, George W. *In the Lena Delta: A Narrative of the Search for Lieut.-Commander DeLong and His Companions Followed by an Account of the Greely Relief Expedition and a Proposed Method of Reaching the North Pole* (Boston: Houghton, Mifflin, 1884).

Mencken, H. L. *Newspaper Days, 1899–1906* (Baltimore: Johns Hopkins University Press, 1996).

Miller, Angela. *The Empire of the Eye: Landscape Representation and American Cultural Politics, 1825–1875* (Ithaca, NY: Cornell University Press, 1993).

Miller, Stuart Creighton. *The Unwelcome Immigrant: The American Image of the Chinese, 1785–1882* (Berkeley: University of California Press, 1969).

Mills, Sara. *Discourses of Difference: An Analysis of Women's Travel Writing and Colonialism* (New York: Routledge, 1993).

Montagu, Lady Mary Wortley, *Lady Mary Wortley Montagu: Selected Letters*. Edited by Isobel Grundy (New York: Penguin, 1997).

_____. "XXXII. to Mrs. T., Adrianople, April 1, O.S. 1718." *Letters of Lady Mary Wortley Montagu, Written During Her Travels in Europe, Asia, and Africa...* (Paris: P. Didot, 1800), 111–116.

Moore, Arthur K. *The Frontier Mind* (New York: McGraw-Hill, 1963).

Moorehead, Alan. *The White Nile* (New York: Perennial, 2000).

Morris, Roy. *American Vandal* (Cambridge: Harvard University Press, 2015).

Mott, Frank Luther. *American Journalism: A History of Newspapers in the United States Through 250 Years, 1690–1940* (New York: Macmillan, 1941).

_____. *A History of American Magazines, 1850–1865*. vol. 2 (Cambridge, MA: Harvard University Press, 1938).

_____. *A History of American Magazines, 1885–1905*. vol. 4 (Cambridge, MA: Harvard University Press, 1957).

Mueller, James. "Stanley Before Livingstone: Henry Morton Stanley's Coverage of Hancock's War Against the Plains Tribes in 1867," *Journalism History* 42, no. 1 (2016): 5–14.

Muller, Nadine, and Joanne Ella Parsons. "The Male Body in Victorian Literature and Culture," *Nineteenth Century Contexts: An Interdisciplinary Journal* 36, no. 4 (2014): 303–06.

Murdoch, David Hamilton. *The American West: The Invention of a Myth* (Las Vegas: University of Nevada Press, 2001).

Murphy, Brenda. *American Realism and American Drama, 1880–1940* (New York: Cambridge University Press, 2008).

Murphy, Deirdre. "'Like Standing on the Edge of the World and Looking Away Into Heaven,'" *Common-Place* 7, no. 3 (2007): common-place.org/book/like-standing-on-the-edge-of-the-world-and-looking-away-into-heaven/.

Nash, Gerald D. "The Census of 1890 and the Closing of the Frontier," *Pacific Northwest Quarterly* 71, no. 3 (1980): 98–100.

Naske, Claus M., and Herman E. Slotnick. *Alaska: A History* (Norman: University of Oklahoma Press, 2014).

National Park Service. "Eliza Scidmore's Faithful Pursuit of a Dream," March 19, 2019, www.nps.gov/articles/scidmore.htm.

Newcombe, Raymond Lee. *Our Lost Explorers: The Narrative of the Jeannette Arctic Expedition, as Related by the Survivors, and in the Records and Last Journals of Lieutenant De Long* (Hartford: American, 1882).

[no author] "Female War Correspondents of World War I: Mapping a Thinly Researched Field in the History of Journalism," *ECREA 6th European Communication Conference—Mediated (Dis)Continuities: Contesting Pasts, Presents and Futures.* November 9–12, 2016, Prague, Czech Republic.

Parsell, Diana. "From Early 'Lady Writer,' Washington Cherry Blossoms and National Geographic Legacy," January 16, 2018, blog.nationalgeographic.org/2018/01/16/from-early-geographic-lady-writer-d-c-cherry-blossoms-and-tsunami/ .

Perkins, Marlin. "Memorable Moments in the Wild Kingdom," www.youtube.com/watch?v=zbJXzwURIRw.

Peterson, Nancy M. "The Unwanted Female Reporter at Wounded Knee," *Wild West.* December 2011, 42–48, www.historynet.com/wild-west-december-2011-table-of-contents.htm.

Pettitt, Clare. *Dr. Livingstone, I Presume? Missionaries, Journalists, Explorers, and Empire* (Cambridge, MA: Harvard University Press, 2007).

Quinn, Katrina J. "'Across the Continent. and Still the Republic!' Inscribing Nationhood in Samuel Bowles's Newspaper Letters of 1865," *American Journalism* 31, no. 4 (2014): 468–489.

_____. "Exploring an Early Version of Literary Journalism: Nineteenth-century Epistolary Journalism," *Literary Journalism Studies* 3, no. 1 (2011): 33–52.

_____. "Narratologies of Autodiegetic Undercover Reportage: Albert Deane Richardson's 'The Secret Service,'" *JNT: Journal of Narrative Theory* 49, no. 1 (2019): 1–26.

_____. "Reconsidering the Public Letter in Epistolary Theory: The Case of Samuel Bowles (1865)," *The CEA Critic* 77, no.1 (2015): 97–119.

_____. "The Rocky Mountains, Yosemite, and Other Natural Wonders: Western Landscape in Travel Correspondence of the Post-Civil War Press" in *After the War: The Press in a Changing America, 1865–1900.* Sachsman, David B., ed. (New York: Transaction, 2017), 127–140.

Reed, David. *The Popular Magazine in Britain and the United States of America, 1880–1960* (Toronto: University of Toronto Press, 1997).

Reinhardt, Richard. *Out West on the Overland Train: Across-the-Continent Excursion with Leslie's Magazine in 1877 and the Overland Trip in 1967* (Secaucus, NJ: Castle Books, 1961).

Rice, Edward. *Captain Sir Richard Francis Burton: A Biography* (Cambridge: De Capo Press, 2001).

Richardson, Albert D. *Beyond the Mississippi: From the Great River to the Great Ocean.* (Hartford: American, 1869).

_____. *The Myth of the Explorer: The Press, Sensationalism, and Geographical Discovery* (New York: Oxford University Press, 1994).

_____. *The Secret Service, the Field, the Dungeon, and the Escape* (Hartford, CT: American, 1865).

Riffenburgh, Beau. "James Gordon Bennett, the 'New York Herald,' and the Arctic," *Polar Record* 27, no. 160 (1991): 9–16.

Rio, Monica. *Nature's Noblemen: Transatlantic Masculinities and the Nineteenth Century American West* (New Haven: Yale University Press, 2013).

Robinson, Michael F. *The Coldest Crucible: Arctic Exploration and American Culture* (Chicago: University of Chicago Press, 2006.

Roediger, David R., and Elizabeth D. Esch. *The Production of Difference: Race and the Management of Labor in U.S. History* (New York: Oxford: 2014).

Romer, Isabella Frances. *A Pilgrimage to the Temples and Tombs of Egypt, Nubia and Palestine in 1845–6* (London: R. Bentley, 1847).

Roosevelt, Theodore. *The Winning of the West.* 4 vols. (New York: G. P. Putnam's, 1889–1896),

Ross, Ishbel. *Ladies of the Press* (New York: Arno, 1974).

Royall, Anne Newport. *Letters from Alabama on Various Subjects* (Washington: 1830).

Ryall, Anka, and Catherine Sandbach-Dahlström. *Mary Wollstonecraft's Journey to Scandinavia: Essays* (Stockholm: Almqvist & Wiksell International, 2003).

Sachsman, David B. "Introduction," *After the War: The Press in a Changing America, 1865–1900* (New Brunswick, NJ: Transaction Publishers, 2017), xv-xxxii.

Sachsman, David B., and David W. Bulla, eds. *Sensationalism: Murder, Mayhem, Mudslinging, Scandals, and Disasters in 19th-Century Reporting* (New Brunswick, NJ: Transaction Publishers, 2013).

Sandler, Martin. *Resolute: The Epic Search for the Northwest Passage and John Franklin, and the Discovery of the Queen's Ghost Ship* (New York: Sterling, 2006).

Saxton, Alexander. *The Rise and Fall of the White Republic: Class Politics and Mass Culture in Nineteenth-Century America* (New York: Verso, 2003).

Scharnhorst, Gary. "Mark Twain Reports the 'Hornet' Disaster," *American Literary Realism* 47, no. 3 (2015): 272–276.

Schoolcraft, Henry Rowe. *Journal of a Tour Into the Interior of Missouri and Arkansaw, from Potosi, or Mine a Burton, in Missouri Territory, in a South-West Direction, Toward the Rocky Mountains; Performed in the Years 1818 and 1819* (London: Sir Richard Phillips, 1821).

Schriber, Mary Suzanne, ed. *Telling Travels: Selected Writings by Nineteenth-Century American Women Abroad* (DeKalb: Northern Illinois University Press, 1994).

Schudson, Michael. *Discovering the News: A Social History of American Newspapers* (New York: Basic, 1978).

Scidmore, Eliza Ruhamah. *Alaska: Its Southern Coast and Sitken Archipelago* (Boston: D. Lothrop, 1885).

_____. *Java, the Garden of the East* (New York: Century, 1899).

_____. *Jinrikisha Days in Japan* (New York: Harper and Brothers Publishers, 1902).

Sears, John. *Sacred Places: American Tourist Attractions in the Nineteenth Century* (New York: Oxford University Press, 1999).

Seed, David. "Nineteenth-Century Travel Writing: An Introduction," *The Yearbook of English Studies* 34 (2004): 1–5.

Shaffer, Marguerite S. *America First: Tourism and National Identity, 1880–1940* (Washington, DC: Smithsonian Institution Press, 2001).

Shelley, Mary, *Rambles in Germany and Italy, in 1840, 1842, and 1843* (Breinigsville, PA: Nabu Pubic Domain Reprints, 2011).

Sides, Hampton. *In the Kingdom of the Ice: The Grand and Terrible Polar Voyage of the USS Jeannette* (New York: Penguin Random House, 2015).

Slotkin, Richard. *Fatal Environment: The Myth of the Frontier in the Age of Industrialization, 1800–1890* (New York: Harper Perennial, 1994).

Smith, Harriet Elinor, ed. *Autobiography of Mark Twain* (Berkeley: University of California Press, 2010).

Smith, Henry Nash. *Virgin Land: The American West as Symbol and Myth* (Cambridge: Harvard University Press, 2001).

Smith, Willard H. *Schuyler Colfax: The Changing Fortunes of a Political Idol* (Indianapolis: Indiana Historical Bureau, 1952).

Smythe, Ted Curtis. "The Reporter, 1880–1890: Working Conditons and Their Influence on the News," *Journalism History* 7, no. 1 (1980): 2–8.

Speake, Jennifer. *Literature of Travel and Exploration: G to P* (Taylor & Francis, 2003).

Spencer, David R. "No Laughing Matter: 19th Century Editorial Cartoons and the Business of Race," *International Journal of Comic Art* 11, no. 1 (2009): 203–228.

Spurr, David. *The Rhetoric of Empire: Colonial Discourse in Journalism, Travel Writing, and Imperial Administration* (Durham, NC: Duke University Press, 1993).

Stanley, Henry M. *The Autobiography of Sir Henry M. Stanley: The Making of a 19th Century Explorer* (Santa Barbara, CA: Narrative Press, 2001).

_____. *My Early Travels and Adventures in America and Asia.* Vol. I (London: Sampson Low, Marston, 1895).

Starr, Paul. *The Creation of the Media: Political Origins of Modern Communications* (New York: Basic Books/ Hachette: 2005).

Stevenson, Robert Lewis. *Travels with a Donkey in the Cévennes* (Boston: Roberts Bros., 1879).

Stillson, Richard Thomas. *Spreading the Word: A History of Information in the California Gold Rush* (Lincoln: University of Nebraska Press, 2006).

Stoddard, Henry Luther. *Horace Greeley, Printer, Editor, Crusader* (New York: G. P. Putnam, 1946).

Strassberg, Richard E., trans. *Inscribed Landscapes: Travel Writing from Imperial China* (Oakland and Berkeley: University of California Press, 1994).

Streeby, Shelly, *American Sensations: Class, Empire and the Production of Popular Culture* (Berkeley: University of California Press, 2002).

Strochlic, Nina. "The Woman Who Shaped *National Geographic*," February 2017, www.nationalgeographic.com/magazine/plus/lost-and-found/woman-shaped-national-geographic-eliza-scidmore/.

Taft, Robert. *Artists and Illustrators of the Old West, 1850–1900* (New York: Bonanza Books, 1953).

Taylor, Benjamin Franklin. *Between the Gates: A Train Journey from Chicago to San Francisco* (Chicago: S. C. Griggs, 1878).

Trachtenberg, Alan. *The Incorporation of America: Culture and Society in the Gilded Age* (New York: Hill and Wang/Macmillan, 2007).

_____. *Shades of Hiawatha: Staging Indians, Making Americans, 1880–1930* (New York: Hill and Wang, 2004).

Twain, Mark. "Jim Smiley and His Jumping Frog," *The Saturday Press.* November 18, 1865, 248–249.

_____. Letters, at www.marktwainproject.org/xtf/search?category=letters;rmode=landing_letters;style=mt, multiple editors, Bancroft Library, University of California at Berkeley, 2007—ongoing.

_____. *Mark Twain's Letters from Hawaii.* Edited by A. Grove Day (New York: Appleton-Century, 1966).

Unruh, John D., Jr. *The Plains Across: The Overland Emigrants and the Trans-Mississippi West, 1840–1860* (Urbana: University of Illinois Press, 1993).

Voynick, S. M. *Colorado Gold* (Missoula: Mountain Press, 1992).

Webb, Melody. *Yukon: The Last Frontier* (Vancouver: University of British Columbia Press, 1993).

Whymper, Frederick. *Travel and Adventure in the Territory of Alaska* (London: John Murray, 1868).

Williams, Robert C. *Horace Greeley: Champion of American Freedom* (New York: New York University Press, 2006).

Wollstonecraft. Mary, *The Complete Works of Mary Wollstonecraft.* Edited by Janet Todd and Marilyn Butler (London: William Pickering, 1989).

_____. *A Vindication of the Rights of Woman* (London: J. Johnson, 1792).

Wood, C. E. S. "Among the Thlinkits [*sic*] in Alaska," *Century Magazine* 24, no. 3, July 1882, 323–339.

Wright, John Stillman, *Letters from the West; or a Caution to Emigrants* (Salem, NY: Dodd & Stevenson, 1819).

Zmijewski, David. "'Hornet': Mark Twain's Interpretations of a Perilous Journey," *Hawaiian Journal of History* 33 (1999): 55–67.

# About the Contributors

Jack **Breslin** is an associate professor at Iona College, New Rochelle, where he teaches media law and ethics, public relations and journalism courses. He earned his BA from St. Alphonsus College in Connecticut and his MA from the University of Georgia. He holds a Ph.D in mass communication from the University of Minnesota, and worked twenty years as a media professional, including newspaper reporting and publicity work with Fox and NBC.

Crompton **Burton,** a graduate of the University of Arizona and Ohio University's Scripps School of Journalism, has a forty-year career in broadcasting and higher education that has included public relations and advancement posts at the University of Maine, Ohio University, and Marietta College. His research has been presented at the Symposium on the Nineteenth Century Press, the Civil War, and Free Expression at the University of Tennessee at Chattanooga.

Mary M. **Cronin** is a professor in the Department of Journalism and Media Studies at New Mexico State University. She has worked as a reporter and editor at newspapers in Florida, New Jersey and Massachusetts, and was a freelance reporter for several magazines. She is coauthor of *The Mass Media: Invention, Development, Application, and Impact*, and editor and co-author of *An Indispensable Liberty: The Fight for Free Speech in Nineteenth-Century America* and *High Private: The Trans-Mississippi Correspondence of Humorist R.R. Gilbert, 1862–1865*.

William E. **Huntzicker** is a Minneapolis writer who has taught journalism and media history at the University of Minnesota in Minneapolis and other colleges in Minnesota and Wisconsin. He has written for the daily *Miles City Star* in Montana and for the Associated Press in Minneapolis and for the University of Minnesota News Service. He has written *The Popular Press 1833–1865* and *Dinkytown: Four Blocks of History*, as well as numerous articles and book chapters on nineteenth-century journalism.

Lee **Jolliffe** is a professor of journalism at Drake University, where she teaches media design and honors courses on the media. She specializes in antebellum abolitionists and self-emancipated slaves, with over eighty academic articles, book chapters, and presentations. She served as first guest editor of *Journalism History*. Prior to her academic career, she worked as a freelance writer and as supervisor of the Writing and Editing Section at Battelle Institute on projects for NASA, the Department of Energy, Department of Defense, National Science Foundation, National Institutes of Health and the Environmental Protection Agency.

Paulette D. **Kilmer** teaches journalism as storytelling, media history and ethics at the University of Toledo. Her research analyzes news as archetype, folklore, and human drama. She has published two books, book chapters, scholarly articles, and essays. She holds a BA and an MA from the University of Wisconsin, Madison; an MA from the University of Kansas, Lawrence; and a Ph.D. from the University of Illinois, Urbana-Champaign.

Jennifer E. **Moore** is an associate professor of journalism in the Department of Communication at the University of Minnesota Duluth. Her research interests include journalism history, visual communication, digital news preservation and participatory news practices. Her research on the nineteenth-century press and participatory news practices appears in academic journals and edited book collections. Prior to academia, Moore worked as a radio reporter and digital content producer and manager.

James E. **Mueller** is a professor and associate dean at the Mayborn School of Journalism at the University of North Texas in Denton. He is the author of four books, including *Ambitious Honor: George Armstrong Custer's Life of Service and Lust for Fame.* He holds a BA in journalism and an MA in journalism from the University of Missouri and a Ph.D. in journalism from the University of Texas. He has ten years of experience as a reporter and editor.

Katrina J. **Quinn** is the communication department chair and a professor at Slippery Rock University in Pennsylvania. With an interdisciplinary research methodology that brings critical literary perspectives to journalistic texts, she has published on topics such as nineteenth-century political reporting, narrative, and journalism of the American frontier. She has worked as a public affairs specialist for the USDA Food and Nutrition Service in Boston.

Michael S. **Sweeney** is a professor at Ohio University's E.W. Scripps School of Journalism and previous editor of *Journalism History.* He worked as a reporter for *National Geographic.* He was a features editor and copy editor at the *Fort Worth Star-Telegram* and a reporter at the *Springfield* (MO) *Daily News.* He has published many academic and popular books, journal articles and encyclopedia entries.

# Index

Numbers in *bold italics* indicate pages with illustrations

CPSIA information can be obtained
at www.ICGtesting.com
Printed in the USA
LVHW020032100723
751961LV00004B/485